PRINCE
OF
PLEASURE

*The Prince of Wales and the
Making of the Regency*

Saul David

LITTLE, BROWN AND COMPANY

A *Little, Brown* Book

First published in Great Britain
by Little, Brown and Company 1998

Copyright © Saul David 1998

The moral right of the author has been asserted.

A CIP catalogue record for this book
is available from the British Library.

ISBN 0 316 64616 4

Typeset in Bembo by M Rules
Printed and bound in Great Britain by
Clays Ltd, St Ives plc

Little, Brown and Company (UK)
Brettenham House
Lancaster Place
London WC2E 7EN

For Cathy

Contents

Acknowledgements

The idea for a book on the life of the Prince Regent (later George IV) came while I was researching my previous biography, *The Homicidal Earl: The Life of Lord Cardigan*. Born in 1797, that infamous aristocrat was described by one reviewer as 'a Regency figure fated to live in the Victorian era'. The critic added: 'Had he been born 40 years earlier, his womanising, duelling and vicious egotism would have been treated as par for the aristocratic course.' The temptation to investigate the life of the man who had shaped the Regency period was irresistible.

No major biography of George IV has been written for almost a quarter of a century – partly because the last author to attempt such a task was the peerless Christopher Hibbert, whose two-volume life was published in 1972/74. I must express my gratitude to Mr Hibbert for the encouragement he has given me, and for the exhaustive nature of his research which has made my job that much easier.

I would also like to thank: Her Majesty Queen Elizabeth II for permission to quote from the Royal Archives; the Marquess of Hertford for permission to quote from the Seymour Papers; Lord Stafford for permission to quote from the Stafford Papers; the Earl of Malmesbury and the Hampshire Record Office for permission to quote from the Malmesbury Papers; the Warwickshire Record Office for permission to quote from the Denbigh Papers; and the Trustees of the British Library for permission to quote from the Hastings Papers, the Liverpool Papers and the Miscellaneous Papers.

The following people were particularly helpful during the course of my research and I am grateful: Cynthia Campbell, the former Curator of the Brighton Pavilion and author of *The Most Polished Gentleman*; Dr William Wheeler, the descendant of George IV's putative son, Henry Hervey; Jeremy Sandford and the Honourable Mary Birkbeck, the descendants of another putative son, Charles Candy; Nicholas Fitzherbert, the family historian and descendant of Mrs Fitzherbert's brother-in-law; the late Diana, Duchess of Newcastle.

I must also acknowledge the assistance given to me by the staffs of the British Library, the Cardiff Central Library and Monmouth Library. Once again I am indebted to Julian Alexander, my literary agent; Richard Beswick and Antonia Hodgson at Little, Brown; and last, but definitely not least, my wife Louise.

Prologue

The infamous first meeting between the betrothed cousins, George, Prince of Wales, and Princess Caroline of Brunswick, took place in St James's Palace on 5 April 1795. She had just arrived by carriage from Greenwich, having been met off the Royal yacht *Augusta* by her new lady-in-waiting, Lady Jersey, who also happened to be the Prince's mistress. He had come directly from his extravagant Pall Mall mansion, Carlton House.

As the handsome but flabby Prince entered the room, his bride-to-be – fair-haired and pretty, yet short and with a head too large for her body – attempted to kneel. 'He raised her (gracefully enough),' recorded Lord Malmesbury, the only witness, 'and embraced her, said barely one word, turned round [and] returned to a distant part of the apartment.'

Calling Malmesbury to him, he said, 'Harris, I am not well; pray get me a glass of brandy.'

'Sir,' replied an embarrassed Malmesbury, 'had you not better have a glass of water?'

'*No*,' said the Prince with an oath, 'I will go directly to the Queen.' And away he went without uttering another word.

The Princess was astonished. 'My God!' she said in French (her

English would never be perfect). 'Does the Prince always act like this? I think he's very fat, and he's nothing like as handsome as his portrait.'

Malmesbury replied that the Prince was 'naturally a good deal affected and flurried at this first interview, but she would certainly find him different at dinner'. And so she did – but it was too late.[1]

The Prince's ungallant reception of his young fiancée – at 26, she was six years his junior – was largely due to her exceptionally low standards of personal hygiene. Malmesbury had noticed these deficiencies during the long journey from Brunswick, and had felt it necessary to advise her that the Prince was 'very delicate' and expected 'a long and very careful *toilette de propreté*' – which meant, at the very least, washing herself well '*all over*'. But this sound advice had made only a 'temporary impression' and she had since returned to her old ways: wearing 'coarse' petticoats and shifts, 'thread stockings, and these never well washed, or changed often enough'. When the fastidious Prince met her for the first time, her pungent body odour was unmistakable.[2]

It did not help that her good looks were offset by a short, stocky physique – whereas the Prince preferred tall, stout women. Or that he was already married (albeit secretly) and had only agreed to a second, official ceremony as a means of reducing his ruinous debts. The final straw came during the farcical wedding night when the Prince discovered that his 'new' wife was not a virgin ('there was no appearance of blood,' he later told Malmesbury, and 'her manners were not those of a novice'). He managed to make love to her just three times – twice that night and once the next – before his repulsion got the better of his sense of duty. A daughter, Charlotte, was conceived in the process; but she died 21 years later in childbirth, leaving him without an heir. Seven years after his death, the daughter of his younger brother, the Duke of Kent, succeeded to the throne as Queen Victoria. Two more contrasting monarchs would be hard to imagine.[3]

The enduring image of George IV is that of 'Prinny', the overweight, overdressed and oversexed buffoon waiting for his periodically deranged father to be declared unfit to rule. This was how he was portrayed in contemporary prints and, more recently, in the TV series *Blackadder* and the film *The Madness of King George*. But like many popular images, it ignores the more serious side of his character. Given his predilection for pleasure, it is probably no coincidence that his lasting achievements were nearly all cultural. The Regency in its widest sense (1800–1830) is remembered today as a devil-may-care period of low morals and high fashion. It was also, thanks to his patronage, a time of great cultural fertility. Probably no monarch in British history has had a more positive influence on so many areas of culture: fine art, sculpture, architecture, literature, music and even science.

The prediction made by his preceptor, the Bishop of Coventry, in 1777 – that his young charge might develop into a combination of 'the most polished gentleman' and 'the most accomplished blackguard in Europe' – proved to be remarkably accurate.[4]

1

A Dissipated Youth

Queen Charlotte of England was just 18, and had been married less than a year, when she fulfilled her dynastic obligations by giving birth to as 'strong, large and pretty boy . . . as ever was seen' at St James's Palace in the early evening of 12 August 1762.

Waiting anxiously in his private apartments, King George III was informed by a breathless Earl of Huntingdon, his bungling Groom of the Stole, that he was the father of a baby girl. The error was doubly unfortunate in that the 24-year-old King had promised £1,000 to the bearer of news that he had a son, but only £500 if it was a daughter. More concerned with his young wife's health than the sex of the child, however, the King hurried to the Queen's bedchamber to hear the glad tidings that both mother and son – the sex of which was no longer in doubt – were alive and well. The lusty infant was then taken into the ante-room and shown to an excited gathering of royal dukes, government ministers, senior peers, bishops and foreign ambassadors.[1]

No heir had been born to a ruling monarch for almost 75 years – since the 'Old Pretender', James II's son, in 1688 – and 'all was joy, merriment, and gladness in London'. A procession of 'immense riches taken in a Spanish galleon', going past St James's Palace on its way to the Bank of England, gave cause for double celebration.

A month later, 'with every circumstance of splendour', the young Prince was baptised George Augustus Frederick by the Archbishop of Canterbury in the Queen's drawing-room. He had already been created Prince of Wales and Earl of Chester and, by right of birth, Duke of Cornwall, Duke of Rothesay, Earl of Carrick and Baron of Renfrew.[2]

In 1762, the year of the Prince's birth, Britain was still on the verge of the great social and economic upheaval that came to be known as the Industrial Revolution. The population of England and Wales was steady at 6.5 million, thanks to the rate of births and deaths being similarly high. But as improvements in agriculture and medicine began to take effect – and people were better fed, better clothed and less likely to catch diseases like smallpox – the death rate plummeted and the population exploded, particularly after 1800. By 1831, the year after George IV's death, it had risen to 16.5 million, with urban areas the principal beneficiaries.

In 1769, however, when George III first came to the throne, the majority of Britons still lived in rural communities. Only two English cities had populations greater than 50,000: London with 750,000, and Bristol with 60,000. The rest were essentially small market towns and little ports.

Trade was the lifeblood of the nation. In 1760, at a time when total government expenditure was just £15.5 million (and that during a war year of exceptional cost), imports were worth £11 million and exports £16 million. The main imports were consumables such as wines, spirits, sugar, tea and coffee. Exports were largely textiles (woollen goods making up a quarter of the total trade), metal goods, tin, pottery and cured fish. One of the most profitable areas of trade was the Atlantic triangle. Merchants would transport manufactured goods to West Africa and exchange them for slaves who, in turn, would be taken to the West Indies and the southern colonies of North America. Sugar, tobacco and timber would be brought back to Britain.

The capital accumulated by trade ultimately helped to finance the

Industrial Revolution; and though Britain in 1760 lagged behind its chief rival, France, in the production of iron, steel, coal and textiles, it was better placed to take advantage of the technical innovations to come – such as the use of the first steam-loom in Manchester in 1806. Its population may have been smaller, but it was more easily reached as one market with fewer internal tolls and better communications. Most parts of the country were less than a day's journey by cart from navigable water.

The improvement of road surfaces had yet to reach its apogee – with the development of Tarmac by the Scottish surveyor, John McAdam, in the early nineteenth century – and the coach or wagon had replaced the pack-horse only on the major routes; from London to fashionable Bath, for example, where a service of fast coaches was already running. In Devonshire, on the other hand, roads were so bad that sledges took the place of wheeled transport; even on a turnpike stretch of the main road south from Newcastle (the future A1), broken stones competed with muddy sand as the most treacherous surface. It was not unusual for villages to be cut off from the rest of the world by mud and water during winter. Nevertheless, these roads were already the best in Europe.

However, they would soon be supplemented by the longest and most efficient canal network. The first was built in 1759 by the Duke of Bridgewater from his coalfield at Worsley to Manchester; it cost £220,000 (£13.2 million today), brought in around £100,000 a year in revenue and halved the price of coal in that area. By 1815, the modern canal system was all but complete and the cost of inland transport had been reduced by about 75 per cent.

Arable agriculture had already been revolutionised in the eastern counties of Essex, Norfolk and Suffolk by Jethro Tull's drill seed and Lord 'Turnip' Townshend's four-course crop rotation and use of marl to give the soil body. The result was a 30 per cent increase in the yield per acre of wheat, for example, during the second half of the eighteenth century. A similar improvement was made in livestock farming by men like Robert Bakewell, a Leicestershire farmer who had been experimenting with stock-breeding for 15 years when he took over his father's modest property in 1760. He replaced the old breeds of sheep, used mainly for wool and the production of manure, with new animals reared specifically for meat; shorter fleeced and more heavily jointed, they matured in two seasons instead of four. Within 50 years the average weight of sheep at Smithfield rose from 28 lb to 50 lb.

At the top of the social pyramid, immediately below the royal family, were the aristocracy; until the end of the century it was very difficult to break into this exclusive club unless you were immensely rich. As members of the House of Lords, holders of senior government office and major landowners – in 1783, 28 peers possessed more than 100,000 acres of land each – they were the dominant political force. The 1st Duke of Newcastle, Prime Minister (or First Lord of the Treasury as he was then known) for much of the 1750s, controlled up to 12 seats in the House of Commons.

As Horace Walpole, the younger son of Sir Robert Walpole, the first Prime Minister, so succinctly put it, 'merit is useless: it is interest alone that can push a man forward. By dint of interest one of my coach-horses might become poet-laureate, and the other, physician to the household.'

When the parliamentary session began in the autumn, society flocked to the capital. But the time spent at the Hanoverian Court could be an irksome duty; for the first three Georges were unostentatious and reserved, unsuited as leaders of English society. 'I am just come from Court,' wrote Lord Hervey in 1728, 'where I saw nothing but blue noses, pale faces, gauze heads and toupets among the younger gentry: lying smiles, forced compliments, careful brows, and made laughs amongst the elders.'[3]

From their mansions in Bloomsbury, Soho and later Mayfair, the ruling élite would emerge to pick up the latest news and gossip in the coffee- and chocolate-houses of St James's Street and Pall Mall; in the second half of the century most evolved into clubs. The best known were White's, Boodle's and Almack's (later known as Brook's) where the main preoccupation was gambling and fantastic amounts were won and lost. At the age of 16, the future statesman Charles James Fox (in league with his elder brother) squandered £32,000 in three days.

Other entertainments included the theatre, the opera, balls, masquerades and dinner parties. All the while, enormous quantities of food and drink were being consumed. Breakfast was a light meal, usually tea and bread and butter. Dinner, the most substantial meal, was between 4 and 5 o'clock. When it was over the ladies retired while the men drank a series of toasts, pausing only to relieve themselves in a chamberpot cunningly concealed in the sideboard drawer. Supper was taken at any time after 9 in the evening. One gargantuan supper – given by the Duke of Marlborough to celebrate the birth of his fourth son – included roast beef, mutton, pork, veal, chicken, duck, goose, boiled tongue, hog's head, plum pudding and apple pie.

The saying 'drunk as a lord' dates from this period – and with good reason. Most of the leading politicians were heavy drinkers; not least the Earl of Northington, Lord Chancellor from 1761 to 1766, who persuaded George III to do away with the evening sessions of Chancery on Wednesdays and Fridays so that he could drink port after dinner.

When the social Season finished in early June, the magnates returned to their country seats. Fortunes were spent on their improvement in the eighteenth century. Between 1747 and 1763, for example, the 4th Duke of Bedford had Woburn Abbey completely rebuilt. Today's Georgian palace was constructed around the Stuart core. Inside were two fixed baths, one hot and one cold, the latter resembling a small swimming-pool. Cipriani painted the library ceiling, Rysbrack made the drawing-room chimney-piece. Total cost: a mere £85,000 (or £5.1 million today).

Hospitality was similarly lavish. It was said to cost £15 a night in candles to illuminate Houghton Hall, the seat of Sir Robert Walpole, Prime Minister from 1721 to 1742. 'Our company at Houghton swelled at last into so numerous a body,' wrote Lord Hervey to the Prince of Wales, father of George III, in 1731, 'that we used to sit down to dinner in a snug little party of about thirty odd, up to the chin in beef, venison, geese, turkeys, etc; and generally over the chin in claret, strong beer and punch. We had Lords spiritual and temporal, besides commoners, parsons and freeholders innumerable.'[4]

For 21 years after the birth of the Prince of Wales, the fecund royal couple produced children at the rate of two every three years – eight boys and six girls in all – although one of each sex died in infancy. The nearest in age to the Prince were Frederick, later Duke of York, born in 1763; William, later Duke of Clarence and ultimately King William IV, born in 1765; Charlotte, later Queen of Württemburg, born in 1766; and Edward, later Duke of Kent and father of Queen Victoria, born in 1767. But it was with Frederick alone that the young Prince shared his nursery and formed the closest friendship. Their sizeable establishment included, at one time or another, two cradle-rockers, a wet-nurse, a dry-nurse, a sempstress and, in charge of all, a governess, Lady Charlotte Finch, the youngest daughter of the Earl of Pomfret, 'a woman of remarkable sense and philosophy'.[5]

In the summer of 1763, the Royal Family moved into Buckingham House (not as yet a palace), a handsome red-brick mansion at the top of St James's Park which the King had bought for his wife the previous year, and henceforth known as the Queen's House. St James's Palace was now used only for official functions. But most of the Prince of Wales's early years were spent in the relatively modest setting of Richmond Lodge, formerly the Keeper's house on the edge of the great park. Of the other available royal residences, Richmond Palace and Windsor Castle had fallen into disrepair, while Hampton Court reminded George III of the strained relationship between his grand-father, George II, and his ill-fated father, Frederick, Prince of Wales.

From earliest infancy the young heir to the throne and his eldest brother were introduced to society at the Queen's Drawing-Rooms at St James's Palace every Thursday. It was soon obvious that the Prince was a singularly precocious child. At the age of four, having been inoc-ulated for smallpox and forced to remain in bed with the curtains drawn, he was asked by Mrs Schwellenberg, one of his mother's

German attendants, if he found the restriction irksome. 'Not at all,' he replied, 'I lie and make reflections.'[6]

Created a Knight of the Garter at the age of three and a half, for his fifth birthday the Prince was given 21 brass cannon, firing 1 lb balls. Little wonder that Lady Sarah Lennox, with whom George III had once been in love, remarked that the King 'has made his brat the proudest little imp you every saw'.[7]

But his young life was not all pomp and ceremony. Both parents were outwardly devout Protestants, determined that their children should grow up in an atmosphere of restraint and rigid application to duty. Lessons began at 7 in the morning, and continued until dinner was taken at 3 o'clock. Even birthdays were not a sufficient excuse to disrupt this monotonous schedule, and any deviation from acceptable behaviour was swiftly chastised with a beating, often administered by the King himself.

At first, such a tough regime seemed to be reaping rewards. By the age of six the Prince was reported to be making good progress with his school work, particularly writing and English grammar (although his spelling was never good). But though intelligent and 'good tempered', he was also something of a milksop, unlike his younger brothers who were 'full of courage'. Years later Joseph Farington, the diarist and Royal Academician, recalled the Prince learning to skate: '[Having] suffered a few falls he could not be induced to expose himself again to the chance of suffering for them.' Prince Frederick, on the other hand, 'did not regard the pain but persisted'.[8]

Despite being one of the Queen's favourites, the young Prince never enjoyed a close relationship with his strait-laced mother. Brought up in the small north German duchy of Mecklenburg-Strelitz, she had led a narrow provincial existence until the unexpected offer of marriage from the King of England and Elector of Hanover. Terrified of being branded unsophisticated, she stuck rigidly to Court etiquette: her sons were rarely permitted to sit in her presence; and even when promenading with their parents, the royal children would be formed into pairs, in descending order of age. So formal was the Queen's relationship with her eldest son that for his eighth birthday she gave him a 'pocket book' (which he had asked for) and a letter containing her wishes about his 'future conduct' (which he had not):

> Above all things I recommend unto you to fear God, a duty which must lead to all the rest with ease . . . Abhor all vice, in private as well as in public, and look upon yourself as obliged to set good examples. Disdain all flattery; it will corrupt your manners and render you contemptible before the world. Do justice unto everybody and avoid partiality . . . We are all equal and become only of consequence by setting good examples to others.
>
> Lastly I recommend unto you the highest love, affection and duty towards the King. Look upon him as a friend, nay, as the greatest, the best, and the most deserving of all friends you can possibly find. Try to imitate his virtues, and look upon everything that is in opposition to that duty as destructive to yourself . . .[9]

Good advice, for the most part, but hardly likely to be absorbed by a wilful eight-year-old. The reference to his 'duty towards the King' was clearly an attempt to break the cycle of father-son animosity which had dogged the Hanoverians since they had succeeded to the English throne; but it was one destined to fail – not least because of their innate differences in character, and the fact that the ascetic father was incapable of revealing genuine affection for his warm-hearted son.

By 1771, the Royal Family had grown to eight children – five boys and three girls – and Richmond Lodge was no longer big enough to accommodate them. The timely death that year of the King's mother, the dowager Princess of Wales, enabled them to move into the newly vacant White House at Kew. To house their many attendants and the various members of their Court, a number of other dwellings close by were leased or borrowed. The whole community was then fenced off, with each house given access into Kew Gardens by a separate gate.

Occupying the houses owned by the Dukes of Cambridge and Cumberland, the King's brothers, were the royal physicians:

> For the Queen [wrote Mrs Papendiek, a member of the Royal Household] would have two of them always on the spot to watch the constitutions of the royal children, to eradicate, if possible, or at least to keep under, the dreadful disease, scrofula, inherited from the King. She herself saw them bathed at six every morning, attended the schoolroom of her daughters, was present at their dinner, and directed their attire, whenever these arrangements did not interfere with public duties, or any plans or wishes of the King, whom she neither contradicted nor kept waiting a moment.

After their own early dinner at 4 o'clock, 'the King and Queen would usually have their family around them,' noted Mrs Papendiek, 'at full liberty, and enjoying themselves with their attendants, and often visitors suited to their different ages. There were birthday entertainments, dances, fireworks . . . and a constant variety of amusements adapted to their several tastes', the 'elder Princes and Princesses attending the small evening parties of the Queen at Kew, upon the same plan as when in London'.[10]

But there was no slackening in their education. At Kew the Prince and his brother Frederick were removed from the royal nursery and put into separate apartments in the White House under the care of a governor. The man selected for this post was Robert D'Arcy, 4th Earl of Holdernesse, a 'formal piece of dullness', according to Horace Walpole, who had served as a Secretary of State in the recent Pelham and Newcastle administrations. He was also Lord Warden of the Cinque Ports, and a year later would be accused by Colonel Luttrell in the House of Commons of using his position to smuggle 'prohibited merchandise'.

'The Prince of Wales is often at the house of the principal smuggler,' continued Luttrell, somewhat melodramatically, 'and as the mob some day or other, provoked past bearing, will indubitably attack and demolish that palace of contraband commerce, the life of the successor himself may be in danger!'[11]

However, until ill-health forced him to spend much of his time abroad, Holdernesse took his duties remarkably seriously. 'I have devoted myself to your service,' he informed his charges in May 1772. 'I have not only given up to that sole duty my time and thoughts but even my little reputation, for if you do not turn out those aimiable Princes nature intended you to be, I shall and perhaps ought to be blamed.'[12]

At times his pupils, the Prince of Wales in particular, were far from 'aimiable'. In July 1772, having failed to treat his governor with the proper respect, the Prince was told that he would not be received by the King until he had made an adequate apology. This was quickly forthcoming. 'Your expressing that the Prince of Wales has given you some marks of sensibility and affection this day is a great comfort to me,' the King wrote to Holdernesse, 'for if he is not susceptible to those feelings but little lasting good can be expected from him.'[13]

Two years later, in a letter to the Prince, Holdernesse stressed the need for honesty: 'I hope you will never forget that a promise once made is sacred and must be kept. *Truth is* the first quality of a man; the higher the rank, the more to be adhered to.'

Again and again, in letters to or concerning the young heir to the throne, there is an implicit fear that not only would he fail to live up to the high moral standards expected by his parents, but that he might even fall short of the more modest levels expected of any gentleman. At least Holdernesse's untimely death in 1778 saved him from the realisation that his efforts, in this field at least, had failed.

The day-to-day business of educating the princes, particularly after Holdernesse first succumbed to illness in 1774, was left to the sub-governor, Leonard Smelt, and the preceptor (or chief tutor), Dr William Markham. Smelt was a talented former officer in the Royal Engineers who had fought against the French at the Battles of Dettingen and Fontenoy, and who had been sent out to survey the defences of Newfoundland. He was also an expert at sketching and plan-drawing, and had a deep knowledge of literature and art. The Prince of Wales's lifelong fascination with the military and love of the arts can be traced to Smelt's influence.

William Markham was no less learned. Of humble origins, he had risen to become the Headmaster of Westminster School by the age of 34, Dean of Christ Church 14 years later, and Bishop of Chester in 1771, just two months before his latest appointment. Jeremy Bentham, one of his former pupils at Westminster, was unimpressed, noting that 'his business was rather in courting the great than in attending to the school.'[14]

In 1772, with more children graduating from the royal nursery and space in the White House at a premium, the Prince and his brother Frederick were given a separate establishment in the Dutch House nearby. A large three-storey, red-brick house – built by a rich London merchant of Dutch descent in 1631 – until recently it had been occupied by Lord Bute, the former Prime Minister. It was here that Smelt and Markham kept their charges busy from 7 in the morning to 8 at night, at which time they were allowed to join their parents for the evening parties until 10 o'clock.

The Prince acquired a good grounding in the classics – finding 'great facility' in learning Greek epigrams by heart – and a reasonable grasp of German, Italian and French, although he became fluent only in the latter. Of the great works of English literature, he was acquainted with Shakespeare but few others, while his father was later to complain that he had 'no insight into the springs' of ancient and modern history, nor 'any comprehensive knowledge of the Constitution, laws, finances, commerce, etc.,' of the two kingdoms he would one day reign: England and Hanover.[15]

But the King was slow to recognise his eldest son's talents, preferring to emphasise his moral shortcomings. Laziness, rudeness and duplicity were punished by beating, although no longer by the King himself. One of the Prince's sisters recalled how she once saw him and Frederick 'held by their tutors to be flogged like dogs with a long whip'.[16]

Fearing, rightly as it turned out, that the Prince's nature was susceptible to corrupting influences, the King tried to seclude him from the
outside world as much as possible. 'It went so absurdly far,' noted
Horace Walpole, that long after other children had been given more
grown-up clothes, 'he was made to wear a shirt with a frilled collar like
that of babies.' Taking hold of his collar one day, he exclaimed to a servant in frustration, '*See how I am treated!*'[17]

In May 1776, ten weeks before the Prince's fourteenth birthday,
Lord Holdernesse resigned his position as governor. According to
Horace Walpole, who heard the story second-hand from Lord
Hertford, Holdernesse had returned from the south of France the pre-
vious autumn, somewhat recovered in health, to discover that 'great
prejudices had been instilled in the mind of his pupils the Prince of
Wales and Prince Frederick'. So bad had this become that since
November they had treated 'his authority with contempt, and often
ridiculed him to his face'. The chief culprit, so Holdernesse had told
Lord Hertford, was Cyril Jackson, the sub-preceptor, 'a very ambitious
man'. But Markham, his superior, was also suspected of undermining
the governor, describing him as a 'a mere dancing-master, fit for nothing but to form a *petit maître*'.

The King, who was understandably distraught at discovering that his
son was 'so headstrong that he has not the least authority over him', had
no option but to dismiss Jackson and Markham. The Prince, who liked
Markham and remained on good terms with him long after he had
been appointed Archbishop of York, tried to intervene on his behalf.
But the King was having none of it, not least because the Prince 'would
secretly feel a kind of victory if the Bishop remained'.

He was more interested in persuading Holdernesse not to resign, and
'used all manner of entreaties' to no avail. 'This spoke the aversion of
the Prince,' wrote Walpole, 'and how far he had carried his disobedience.' As Smelt had been appointed on the recommendation of
Holdernesse, he too resigned.

Thus ended the so-called 'Nursery Revolution'. The new governor
was the recently created Earl of Ailesbury (formerly Lord Bruce),

described by Walpole as 'a formal, dull man, totally ignorant of and unversed in the world' and 'totally unfit to educate the Prince of Wales'. He had 'barely taken possession of his post, and dined once with the Prince', when he too resigned, giving as the reason his wife's ill-health. His elder brother, the Duke of Montagu, took his place, 'one of the weakest and most ignorant men living' who, according to his wife, 'was not fit for any of the great offices of State'.

Markham was succeeded as Preceptor by Dr Richard Hurd, Bishop of Lichfield and Coventry, a 'stiff and cold, but correct gentleman', who had 'acquired a great name by several works' of literary criticism and philosophy 'of slender merit'. His chaplain, the Reverend William Arnold, replaced Jackson as Sub-Preceptor, while Lieutenant-Colonel George Hotham became Sub-Governor. The replacement of all the Prince's servants – who, the King felt, had become too pliable – completed the 'revolution'.[18]

Hurd's first act was to draw up his exacting *Plans of Study for the Princes*, which included the fields of religion, morals, government and laws, mathematics, natural philosophy, history and 'polite literature' (mainly Greek and Latin authors, but also Shakespeare, Milton and Pope). In addition, the Prince was taught to play the cello by John Crosdill, to fence and box by Henry Angelo, and to draw by Alexander Cozens. He was encouraged to appreciate fine art, and shown how to sow and harvest his own crops. He even baked his own bread. In short, he was well on his way to becoming the most versatile and cultured prince of his time.

Not to mention one of the most alluring. 'He was not so handsome as his brother,' wrote Mrs Papendiek of the Prince as he approached manhood, 'but his countenance was of a sweetness and intelligence quite irresistable. He had an elegant person, engaging and distinguished manners, added to an affectionate disposition and the cheerfulness of youth. In accomplishments the brothers were unequal, as well as in acquired knowledge, the scale turning always in favour of the Prince of Wales.'[19]

But the Prince also had less attractive traits. For example, he was much given to thoughtless practical jokes, like the time when he served up a live rabbit to the greedy oboist, Johann Fischer; on another occasion he squeezed the frail hand of the Bishop of Winchester, his father's former tutor, so hard that it hurt him for days.

He also had a tendency to fall in with the wrong people. 'Much do I lament,' wrote Mrs Papendiek, 'that some of those about the young Princes swerved from principle, and introduced improper company when their Majesties supposed them to be at rest, and after the divines had closed their day with prayer.' The two men she blamed for introducing the two eldest princes to women and wine were their attendants, Colonels Gerard Lake and Samuel Hulse, 'the very men who should have been avoided'. However, neither the beautiful Duchess of Devonshire, a close friend of the Prince, nor the diarist Nathaniel Wraxall agreed with this condemnation of Lake, who later achieved fame as a successful general and died a viscount. The Duchess thought him a man 'such as ought to have been about the Prince, sensible, worthy and a gentleman', while Wraxall described him as a 'pleasing exception' to the Prince's list of undesirable companions.[20]

On the threshold of manhood, the Prince was very much an enigma. Asked for an assessment of his 15-year-old pupil, Hurd replied, 'I can hardly tell. He will either be the most polished gentleman or the most accomplished blackguard in Europe, possibly an admixture of both.' It was a particularly prescient remark.'[21]

In April 1779, the 16-year-old Prince fell in love for the first time, with 23-year-old Mary Hamilton, the great-grand-daughter of the 3rd Duke of Hamilton and his sisters' sub-governess, 'whose virtue was as unblemished as her beauty'. On 25 May, no longer able to hide his feelings, he came clean in a letter:

As you have bound yourself to me by such solemn promises of secrecy and of friendship, I dare now reveal to you the most secret thoughts of my Soul, such is the confidence I place in you. When I promised to name you the Lady, you declared you would not think the worse of me on her account, or indeed of any. Therefore trusting totally to your honour I now declare that my fair incognita is your dear, dear, dear Self. Your manners, your sentiments, the tender feelings of your heart so totally coincide with my ideas, not to mention the many advantages you have in person over many other ladies, that I not only highly esteem you, but even love you more than words or ideas can express.

Miss Hamilton's response five days later was guarded. While she could, without threat to her honour, accept his '*friendship*', anything more was out of the question. She begged him not to 'offend' her 'delicacy' by sending her presents. '*Friends are not to be bought.*' 'Your heart I believe is excellent,' she concluded with some perception, 'follow its dictates and you will be less likely to err than if you suffer yourself to be led away by a number of interested wretches that will surround you.'

Undeterred, the Prince wrote almost daily in the hope that Miss Hamilton would change her mind. He even threatened suicide if his love was not reciprocated. 'Think not that this is the resolution of a giddy, rash, wild young man,' he added, 'it has arisen from the long constant contemplation of a strong and sound mind.' He would, however, 'sooner go to immediate perdition' than attempt anything 'detrimental' to her 'reputation, honour and virtue'.

But Miss Hamilton would not be swayed by the passionate words of her youthful suitor. However imprudent she had been in acknowledging his 'friendship', she would never 'act so base a part as to encourage such warm declarations'. 'You fancy yourself attached. Shall I paint the Object?' she asked rhetorically. 'Inferior in Birth − no beauty to attract − no person to captivate − possessed only of the most common accomplishments − an honest heart we will allow. This may be sufficient for a Friend, but . . . how disgraceful for you to pretend to feel anything more!'

Only after she had threatened to resign her duties at Court if he did not stop pestering her, did the Prince finally agree to address her 'by the endearing names of *friend & Sister*, & no longer with the impetuous passion of a Lover urging his Suit'.

Relieved, she continued to act as his mentor, pointing out such 'reprehensible' traits as his preference for low companions and his 'indelicate, ungentlemanlike & wicked practise . . . of swearing'. He accepted the criticism, defending himself on the grounds that he had picked up the habit 'from hearing people in the Army do so', and that he had reciprocated to 'show that I was now become a Man'.

Encouraged by this climate of self-examination, in September the Prince sent Miss Hamilton an extraordinarily honest appraisal of how he saw his own nature:

> His sentiments and thoughts are open and generous, above doing any thing that is mean (too susceptible, even to believing people his friends, & placing too much confidence in them . . .), grateful and friendly to an excess where he finds a real *friend*. [He] has a *strict notion of honor*, rather too familiar with his inferiors, but will not suffer himself to be browbeaten or treated with haughtiness by his superiors. Now for his vices, or rather let us call them weaknesses – too subject to give . . . vent to his passions of every kind. . . ., but he never bears malice or rancour in his heart . . . he is rather too fond of Wine and Women but upon the whole his Character is open free and generous, susceptible of good impressions, ready to follow good advice.

The Prince was only half correct in this last assessment, for his greatest weakness was his susceptibility to people who did not have his best interests at heart. Miss Hamilton was well aware of this, noting in her reply that her 'greatest apprehension' was that 'the openness and ingen-uousness' of his 'temper' would make him 'a dupe to designing, interested, artful people of both sexes'.[22]

Had he been exposed much longer to the sensible advice of this perceptive and honourable woman, the Prince might have turned out very differently. But, as Miss Hamilton had rightly pointed out, the gap in rank between them was too great, marriage was out of the question, and it was only a matter of time before the Prince's youthful ardour was directed elsewhere.

The next object of his passion was Mary Robinson, 21, a young actress 'more admir'd for her beauty than for her talents'. Though she often hinted that she was the natural daughter of the 1st Earl of Northington, her actual father was almost certainly Nicholas Darby, a Newfoundland-born ship captain, who had abandoned his family after a failed attempt to establish a whale fishery on the coast of Labrador. Married at 15 to Thomas Robinson, an extravagant articled clerk who lived beyond his means, she had been 'driven to the stage' to make ends meet. After being released from a long spell in the Fleet debtors' prison, a mutual friend had introduced her to Richard Brinsley Sheridan, the successful playwright who had just taken over from David Garrick as the manager of the Drury Lane Theatre. Sheridan saw her potential, and in December 1776 she made her stage début as the lead in *Romeo and Juliet* to great acclaim. Within three years she was one of the most celebrated actresses in London, with a habit of riding about town in a carriage adorned by a fake coat of arms, dressed in an array of bizarre yet alluring costumes, and accompanied by her disreputable husband and a host of would-be lovers.[23]

On 3 December 1779, Mrs Robinson appeared as Perdita in a Royal Command Performance of *The Winter's Tale* at Drury Lane, attended by the Prince of Wales. He was bewitched – as William Smith, the actor playing Leontes, had predicted he would be. Unable to take his eyes off her, he made a number of flattering remarks as she stood beneath his box, overwhelming her (so she claimed) with confusion. When the performance ended, he stood up and bowed to her. 'As the curtain was falling,' she recalled, 'my eyes met [his]; and with a look that *I shall never forget*, he gently inclined his head a second time; I felt the compliment, and blushed my gratitude.'

A couple of days later – using his friend Lord Malden, the son of the

Earl of Essex, as a go-between – the Prince sent the first of a number of painfully sentimental letters addressed to 'Perdita' and signed 'Florizel'. One contained a lock of his hair with the promise, 'To be redeemed', another a miniature of himself and a paper heart with the motto, 'Unalterable to my Perdita through life'.[24]

Miss Hamilton, to whom he had so recently expressed identical sentiments, was conveniently forgotten. 'Adieu, Adieu, Adieu, *toujours chère*,' he wrote to her on 5 December. 'Oh! Mrs. Robinson.' But she was too good a friend not to try to prevent such an unsuitable liaison. An actress like Mrs Robinson, she warned, 'has too much trick and art not to be a very dangerous object'. Details of Mary Robinson's private life followed, including the existence of her husband and child – but the Prince would not be discouraged. On New Year's Eve, Miss Hamilton made one last appeal: 'For the love of Heaven, Stop, O stop my friend! and do not thus headlong plunge yourself into vice.' It fell on deaf ears.

Thus ended the brief but intense period of correspondence between the Prince and Miss Hamilton (he alone had written 75 letters). But they remained on friendly terms for many years, and one of his attendants later claimed that she was 'the only woman he ever heard the Prince speak of with proper respect, except the Queen'.[25]

Mrs Robinson, meanwhile, was playing a clever game. She refused to agree to the Prince's suggestion that she should come to his private apartments in the Queen's House disguised as a boy because of 'the indelicacy of such a step, as well as the dangers of detection'. She later claimed that she only agreed to meet the Prince after discovering her husband in bed with one of her maids. In truth she was already a skilled courtesan, not about to let such an enviable – not to say potentially lucrative – prize slip from her grasp, and was merely heightening the Prince's appetite.

Their first meeting – fixed for the Prince's house at Kew – was postponed when Mrs Robinson's arrival by boat at the royal landing-place was interrupted by people approaching from the White House. But a subsequent tryst in June 1780 was more successful, and the relationship was consummated with mutual satisfaction. The Prince had already promised in writing to give her the enormous sum of £20,000 (the equivalent of £1 million today) once he had come of age. He now said that he would set her up in her own house if she gave up her career on the stage and became his mistress. Not surprisingly, she agreed.

Their affair was soon the talk of the town, with the papers full of speculative gossip, shop windows adorned with irreverent cartoons of 'Perdita' and 'Florizel', and Mrs Robinson 'overwhelmed by the gazing of the multitude' wherever she went. The King was horrified, but knew his son well enough not to force the issue. On 14 August, two days after the Prince's eighteenth birthday, he wrote him a long letter. 'No one feels with more pleasure than I do your nearer approach to manhood,' he began, 'but the parent's joy must be mixed with the anxiety that this period may be ill spent.'

> Your own good sense must make you feel that you have not made that progress in your studies which, from the ability and assiduity of those placed for that purpose about you, I might have had reason to expect; whilst you have been out of the sight of the world . . . your foibles have less been percieved than I could have expected; yet your love of dissipation has for some months been with enough ill nature trumpeted in the public papers, and there are those ready to wound me in the severest place by ripping up every error they may be able to find in you.

Other than assuring the King that 'it will be my principal object through life to merit' the 'parental attachment & kindness you profess towards me', the Prince made little effort to mend his ways. Now living with his eldest brother in apartments along the east side of Windsor Castle – while the rest of the Royal Family inhabited the house of Lord Talbot opposite – he would wait until the King had gone to bed before meeting his mistress.[26]

But it was only a matter of time before the Prince tired of the eccentric Mrs Robinson. Unsavoury incidents, as when she attacked her husband in public after discovering him making love to a '*fillette*' in a box at Covent Garden, hardly endeared her to her royal lover. As the year drew to its close, the Prince wrote to tell her that they must 'meet no more', citing her rudeness to a friend of his in public as the reason. Others believed the rumour that she was also sleeping with his friend Lord Malden. In any case, the Prince had fallen for another woman: the alluring Elizabeth Armistead.

When her liaison with the Prince began, Mrs Armistead was still the mistress of Lord George Cavendish, the brother of the Duke of Devonshire. One night, according to the Duchess of Devonshire, Lord George returned to Mrs Armistead's house 'rather drunk'. On entering her room, 'he perceiv'd some unaccustomed light in another, and much against her entreaties went in'. There, hiding behind the door, he discovered the Prince of Wales. In his inebriated condition, Lord George might not have been 'quite so respectable as he ought, but it had luckily another effect – he burst out laughing, made [the Prince] a low bow and retired'.[27]

However, Mrs Robinson was not prepared to be supplanted without a fight and she wrote the Prince a furious letter, railing against the 'calumnies' her enemies had fabricated. He responded with a 'most eloquent' letter, 'fully acquitting' her of 'the charges which had been propagated to destroy her'. They met once more and 'passed some hours in the most friendly and delightful conversation'. 'I began to flatter myself,' wrote Mrs Robinson, 'that all our differences were adjusted. But no words can express my surprise and chagrin, when, on meeting his Royal Highness *the very next day* in Hyde Park, he turned his head to avoid seeing me, and even affected *not to know me!*'[28]

When further attempts to see him were unsuccessful, she wrote more angry letters, accusing him of destroying her career with false promises which had left her heavily in debt. Desperate, she even resorted to blackmail:

> A certain *amour royal is* now totally at an end [stated the *Morning Herald*]; a separation has taken place a *thoro* for more than three

weeks, and a *settlement* worthy of such a *sultana* is the only thing
now wanting to break off all intercourse whatever. Mrs Robinson
thinking the adjustment of this part of the *divorce* too essential to
be trifled with, has roundly written to her once *ardent lover*, 'That
if her establishment is not duly arranged within the space of four-
teen days from the commencement of the new year, his —————
————— must not be surprised if he sees a full publication of all
those *seductory epistles* which alone estranged her from *virtue* and
the *marriage vow*![29]

The threat had the desired effect, not least because the letters contained a number of less than complimentary remarks about the King.
Colonel Hotham, the Prince's Treasurer, was authorised to make a settlement with Lord Malden, Mrs Robinson's representative. After much
wrangling, it was agreed that Mrs Robinson would receive a lump
sum of £5,000 and an annuity of £500, half of which would continue
to be paid to her daughter after her death.

The King, who was forced to go cap in hand to his Prime Minister
for the money, was more determined than ever to keep his son on a
tight leash. He had already, in December 1780, informed the Prince of
the limitations that would accompany the retirement of his Governor
and the formation of his own Establishment:

> My inclination [wrote the King] is to grant you all the rational
> amusement I can, and keep you out of what is improper, and so
> to steer you, that when you arrived at the full stage of man-
> hood, you may thank me for having made you escape evils that
> ill become a young man of rank, but in your exalted situation
> are criminal.

The Prince would be allowed to dine with his attendants in his apartments twice a week, and to attend plays, operas and balls having first
informed his parents. But he would not be permitted to go to balls or
assemblies in private houses – 'which never has been the custom for the

Prince of Wales' – nor masquerades – 'you already know my disapprobation of them.'

He would be expected to attend church on Sunday and the
Drawing-Room at St James's when the King was present, as well as the
Queen's Thursday Drawing-Room. When the King rode out of a
morning, he would accompany him. If the Prince went out alone,
whether on horseback or in a carriage, at least one of his attendants
would go with him. For those evenings when he was not attending
plays or operas, the King would invite a 'variety of company' so that he
would have a choice 'of playing cards or conversing . . . in the musick
room'.

'Be but open with me,' the King concluded, 'and you will ever find
me desirous of making you as happy as I can, but I must not forget, nor
must you, that in the exalted station you are placed in, every step is of
consequence, and that your future character will greatly depend in the
world on the propriety of your conduct at the present period.'[30]

Within a matter of weeks – as if to ensure his future good behaviour – the Prince had been deprived of his two closest friends.
Frederick, his adored brother, the 'sole companion of his youth', was
sent to Hanover to complete his military training. Colonel Lake, his
'best friend' and recently appointed his First Equerry, went to fight the
American rebels. So upset was the Prince at being separated from his
brother 'that he stood in a state of entire insensibility, totally unable to
speak'. His parting from Lake was just as painful. 'You know how
much I love him,' he wrote to Frederick on 20 January 1781, 'and
therefore will easily conceive what a loss he is to me at the present
moment, more especially as I have not you, my dear brother, with me,
from whom I could always meet with disinterested advice.'[31]

But the new restrictive regime was never likely to work. The more
the King tried to curb his wayward son, the more the Prince rebelled.
He was by nature a free spirit, a hedonist, and could not be expected to
thrive within the narrow boundaries prescribed by a stern father he neither liked nor respected. Ironically, his separation from Prince Frederick
and Colonel Lake had the opposite effect to that intended by the King.

Frederick, too, had had affairs – most notably with Letitia Smith, the former wife of the hanged highwayman Jack Rann, who was soon to marry the equally disreputable Sir John Lade – and would continue to do so in Hanover, but he was also capable of offering useful counsel. 'For God's sake,' he wrote later that year, 'do everything which you can to keep well with [the King], at least upon decent terms; consider he is vexed enough in public affairs.'[32]

Lake was also a moderating influence, full of sensible advice. In a letter written on 23 January 1781, shortly before his departure to America, he warned the Prince that his 'great good nature' was 'liable to be imposed upon by people who have not the smallest pretensions to your civility or attention'. A 'knowledge of the world and of men' was essential, but difficult to acquire given the 'retired and private education unavoidably chalked out for a Prince' while most other young men had 'reaped the benefit of a public school'. Furthermore, because of his 'situation', many people would try to gain his 'favor' by encouraging him to do 'things that they would perhaps be the first to condemn, and when they find the world disapproving your conduct, will lay the blame entirely upon yourself'.

Involvement in politics was to be avoided at all costs. 'Your own good sense (of which no one has a greater share) if properly employed,' wrote Lake, 'will prevent your becoming the dupe of those who have no other design than to make use of you for their own advantage.' This would prevent friction within his family, for it was in his 'own interest' for them 'all to live well together'.

Lastly, he was to refrain from writing 'any more letters to a certain sort of ladies'. 'I should hope,' Lake concluded, 'that what you have already suffered will be a sufficient warning.'[33]

But it was not. Ignoring Lake's advice, the Prince fell in with Charles Wyndham and Anthony St Leger, two young rakes notorious for their outrageous behaviour, and spent much of the early months of 1781 engaged in drunken and debauched escapades. During one particularly raucous night at the Blackheath house of Lord Chesterfield – a man later described by one of the Queen's attendants as having 'as little good breeding as any man I ever met with!' – they got so drunk that George Pitt, the son of Lord Rivers, tried to tear the tongue out of a fierce house-dog. The dog responded by savaging a footman's leg and Wyndham's arm. As if that was not enough, Chesterfield fell down the stairs, while the Prince was incapable of driving home and had to leave the reins of his phaeton to his disreputable uncle, the Duke of Cumberland.[34]

It was all too much for the Prince's frail constitution. 'Drinking and living too freely,' recalled the Duchess of Devonshire, 'brought on a violent fever . . . which soon however spent itself in a hideous humour in his face.' For most of March he was in the care of his physician, Sir Richard Jebb, who for two days even feared for his life. 'I remained cooped up in my bedchamber an entire fortnight,' the Prince informed his eldest brother, 'without ever tasting anything but barley water or some damned wishy washy stuff of that sort.'[35]

But having recovered, the Prince made no attempt to moderate his depraved lifestyle. In addition to Mrs Armistead, he is said to have had affairs with Mrs Grace Dalrymple Eliot, the divorced wife of a rich physician who had recently returned from France; Lady Melbourne, the famous hostess and mother of the future Prime Minister; and Elizabeth Billington, the wife of a double-bass player in the Drury Lane orchestra. Both Mrs Eliot and Lady Melbourne are reputed to have had children by the Prince: in March 1782, Mrs Eliot gave birth to a daughter and christened her Georgiana Frederica Augusta Seymour in honour of her putative father; Lady Melbourne's fourth son, George Lamb, born in July 1784, was also said to be his (Lord Minto, who met him in 1805, noted that he was 'a good-natured lad', something like the Prince of Wales). But the paternity of either is impossible to prove because both ladies had other lovers at this time.[36]

The Prince also had an ill-advised liaison with Countess von Hardenburg, the artful wife of Count Karl who had come to London in the hope of being appointed Hanoverian Envoy. His first meeting with the Countess was at a concert in the Queen's apartment in Buckingham House during the spring of 1781. 'After having conversed with her some time I perceived that she was a very sensible, agreable, pleasant woman, but devilish severe,' he wrote to his brother Frederick in July, after the affair was over. 'I thought no more of her at that time.'

But at a second meeting at one of the Queen's card parties at Windsor, the Prince revised his earlier opinion. She looked 'devinely pretty' and he 'could not keep' his 'eyes off her'. The fact that she, like him, was clearly bored, preferring to play cards for money, served only to increase the attraction. 'From that moment,' he wrote, 'the fatal though delightful passion arose in my bosom for her, which has made me since the most miserable and wretched of men.'

The infatuated Prince made his move soon after, during the fortnight when the Count was the hunting guest of the King at Windsor. Suggesting to the Countess that they meet alone in her husband's house in London, he was taken aback by her angry response that he had forgotten to whom he was talking, and was forced to apologise. But it was all for effect. The Countess was a capricious minx, by turns seductive and aloof, who, soon after Prince Frederick's arrival in Hanover, had tried to make love to him at a dance. When the moment proved inopportune – the room to which they retired was already occupied – the Countess flounced off and told an acquaintance that Prince Frederick was 'the most tiresome fellow' and 'never would leave her alone'.

The pattern of seduction used for the Prince of Wales was the reverse. For he was a greater conquest than his brother, with more influence, and needed a more subtle ensnarement. With the Prince lovesick to the point of endangering his health – 'I have spit blood and am so much emaciated you would hardly know me' – the Countess finally agreed to let him visit her alone at her house in Old Windsor. There she told him that she was 'very much attached' to him and loved him 'most sincerely', but that she had once been 'very much attached to another person' and did not think that a woman could truly love more than one person in her life. If, after such a declaration, he could still attach himself to her, it would be 'an additional proof' of his love.

The Prince's response was as expected. Far from lessening his affection, it had 'increased it if possible', and made him 'entertain a higher idea of her honour'. Nevertheless, it still took another two or three visits before the scheming Countess would let him make love to her. 'However,' he informed Prince Frederick, 'at last she did. O my beloved brother, I enjoyed beforehand the pleasures of Elyssium . . . Thus did our connexion go forward in the most delightful manner. . .'

At this stage, the only third party who knew about the affair was the Prince's equerry, Colonel Hulse. Then 'an unfortunate article' appeared in the *Morning Herald*, stating that the Prince's carriage was constantly to be seen at the door of a German Baroness who had taken a house next to Mrs Robinson's in Cork Street. In fact, it was the Duke of Gloucester's carriage which had been seen outside the door of a *Polish Countess*, but the damage had been done. Already suspicious, Count von Hardenburg now ordered his wife to write to the Prince, telling him that they could meet no more. At first she refused, denying her guilt. But so angry did the Count become that she eventually confessed that the Prince had made advances to her, though she had not succumbed. She also agreed to write to the Prince, while the Count included a suitably outraged missive of his own.

The Prince 'fell into fits' when he received the packet containing the two letters, but soon recovered enough to reply to the Count. He was indeed 'very strongly attached to his wife', but she had always treated him with the 'utmost coolness'. If anyone was at fault, it was him. At the same time, the Prince sent the Countess 'the most passionate of letters'. Next morning, having just been told by Lord Southampton, the head of his Household, that the King would not consent to let him go abroad to get over his unhappiness, the Prince received a reply from the Countess. Disowning her previous letter on the grounds that her husband had forced her to write it, she reaffirmed her love for the Prince and suggested that they elope that very night.

Torn between his passion for the Countess and the consequences of such an elopement, the Prince 'lost' his 'senses entirely' for a time. At first he agreed to go away; but the thought of the Countess – 'the only woman upon earth I can and do only love' – 'perishing for want' made him change his mind. In desperation, he 'threw' himself at his 'mother's feet and confessed the whole truth to her'. Having 'cried excessively' and shown herself much moved by her son's predicament, she advised him to send Hulse to tell the Countess that an 'unforeseen accident' prevented the Prince going with her. She also insisted that the King be informed.

A couple of days later, having been sent for by the King, Count von Hardenburg was on his way back to the Continent with his errant wife. For a time, he worked for the Duke of Brunswick; but his wife's increasingly loose morals eventually caused him to divorce her and join the Prussian diplomatic corps in Berlin. It was there that he eventually rose to the post of State Chancellor and achieved lasting fame as one of the 'Liberators of Europe'.

The Prince, meanwhile, was heartbroken. 'O did you but know how I adore her, how I love her, how I would sacrifice every earthly thing to her,' he wrote to Prince Frederick in July, 'by Heavens I shall go distracted: my brain will split.' But this did not last. Informed by his brother Frederick of the Countess's true nature, the Prince admitted that he had always harboured doubts about her, and that she had appeared to be 'very capricious and very singular in some things, and very cheerful and agreeable in others'. Though he still asked after her from time to time, he had other fish to fry: Lady Augusta Campbell, the beautiful and headstrong daughter of the 5th Duke of Argyll, for one. It was generally supposed not to have been an accident, wrote the Honourable Robert Fulke Greville, the King's favourite equerry, that Lady Augusta was placed next to the Prince at a ball given by the King and Queen to celebrate his nineteenth birthday.'[37]

———— •◆• ————

2

Into Opposition

By the autumn of 1781, the Prince's relationship with his parents had deteriorated still further. 'The King,' he informed Prince Frederick in September, 'is excessively cross and ill tempered and uncommonly grumpy, snubbing everybody, in everything.' A month later, he wrote: 'I am sorry to tell you that the unkind behaviour of both their Majesties, but in particular of the Queen, is such that it is hardly bearable.'[1]

One particular cause of tension between the Prince and his parents was his friendship with his two disgraced uncles, the Dukes of Cumberland and Gloucester. Both had made unsuitable marriages against the King's will: Gloucester in 1766 to the Dowager Countess Waldegrave, the widow of the King's former (and hated) governor, and the bastard daughter of Sir Edward Walpole and a clothing apprentice; Cumberland in 1771 to Mrs Anne Horton, the widowed daughter of the infamous Simon Luttrell, later the 1st Earl of Carhampton, whom Lady Louisa Stuart dubbed 'the greatest reprobate in England'. She added:

> He once challenged his eldest son, the late Lord Carhampton, who in return sent his word that if he (the father) could prevail

on any gentleman to be his second, he would fight him with all
his heart. Such was the style of the family. The daughters had
habits suited to it, noisy, vulgar, indelicate, and intrepid: utter
strangers to good company, they were never to be seen in any
woman of fashion's house, though often leaders of riotous parties at Vauxhall or Ranelagh.[2]

It was to prevent a repetition of such unseemly unions, so potentially
damaging to the reputation of the Royal Family, that the King had
sponsored the passing of the Royal Marriage Act in 1772.

The Act prohibited any descendant of George II, except those who
were the issue of Princesses wedded into foreign houses, from marrying before the age of 25 without the King's consent. Thereafter, they
could marry if they had given the Privy Council twelve months' notice,
and provided the Houses of Parliament did not object. Any marriages
contracted in contravention of the Act were null and void.

What made the Act so bizarre was the fact that two years before his
own state wedding to Charlotte of Mecklenburg-Strelitz, George III
himself, when Prince of Wales, appears to have secretly married
Hannah Lightfoot, the daughter of a Quaker tradesman. A witness
statement to their marriage in Kew Chapel on 17 April 1759, signed by
J. Wilmot, a clergyman and confidant of the Prince, was recently found
in Court of Chancery files by Kenneth Griffith, a film-maker and ama-
teur historian. It states that the marriage was 'solemnised this day
according to the rites and ceremonies of the Church of England'. A
second statement confirms that Wilmot conducted the ceremony.
Lightfoot died in 1768, describing herself in her will as Hannah
Regina. If genuine, these documents prove that George III was not
only a bigamist but also a hypocrite.

His union with Lightfoot has an even greater implication. For
Griffith believes that the couple had a son, also named George, who
was sent away to South Africa to avoid a scandal. His alleged gravestone
bears the words: 'In Memory of George Rex Esquire'. If George Rex
was indeed born after the lawful marriage of the Prince of Wales and

Hannah Lightfoot, then he, rather than the subject of this book, was the rightful heir to the throne. It is just as well for the Windsors that he is said to have died without issue.[3]

Of course, the Royal Marriage Act was not retrospective and could do nothing about those unsuitable marriages which had already taken place, including his own to Hannah Lightfoot and those of his two brothers. But he may well have genuinely regretted his youthful impetuosity, and chose to punish his brothers by excluding them from Court. The ban was eventually lifted in 1780: but relations between the King and Cumberland, in particular, remained less than cordial. This was hardly surprising given the fact that, according to Horace Walpole, 'unbounded freedom reigned at Cumberland House, as its mistress, laughing forms and etiquettes to scorn, was better pleased that rag, tag and bobtail . . . should flock in, than that numbers should ever be want-ing.' A centre of Whig opposition to the King's Tory ministers, its raucous guests could often be heard mocking the royal couple. Walpole wrote:

> A mighty scope for satire was afforded by the Queen's wide mouth and occasionally imperfect English, as well as by the King's trick of saying What? What? his ill-made coats, and general antipathy to the fashion. But the marks preferably aimed at were his *virtues*; his freedom from vice as a man; his discouragement of it as a sovereign; the exclusion of divorced women from his Court; beyond all his religious *prejudices* – that is to say, his sincere piety and humble reliance on God.[4]

Hardly surprising, then, that the wayward son was drawn towards his disrespectful aunt and uncle. By the autumn of 1781, the Duke and his nephew were hunting together twice a week. In December, the King told his now-reconciled brother, Gloucester, that he feared the Duke of Cumberland's influence over his son. 'When we hunt together,' complained the King, 'neither my son nor my brother speak to me; and lately, when the chase ended at a little village where there was but a single post-chaise to be hired, my son and brother got into it and drove to London, leaving me to go home in a cart if I could find one.'

Since the Court had come to town, the King added, the Duke had taken the Prince 'to the lowest places of debauchery, where they got dead drunk, and were often carried home in that condition.'

'I wonder,' said Gloucester, 'that your Majesty bears all this.'

'What would you have me do in my *present distress*?' asked the King. 'If I did not bear it, it would only drive my son into Opposition, which would increase my distresses.'[5]

At first, the King's softly-softly approach made little difference. By February 1782, the Prince was a frequent visitor to Cumberland House where a faro bank was kept for his amusement; the Duke, in turn, 'carried bankers and very bad company to the Prince's apartments' in Buckingham House. 'This behaviour,' noted Walpole, 'was very grating to the King, and the offences increased.' He added:

> But it was not long before the folly and vulgarity of the Duke of Cumberland disgusted the Prince. His style was so low that, alluding to the Principality of Wales, the Duke called his nephew *Taffy*. The Prince was offended at such indecent familiarity, and begged it might not be repeated – but in vain . . . Yet though the Prince had too much pride to be treated vulgarly, he had not enough to disuse the same style. Nothing was coarser than his conversation and phrases; and it made men smile to find that in the palace of piety and pride his Royal Highness had learnt nothing but the dialect of footmen and grooms.[6]

Unfortunately, the Prince was showing no sign of dropping his other undesirable friends. In March 1782, the King castigated him for missing one of his Levées without permission so that he could hunt in Northamptonshire with Anthony St Leger. If the Prince did not amend his conduct, the King warned, he would be obliged 'to take steps that certainly will be disagreable'. Such 'improper behaviour' was 'doubly severe' to the King at a time when he was being 'harassed' by certain political events. For the government was about to fall over its poor handling of the American War.[7]

Lord North, a Tory, had been Prime Minister since 1770. A former Chancellor of the Exchequer, North had supported Charles Townshend's Revenue Act of 1767 which imposed duty on glass, lead, paper, paint and tea imported into the 13 colonies of America. When the colonists raised the cry of 'No taxation without representation!', North declared: 'I will never yield till I have seen America at my feet.'

Once at the head of government, however, he agreed to the repeal of all Townshend's duties except that on tea, which was then drunk in relatively small volumes in America and only raised about £3,000 a year in tax. Furthermore, the level of duty was only 3d per pound, a quarter of the tax paid by British tea-drinkers.

But the colonists' objection to taxation was one of principle, and in December 1773 a mob of Boston citizens attacked three tea-ships owned by the East India Company and emptied their cargo, worth £18,000, into the harbour. The so-called 'Boston Tea Party' outraged opinion in Britain, causing North to introduce measures that would suspend the Massachusetts Charter, close Boston harbour and transfer its trade to Salem, replace the elected Council of Massachusetts with one nominated by the Crown, and give the Governor the power to choose all judges and magistrates. The proposals were passed by both Houses of Parliament with large majorities.

It was the point of no return. Angered by these repressive measures, the other 12 American colonies – hitherto lukewarm in their opposition to the British Crown – rallied behind Massachusetts. In September 1774, at the First Continental Congress in Philadelphia, the radical majority agreed to an outright rejection of Britain's powers of taxation and right of legislation. North's government responded by sending more troops to America, causing the colonists to raise local militia.

War duly broke out on 19 April 1775 when a party of British troops, on their way to seize a cache of rebel arms at Concord, Massachusetts, were engaged by a small body of militia at Lexington. At the Second Continental Congress, which met in early May, the country was put on a war footing and George Washington, a Virginian gentleman-farmer and politician who had served with the British in the war against the French in Canada in 1759, was appointed Commander-in-Chief of the Continental Army. Meanwhile, more British troops had arrived in Boston. In an attempt to hem them in, the rebels constructed a series of earthworks on Bunker Hill at the neck of the peninsula. These were eventually taken by General Howe on 17 June, but at a cost of more than half his 2,000 men.

A year later, during which time the British had evacuated Boston, lost Montreal but repulsed the rebels from Quebec, the legislatures of the 13 American colonies signed the Declaration of Independence on 4 July 1776. For a time the fortunes of the British improved. In August, General Howe landed at Long Island, New York, defeated Washington at Brooklyn and forced him to retreat over the Delaware. American defeatism was rife and militiamen began to desert; but their morale was restored in December when Washington recrossed the river and beat a British force at Trenton, New Jersey.

The new British plan was to drive a wedge through the middle of the American colonies, so that each half could be pacified separately. The line chosen was the River Hudson, which would be taken by a two-pronged assault – southwards from Canada and northwards from New York. But with General Burgoyne making heavy going of his descent from Canada, Howe in New York decided to take Philadelphia, which he achieved on 25 September 1777 after defeating Washington at Brandywine Creek. It was now too late to assist Burgoyne, who was forced to surrender to General Gates at Saratoga on 17 October.

The tide was turning. On 6 February 1778, France signed an alliance with the rebels; Spain followed suit 16 months later. By now British troops had abandoned Philadelphia and invaded Georgia, taking

Savannah in December 1778. After Charleston had fallen in May 1780, the victorious British troops under General Cornwallis fought their way up through North Carolina and into Virginia, where they established a base at Yorktown, near the mouth of the Chesapeake River. But when Washington's army arrived from the north, after feinting an attack against New York, and a superior French fleet forced Admiral Hood's squadron to withdraw, Cornwallis's 7,000 men were cut off. On 19 October 1781, after fierce resistance, his entire army capitulated. 'Oh God!' cried Lord North on hearing the news. 'It is all over.'[8]

His belief in ultimate victory gone, the Prime Minister now tried to convince George III that to continue the war was pointless. But the King was determined to fight on, and told Parliament so when he reopened it on 27 November. He reckoned without the stirring oratory of the brilliant Charles James Fox, a leading member of the Whig opposition. If members were asked, said Fox, to put their hands on their hearts and declare that they truly believed Britain could ever conquer America, North and he would be in agreement because he 'believed in his soul that the [Prime] Minister himself would vote against . . . this accursed and abominable war'. The real villain was the 'influence of the Crown': to it could be attributed the 'loss of the thirteen provinces of America', for it was 'the influence of the Crown in the two Houses of Parliament that enabled his Majesty's ministers to persevere against the voice of reason, the voice of truth, the voice of the people'.[9]

This was no exaggeration. In theory, the British political system was neither an absolute monarchy, an aristocratic oligarchy nor a democracy, but a mixed Constitution in which all three elements shared power. The Revolution of 1688 had done away with the absolutism of the Crown and made it impossible for a monarch to govern without the consent of Parliament. An elaborate system of checks and balances safeguarded the system: the House of Commons' control over finance was an effective check on the sovereign; the right of the Crown to create peers was an effective check on the House of Lords; the right of the Crown to dissolve Parliament and to veto Bills was an effective check on the Legislature as a whole.

But in truth, the Crown wielded the greatest power because of the enormous amount of patronage at its disposal. At any one time, therefore, up to a third of the members of the House of Commons were 'placemen', bound to support the ministry that retained the King's favour. The rest were equally divided between factions of politicans loosely grouped under the terms Tory and Whig (the 'ins' and the 'outs') and the Independents, members unconnected with any faction. No government, therefore, could be a party government because all Prime Ministers were dependent on the support of the Crown and the goodwill of at least some unattached Independents. It followed that only in exceptional circumstances could the King's servants be ousted from power against his will.

The year 1782 was just such an occasion. Criticised almost daily on its conduct of the war, Lord North's government tottered and then fell. On 20 March, exactly a month after narrowly defeating a vote of no confidence in the way the naval war was being conducted, North offered his resignation. 'Remember my Lord, it is you that desert me, not I you,' remarked a bitter George III, who was now at the mercy of his political enemies – the Whigs.[10]

The political descendants of the leaders of the Glorious Revolution, the Whigs were divided into two main factions: one led by the second Earl of Shelburne, the other by the second Marquess of Rockingham. For the King, the more acceptable of the two was Shelburne, but he did not have enough parliamentary support to form a government. Therefore Rockingham became Prime Minister by default. His price: no royal veto on American independence, economies in all departments of state, and the reduction of Court influence by excluding government contractors from the Commons and abolishing sinecures.

Among Rockingham's senior appointments were Shelburne and Charles James Fox as Home and Foreign Secretaries respectively. The latter, just 33, was the brilliant but dissolute younger son of the late

Henry Fox, 1st Baron Holland, whose tenure as Paymaster-General during the Seven Years' War had enabled him to accumulate an enormous fortune. Twenty years after his death, in a petition to the King from the Livery Company of London, Holland was described as 'the public defaulter of unaccounted millions'.[11]

A heavy drinker and an inveterate gambler, an M.P. since the age of 19 (the minimum age of 20 having been overlooked), Charles Fox had made a name for himself in Parliament by his acid condemnation of North's handling of the American War. He was, as a consequence, particularly repugnant to George III. 'That young man,' wrote the King to Lord North in 1774, 'has so thoroughly cast off every principle of common honour and honesty, that he must become as contemptible as he is odious.'[12]

Three weeks before joining the new government, Fox presented the King with an Address from his Westminster constituency. He 'took it', noted a bitter George Selwyn, who was about to lose his sinecure 'place' on account of the change of ministry, 'as you would take a pocket handkerchief from your *valet de chambre* . . . and passed it to his Lord in Waiting'.[13]

However, Fox would not be in a position to torment the King for long. On 1 July 1782, with his government just three months old, Rockingham died – but not before his administration had passed legislation which substantially weakened the hold of the Crown over the Executive by limiting the amount of patronage at the latter's disposal. One act had disenfranchised the revenue officers of the Crown, thereby removing the vote from those most susceptible to government pressure; another had disqualified those holding government contracts from becoming M.P.s.

With Rockingham gone, the King appointed Shelburne as his successor. This, in turn, led to Fox's resignation. The ostensible reason was a conflict over policy (Fox wanted the Americans to be granted independence *before* the conclusion of a peace treaty), but the reality was that he distrusted Shelburne – as his father had done before him – and would not serve under him. Of the remaining four Rockinghamite

Cabinet ministers, only Lord John Cavendish, the Chancellor of the Exchequer, followed him into Opposition. Cavendish was replaced by William Pitt the Younger, 23, the exceptionally gifted second son of the great statesman, his namesake (latterly the Earl of Chatham), who had died in 1778.

It was about this time that Fox's long intimacy with the heir to the throne began. 'The Prince of Wales dined with Mr Fox yesterday by previous engagement,' noted Horace Walpole, shortly after Fox's resignation, 'they drank royally.'

Fox may have been having an affair with the Prince's former mistress, Mrs Robinson, but their common ground was more than just a shared taste in women: 'The Prince,' wrote Fox's most recent biographer,

> was a man of as many gifts as frailties, and there was much about him which Fox found genuinely attractive; but another motive for the ripening friendship must realistically be seen in the Prince's position as heir apparent. It was well to be on good terms with the future king, and opposition politicians had traditionally cultivated Georgian Princes of Wales.[14]

Fox, in turn, held many attractions for the impressionable Prince: a brilliant mind, dazzling conversation and a rebellious nature, not to mention the fact that his politics were anathema to the King. By December, as the possibility of an unholy alliance between the Rockinghamite Whigs (now nominally led by the Duke of Portland, but in reality by Fox) and Lord North's Tories became increasingly likely, Fox was seeking the Prince's views on a change of government. 'What I meant to say,' wrote Fox on the 18th, 'was only that I thought from the appearance of things that there was a great probability of change, and that on that account I wished very much for an opportunity of conversing with your Royal Highness in order to know your wishes upon matters in which (in any situation) it would be my happiness to obey your commands.'[15]

Whereas Shelburne could count on only about 140 solid supporters in the 558-strong House of Commons, North had 120 followers and Fox 90. If the latter pair combined, and enough Independents voted with them, the government could be ousted. Their opportunity came in February 1783 during debates over the terms of the peace treaty with America and her allies. On the 24th, having suffered two narrow defeats in the House of Commons, Shelburne resigned.

The King was now in a particularly unenviable position; twice in the space of a year his chosen ministry had been ousted by pressure from the House of Commons, which left a Fox–North Coalition as the only viable alternative. As its leaders had agreed to be equal partners in any new government, they put forward the unexceptional Duke of Portland as the Prime Minister. On 4 March, so Fox told the Prince, North wrote to inform the King of this condition. His subsequent 'interview with his Majesty was short,' wrote Fox, 'and the substance of the conversation was merely this: that as we could not give up the point of the Treasury, and as Lord North could not take it nor act without us, that his Majesty had no further commands for his Lordship. This negotiation is therefore entirely at an end, and not only the country is now without a Ministry, but there does not appear at present any prospect of making one.'[16]

By now, according to Horace Walpole, the Prince had 'thrown himself into the arms of Charles Fox . . . in the most indecent and undisguised manner'. As soon as Fox rose from his lodgings in St James's Street, which was often very late, he would proceed to nearby Brook's Club where he held court. Walpole noted:

> His bristly black person, and shagged breast quite open, and rarely purified by any ablutions, was wrapped in a foul linen night-gown, and his bushy hair dishevelled. In these cynic weeds, and with epicurean good humour, did he dictate politics – and in this school did the heir of the Crown attend his lessons and imbibe them . . . The Prince not only espoused the cause of the Coalition, but was not at all guarded in his expressions: he was even reported to have said aloud in the

Drawing-room, 'that his father had not yet agreed to the plan of the Coalition, but, by God, he should be made to agree to it'.[17]

The King, meanwhile, was sounding out every possible alternative. He offered the premiership without success to young Pitt, Lord Weymouth, Lord Temple (the Lord-Lieutenant of Ireland) and Lord Gower (the head of the old Duke of Bedford's faction). None could muster sufficient backing in the House of Commons. When Gower suggested trying Thomas Pitt, the nephew of Lord Chatham, the King replied, 'Yes, Mr Thomas Pitt or Mr Thomas *Anybody*.'[18]

But Thomas Pitt, too, had no option but to refuse. By 12 March, the King had been forced to accept Portland as the head of government, with Fox and North as Foreign and Home Secretaries respectively. What he could not agree to was Fox's demand, made through Portland, that the Coalition be allowed to nominate all seven principal ministers. Nearing the end of his tether, the King even contemplated abdicating in favour of his eldest son and returning to Hanover. He even wrote, but never sent, letters of abdication to his son and the Houses of Parliament.

'The situation of the times are such,' read the former, 'that I must, if I attempt to carry on the business of the nation, give up every political principle . . . ; and must form a Ministry from among men who know I cannot trust them and therefore will not accept office without making me a kind of a slave.' Only by abdicating could he avoid the destruction of his 'principles and honour'.[19]

As the members of Brook's laid bets on the duration of his reign, the King – according to Walpole – went to the extreme of consulting Lord Thurlow, the Chancellor, on what legal 'redress he could have against a man who alienated him from the affection of his son'. Thurlow is said to have replied 'that he would have no peace till his son and Fox were secured in the Tower'.[20]

After Pitt's second refusal, the King caved in. He had held out, so he told Lord Temple on 1 April:

> . . . till not a single man is willing to come to my assistance and
> till the House of Commons has taken every step but insisting
> on this faction by name being appointed ministers. To end the
> conflict which stops every wheel of government . . . I intend
> this night to acquaint that *grateful* man Lord North that the
> seven cabinet counsellors that the coalition had named shall kiss
> hands tomorrow.

But the new government, he continued, would not enjoy either his
favour or his confidence. He would 'refuse any honours that may be
asked by them' and hoped that not many months would 'elapse before
the Grenvilles [Temple was one], the Pitts and other men of ability and
character' would relieve him of such an intolerable situation.[21]

The following day, the seven principal Cabinet ministers – four
Foxites (as the Rockinghamites had now become) and three of North's
faction – were received by the King. He was, said Walpole, remarkably
gracious to the Duke of Portland and Fox, although Lord North was
treated with the 'utmost coldness'. Lord Townshend, an eyewitness,
gives a slightly different slant to the occasion. As Fox was presented, the
King 'turned back his ears and eyes just like the horse at Astley's when
the tailor he had determined to throw was getting on him'.[22]

The fact that the King refused to grant any new peerages (or even
promotions within the peerage) was a serious blow to the new government. This diminution of its powers of patronage – and therefore its
ability to secure votes in both Houses – was compounded by the effects
of the reforms passed during Rockingham's administration.

As a result, even Fox was prepared to tread cautiously. At his first
royal audience, responding to the rumours that he had encouraged the
Prince in his filial disobedience, he told the King that 'he had never said
a word to the Prince which he would not have been glad to have his
Majesty hear'. He had only promised, he continued, to settle the question of the Prince's separate Establishment when he gained his majority
that August. 'Oh,' replied the King, 'that will all be in good time.'[23]

When the matter first arose in Cabinet in early June – the King having agreed to leave it to Portland – Fox suggested the fantastic annual figure of £100,000, to include £12,000 from the revenue of the Duchy of Cornwall. At first only Portland and Lord Keppel, the First Lord of the Admiralty, were enthusiastic; but the remaining members of the Cabinet were won over when they were told that Shelburne had promised a similar sum. How, then, could his 'friends' offer less?

According to Richard Fitzpatrick, the Secretary at War, the King gave his consent to the initial proposal that Parliament would be applied to for the whole £100,000. But when the Cabinet then decided that 'a part from Parliament, and a part from the Civil List, would be more palatable', and amended the proposal accordingly, the King demurred. Not then on speaking terms with the Prince, he drafted a letter to Colonel Hotham, his Treasurer, telling him that £100,000 was the amount granted to his grandfather when he had a wife and nine children to support, and that the burden of taxes on the people made such a figure wholly unjustifiable.

Next day, 16 June, the King received another letter from Portland, detailing the government's intention to include the Prince's debts of £29,000 in the settlement. It was the final straw:

> It is impossible [he wrote in reply] for me to find words expressive enough of my utter indignation and astonishment . . . When the Duke of Portland came into office I had at least hoped he would have thought himself obliged to have my interest and that of the public at heart, and not have neglected both to the passions of an ill-advised young man . . . If the Prince of Wales's establishment falls on me, it is a weight I am unable to bear; if on the public I cannot in conscience give my acquiescence to what I deem a shameful squandering of public money.[24]

The Cabinet was 'thunderstruck', wrote Walpole, and met to consider resigning *en bloc*. Before they could come to a decision, however, 'the Duke of Portland was summoned to the King, who in an agony of tears kissed the Duke' and 'confessed he had gone too far'. But when Portland then suggested resurrecting the original proposal, whereby Parliament would be asked for the whole £100,000, the King would not have it. The most he would agree to was £50,000 a year from the Civil List, an additional £12,000 from the Duchy of Cornwall revenue (which was the Prince's by right) and a one-off parliamentary grant of £50,000 (it became £60,000) to settle his debts and set up his own Establishment.[25]

The majority in the Cabinet were all for accepting the King's offer; only Fox and, to a lesser extent, Portland felt honour bound to resign unless the prince consented to this drop in his future income. At last he did, thanks to the coaxing of his close friend, the Duchess of Devonshire, who asked him to consider 'whether it is not in the power of the present administration to serve you more by staying in than going out'.[26]

Colonel Lake, recently returned from America, was also prominent in persuading the Prince to release Fox from his obligation by accepting a measure he was 'naturally very averse to'.

The King, needless to say, was not slow in rubbing salt into the Prince's wounds by sending Hotham, his Treasurer, an amended version of the earlier draft letter on 21 June. He did not see any merit, he wrote, in applying to Parliament to increase the Prince's income beyond £62,000; that in itself was £27,000 more than he himself had received at a similar age. In any case, the prince's disgraceful conduct over the previous three years – 'his neglect of every religious duty . . . want of even common civility to the Queen and me . . . and his total disobedience of every injunction I have given' – had forfeited any sympathy that he, the King, might otherwise have felt.

But despite this minor victory, the King could not 'forgive or forget' the conduct of his ministers towards him. He would sack them as soon as the opportunity arose.[27]

On reaching his majority on 12 August 1783, the Prince was given Carlton House in Pall Mall as his official residence. It had not been inhabited since the death of his grandmother, the Princess Dowager of Wales, 11 years earlier. An undistinguished stone-faced mansion, designed by the 3rd Earl of Burlington in the early eighteenth century for his uncle, Baron Carleton, its only outstanding feature was its beautiful gardens. Laid out by Burlington's protégé, William Kent, in imitation of Alexander Pope's beautiful grounds at Twickenham, they ran westward as far as Marlborough House, the tasteful mansion built by Sir Christopher Wren for the first Duchess.

To enlarge and refurbish Carlton House, the Prince engaged Henry Holland, who had married the daughter – and taken over the architectural practice – of Lancelot 'Capability' Brown. The designer of Brook's Club in the late 1770s, Holland's French-influenced interiors would soon be the hallmark of the Prince's new house. The work begun by Holland in the early autumn of 1783 continued on and off for nearly 30 years, at an eventual cost of more than £500,000.

In November 1783, the Prince moved in as the work continued around him; within a few months, the first stages of the alteration were complete. The new façade, with its elegant Corinthian portico, was generally admired – Horace Walpole praising its 'august simplicity' – though Captain Rees Gronow, the diarist and dandy, would later condemn the whole building as 'one of the meanest and most ugly . . . that ever disfigured London, notwithstanding it was screened by a row of columns'.[28]

Opinions about the magnificent interior were similarly divided. Beyond the impressive entrance hall, fringed with Ionic columns of Siena marble, was an octagon with a sweeping double staircase which led up to the state apartments, the Prince's bow-windowed bedroom, his dressing-room and bathroom. The ground floor accommodated the music room and the prince's famous Chinese drawing-room, for which the authentic lanterns alone cost £441.

Over the years, adjoining properties were bought up and demolished; new wings, servants' quarters and stables were added. Part of one new suite of rooms was a fan-vaulted Gothic conservatory which could have been mistaken for a small cathedral. The gardens acquired more statues, a waterfall, a marble-floored temple, even an observatory. Craftsmen and decorators were brought in from all over Europe; the exquisite furniture, most of which came from France, was supplemented by fine English and Dutch oil paintings, Sèvres china, Gobelin tapestries, bronzes, clocks and marble busts. In the opinion of the novelist Robert Plumer Ward, it became the equal of the Palace of Versailles. Others, like Robert Smirke, the dour architect of many of London's public buildings, thought the apartments were vulgar and 'overdone with finery'.[29]

On 11 November 1783, at the opening of the new session of Parliament, the Prince made his first appearance in the House of Lords. Extravagantly attired in black velvet lined with pink satin and embroidered with gold and pink spangle, pink high-heeled shoes, his hair frizzed 'with two very full curls at the sides', he took his seat in the chair of state on the right side of the throne as the King made his traditional Speech.[30]

He then went to the House of Commons to add his moral support as Fox sought to defend the peace treaties which the government had recently concluded with France, Spain and the United States. But he need not have bothered. Fox's speech was a triumph, 'allowed by all those who heard it,' reported the *Morning Chronicle*, 'to be one of the ablest, and at the same time one of the most fair and honest ever delivered from the mouth of a Minister at the opening of a session of Parliament'.[31]

But Fox would soon be brought down by a separate piece of legislation referred to in the King's Speech: his Government of India Bill, introduced to the House of Commons a week after the opening of Parliament, which sought to increase domestic control over the Honourable East India Company, the dominant force in the sub-continent. Originally a trading house, granted an exclusive charter by Elizabeth I, the Company had taken to enlisting soldiers in the early eighteenth century as the break-up of the great Moghul Empire in north and central India began to threaten its lucrative business. So began a long period of territorial expansion, as obdurate rulers were defeated and the more biddable ones were recognised as clients.

In 1773, alarmed by this growth, Parliament passed a Regulating Act which made the Company responsible for civil government in its territories and gave the Governor-General of Bengal, the largest of the three presidencies ruled by the Company, supervisory control over the other two: Bombay and Madras. A year later, the India Act brought the Company's Board of Directors under the authority of a newly created Cabinet minister, the President of the Board of Control. But by the early 1780s, with the finances of the Company in turmoil, it was generally accepted that Parliament would have to have more of a say in the government of the Company's territories. The question was, how much more?

Fox's Bill – heavily influenced by the work of Edmund Burke, the chairman of a parliamentary sub-committee on India – was ingenuous. It aimed to strengthen domestic control over the Company without increasing the power of the King's government by appointing a seven-member commission with executive authority. These commissioners – named in the Bill and all supporters of the Fox-North Coalition – would serve in London for no fewer than three or more than five years, after which time their successors would be governmentally appointed. Another parliamentary sub-committee, chaired by Henry Dundas, had suggested increasing the power of the Governor-General as a remedy to the Company's misdeeds, but this was just what Fox and Burke wanted to avoid. Replying to Opposition criticism that his Bill would undermine strong government in India by ceding ultimate power to commissioners separated by a voyage of six months, Fox replied that every line of his Bill 'presumes the possibility of bad administration, for every word breathes suspicion'.

Pitt's charge that the Bill combined 'absolute despotism' with 'gross corruption', and was 'one of the boldest and most alarming attempts at the exercise of tyranny that ever disgraced the annals of this or any other country', failed to win over enough Independent M.P.s, and it passed its third reading in the House of Commons in November by 229 votes to 120.

But those outside Parliament feared the effect of the transfer of patronage from the Company to the commissioners, seeing this as an attempt to ensure the continuation of the Coalition government by substituting the legitimate influence of the Crown for the illegitimate influence of faction. The most celebrated cartoon of many, by James Sayer and entitled 'Carlo Khan, the Great Potentate of Leadenhall Street', depicted an enormously fat Fox making a triumphal entry into the London headquarters of the East India Company astride an elephant with the face of Lord North, and preceded by Burke as herald.

At the beginning of December, as the Bill was about to be sent up to the House of Lords, former Lord Chancellor Thurlow sent the King a memorandum, co-drafted with Earl Temple, suggesting that the House of Lords should be 'informed of his feelings' about the proposed legislation. The King, who had already received Pitt's secret agreement to form an alternative administration if the Bill was defeated, was only too happy to comply. On 11 December, in a written statement, Temple was authorised to tell the members of the Upper House that 'whoever voted for the India Bill was not only not his friend, but would be considered by him an enemy'.

Such an interference by the King in the passage of legislation sponsored by his own ministers was unprecedented; it was also decisive. When the Lords divided for the first time in the early hours of 16 December, the Bill was defeated by 69 votes to 57. Among those voting with the government was the Prince of Wales, though it is unlikely that he was then aware of the exact form of words used by his father to Lord Temple; when he did discover that his vote put him among his father's 'enemies', he made a hasty apology and promised not to support the Bill a second time. He was not the only one. On 17 December, when the House divided once again, the majority against the Bill had increased to 19.

The government was dismissed the following evening. 'Lord North is by this required,' read the King's letter (he could not bring himself to write to Fox), 'to send me the seals of his department, and to acquaint Mr Fox to send me the seals of the Foreign Department. [The under-secretaries] will be the proper channel of delivering them to me this night. I choose this method as audiences on such occasions must be unpleasant.'[32]

Next day, the 24-year-old Pitt kissed hands as First Lord of the Treasury and Chancellor of the Exchequer (the youngest Prime Minister in history); Fox would not see office again for more than 22 years.

A description of the Prince at this time, by the diarist Nathaniel Wraxall, is particularly revealing:

> Nature had bestowed uncommon graces on his figure and person, nor were his manners less highly distinguished than his birth . . . Like the princes of the House of Brunswick, he manifested an early tendency to become corpulent; nor did he, like George III, repress that disposition by abstinence or renunciation. Convivial as well as social in his temper, destitute of all reserve, . . . he presented in these respects a contrast to the shy, correct, and distant manners of the King, his father. Endowed with all the aptitudes to profit by instruction, his mind had been cultivated with great care, and he was probably the only prince in Europe, heir to a powerful monarchy, competent to peruse the Greek as well as the Roman poets and historians in their own language. Capable of warm and steady friendship, he possessed a heart not less susceptible of love and live to the impressions as well as to the seduction of female charms. Humane and compassionate, his purse was open to every application of distress, nor was it ever shut against genius or merit.[33]

One woman to whom his purse was never closed was Georgiana, the

beautiful Duchess of Devonshire. Born in 1757, the daughter of the 1st
Earl Spencer, she had married the 5th Duke when she was 17. But even
his fantastic wealth was hard put to keep pace with the gambling debts
his young wife managed to accumulate. To hide the extent of her
indebtedness from the Duke, she was forced to borrow ever more sums
from moneylenders at increasingly exorbitant rates of interest.

Her greatest benefactor over the years was the Prince, who lent her
thousands of pounds without ever expecting it to be repaid. He
undoubtedly desired the Duchess, as his attempted seduction of her in
later years proves, but he was not the sort of man to temper his generosity by *expecting* anything in return. This did not, however, put a stop
to the inevitable gossip, particularly as the Prince was a regular visitor
at Devonshire House, the Duke's imposing London mansion. Mr
Heaton, the Duke's agent, was one of the first to drop hints. 'This man,'
wrote the Duchess to Lady Elizabeth Foster on 6 January 1784, 'I was
obliged to have a dispute with this year because I thought he had ill
used some people employed at Chatsworth. His revenge was insinuat-
ing to [the Duke] that people thought the P[rince] of W[ales] liked
me.'[34]

On 10 March 1784, with the initial alterations to Carlton House
almost complete, the Prince gave a celebratory ball. Among the guests
was his first love, Mary Hamilton, who had 'two long conversations'
with him 'in the old friendly style'. There were, she noted in her diary,
'between 5–600 people, no distinction of party, as there were both the
ins & outs'. Having begun the ball by dancing with Lady Charlotte
Bertie, the daughter of the late Duke of Ancaster, the Prince quit the
floor 'as he had not been well'. But he returned at about 2 in the morning to dance a minuet with the same partner. 'He dances *very finely*.'

Supper finally got under way at 2.30. 'I went to the lower rooms,'
wrote Hamilton, 'everything handsome and *proper* and well attended.'
The pages were dressed in a dark-coloured uniform trimmed with
gold lace; the footmen, who waited on the tables, in the royal livery. 'In
short it was a fine entertainment and as well conducted as possible for
so great a number of People. The Prince's attentions were *properly*

divided, and nothing in my opinion could be more proper than his behaviour – *what a pity that one who knows so well how to do what is right, ever fails of doing so!*[35]

Two days earlier, the House of Commons had passed by a single vote a motion to submit to the King an Address calling for the dismissal of Pitt's ministry on the grounds that it had adopted principles 'unfriendly to the privileges of the House and to the freedom of our excellent constitution'. This was the final straw. On 25 March 1784, the King granted Pitt's request for a dissolution of Parliament and a General Election. Thanks to the government's monopoly of patronage and electoral management, there was never any doubt that it would come out on top.

Like all eighteenth-century elections, that of 1784 was corrupt in that many 'rotten' or 'pocket' boroughs – those with a handful of voters in the thrall of a single great landlord – were available in return for peerages, other honours and money. Even voters in the 'open' boroughs and counties were not immune to financial and alcoholic inducements. However, compared with the 1780 election when £62,000 of Treasury money was spent to secure a government victory, that of 1784 was relatively 'clean' in that only half that sum was spent. Large-scale bribery was unnecessary because middle-class opinion – identifying Fox as a threat to the monarchy – was generally against the Coalition candidates in the seats where it could prevail: the counties and the 'open' boroughs.

The hardest-fought contest, and the one in which the Prince took the closest interest, was in Fox's Westminster constituency where three strong candidates were competing for two seats. Admiral Lord Hood, a government supporter and naval hero, was expected to top the poll; the fight would then be between Fox and Sir Cecil Wray, a rich landowner who had only recently abandoned his Whig principles to support Pitt. The administration was particularly keen to win this second seat, partly because it was Westminster and partly because it would be a blow to the prestige of its most dangerous opponent. It would not, however, remove him from Parliament because he had already taken the precaution of being nominated for the borough of Tain in northern Scotland, in the 'pocket' of a sympathetic Whig patron, Sir Thomas Dundas.

Unlike many borough constituencies, Westminster was as close as you could get to a genuine contest. Uniquely it provided the vote to every 'inhabitant householder', giving it the largest electorate in the land which included the members of fashionable society and the political élite, as well as a number of middle and lower-class voters.

In the event, the Westminster poll went on for 40 days, the longest of the election. It was, remarked Hood, the veteran of numerous sea battles, 'the most arduous and unpleasant business I ever took in hand'. Rival supporters with their bands and banners roamed the streets, and several clashes occurred. In one, a 'gang of fellows headed by naval officers' and 'carrying his Majesty's colours' fought with 'a mob of Irish chairmen and pickpockets'. In another a constable was killed, each side blaming the other for his death.'[36]

Many fashionable ladies turned out to canvass for both sides, but the Foxites had the edge in the glamour department with the support of the gorgeous Spencer sisters, the Duchess of Devonshire and Lady Duncannon (later the Countess of Bessborough), as well as the Duchess of Portland. Of the three, Georgiana Devonshire was far and away the biggest asset. 'She was very beautiful,' wrote Mrs Papendiek, 'and her manner was so engaging, so sprightly, and withal so gentle and polite, that all who came into contact with her at once became subservient to her influence.'[37]

Despite withdrawing from the contest for a time at the behest of her mother, Lady Spencer, who felt she was disgracing herself and her family, the Duchess was soon back canvassing, clad in Foxite buff and blue, the colours of Washington's volunteers. It was said that she shook hands with a cobbler and, worse, kissed a butcher. She denied the latter charge: it was her sister and another lady who had been kissed.

When the poll finally closed on 17 May, Hood was the winner with 6,694 votes. Fox, after a shaky start, had come second with 6,234; Wray a narrow last with 5,998. However, Hood and Fox were not declared elected by the High Bailiff because Wray had demanded a scrutiny. Unlike a recount today, a scrutiny looked at each ballot paper in some detail to decide if a vote was genuine. It could take months, and on this occasion did. Hood and Fox would have to wait until 3 March 1785 before they were formally declared elected.

But this did little to dampen the celebrations of Fox's supporters as they carried him in a laurel-decked chair through the streets of the constituency. Leading this pre-planned triumphal procession were heralds on horseback, 24 butchers wielding marrow-bones and cleavers, 'bands of music, cat-call noises of all kinds, emblems of every insignia of a fox, twelve carriages of commoners and gentry, with their best liveries and every possible decoration', 24 horsemen, wearing blue coats and buff waistcoats. Then came Fox himself, followed by 24 gentlemen of the Prince's Household, the Liberty Boys of Newport Market, the state carriages of the Duchesses of Portland and Devonshire and finally, bringing up the rear, the Prince's state carriage 'with the full equipment of horses, men, dress'.

Having reached Carlton House, the procession did three rounds of the courtyard as the Prince and his friends cheered from the windows. Then it moved off down Pall Mall and up St James's Street to Devonshire House, where the Prince was once again waiting to greet it after having raced through the back streets in his private carriage. Standing on a platform behind the wall of the courtyard, flanked by the Duchesses of Portland and Devonshire, the Prince was wearing a wreath of laurel and a fox's brush.

After speeches, dinner at Devonshire House and more speeches at Willis's Rooms, the festivities were continued the following day when the Prince gave a magnificent fête in the gardens of Carlton House which went on until 6 in the evening. This was followed by a ball at the house of Mrs Anne Crewe, the wife of the Foxite M.P. for Cheshire and a celebrated beauty. At some point during the evening, the Prince proposed the toast, 'Here's buff and blue and Mrs Crewe!', to which his hostess responded, quick as a flash, 'Here's buff and blue and all of *you!*'[38]

More parties followed, at one of which the sozzled Prince collapsed while dancing a quadrille; no sooner had he been helped to his feet than he was violently sick. Clearly, he was no more capable of holding his drink now than he had been as a teenager. Only a month earlier, he and three companions had been arrested for drunkenness in Mount Street and confined in the watch-house. When the tailor of one of the party arrived to post bail, he goggled at the sight of the Prince. Did the constable and watchmen not realise that they had detained the heir to the throne, he asked? Horrified, they went straight to the Prince and expressed the hope that he had not been offended by their actions.

'Offended, my good fellows. By no means!' he replied. 'Thank God the laws of this country are superior to rank; and when men from high station forget the decorums of community, it is fit that no distinction should be made with respect to them. It should make an Englishman proud to see the Prince of Wales obliged to send for a tailor to bail him.'[39]

3

Mrs Fitzherbert

'The Prince of Wales has given several parties and means to continue them for a week,' wrote the Duchess of Devonshire to a friend on 18 May, the day after Fox's victory in the Westminster election. 'His flirt, Mrs Hodges, has gone out of town; her brother behaved vastly well about it, and said if her husband would not take her out of town he would, for he didn't choose his sister should be talked of in such a manner. Mrs Fitzherbert is at present his favourite, but she seems, I think, rather to cut him than otherwise.'[1]

So reads one of the earliest references to the woman who was to become the love of the Prince's life. Born Maria Anne Smythe on 26 July 1756, the eldest daughter of Walter Smythe of Brambridge in Hampshire, Mrs Fitzherbert was of Catholic Royalist stock. The baronetcy of her paternal grandfather, Sir John, had been bestowed by Charles II in 1660 for his family's loyal support during the Civil War. Her mother, Maria Errington, descended from an old Northumberland Catholic family, was the half-sister of the 1st Earl of Sefton.

From the age of 12 to 16, Maria was educated at an English convent run by Conceptionist nuns in Paris. During one of her parents' visits, she was taken to Versailles to see King Louis XV dine. But the sight of such an all-powerful monarch pulling apart a chicken with his fingers was too much for young Maria to bear – and she burst out laughing. Fortunately the King was charmed rather than insulted by this harmless instance of *lèse majesté*, and he ordered the Duc de Soubise, one of his courtiers, to present her with a 'dish of sugarplums'.

At 18, with suitors from the closed world of the Catholic gentry queueing up, she married Edward Weld of Lulworth Castle, Dorset, a rich landowner 26 years her senior. Three months later Weld was dead, having fallen from his horse. Though he intended to leave all his property to his wife, he had forgotten to sign the will and everything went to his brother.

Three years later, in 1777, she married Thomas Fitzherbert of Swynnerton Park in Staffordshire, the head of another ancient Catholic family. He was among the first Catholic gentlemen to forsake the Stuarts and openly declare allegiance to England's Hanoverian Kings. In his London house in Park Street, like-minded members of his faith would meet to discuss ways to lobby for the repeal of laws which excluded Catholics from the Bar, the armed services and all government appointments of trust. This lobbying bore partial fruit in 1778 with the passing of the Roman Catholic Relief Act, which made it possible for Catholics to join the army and the navy by removing the Protestant oath of allegiance; now they simply had to swear fidelity to the Crown. (Of course the primary motive behind the Act was to accelerate recruitment for the American War.)

An Anglican backlash was inevitable. Fearing that this legislation was the precursor to more concessions, the ultra-Protestants formed an association under the leadership of Lord George Gordon, 28, the third son of the Duke of Gordon and M.P. for the rotten borough of Ludgershall. On 2 June 1780, while supporters of the Protestant Association blocked the entrances to the Houses of Parliament, Gordon and eight other M.P.s moved that a Protestant petition, objecting to Roman Catholic influence in public life, be taken into immediate consideration. That night, with the mob swelled by criminal elements, the Sardinian chapel in Lincoln's Inn Fields was razed to the ground. The so-called Gordon Riots had begun.

Over the next few days, the rioting became increasingly violent: Roman Catholics and those identified as their sympathisers were attacked in the streets; more foreign chapels and private Catholic houses were looted and burned; Newgate Prison was stormed and its inmates released. The lawlessness continued for a week, partly because the troops could not act without the sanction of civil magistrates who feared for their own property. One Middlesex magistrate who *did* authorise intervention, the blind Sir John Fielding (brother of the novelist Henry Fielding), had his house razed to the ground. It was not until 9 June – after the King had authorised soldiers to open fire – that the riots were finally brought under control.

The killed and wounded – rioters and victims alike – numbered 458; a further 59 rioters were sentenced to death, although only 21 were actually executed. Lord George was imprisoned in the Tower and tried for high treason; but thanks to the eloquence of his counsel, Thomas Erskine, he was acquitted on the ground that he had no treasonable intentions. In 1788, by which time he had converted to Judaism, he was back behind bars: this time for libelling Marie Antoinette, the Queen of France, and the administration of English justice. Unable to find sureties for his future good behaviour, he died of prison fever five years later.

It was in 1780, shortly before the Gordon Riots, that Mrs Fitzherbert first set eyes on the Prince. She was driving down Park Lane in a carriage when her husband pointed out the heir to the throne. A few days later, the Fitzherberts were on their way to a breakfast in Chiswick. 'As they were turning down the Lane,' wrote George Dawson-Damer, who was told the story by Mrs Fitzherbert a year before her death, 'she perceived that the Prince had followed her, and had stopped to look at her.'[2]

Nothing came of the incident. Mrs Fitzherbert was happily married and the Prince was still embroiled with Mrs Robinson. But he had registered his interest. When he next saw her, almost four years later, she was 27, childless and twice a widow, her second husband and infant son having died in the south of France in 1781. Bequeathed a sizeable annuity of £1,000 and a town house in Park Street, she chose to spend her time out of London and away from society.

It was her half-uncle, Lord Sefton, who persuaded her to return to the capital. 'Mrs Fitzherbert is arrived in London for the season,' announced the *Morning Herald* in early March 1784. The meeting with the Prince that was to change both their lives took place at the Opera. Still in widow's weeds and loth to show herself in society, Mrs Fitzherbert had only agreed to go with her uncle, Henry Errington, on condition that she be allowed to wear a bonnet and veil.[3]

Describing the occasion, Dawson-Damer wrote:

> She left the Opera leaning on Henry Errington's arm, and when at the door, with her veil down waiting for the carriage, the Prince came up to him and said, 'Who the devil is that pretty girl you have on your arm, Henry?' On being introduced, the Prince is said to have been transfixed, unable to tear his eyes away from the lovely face half hidden by the veil. Then her carriage drew up and she was able to make her escape.[4]

It would not be for long. On 10 March, Lord Wentworth received a letter from his sister informing him that the Prince was making 'fierce love to the widow Fitzherbert' and was expected to succeed. Though not a traditional beauty – her aquiline nose was too long and her chin too determined – she was undoubtedly striking with her large hazel eyes, golden hair and flawless complexion. But her greatest asset was her demure nature and sweetness of temper. To a Prince who was used to scheming, artful women, this made her irresistible.[5]

He began to lay siege to her affections by bombarding her with invitations to events at Carlton House. Some she accepted, others – as when he planned to make her Queen of the Ball – she did not. This only served to inflame his desire. When she made it clear that there was no question of her becoming his mistress, he proposed marriage, knowing full well that the King would never consent to him marrying a Catholic commoner. Yet if he married secretly, not only would such a union disqualify him from ever becoming King, thanks to the terms of the Act of Settlement of 1701, it would also be in contravention of the 1772 Royal Marriages Act and therefore illegal.

All these arguments were put to the Prince by Mrs Fitzherbert. She was flattered by his attention, even attracted to him, but she could see no future in such a connection. Undeterred, he kept up his entreaties. He could not live without the woman who could be his moral redemption, and would give up everything if only they could be together. He would kill himself, he told the Duchess of Devonshire, if he could not have Mrs Fitzherbert. Understandably alarmed, she agreed to act as a go-between and was relieved when Mrs Fitzherbert concurred with her belief that the match was impossible. 'Her good sense and resolution seemed so strong,' wrote the Duchess, 'that I own I felt secure of her never giving way.' To make the task easier, Mrs Fitzherbert resolved to go abroad.

On the night of 8 July 1784, in a desperate attempt to stop her, the Prince stabbed himself and made out that it was a suicide attempt. Mrs Fitzherbert was preparing for bed when four members of the Prince's Household – Lord Southampton, Tom Onslow, Edward Bouverie and Thomas Keate, his surgeon – arrived at her house 'in the utmost consternation'. They told her what the Prince had done, that he was in mortal danger and that 'only *her* immediate presence would save him'.

At first, suspecting a ruse, she said 'that nothing should induce her to enter Carlton House at this hour'. But the distraught faces and desperate pleas of the Prince's men finally brought her round. She would go, but only if another lady of high character, preferably the Duchess of Devonshire, accompanied her. When they arrived at Devonshire House, the Duchess was in the middle of a dinner party; but no sooner had she been informed of the Prince's injury than she agreed to accompany Mrs Fitzherbert in her carriage.

Arriving at Carlton House, they 'found the Prince in bed, his wound still bleeding'. Mrs Fitzherbert was so overcome that she almost fainted. Before she had had enough time to recover her senses, the Prince told her that 'nothing would induce him to live unless she promised to become his wife'. She meekly agreed, and even allowed the Prince to place one of the Duchess's rings on her finger.

But it was never her intention to go ahead with the marriage. Once back at Devonshire House, she and the Duchess signed a joint statement declaring that 'promises obtained in such a manner are entirely void'. Then she returned home and ordered her servants to pack her trunks; by dawn, she was on her way to the Continent.[6]

Fortunately for the Prince, Mrs Fitzherbert's travelling companion was, the 34-year-old daughter of the Earl of Balcarres, Lady Anne Lindsay, a good friend of his who kept him informed of their whereabouts. On 17 July, while recovering from his wound at a rented house in Brighton, he sent Mrs Fitzherbert – then in Paris – an 18-page letter. Ever since that night at Carlton House, he declared, he had 'looked upon [himself] as married'. Other women no longer held any interest for him. He could not live without her and would kill himself unless she returned. He added: 'You know I never presumed to make you any offer with a view of purchasing your Virtue. I know you too well.' The letter was signed 'not only the most affectionate of Lovers but the tenderest of Husbands'.[7]

More letters followed by special courier – so many, in fact, that for a time the French government suspected espionage and arrested three messengers – but Mrs Fitzherbert steadfastly refused to respond. In desperation, the Prince took to consulting his good friend Charles James Fox at the home of Fox's latest mistress (and future wife) Mrs Armistead. According to Lord Holland, Fox's nephew, who heard the story direct from Mrs Armistead, the Prince:

> . . . cried by the hour [and] testified to the sincerity and violence of his passion and his despair by the most extravagant expressions and actions, rolling on the floor, striking his forehead, tearing his hair, falling into hysterics, and swearing that he would abandon the country, forgo the Crown, sell his jewels

and plate, and scrape together a competence to fly with the object of his affections to America.[8]

On one occasion, the Prince is said to have set off from Brighton on horseback at 4 in the morning, accompanied by Colonel Lake and two grooms. That same day, having spoken to Fox and Mrs Armistead, he returned to Brighton: a total distance of more than 100 miles and ten hours in the saddle. Much to the disappointment of Brighton's worthies, he was too weary to attend a ball in Shergold's Assembly Rooms that evening.

The advice that Fox gave the Prince was motivated as much by political ambition as by personal friendship. Pitt's victory in the recent General Election and the King's avowed intention not to employ him again meant his best chance of future office lay with the heir-apparent. The King was 46 (in an age when few people lived much beyond 50) and would not live for ever. But if the Prince disqualified himself from the throne before his father's death, Fox's hopes would come to nothing.

To calm the Prince, therefore, Fox appears to have suggested some form of marriage that would not be legally binding. Certainly, this is what the Duchess of Devonshire hinted at in a letter to Mrs Fitzherbert. The reply was suitably indignant:

> I am a good deal surprised at your desiring me to finish this affair one way or the other; you cannot be ignorant, my dear Duchess, that from the first moment it was proposed my sentiments have never varied; does not the same reasons now subsist and must they not always be the same? I should think I used him very ill had I ever endeavoured to deceive him . . . In regard of my coming to England I must beg to differ with you in opinion, as I cannot see the least good effect it could possibly have. I am perfectly well acquainted with every Circumstance, and why should I appear to give into measures I can never consent to? Whatever Mr. F——— or his friends say

to him they know in their breasts they cannot approve of, and I am confident there is not one of them that will take it upon themselves to say it is a legal proceeding . . .[9]

Realising that Mrs Fitzherbert had no intention of returning, the Prince now made plans to follow her. In a letter to his brother Frederick in Hanover, he mentioned his latest quarrel with the King (over his championing of the Foxite Whigs) and gave the reason for his journey as an attempt to economise. 'For Heaven's sake,' replied Frederick on 28 July:

do everything in your power to put an end to [your differences with the King], for it would be a dreadful calamity not only for us, but for the whole country if it was to continue. Let me also entreat of you, my dearest brother, to give up the idea of trav-elling. Indeed, you know not all the inconveniences to which you would be subjected, and as for saving money I can assure you you are very much mistaken if you think that you will be able to do that.[10]

Led by his heart, the Prince ignored these objections. But before he could leave England, he needed the permission of a father with whom he was barely on speaking terms. On 24 August, twelve days after his 22nd birthday (which his father had studiously ignored), he wrote to the King from Brighton:

I . . . think it my duty to inform your Majesty of a resolution I have been induced to take, from the peculiar and very embarrased situation of my affairs, arising from the necessary expenses I incurred during the course of last year; I mean the putting in full practice a system of economy by immediately going abroad.

The King, who may already have known the real reason for his son wanting to go abroad, wrote an angry reply. The Prince's letter had occasioned 'unpleasant sensations . . . in addition to what I constantly suffer from his reprehensible conduct, which has grown worse every year, and in a more glaring manner since his removal to Carlton House'. As if his support for the King's political enemies was not bad enough, he had also spent a fortune on his new house after having proposed 'only painting it and putting handsome furniture where necessary'.

As to the Prince's intention to go abroad, if such 'an improper plan was put into execution his character would be forever blasted in this country, and also in all Europe'. The King therefore insisted that his son gave up 'a measure' that could only lead to a 'public breach' between them; if the Prince agreed, he would see what he could do about helping to pay off his debts.

But the Prince was adamant. 'I see no fresh reason for altering my resolution of travelling,' he replied on 30 August. 'With regard to my retrenchments . . . nothing but my going abroad can possibly put me in the situation I should wish.'

The King, however, was equally determined that the Prince would not go. On 2 September, in a short note, he commanded his son 'not to leave the realm without having obtained my particular leave'. The threat of arrest and a public breach with the King were too much even for this lovelorn Prince to risk. Unable to leave the country, his attempts to persuade the obdurate Mrs Fitzherbert to return were confined to letters.[11]

Nevertheless, he was keen to make the best of a bad job. The King had expressed a willingness to help him out of his financial difficulties, and he intended to hold him to it. On 17 September, therefore, he told Lord Southampton to 'order Colonel Hotham to make out as near a state as he can of my debts in order that you may transmit them to the King'.

Hotham's anxious response, on 27 October, was that his debts had already reached the enormous sum of £147,293. Yet even this total could only be an estimate because 'every day brought on some charge

in every department which I could neither account for nor control.'
The 'amazing expense' of his stables alone was costing £31,000 a year,
'double what Colonel Lake thought would be sufficient sixteen months
ago!' Holland's estimate of future works on Carlton House had risen
from £18,000 to £30,250. He had borrowed £15,000, but had not
'been pleased to inform' Hotham about the 'particulars'. The Prince
was, in addition, 'totally in the hands, and at the mercy of' his builder,
his upholsterer, his jeweller and his tailor, from whose 'charges there is
no appeal'. To meet 'so many torrents of expense', his income of
£50,000 a year plus the 'precarious supply' of the Duchy of Cornwall
was patently inadequate.[12]

As it happened, the negotiations to pay off the Prince's debts made
little progress because he refused to make a full financial disclosure. The
King – who suspected his son of using money for political purposes –
wanted him to break with the Opposition and allot a part of his income
(£10,000) to pay his debts. He would do neither. Even 'with the
strictest economy,' he told the diplomat Sir James Harris (later Earl of
Malmesbury), who was acting for the government, on 27 April 1785,
'my expenses are twice my income. I am ruined if I stay in England.'

Surely the King 'could not object to any increase of income
Parliament thought proper to allow,' asked Harris.

'I believe he would,' said the Prince. 'He hates me; he always did,
from seven years old.'

On 23 May, the Prince told Harris that he had at last given up all
intention of travelling abroad. 'I see all my other friends, as well as yourself, are against it, and I subscribe to their opinion.'

Relieved, Harris then suggested ways of easing his financial burden.
'I thank you,' replied the Prince, 'but it will not do. The King . . .
would turn out Pitt for entertaining such an idea; besides, I cannot
abandon Charles Fox and my friends.'

Harris's response was that Fox and the Duke of Portland had 'repeatedly declared that a Prince of Wales ought to be of no party'.

Ignoring this point, the Prince continued to complain about the
harshness of his father's treatment of him.

'May I suggest, Sir,' said Harris, 'the idea of your marrying? It would, I think, be most agreeable to the King, and, I am certain, most grateful to the nation.'

'I never will marry!' came the angry reply. 'My resolution is taken on that subject. I have settled it with Frederick. No. I never will marry!'[13]

Little did Harris know that the Prince still had every intention of marrying Mrs Fitzherbert in secret, and that she had recently written to say that she *might* come home. In the meantime, he was only too glad to receive temporary solace from other women. 'He came to the ball on Wednesday last and made the town mad,' wrote Mary Noël of the Prince's stay at Lord Radnor's for the Salisbury races in the spring of 1785. 'He has got his present déesse, Lady Bamfylde, with him at Lady Radnor's . . . Lady Bamfylde is the only woman in the house and the Prince opened the ball with her . . . and drove her all the time the next day in Mr Bouverie's phaeton. She is grown fat, old and ugly but his Royal Highness is not noted for his taste in females.'[14]

But the occasional dalliance did not lessen his determination to have Mrs Fitzherbert. To this end he badgered her parents, her brothers and even her uncle, Henry Errington – and he continued to write her passionate letters. Finally, in October, after yet more threats to commit suicide, she wrote back saying she *might* consent to a secret marriage.

The Prince was ecstatic. 'I hardly know, *my dearest and only beloved Maria*, how I am to begin this letter to you,' he wrote on 3 November, the first of 42 pages. 'Such a train of extraordinary and wonderful events have happened lately, which at first created the greatest apprehensions and alarms in my bosom, and since have tended to the facilitating and entire arrangement of our plan, so that nothing now is wanting but the arrival of my adored Wife in this Country to make me the happiest of Men.'[15]

By late November, Mrs Fitzherbert was finalising her plans to return. 'I have told him I will be his,' she informed Lady Anne Lindsay, who had come back to England before her. 'I know I injure him and perhaps destroy for ever my own tranquillity.'[16]

Why then, if she was fully aware of the consequences, did she change her mind? Was it because she feared that the strength of the Prince's passion – which had shown no signs of abating during the 16 months they had been apart – might actually cause him to take his own life if it was permanently thwarted? Had she tired of a life of exile? Or was she simply in love with the most eligible bachelor in England? We will never know, but the truth is probably an amalgam of all three factors.

The simplest solution would have been for Mrs Fitzherbert to become the Prince's mistress; but this her devout Roman Catholicism would not allow. The only alternative was to wed in secret. Such a union – and the issue therefrom – would not be recognised by the laws of the land (thanks to the Royal Marriages Act), but it would be legit- imate in canonical law, and therefore in the eyes of God, and that was enough for Mrs Fitzherbert. The likelihood that the marriage would, if discovered, destroy the Prince's chances of succeeding to the throne and, even worse, threaten the very fabric of society by provoking a Protestant backlash, does not seem to have concerned her overmuch. She was more preoccupied with the moral and spiritual ramifications.

Even with Mrs Fitzherbert's consent, however, there were still one or two obstacles to be cleared before the marriage could take place: Charles James Fox, in particular. On 10 December, having learned of Mrs Fitzherbert's return, he wrote to warn the Prince against taking the 'very desperate step of marrying her' which he assumed was imminent. For by marrying a Catholic, the Prince would exclude himself from 'the succession of the Crown'.

Would he not consider the circumstances in which he stood? implored Fox. 'The King not feeling for you as a father ought, the Duke of York professedly his favourite, and likely to be married agree- ably to the King's wishes; the nation full of its old prejudices against Catholics; and justly dreading all disputes about succession; – in all these circumstances your enemies might take such advantage as I shudder to think of.'

Neither the marriage nor its offspring would be legitimate, Fox pointed out, adding:

The sum of my humble advice, nay of my most earnest entreaty, is this – that your Royal Highness would not think of marrying until you can marry legally . . . In the meanwhile, a mock Marriage (for it can be no other) is neither honourable . . . nor . . . even safe. This appears so clear to me, that, if I were Mrs Fitzherbert's father or brother, I would advise her not by any means to agree to it, and to prefer any species of connection with you to one leading to so much misery and mischief.

In other words – if they had any sense – even her family would prefer that she became his mistress rather than his illegal wife. Unfortunately for the Prince, this was not an option. So that night, to soothe Fox and prevent him from interfering further, he wrote a deliberately misleading reply. 'Make yourself easy, my dear friend. Believe me, the world will now soon be convinced, that there not only is, but never was, any grounds for these reports [that a marriage was imminent].'

If he had stopped just short of a barefaced lie, it was only because he had not actually specified the type of 'reports' he was referring to. But Fox would be deceived nonetheless, as he was meant to be. The only clue to the Prince's deception lay in an additional comment: that he ever intended 'to adhere to' the maxim of 'swimming or sinking' with his 'friends'.[17]

The final difficulty was presented by the service itself. A Church of England clergyman was required because, until the second Relief Act of 1791, even marriages between two Roman Catholics were not legally binding unless they had been solemnised by an Anglican parson. But finding such a priest willing to officiate was not easy; the terms of the Royal Marriage Act meant that he (and the witnesses for that matter) would be committing a felony. Two had already turned the Prince down (one after having second thoughts) by the time the Reverend John Burt was approached. A young curate languishing in Fleet debtors' prison, he agreed to conduct the service in return for £500, an appointment as one of the Prince's chaplains, and a promise that he would be made a bishop when the Prince became King. (He was duly paid and made a chaplain; but in October 1791, as the Prince was in the process of persuading Lord Chancellor Thurlow to appoint him Prebendary of Rochester, he died suddenly of a 'putrid fever', aged just 30.)[18]

The marriage took place during the early evening of 15 December 1785 in the locked drawing-room of Mrs Fitzherbert's house in Park Street. Aside from Burt, the only witnesses were Henry Errington, Mrs Fitzherbert's uncle and guardian since the protracted illness of her father, and John Smythe, her younger brother. After the ceremony, the Prince wrote out a certificate of marriage which he, Mrs Fitzherbert and the two witnesses signed; it was given to Mrs Fitzherbert for safe keeping. The newlyweds then left for a week-long honeymoon at Mrs Fitzherbert's villa, Ormeley Lodge, near Richmond.

Other than those present, only the Duke and Duchess of Cumberland, a couple of members of the Prince's Household and Sir James Harris, the British Minister at The Hague (who had gained the Prince's confidence during the recent negotiations over his debts), knew for certain that the wedding had taken place. Prince William, the Prince of Wales's second brother and a captain in the Royal Navy, was told by letter in January 1786. 'My best compliments to M[aria],' he replied from Plymouth on 30 January, 'and tell her she may rely in my secrecy.'[19]

Rumours were soon rife. 'Surely there cannot be any truth in the Report of the Prince being married to a Catholic Widow,' wrote the Earl of Denbigh to Major Bulkeley on 4 March 1786. 'Is it believed or not? If true the consequences of it may be dreadful to our Posterity.'

The same question was put by Denbigh to Matthew Arnott, the Reading Clerk to the House of Lords. Arnott replied on 14 March: 'The marriage you allude to, I fear is but too well founded in fact.'

Viscount Wentworth, Denbigh's son, went further. 'I agree with you that a late supposed transaction is an alarming subject,' he wrote on 17 March, 'especially as pregnancy is said to be already visible.'[20]

By now, a large number of scurrilous prints depicting the marriage had appeared. The most popular, by James Gillray, the political satirist, portrayed the Prince and Mrs Fitzherbert being married in a French church by Edmund Burke, a strong supporter of Catholic emancipation. The bride is being given away by Fox, who was wrongly assumed to have encouraged the wedding. Two of the Prince's dissolute friends – the Honourable George Hanger and Richard Brinsley Sheridan, the dramatist and Foxite M.P. – are standing as witnesses; Sheridan, with a napkin over his arm and a bottle of wine in each coat pocket, is ready to serve the wedding breakfast. Another Gillray print, 'The Morning after the Marriage', showed the Prince stretching and scratching his head while Mrs Fitzherbert, sitting on the bed, is pulling on one of her stockings.

The Prince was too blissfully happy to care. Mrs Fitzherbert had rented Lord Uxbridge's mansion in St James's Square so that she could be nearer to Carlton House; he, in turn, had let it be known that any invitations to him were also to be extended to her. Society on the whole complied. Taking their cue from the Duchess of Devonshire, the leading Whig ladies continued to receive Mrs Fitzherbert, as did a number of Tory hostesses including the normally staid Countess of Salisbury. Only a few were unable to pretend that nothing had happened. 'God knows how it will turn out,' wrote Lady Jerningham, a Roman Catholic, to her daughter in Paris. 'It may be to the glory of our belief, or it may be to the great dismay and destruction of it! She has taken a box to herself at the opera, a thing which no lady but the Duchess of Cumberland ever did – a hundred guineas a year! The Prince is very assiduous in attending her in all publick places, but she lives at her own house.'[21]

The one cloud on the Prince's horizon was his mounting debt. By the summer of 1786, it had risen to more than £160,000, with a further £80,000 needed to pay for work in hand on Carlton House and £30,000 'for incidental charges not yet come in'. The grand total was just under £270,000. 'I confess the sum is large,' wrote the unchastened Prince to his father on 15 June, 'but what adds more to my distress is, that the longer it continues unpaid, so much the more it will continue to augment. I therefore have nothing to do but to throw myself upon your Majesty's benevolence, hoping for your gracious assistance, which if I am so unfortunate as not to meet with, will throw me into a situation below that of the lowest individual in the country.'

But the King was unimpressed with the Prince's 'statement of arrears', particularly as it failed to specify where the money had gone. 'Without some examination of the expenses which have led him into his present situation,' he replied, 'it is scarcely possible to conceive a sufficient security that the same abuses will not recur. But then instead of proposing or expressing a readiness to conform to any future regulations for this purpose, this unsatisfactory account is followed by a demand of above £100,000 more to support farther extravagance; assistance from me, is, under such circumstances, out of the question.'

The Prince's bitter response was that, as he had 'no reason to expect either at present or in future the smallest assistance' from his father, the King would hear no more from him on the subject.

His only option now, he told Lord Southampton on 7 July, would be to shut up Carlton House, sell his stud and most of his carriages, and dismiss the gentlemen of his Household with the exception of Hotham, Lake, Samuel Hulse (one of his equerries) and Henry Lyte, his Keeper of the Privy Purse. They would henceforth be known as 'Inspectors of Accounts'. But whenever it was in his power 'to reassume that splendid situation' in which his birth had placed him, he would be only too glad to welcome his Household back 'with open arms'.[22]

In the meantime, he would – at Fox's suggestion – put by the majority of his income (£40,000) to pay off his debts, and live off the rest as a private gentleman in Brighton.

On Wednesday 2 August 1786, on his way to the weekly Levée, the King was getting out of his carriage at the garden door to St James's Palace when he was approached by a well-dressed woman holding a rolled-up petition in her right hand. As 'the King bent forward to take it,' wrote Fanny Burney, the celebrated novelist and Second Keeper of the Queen's Robes, 'she drew from it, with her left hand, a knife, with which she aimed straight at his heart!'

Seeing her intent, the King started back, causing the knife to miss. A second thrust was made, this time on target, but the knife was so thin and worn that it bent on the King's waistcoat. Before a third strike could be attempted, the woman was disarmed by a Yeoman of the Guard.

'Has she cut my waistcoat?' cried the shocked monarch. 'Look! For I have had no time to examine.'

On hearing that the material had not been severed, the King thanked God. 'Though nothing,' he later told his wife, 'could have been sooner done, for there was nothing for her to go through but a thin linen, and fat.'

By now, with the King protected by a ring of guards, the assassin was being roughly manhandled by onlookers. They seemed to be about to administer mob justice when the King, 'the only calm and moderate person then present', called out: 'The poor creature is mad! Do not hurt her! She has not hurt me!'

At which he strode forward, showing himself to the mob and declaring that he was 'perfectly safe and unhurt'. Having given orders 'that the woman should be taken care of', he went into the palace and held his afternoon Levée as if nothing had happened. 'There is something in the whole of his behaviour upon this occasion,' wrote Burney, 'that strikes me as proof indisputable of a true and noble courage.'[23]

The assassin, meanwhile, had been taken to the Queen's antechamber 'where she remained from twelve till near five, during which time, though spoken to by several of the nobility, she did not once condescend to open her lips, but appeared totally unmoved by any representations of the atrocity of her crime'.

On 4 August she was brought before members of the Privy Council, including the Archbishop of Canterbury and nine peers. They took depositions and adjourned until 8 August when they were joined by Pitt and William Grenville, the Paymaster-General. They discovered that the woman was Margaret Nicholson, a spinster in her early forties from Stockton-on-Tees, who had spent most of her life in domestic service. She told the Privy Counsellors that her motive for carrying out the attack was because she had a right to 'a property due to her from the Crown of England'. Having failed to acquire it by numerous petitions, she had carried out her assault 'not to kill the King but merely to shew the Cause'.

Dr Munro, the physician at the Bethlem lunatic asylum (popularly known as 'Bedlam'), was called next. The prisoner, whom he had examined daily since the attack, 'appeared to have a consciousness of what she had done, but did not seem sensible of having committed any crime'. From what she had told him, he had concluded that 'she must have been in this situation about ten years'. She could talk about nothing else but 'her right to the Crown and the mystery'. He had, in conclusion, hardly ever seen 'a clearer case of insanity'.

This expert evidence clinched it. The Privy Councillors concluded 'clearly and unanimously' that Margaret Nicholson was insane. The following day, she was taken to Bethlem Hospital 'to be confined for life; to be supported in case of sickness; but while in health to be employed, and made useful', her 'insanity' being 'of that kind as not to affect her manual operations'. She eventually died in custody in May 1828, having outlived the King she had tried to assassinate by eight years.[24]

In September 1783, when the Prince paid his first visit to Brighton – or Brightelmstone as it was then called – to stay with his uncle and aunt, the Duke and Duchess of Cumberland, it was little more than a small fishing town. Delightfully situated in a large Sussex bay, it consisted of just eight streets, with the Steine, an irregular piece of common land used for boat-building and drying nets, forming its eastern boundary. The town had begun its rise to prominence 31 years earlier when Dr Richard Russell – an advocate of bathing in, and even drinking, sea-water as a cure for various maladies – published his famous *Dissertation Concerning the Use of Sea Water in Diseases of the Glands*. After Russell had moved to the town the following year, and a mineral spring was discovered in nearby Hove, Brighton's popularity as a coastal spa was assured.

It was for reasons of health that the Prince returned to Brighton in the summer of 1784, partly to recuperate from his self-inflicted stabbing wound, and partly to relieve his badly swollen throat glands – said to be a pyschosomatic reaction to Mrs Fitzherbert's flight – by taking Russell's cure. As before, he stayed at Grove House, the Honourable George Wyndham's red-brick mansion on the Steine. But so enjoyable did he find this visit – riding on the Downs, shooting partridges at Falmer, swimming under the watchful eye of 'Snoaker' John Miles, the veteran bathing-machine attendant, and seducing the local girls – that he instructed Louis Weltje, his Comptroller, to find him a house of his own. Weltje chose 'a respectable farmhouse' on the west side of the Steine which he leased from Thomas Kemp, the M.P. for Lewes. It was to this house that the Prince retired in the summer of 1786, while Mrs Fitzherbert was set up in a small villa nearby.

On 18 July 1786, the Earl of Mornington (the elder brother of the future Duke of Wellington) wrote to the Duke of Rutland from Brighton: 'People talk much of the Prince of Wales's reform, particularly in this spot, which he has chosen as his place of retreat . . . Mrs. Fitzherbert is here, and they say with child.'

In the spring, both Viscount Wentworth (as we have seen) and the Duke of Gloucester had written letters referring to her alleged pregnancy. Gloucester's read: 'I think, Sir, by a certain paragraph, you do not think it impossible that a son & heir may be upon the stocks already.'[25]

It is now generally accepted that the Prince and Mrs Fitzherbert had at least one child, and possibly two. Mrs Fitzherbert herself never denied having had children by the future George IV. In 1833, after the King's death, one of Mrs Fitzherbert's executors, Lord Stourton, asked her to sign a declaration he had written on the back of her marriage certificate. It read: 'I Mary Fitzherbert . . . testify that my Union with George P. of Wales was without issue.' According to Stourton, 'she smilingly objected, on the score of delicacy'.[26]

The identity of the unborn child referred to by Wentworth, Gloucester and Mornington has never been proved, but the most likely candidate is James Ord. Born in the early autumn of 1786 (a date which fits with the marriage of his putative parents), he was taken out of the country to Bilbao in Spain a couple of months later by a Catholic man, also known as James Ord, his sister and his mother. The sister, Mary, young Ord was taught to call 'mother'; Ord senior he knew as 'Uncle'.

Towards the end of 1790, with war threatening between Britain and Spain, the Ords set sail for America, landing at Norfolk, Virginia. It is possible that they travelled on the same ship as Archbishop John Carroll of Baltimore, who was returning from England where he had been consecrated as the first American Catholic bishop. The ceremony had taken place on 15 August 1790 in the chapel of Lulworth Castle, the home of Thomas Weld, Mrs Fitzherbert's brother-in-law by her first marriage. Carroll had left England for America on 9 October, and may well have been charged by Mrs Fitzherbert to collect the Ords en route. She certainly knew Carroll well. As a young Jesuit priest, he had taught the eldest son of Lord Stourton (the son of this pupil later married the sister of Mrs Fitzherbert's first husband, Edward Weld). When the Jesuit Order was suppressed in 1773, Carroll continued to live in England with the Earl of Arundel, Lord Stourton and the Weld family. He would have been well acquainted with Mrs Fitzherbert, who was then Mrs Weld.

Following the death of his 'mother', Mary Ord, in 1792, young James spent the next eight years with various members of the Carroll family. Then, in April 1800, he was enrolled in the Jesuit College at Georgetown, D.C., entering the Jesuit Order six years later. His college fees were paid by Notley Young, another prominent Catholic and a close friend of Archbishop Carroll. Why such distinguished American Catholic families would have bothered with an obscure young foreigner is an enigma – unless Archbishop Carroll's connection with the family of Mrs Fitzherbert in England and James Ord in America was not a coincidence. Other circumstantial evidence would seem to suggest so.

When the Ords arrived in Spain in 1786, for example, the British Ambassador in Madrid was none other than Alleyne Fitzherbert (later Lord St Helens), a cousin of Mrs Fitzherbert's second husband. He, like the Ords, left Spain towards the end of 1790 when war with Britain seemed likely.

There were also two letters from Count Florida Blanca, Prime Minister of Spain, written while the Ords were living in Bilbao, which came into young Ord's possession 20 years after the death of his 'uncle' in 1810. The first, noted Ord, was an 'official communication, saying that James Ord [senior], an Englishman and a Catholic, had signed an agreement before the Spanish Ambassador in London . . . to serve the King of Spain for a period of four years; . . . that he was to report directly to him (Florida Blanca) and that every civility was to be shown him'. The second letter was addressed to Ord senior, 'congratulating him upon the zeal and ability he shows'.

'Why an obscure Englishman,' commented young Ord, 'who had a few years before been a common British seaman, should have received such an appointment under the Spanish Government, whose very language he apparently did not understand, and should, moreover, have been personally written to by the Prime Minister, seemed a most extraordinary circumstance.'

Convinced that at least one of his parents must have been extremely influential, Ord spoke to Father William Matthews, 'an intimate friend' of his 'uncle', in the hope that he would 'be able to throw some light on the subject'. He was right. Ord's recollection of the conversation is as follows:

> He [Matthews] . . . said that my uncle really knew very little –
> only that I was a child of *one* of the sons of George III, and he
> (James Ord) thought it probable that it was the Duke of York,
> as he had obtained the position in Spain for him; and, also,
> because the negotiations for my transfer to the Ords were car-
> ried on by the Duke of York and a Mr Farmer.
>
> I then told Father Matthews that I thought the probabilities

were that I was the child of Mrs Fitzherbert and the Prince of
Wales, to which he replied that he *had heard this stated by others*,
but he declined to say by whom.[27]

Ord then wrote to Mrs Fitzherbert, who was still alive, asking her to
confirm that he was indeed her son. She never replied. Nevertheless,
Ord's claim should be taken seriously. It makes complete sense that he
was spirited out of the country soon after his birth (however painful this
must have been for his mother). The Prince's illegal marriage to a widowed Catholic was bad enough; but the existence of a son, if known,
would surely have ended any chance he had of becoming King.

The fact that young Ord was assisted in Spain and America by families connected to Mrs Fitzherbert, and was brought up a Catholic,
surely makes him more likely to have been the son of the Prince of
Wales than the Duke of York – particularly as the Duke did not return
to England until the summer of 1787. Then again, are we to believe
that the Duke was able to obtain for James Ord senior the position of
Superintendent of the Royal Dockyard at Bilbao while he was resident
in Hanover? It seems possible, if not particularly likely.

Another child said to have been fathered by the Prince of Wales was
Henry Augustus Frederick Hervey, born on 1 December 1786. His
descendants have always believed that his mother was Mrs Fitzherbert –
but the evidence suggests that she was none other than Lady Anne
Lindsay. To conceal his identity, the infant was named after the 4th Earl
of Bristol (whose family name was Hervey), a close friend of Lady
Anne Lindsay and her future husband, Andrew Barnard, the son of the
Anglican Bishop of Limerick.

According to church records, young Hervey was baptised at St
Marylebone Parish Church on 31 December 1786. His parents are
given as Andrew Barnard (presumably to hide the Prince's identity) and
Maria Coghlan, Barnard's then mistress. In 1803, at the age of 16,
Hervey was nominated as an Officer Cadet in the Bombay Army of the
Honourable East India Company Army by Lord Hardwicke, the Lord
Lieutenant of Ireland, a friend of Andrew Barnard and the husband of

Lady Anne's sister, Lady Elizabeth. On 11 July 1810, he married Margaritha Adrians Geisler in Colombo. By the time she died in October 1818, they had had four children: Margaret Anne, Albert Henry, Gerald Augustus and Charles Robert. Hervey himself was drowned when the brig HMS *Lion* went down off the Coramandel coast of India in 1824. He was 38, a Captain in the Army of the East India Company.[28]

On Good Friday the previous year, Lord Eldon, the Lord Chancellor, had had an audience with George IV to discuss the latter's will. 'He . . . mentioned that he had a natural son,' noted Eldon in a memorandum of the meeting, 'an officer in the East Indies, to whom he thought himself bound to give a legacy of £30,000.'[29]

This officer may well have been Captain Hervey. He certainly appears to have been the son of Lady Anne Barnard (formerly Lindsay). After his death, she altered her will to provide for his children: his sons received £1,000 each; his daughter an annuity of £250. She also appointed her brother, the Honourable Hugh Lindsay, to act as their guardian in the event of her death.[30]

In later life, the sons of Captain Hervey – all of whom followed him into the service of the East India company – would often speculate about the identity of their grandfather. 'Another notion,' wrote Charles Hervey to his brother Albert in 1845, 'might be that . . . the King seduced the Lady [Anne] while she was in love on the one hand with Mr Barnard and engaged on the other with Mr Atkinson, who dying, the King got the former to marry Lady Anne, and to father the off-spring of the seduction as his own bastard.'

However, Gerald Hervey, the middle brother, was not entirely convinced. 'That story of Charly's about our granddad is all a fudge in my opinion,' he replied to Albert in June of that year:

> . . . The fact was Lady Anne had great influence with his late Majesty King George IV when he was Prince of Wales – and many say that she was secret to many of his intrigues and our poor father's influential letters was entirely owing to her . . . Yet

it may be as Charly says – but whether it is or not I shall give but little attention to it. Would it in any way better us by its being discovered. King George had a whole host of these kind of children . . . and these we all know to be but little better off than ourselves.[31]

A number of other people claim descent from the future George IV. Among the more believable are Major G.S. Crole, William Hampshire and Charles Candy. The Major was the third child of Eliza Crole, with whom the Prince had an affair in 1798. She was sometimes known by the name of Miss Fox, and her late father had once managed Brighton Theatre. She received an annuity from the Prince of £500 a year; her son eventually sold out of the Army in 1832, telling King William IV's private secretary that he was 'heartily tired of the service' and had never had 'much partiality for it'.[32]

Hampshire's mother was Sarah Brown, the daughter of an East End publican (he ran the White Hart Hotel in Mile End Road), who was said to have been the Prince's mistress for 15 years. In 1832, two years after George IV's death, Hampshire was appointed a clerk by the Duke of Devonshire, William IV's Lord Chamberlain. Despite his apparently humble origins, he rose rapidly in the Royal Household and became Queen Victoria's Paymaster in 1854.

Charles 'Beau' Candy is reputed to have been the result of a liaison between the Prince and a French lady of that name. With money provided by his father, he became a successful merchant and lived in some style in Streatham (then very fashionable). In the 1830s he married Margaret Papineau, a member of Queen Adelaide's household. They had two children: Alice and Henry, born in 1838 and 1843 respectively.

By the spring of 1787, the Prince was in desperate need of money. What he had saved by closing Carlton House, and more, was being spent on improvements to his house in Brighton. So hard-up had he become that he was forced to use the common post-chaise for his occasional visits to London, while trips to the races at Newmarket were said to be financed by Mrs Fitzherbert.

As the King had said his last word on the subject of his son's debts, the Prince 'authorized an application' directly to Parliament 'as his last resort'. But his Whig friends were not enthusiastic. The rank and file of the party were unsympathetic towards his straitened circumstances, while Portland and Fox feared that a debate about his debts would lead to questions about Mrs Fitzherbert's status. But the Prince was desperate: if the Whigs would not help him, he must find an Independent M.P. who could. The man selected was Alderman Nathaniel Newnham, who sat for the City of London.

On 20 April 1787, Newnham rose to ask 'whether it was the design of Ministers to bring forward any proposition to rescue the Prince of Wales from his present very embarrassed situation'. Pitt's peremptory reply was that the government could only involve itself in such a matter at the command of the King and they 'had not been honoured with such a command'. So Newnham then gave notice that he would propose a motion himself on 4 May.

A week later, in response to Pitt's request to know the 'scope and tendency' of his motion, he told the House that it would 'run somewhat to the following purport, "That an humble Address be presented to his Majesty, praying him to take into his royal consideration the present embarrassed state of the affairs of . . . the Prince of Wales, and to grant him such relief as his royal wisdom should think fit, and that the House would make good the same"'.

As the Whig leaders had feared, this gave the Tory squires their opportunity. Their mouthpiece was John Rolle, the stout M.P. for Devonshire who had recently been lampooned in Richard Fitzpatrick's *Rolliad*. He was much concerned, he said, that 'the worthy magistrate still persisted in his intentions to bring forward a motion of so delicate a nature'. If ever there was a question which demanded the attention of the country squires, it was the one which 'the honourable alderman had declared his intention to agitate, because it was a question which went immediately to affect our constitution in Church and State'. The reference to the alleged marriage of the Prince to Mrs Fitzherbert was obvious.

With Fox absent that day, Sheridan took it upon himself to defend the Prince. At first he pretended not to understand Rolle's implication. He could not, he told the House, see how such a motion 'endangered' the 'existence of the Church and State'. Instead it was his opinion that 'the motion originated only in a consciousness of the unparalleled difficulties under which the Heir of the Crown was so long suffered to Labour.'

Pitt had heard enough. If Newnham stood by his motion, he announced, he 'should be driven, though with infinite reluctance, to the disclosure of circumstances which he would otherwise think it his duty to conceal'. The threat to expose the Prince was clear. But Sheridan – under the illusion that the marriage had not taken place – was not to be browbeaten. It was impossible to withdraw the motion 'after what had passed', he replied. 'Insinuations had been thrown out . . . and converted into assertions that day, which the honour and feelings of the parties made it necessary to have explained.'

Realising that he had gone too far, Pitt took the opportunity to explain to the House, later in the evening, that he had been 'perfectly misunderstood' with 'regard to the insinuation he was accused of making'. The 'particulars to which he alluded . . . related only to the pecuniary situation of the Prince of Wales' and not to any 'extraneous circumstances'.

A triumphant Sheridan thanked him for his clarification, adding that 'any sort of allusion' to 'that matter' would have been 'in the extremest degree indelicate and disrespectful'.[33]

The Prince was understandably anxious when Sheridan informed him what had taken place. Rolle and his friends were bound to refer to his alleged marriage when the debate resumed; some form of denial was essential. But it had to be kept from Mrs Fitzherbert. So Sheridan was sent to explain to her the peril the Prince was in, and how the smallest hint from her that they were married would ruin them both. Her response was that she had no intention of saying anything. She was 'like a dog with a log tied round its neck' and they 'must protect' her.

Unfortunately, Fox was not privy to these conversations. Mrs Fitzherbert had never forgiven him for suggesting that she should become the Prince's mistress, and as a result he had seen less of the Prince since her return. Furthermore, he had every reason to assume that the marriage had not taken place, and that he was at perfect liberty to deny it. Not only had the Prince's letter of 11 December 1785 assured him that 'there not only is, but never was, any grounds for these reports . . . so malevolently circulated', but the Prince himself had 'contradicted the supposition' of his marriage a number of times since in Fox's presence.[34]

On Monday 30 April, therefore, when the debate on the Prince's debts resumed, Fox described Rolle's insinuation as a 'low malicious falsehood'. He 'was at a loss,' he added, 'to imagine what species of party it was that could have fabricated so base and scandalous a calumny'.

Rolle, however, was unconvinced. Though such a marriage could not have gone ahead 'under the formal sanction of the law, there were ways in which it might have been satisfactorily evaded'. No, replied Fox. He 'did not deny the calumny in question merely with regard to the effect of certain existing laws . . .; but he denied it *in toto*, in point of fact, as well as law. The fact not only never could have happened legally, but never did happen in any way whatsoever.'

Did Fox speak 'from direct authority', asked Rolle. Yes, came the reply. Goaded by Sheridan into a response, Rolle said that 'the House would judge for themselves of the propriety of the answer'.[35]

It was only later, in Brook's, that Fox realised he had been deceived. 'Mr Fox,' said Henry Errington, 'I hear that you have denied in the House the Prince's marriage to Mrs Fitzherbert. You have been misinformed. I was present at the marriage.'[36]

Fox was aghast – but helpless. If he recanted, the Prince would be ruined and his own political aspirations dashed (so he thought). If he did nothing, *his* reputation would be on the line and Mrs Fitzherbert would have further cause to hate him for destroying her character (she was now assumed to be the Prince's mistress). There was no contest: he did nothing.

The Prince's reaction was mixed: he was relieved that a denial had been made, but anxious that it had been so categorical. His first priority was to placate Mrs Fitzherbert. Arriving at St James's Square, he found her 'in an agony of tears' and 'deeply afflicted and furious against Fox'. He, in turn, railed 'at the liberty Fox had taken in exceeding his commission'. But Mrs Fitzherbert was not taken in by this performance and told the Prince that she had no alternative but to cease all contact with him.[37]

Distraught, he returned to Carlton House and sent for Charles (later Earl) Grey, a leading Whig. In the course of a 'long conversation,' wrote Grey, the 'dreadfully agitated' Prince 'confessed' to the secret marriage. Grey continued: 'The object was to get me to say something in Parliament for the satisfaction of Mrs. Fitzherbert, which might take off the effect of Fox's declaration. I expressly told him how prejudicial a continuance of the discussion must be to him, and positively refused to do what he desired. He put an end to the conversation abruptly by saying, "Well, if nobody else will, Sheridan must." '[38]

Though a successful playwright – his hits included *The Rivals*, *The School for Scandal* and *The Critic* – Sheridan went through money like water and was not a rich man. He had gained his first seat in Parliament with the help of the Duchess of Devonshire and would need the patronage of great men to remain there. He could not, therefore, afford to turn down a request by the Prince of Wales. On being summoned to Carlton House, he told the Prince that he would do his best to salvage Mrs Fitzherbert's reputation without implying that the marriage had actually taken place (not an easy feat).

Meanwhile, far from blaming Fox for his denial, the Prince had sent him a typically warm letter – 'My dear Charles . . . Ever affectionately yours' – summoning him to an interview at Carlton House the following day. 'When I see you,' wrote the Prince, 'I will relate to what has passed between *my friend and me* relative to me seeing *you*. I feel more comfortable by Sheridan's and Grey's account of what has passed to-day. I have had a distant insinuation that some sort of message or terms are also to be proposed to me to-morrow.'[39]

The 'insinuation' had come from Henry Dundas, the Treasurer of the Navy and Pitt's right-hand man in government (though he was not yet in the Cabinet). The Prince met Dundas on Wednesday, 2 May 1787, and was told that Pitt was now anxious to arrange a settlement of his debts. Although Dundas did not say it, Fox's denial of the marriage had made a number of Independent M.P.s more sympathetic to the Prince's plight; Pitt realised that he had to act or lose their support. 'There existed,' in addition, wrote the diarist Wraxall, 'a disposition to accommodate matters, without making disclosures in the House of Commons, equally painful to the King and to the Prince.'[40]

On 3 May, during a two-hour interview at Carlton House, Pitt told the Prince that he would lay all the circumstances of his debt before the King and 'return an answer as speedily as possible'. It arrived, 'by his Majesty's command', in the early hours of the following morning and stated that if the Prince 'thought proper to withdraw the motion intended to be made the next day in the House of Commons, every thing should be settled to his Royal Highness's satisfaction'.[41]

Next morning, in front of more than 400 M.P.s, Newnham duly announced with the 'most sincere and heartfelt satisfaction' that his motion was 'now no longer necessary'. Rolle was inevitably suspicious. If 'it should hereafter appear that any concessions had been made humiliating to the country, or dishonourable in themselves,' he announced, 'he would be the first man to stand up and stigmatize them.'

Pitt's response, which amazed the House, was that he 'knew of nothing which could make the motion less necessary now than it had ever been'. As to the 'terms and conditions' which Rolle had alluded to, he 'knew of none which had been made'. When questioned further by Rolle, he stated that the King had made 'no concessions of any sort' and 'had not, in any one instance, departed from those principles which had all along influenced him'.

Hearing this, Fox stood up to point out that 'the conduct of the other party alluded to [the Whigs] had been equally uniform' and that 'nothing but what was most respectful and most proper had ever been intended'.

Then it was Sheridan's turn. He would, he said, 'not enter into distinctions which the right honourable gentleman had attempted to make. If it was meant to be insinuated that the merit of the presumed reconciliation belonged exclusively to his Majesty's ministers, be it so.' But, 'in truth, the measures which had been adopted were the result of his Royal Highness's own judgement.' He ended his short speech with a reference to Mrs Fitzherbert, 'the lady to whom it was supposed some late parliamentary allusions had been pointed'. 'Ignorance and folly alone,' said he, 'could have persevered in attempting to detract from a character upon which truth could fix no just reproach, and which was in reality entitled to the truest and most general respect'.[42]

According to the Independent M.P. Daniel Pulteney, 'everyone smiled' at this brave attempt to resurrect Mrs Fitzherbert's reputation. But the Prince was not smiling when he heard a report of the day's proceedings. Not because Sheridan's words had displeased him – he had done as well as could be expected, under the circumstances – but because Pitt's had.[43]

Having demanded and not received an adequate explanation, the Prince requested an audience with Pitt at Carlton House the following day at which he gave him a written proposal for the King. In return for an additional £40,000 per year and a lump sum to cover the cost of the work done on Carlton House, the Prince would take care of the rest of his debts and would resume his Establishment. He would, in addition, 'engage not to apply hereafter for the payment of any farther debts'. If the King could only agree to part of the above, he 'should prefer the increase of income . . . without the payment of debts', rather than the other way round. This would enable him, after a course of years, to have 'a proper Establishment' and 'to pay his respects again at Court'.

The King's response was brief. He wanted an immediate 'examination' of the particulars of the Prince's finances, 'as the nature and mode of relief as well as the measures necessary to prevent debts in future' would depend upon the result. He added, somewhat mischievously, that 'while the Prince of Wales continues unmarried' he did not con-sider any increase in income was necessary.[44]

Finally, on 21 May, after much wrangling, Pitt read out the King's Message respecting the Prince of Wales's debts to the House of Commons. If his 'faithful Commons' were prepared to consider grant-ing a sum that would cover his debts and the amount needed to complete Carlton House, he would finance an increase in the Prince's income of £10,000 a year from the Civil List; in return, the Prince 'had given his Majesty the fullest assurances of his firm determination to confine his future expenses within his income' and had 'settled a plan for arranging those expenses in the several departments'. Three days later, the House of Commons duly voted the Prince £161,000 to pay his debts (which were not quite as large as he had estimated the year before) and an initial £20,000 – it became £60,000 – to finish Carlton House.[45]

The final settlement fell short of what the Prince had hoped for, but it was better than nothing. On 21 May, he wrote to the Queen asking for permission to pay his respects at Buckingham House now that this 'unpleasant business' was 'entirely concluded'.[46]

But there was still one other person he needed to mollify: Mrs Fitzherbert. In her opinion, Sheridan's speech had done little to repair the terminal damage done to her reputation by Fox's denial of her marriage. Also, in the cold light of day, she had come to the conclu-sion that Fox would never have spoken so plainly without the authority of the Prince. Her husband was therefore partly to blame, and she refused to see him.

So distressed did the Prince become that on 27 May he fell 'exceed-ingly ill' with 'an inward complaint' and a violent fever. Though brought on by emotional stress, this attack was remarkably similar to others which incapacitated him during the course of his life. The symp-toms were always the same: abdominal colic, painful weakness of the limbs, fever, and excitability or lowness of spirits.

On 4 June, the King's 49th birthday, the traditional 21-gun salute in Hyde Park was cancelled so that the 'Prince of Wales might not be disturbed', noted the Earl of Ailesbury, his former Governor. A few days earlier Ailesbury had been informed that the Prince 'was exceedingly ill and worse than Mr. Keate [his surgeon] had ever known him, and besides Sir Richard Jebb and Halifax, Dr. Warren [the Prince's physician] had been called'.[47]

According to Wraxall, whenever the Prince fell ill with a fever he made use of 'a fatal expedient – the lancet'. Long before he was 30 'he had been bled above a hundred times'. When his physician refused to perform such an operation, arguing that it provided only 'momentary relief' and dire long-term consequences, the Prince would open a vein himself.

'The unavoidable result of a perpetual recurrence of such disorders, when followed by the lancet,' wrote Wraxall, 'was a debility of the nervous system, and a necessity for resorting to the same stimulant, wine. Even wine not being found sufficiently strong to produce the desired effect, and his stomach demanding more powerful aid, liquers successed of every description.'[48]

With the Prince so ill – and threatening, in addition, to commit suicide – Mrs Fitzherbert began to waver. The warmth with which she was now received by London Society undoubtedly helped. When the Tory Duchess of Gordon, having declared her belief that Fox had lied, invited the Prince – now partially recovered – and Mrs Fitzherbert to a ball, they both accepted and were seen dancing together. The separation was over.

In early July they returned to their respective residences in Brighton. The pretty farmhouse on the Steine had been transformed by Henry Holland into the impressive structure known as the Marine Pavilion (not to be confused with its replacement, the Royal Pavilion, which was designed by John Nash almost 30 years later). Graeco-Roman in style, it was a long, low building with two bow-fronted wings flanking a central domed rotunda. Its interior, like Carlton House, was French in influence – both in decoration and in furniture. The corridors, for example, were painted French blue, while the Prince's bedroom, over the breakfast room in the wing nearest to the sea, was hung with quilted chintz and contained a curtained bed hung with green and white chequered silk.

The Prince spent his days walking on the Steine, bathing in the sea, playing cricket in the Pavilion grounds and travelling to Newmarket to watch the races. At night he would dine with Mrs Fitzherbert, and often go on to the theatre or a local ball. He had never been seen 'in better health or more buoyant spirits', reported the *Morning Herald* on 24 July.

His joy was complete when, during the evening of 2 August, he received word that his eldest brother, Prince Frederick (recently created the Duke of York) had at last returned from Hanover. Not having seen him for more than six years, the Prince immediately sent for his carriage and travelled through the night to Windsor. As the two brothers hugged each other warmly, the Prince was reduced to tears of joy. 'The day was a day of complete happiness to the whole of the Royal Family,' wrote Fanny Burney. 'The King was in one transport of delight, unceasing, invariable; and though the newly-arrived Duke was its source and support, the kindness of his heart extended and expanded to his Eldest-Born, whom he seemed ready again to take to his paternal breast.'[49]

It could not last.

Making up for lost time, the Prince saw much of his brother in what was left of the year. He gave a party in his honour at Brighton, introducing him to Mrs Fitzherbert (with whom the Duke formed an instant friendship which lasted until his death). He invited him to shoot at Bagshot and to go racing at Newmarket. When he returned to London to immerse himself in the kind of dissolute life to which his marriage had put a temporary stop, the Duke accompanied him.

'We are totally guided by [the Prince of Wales],' wrote Major-General Richard Grenville, head of the Duke's Household, to Lord Cornwallis on 20 December, 'and thoroughly initiated into all the extravagances and debaucheries of this most *virtuous* metropolis.' He added: 'Our visits to Windsor are less frequent, and I am afraid will at last be totally given up. I flatter myself still, however, with the hopes that when the first burst is passed, some little reflection will come to our assistance, and we shall perceive before *it is too late* that we are losing ourselves in the eyes of the world, and throwing away the finest game that ever man had presented to him.'[50]

After Christmas, the Prince and the Duke of York infuriated the King further by travelling to Plymouth to welcome home Prince William, their next eldest brother. William's early life had given his father almost as many headaches as that of the Prince. Sent to sea in 1781 at the age of 15, he had returned home two years later to a cool reception by his parents. Appalled by his bad language and uncouth behaviour, the King despatched him to Hanover in an effort to polish his manners. This had the opposite effect. William felt suffocated by the strict conventions of the Hanoverian Court, and spent his time gambling and womanising. After a year – during which time he had fathered at least one illegitimate son – he informed the Prince how frustrated he was at being compelled to stay in Hanover, 'this damnable country, smoking, playing at twopenny whist and wearing great thick boots. Oh, for England and the pretty girls of Westminster; at least to such as would not clap or pox me every time I fucked.'[51]

By April 1785, William was desperate to return to the Navy if only to relieve his boredom. He got his wish after his brother Frederick had written to the King saying that only the discipline of service could save William from 'his natural inclination for all kinds of dissipation'. But his second spell at sea was hardly more successful than the first. He was constantly in debt and went from one injudicious liaison to another. Having been promoted to captain and given command of his own frigate, the *Pegasus*, he over-disciplined his men and fell out with his First Lieutenant, Schomberg. The Admiralty sided with Schomberg, and chastised William for threatening his junior officer with a court-martial. With this cloud hanging over his future, he returned to Plymouth on 27 December 1787, to be met by the Prince and the Duke of York. The next two days were a blur of alcohol and women.

Nor did the poor example set by the Prince end there. In early April 1788, General James Grant, the M.P. for Sutherlandshire, wrote to Lord Cornwallis:

> The Prince has taught the Duke to *drink* in the most liberal and copious way, and the Duke in return has been equally success-ful in teaching his brother to lose his money at all sorts of play – quinze, hazard etc . . . These play parties have chiefly taken place at a new Club, formed this winter by the Prince of Wales in opposition to Brook's, because Tarleton and Jack Payne, proposed by his Royal Highness, were blackballed.[52]

So much money did the Duke lose – more than £40,000 by March 1788 according to T.F. Fremantle – that he was eventually forced to sell Allerton, the valuable estate in the West Riding of Yorkshire which he had bought just before returning to England with the accumulated revenues of the bishopric of Osnaburg (to which his father had appointed him at the age of six months).[53]

———•—

4

The Mad King

By the early summer of 1788, the King was forced to accept that he had lost his second and favourite son, the Duke of York, to the corrupting influence of the Prince of Wales. If the Duke's ruinous gambling debts were not bad enough, he had chosen as his mistress the notorious Countess of Tyrconnell, a lady whom even the equivocally placed Mrs Fitzherbert could not bring herself to receive on the grounds that she was 'contaminate'.[1]

But far worse was in store for the long-suffering monarch. On 11 June 1788, at Kew House, he was 'siezed with a bilious fever, attended with violent spasms in his stomach and bowels'. His doctor, Sir George Baker (President of the Royal College of Physicians), prescribed 'a pretty smart purge' which seemed to relieve the symptoms. He was unwell for a fortnight nonetheless. 'It is supposed,' wrote the Queen, 'that the dryness and heat of the season has occasioned these violent attacks.'[2]

Nathaniel Wraxall, on the other hand, blamed the King's scanty diet:

Probably the humour might have exhausted its force in the

extremities, in the shape of gout, if his Majesty had eat and drunk like almost any other gentleman. But his natural disposition to temperance . . . impelled him to adopt the habits of an ascetic. The most simple food, taken in very moderate quantity, constituted his repasts. Yet his German origin showed itself in his predilections: for sour crout [sic] was one of his favourite dishes . . . His ordinary beverage at table was only composed of a sort of lemonade, which he dignified with the name of *cup*; though a monk of La Trappe might have drunk it without any infraction of his monastic vow.[3]

To speed the King's recovery, Baker recommended a stay at the small spa town of Cheltenham where the waters were 'particularly good for all bilious complaints'. The Royal Family left on 12 July, the day after Parliament had broken up for the summer recess, and spent a relaxing month at Bays Hill Lodge, the house of Lord Fauconberg. The King's routine was fixed. Having visited the spring in the early morning, so as not to draw attention to himself, he would ride until 3 in the afternoon. Dinner was taken at 4 o'clock, followed by a stroll with his family at 7. By 11 p.m. the house was quiet.

He would often ride alone and 'enter into conversation with persons who accidentally fell in his way'. One such dialogue, with a farmer driving a flock of sheep, took in 'the value and properties of land, the prices of sheep and of cattle'. Put at ease, the farmer 'asked the gentleman, as he thought, if he had seen the King; and being answered in the affirmative, the farmer said, "Our neighbours say, he's a good sort of man, but dresses very plain." "Aye," said his Majesty, "as *plain* as you see me now"; and rode on.'[4]

Part of the reason for the King's good humour was his conviction that the waters were doing him good. '[They] are more efficacious than I possibly could have expected,' he wrote to Pitt on 22 July, 'for while they remove byle in a very gentle manner they strengthen the stomach and are a general bracer to the constitution.'[5]

On 16 August, the King returned to Windsor and enjoyed two

months of improved health. But in the early morning of 17 October, at Kew, he suffered a recurrence of his earlier 'bilious' attack. Once again, Sir George Baker was sent for:

> I found his Majesty sitting up in his bed, his body bent forward. He complained of a very acute pain in the pit of the stomach shooting to the back and sides, and making respiration difficult and uneasy. This pain continued all the day, though in a less degree of acuteness towards the evening; but it did not cease entirely until the bowels had been emptied . . .
>
> His Majesty informed me . . . that of late he had been much tormented in the night by a cramp in the muscles of his legs, and that he had suffered much from the rheumatism, which affected all his limbs . . . It was likewise mentioned that he had had a rash.

Attributing the cause to the fact that the day before, the King had failed to change his stockings after getting his feet wet (an omission made worse when he then ate 'four large pears for supper'!), Baker prescribed the purgatives of castor oil and senna. But they simply aggravated his already 'excruciating pain', and laudanum (tincture of opium) had to be given to relieve it.

The following day, his eyes yellow and his urine dark, the King was suffering from a 'slight' fever and a pain in his left foot. On 20 October, hardly able to stand straight because of a painful stomach, he tried to reply to a dispatch which Pitt had sent. But his mind kept wandering and he was unable to keep to the point. His handwriting, moreover, was shaky and larger than normal. He was, he informed Pitt at the end of the letter, 'not quite in a situation to write at present'.[6]

Two days later, the first signs of mental derangement were evident. 'The look of his eyes, the tone of his voice, every gesture and his whole deportment represented a person in a most furious passion of anger,' wrote Baker. Part of his purgative had been 'too powerful', the other part 'had only teazed him without effect', the King told him.

Repeating these and other criticisms again and again, the King kept him 'detained' for three hours. That evening, Baker informed Pitt that he had 'just left the King in an agitation of spirits bordering on delirium'.

On Friday 24 October, having seen the King in the morning, the Duke of York informed the Prince that he thought 'him getting well very fast'. The King thought so too and, in an attempt to end the rumours that he was seriously ill, he appeared at the weekly Levée at St James's. But his disordered dress, flannel-wrapped legs and hurried speech seemed to confirm the opposite.[7]

Two days later at Windsor – Baker having authorised the move – the King stopped Fanny Burney in the passage outside the Queen's room and 'conversed upon his health' for almost half an hour. Speaking 'with that extreme quickness of speech that belongs to fever', he told Burney that he hardly slept 'one minute all night' and that if he could not get any rest 'a most delirious fever' was awaiting him.

On 28 October, when the Prince visited for the first time, the King's 'agitation of spirits, & inordinate flow of words' were as bad as ever. Next day, Burney was more optimistic: 'The dear and good King again gains ground, and the Queen becomes easier.'[8]

The Duke of York was similarly upbeat in a letter to the Prince the following day:

> I found him with respect to his rheumatic complaint certainly better, though still very weak, but it appears now as if everything has thrown itself upon his nerves, which has given him a very violent degree of agitation which nothing but rest and quiet will remove. I cannot help adding that he spoke with tears in his eyes and with the greatest affection concerning you and said how happy you had made him by coming to see him.[9]

But all was not well by the evening. 'My medical advice had not been followed,' noted Sir George Baker. 'I found His Majesty at his concert, not seeming to attend to the music, but talking incessantly. His pulse was 84. He now complained, that [he] was of late become near-sighted; that his vision was confused, and that whenever he attempted to read a mist floated before his eyes.'[10]

By 3 November, a pattern had set in. 'The King is better and worse so frequently, and changes so, daily, backwards and forwards,' wrote Burney, 'that everything is to be apprehended, if his nerves are not some way quieted. I dreadfully fear he is on the eve of some severe fever. The Queen is almost overpowered with some secret terror.'[11]

That day, the King wrote to Pitt to convince him that he could still 'sign warrants without inconvenience' and had 'no objection to receive any large number'. He was, he insisted, attempting to read 'the despatches daily, but as yet without success; but he eats well, sleeps well, and is not in the least fatigued with riding . . . Having gained so much, the rest will soon follow.'[12]

It would be his last letter to his Prime Minister for almost four months.

On 5 November, when the dam finally broke, the Prince was the inevitable catalyst. Arriving at Windsor that day from Brighton, he joined the Royal Family at dinner. But his presence must have been too much for his distressed father who, having become increasingly agitated during the meal, suddenly leapt out of his chair, grabbed the Prince's collar and threw him against a wall. The Queen at once fell into 'violent hysterics', while the Prince 'burst into tears' and had to be comforted by his marginally less distressed sisters.[13]

The King was now 'under an intire alienation of mind, and much more agitated than he had ever been', noted Baker. His eyes, the Queen told Lady Harcourt, her Lady of the Bedchamber, 'she could compare to nothing but black currant jelly, the veins in his face were swelled, the sound of his voice was dreadful; he often spoke till he was exhausted . . . while the foam ran out of his mouth.'[14]

That night, on the pretext that the Queen was ill, he was moved out of her bedroom into the dressing-room next door. This did not prevent him from going into her room in the middle of the night to satisfy himself that she was still there. During the half-hour that he remained there, the Queen was scared witless, despite the presence of Miss Goldsworthy, one of her attendants, who was sleeping next to her.

To give the Queen peace of mind, she was moved to an apartment further down the corridor. It was just as well. The following night, the King made a second visit and was astonished to discover the Prince of Wales, the Duke of York, the physicians and a host of attendants sitting on sofas and chairs round the walls of his wife's bedroom. When Sir George Baker made a hesitant suggestion that he should return to bed, the King 'penned him in a corner' and told him that he was 'a mere old woman' and could not understand why he had 'ever followed his advice'. Eventually, with the Prince desperately making 'signs and whispers' for someone to do so, Mr Fairly, one of the attendants, took the King by the arm and led him back to bed.[15]

Over the next few weeks, the King's condition steadily worsened. He got little sleep, sweated heavily and became increasingly violent; his pulse fluctuated wildly and he was prone to powerful convulsions of his arms and legs; he talked constantly, once for 'nineteen hours without scarce any intermission'. At times he was rational, but more often deluded. 'He fancies London is drowned and orders his yacht to go there,' noted Lord Sheffield. He wrote despatches to foreign courts 'founded upon imaginary causes' and 'lavished honours upon all who approached him; elevating to the highest dignities, pages, gentlemen of the bed-chamber, or any occasional attendant'. After refusing to be shaved for a fortnight, he allowed one of his pages to shave his cheeks but not his throat, chin or upper lip; to complete the job the page had to wait a few days longer.[16]

Meanwhile, on 6 November, Dr Richard Warren had arrived to assist Baker and Dr William Heberden, 78, a retired physician of some repute who lived near Windsor and who had been called in by Baker three days earlier. Warren, physician to the Prince of Wales and many 'leading men in opposition' such as the Dukes of Devonshire and Portland, Earl Fitzwilliam and Charles James Fox, had come at the request of the Prince and 'unknown to the Queen, who would never have consented to the calling in a physician to whom the King had a particular objection'.

'From this fatal step,' wrote Lady Harcourt, 'many of the evils that followed resulted . . . [Warren] being sent for to Windsor gave dissatisfaction to many of the King's most attached friends, and his Majesty said to him, the first time he went into his room, "You may come here as an acquaintance but not as *my* physician; no man can serve two masters; you are the Prince of Wales's physician, you cannot be mine."'[17]

But Warren did not let his patient's lack of cooperation prevent him from making an immediate diagnosis. Ignoring the Queen, he went directly to Windsor Castle to tell the Prince that the King's life was 'in the utmost danger' and that 'the seizure upon the brain was so violent, that, if he did live, there was little reason to hope that his intellects would be restored.'[18]

This was the Prince's first indication that the King's mental derangement might be permanent and that, in the event, a Regency would be necessary. While genuinely sympathetic towards his ailing father, he was at the same time keenly aware of the political opportunities which such an eventuality would present. As Regent, he would be in a position to dismiss Pitt and replace him with Portland or Fox. The Whigs could then request the dissolution of Parliament and the holding of a General Election (as Pitt had done with such success in March 1784). By using the influence of the Treasury and the promise of honours – and assuming the support of at least a sizeable proportion of Independent M.P.s – the Whigs would be able to secure a working majority in the next House of Commons.

Pitt and his ministers were not under any illusions as to the consequences if the King did not recover. 'If his indisposition of mind continues,' William Grenville, the Paymaster-General, informed his brother Buckingham on 7 November, 'without some more material bodily illness, he may live years in this melancholy state; and this, of all events that can happen, is perhaps the most to be feared. He was, however, thought yesterday to be in imminent danger of death. Should this not happen, but the other, it seems generally agreed that the Prince of Wales must be appointed Regent, with kingly power.'[19]

The following day, during a conversation with the Prince at Windsor, Pitt was told of the 'many instances of conversation and conduct which showed the derangement of [the King's] mind'. Three of the doctors – Baker, Warren and Henry Revell Reynolds (who had joined them on the 7th) – were then sent for, and they confirmed that the King was incapable of acting rationally. They could not decide, however, whether the 'disorder' was 'one locally fixed on the brain' or a 'translation of a disorder from one part to another'. If it was the latter, 'there might be a hope of removing it, but there would then be a possibility that it might attack some part where it might be dangerous to life.' If it was the former, 'there was more reason to think the disorder would be permanent, without affecting life.' On balance, though, they thought 'there was more ground to fear than to hope, and more reason to apprehend durable insanity than death.'[20]

The royal physicians had no real understanding of the nature of George III's malady – and therefore no idea how to treat it – because they had never come across an illness with such an unusual combination of physical and mental manifestations. The mental derangement was particularly perplexing because, unlike a delirium, it outlasted the improvement in physical health. But it could not be simply insanity, they reasoned, because that would not explain the physical symptoms with which the illness had begun.

The most convincing explanation for both these conundrums was provided by two psychiatrists, Ida Macalpine and Richard Hunter, in 1966: the King was suffering from a rare metabolic disorder called porphyria. Not clinically defined until the 1930s, it is one of a group of disorders in which 'inherited defects of body chemistry lead to an abnormal accumulation of toxic chemical substances which damage the nervous system'. Porphyria is so-called because the 'biochemical lesion is a disturbance of porphyrin metabolism', the purple-red pigments which are found in every body cell and which give blood its colour. An attack of porphyria will result in a huge increase in the formation and excretion of these pigments. Such an 'excess in the blood causes widespread intoxication of all parts of the nervous system peripheral and central'; it also turns the victim's faeces and urine purple or dark in colour 'either when it is passed or after it has been left to stand'.

Porphyria is an hereditary disease that is transmitted to about half the offspring of an affected parent. It can remain latent throughout life, or cause intermittent attacks of varying severity 'which are always dangerous and may be fatal'. The acute sufferer has been described as 'ill, paralyzed, delirious, and in agonizing pain'. These are exactly the symptoms, say Macalpine and Hunter, that George III displayed at intervals throughout his life.

The disorder of his nervous system, they claim, affected the 'peripheral nerves, which supply movement and sensation to all parts of the body, causing painful weakness of the arms and legs, so that he could not hold a cup or pen, or walk or stand unaided . . ., hoarseness and difficulty in swallowing.' A disruption of his 'autonomic nervous system, which controls the heart, blood vessels, gastro-intestinal system and sweat-glands, led to nausea, colic and constipation due to paralysis of the gut'. When these 'attacks became more severe the brain was involved, leading to giddiness, visual and auditory disturbances, mounting agitation, excitement, over-activity, non-stop rambling, irritability and persistent sleeplessness, confusion typically first by night and then also by day, producing delirium, tremor, rapid movements of his eyes, rigors, stupor and convulsions.' It is easy to see how anyone unaware of such a disease would have concluded that the King was mad.

Macalpine and Hunter also point to the fact that 'the records of the royal physicians contain six instances in which they describe his urine at the height of attacks as "dark", "bilious" or "bloody", and even noted on occasion that it left a bluish stain on the vessel after it had been poured away'.

The psychiatrists trace the disorder back to James VI of Scotland and I of England, claiming that it was transmitted to the Hanoverians by his grand-daughter Electress Sophia, the mother of George I. Of particular interest to this study is their suspicion that the Prince of Wales (later George IV) was from time to time afflicted by porphyria, albeit in a less virulent form than the one which affected his father. 'In essence,' they wrote, 'the attacks which incapacitated him periodically from his teens throughout his life consisted of abdominal colic, painful weakness of the limbs so that at times he was almost paralysed, and excitability and impulsiveness or lowness of spirits. Both father and son were dangerously ill for short periods, but each attack was followed by prolonged debility.' Their respective medical histories were distinguished only by the fact that 'George IV did not suffer from episodes of *obvious* [my italics] derangement'.

But George III, too, had been periodically stricken by the physical symptoms of porphyria without any accompanying mental impairment. This occurred in the summer of 1762, for example, shortly before the birth of the Prince of Wales, and again in 1765 and 1766. Each time the symptoms were abdominal pain, fever, a fast pulse and fatigue.[21]

With his father not expected to recover from his derangement in the near future, if at all, the Prince began to behave as if he was already Regent. On 8 November, he 'took the government of the [Queen's Lodge] into his own hands', wrote Miss Burney. 'Nothing was done but by his orders, and he was applied to in every difficulty. The Queen interfered not in anything; she lived entirely in her two new rooms, and spent the whole day in patient sorrow and retirement with her daughters.'[22]

The Prince even began to contemplate the formation of a future Whig government. During the evening of 9 November, Captain John Payne, the new Comptroller of the Prince's Household, wrote to Lord Loughborough, a prospective Lord Chancellor:

> I took the liberty of mentioning to the Prince the very liberal accommodation of your conduct in promotion of his service.

He said, 'Well if the C[hancellor Thurlow] chooses to remain where he is, Lord L[oughborough] can have the Privy Seal or President for the present, and settle the other arrangements afterwards, if it is more to his mind.'[23]

Such a transition of power, however, would not be easy, nor necessarily popular. 'I cannot help thinking,' wrote Lord Bulkeley at Windsor to the Marquess of Buckingham on 11 November, 'that the Prince will find a greater difficulty in making a sweep of the present Ministry, in his quality of Fiduciary Regent, than in that of King. The Stocks are already fallen 2 per cent, and the alarms of the people of London are very little flattering to the Prince.'[24]

Unconcerned, the Prince stepped up his secret negotiations with potential ministers. With Fox holidaying on the Continent with Mrs Armistead, Sheridan took on the role of go-between. It was he who first contacted Lord Chancellor Thurlow, the Cabinet minister seen – correctly – as the most likely to abandon Pitt for any future Portland-Fox Whig ministry. On 28 November, the *Morning Post* even went so far as to print a list of the expected Cabinet, naming Portland as Prime Minister, Fox and Lord Stormont as Secretaries of State, Sheridan as Navy Treasurer, Lord John Cavendish as Chancellor of the Exchequer and Edmund Burke as Paymaster-General.

The obstacles, however, were many. The Prince had yet to forgive Portland for opposing the parliamentary motion to pay off his debts, and he had seen little of Fox since the latter's discovery of his deception about his marriage the previous year. In addition, Charles Grey was claiming that he and not Cavendish should be Chancellor of the Exchequer, while Loughborough was indignant that Thurlow might be asked to remain Lord Chancellor. The putative Whig Cabinet was, in short, far from united.

Furthermore, not all the medical experts were of the opinion that the King would never regain his senses. On 19 November, the day after he had become the fifth physician to attend the King, Sir Lucas Pepys told Fanny Burney that 'there was nothing desponding in the case, and that his Royal Patient would certainly recover, though not immediately'. Dr Anthony Addington, 75, the Pitt family doctor and former proprietor of a private madhouse in Reading who joined the medical team in the last week of November, told the Prime Minister that he was 'favourable as to a possibility, and even a prospect of recovery'.[25]

Officially, however, the prognosis was grim. On 26 November, the daily medical bulletin announced that the King had 'had sufficient sleep in the night, but does not appear to have been relieved by it'. Reading between the lines, this meant that the King was recovering his physical health while his mental impairment remained; his delirium was no longer accompanied by fever. 'By definition,' wrote Macalpine and Hunter, 'it meant insanity, that is a derangement of the mind . . . due directly to disease of the brain, the other bodily functions remaining healthy.'[26]

On 24 November, by which time 'restraints' were being used to keep the King 'quiet' – first an 'envelopement' of linen, then a straitwaistcoat – the physicians had decided that it would make more sense to move him from Windsor to Kew. Closer to London, Kew had a private garden where the King would be able to take exercise without being disturbed. But the patient himself did not want to go, so the Prince asked the Cabinet up to Windsor to examine 'his Majesty's situation'.

Assembling on 27 November, they took statements from all the royal physicians bar Heberden who was no longer in attendance. Addington, the most upbeat about the King's recovery, was supported by Pepys and Reynolds. Warren and Baker 'did not seem to entertain so much favourable expectation', noted the Duke of Leeds, the Foreign Secretary. All agreed, however, that 'restraint' was 'necessary, and that the degree in which they thought it expedient could be much better observed at Kew'. Such a move would, in addition, provide a welcome 'change of air and objects'.[27]

The move took place on Saturday, 29 November, but only after a lengthy struggle. 'The poor King had been prevailed upon to quit Windsor with the utmost difficulty,' wrote Miss Burney. As well as threatening the use of force, the physicians had told the King that he would be allowed to see the Queen, who had preceded him, but when he arrived at Kew he was instantly hustled into secure apartments. Complaining that he had been deceived, he refused to go to bed; when his pages tried to force him, he pulled the hair of one and kicked another. From now on his condition worsened. By day he ate very little, refused his medicine, swore and uttered 'indecencies'; at night he was 'almost unmanageable' and had to be tied to his bed; he became so depressed he even asked his pages to end his life.[28]

His misery was compounded by the fact that Kew Palace 'had never been a winter residence, and there was nothing prepared for its becoming one'. It was 'in a state of cold and discomfort passed all imagination', wrote Fanny Burney. There were no carpets or rugs on its bare boards and sandbags had to be used to keep out draughts.

Then, on 30 November, a meeting was held at Kew between the Prince, the Duke of York, Lord Chancellor Thurlow and the doctors to discuss the 'system' by which the King would be managed in the future. With the regular physicians clearly at a loss how to treat the King's illness, it was decided to send for a specialist 'mad-doctor'. The Queen reluctantly agreed. The man chosen, on Lady Harcourt's recommendation (he had previously cured her mother), was the Reverend Dr Francis Willis, 73, the celebrated owner of a private asylum at Greatford in Lincolnshire where, he claimed, nine out of ten patients recovered. Not everyone was convinced of his bona fides though. He was 'considered by some not much better than a mountebank,' Lord Sheffield told William Eden (the future Baron Auckland), 'and not far different from some of those' confined in his asylum.[29]

Willis arrived on 5 December, accompanied by his son John and three of his 'physical assistants'. His technique, he told a horrified Robert Fulke Greville, the King's equerry, was to break in patients like 'horses in a manège'. Madness was no more than over-excitability; it needed to be calmed. That evening, Willis told the King 'that his ideas were now deranged, and that he required attention and management'. When the King responded violently by attempting to charge at Willis, he was restrained and threatened with a strait-waistcoat. It was used often. According to Fulke Greville, after his first night wearing it, the King 'repeatedly said, that he would never more wear the Crown, & desired his eldest son might be sent for'.[30]

So began the new 'system' of coercion and control. Whenever the King refused to cooperate – by rejecting his food, resisting going to bed or throwing off his bedclothes (even if he had a genuine reason, such as a sweating attack) – he was put in the strait-waistcoat. Once, when he made indecent remarks about Lady Pembroke, the Queen's Lady of the Bedchamber and a grandmother, Willis stuffed a handkerchief in his mouth.[31]

Fox was in Bologna when the Duke of Portland's messenger reached him on 15 November. Hearing the news of the King's illness, he set off immediately, reaching England nine days later. Already suffering from dysentery, the exhausting journey weakened him further. 'I never saw Fox . . . exhibit so broken and shattered an aspect,' wrote Wraxall when he saw him in the House of Commons some days later. 'His body seemed to be emaciated, his countenance sallow and sickly, his eyes swollen, while his stockings hung upon his legs, and he rather dragged himself along than walked up the floor to take his seat.'[32]

But despite his illness, Fox wasted no time in immersing himself in the secret negotiations for a new ministry. The day after his return, he was sent by the Prince to speak to Lord Thurlow. Lord Chancellor since 1778 (with a brief gap during the Fox-North ministry in 1783 when the seal was in commission), Thurlow would provide experience and continuity for any future government; he would also bring with him some much needed support. Having spoken to Thurlow, Fox reported back to the Prince. While the Lord Chancellor did not think it fit 'to enter into anything like negotiation with any other persons,' wrote Fox, he was 'very open in declaring that he has no further connection with [the present government] than that which arises from the accident of the moment, and upon the whole it is my opinion that it is his present intention to treat with us as soon as that connection is dissolved.' Under the circumstances, it was now best 'to let the matter rest where it is and when your Royal Highness has the power, to make such offers as may be thought advisable'.[33]

Clearly, Thurlow was prepared to desert Pitt if it meant he could remain as Lord Chancellor. That would not please Lord Loughborough, who had been as good as offered the post, but Thurlow was too big an asset to let slip. Then there was the small matter of the future Prime Minister to take care of. The obvious choice was the Duke of Portland, the nominal head of the Whig party, with whom the Prince had had little contact since their disagreement a year earlier. On Sheridan's advice, the Prince wrote to the Duke, informing him that he was anxious to 'cancel all former discontents'. The Duke was only too happy to accept. When the Prince called on him at Burlington House on 30 November, offering to shake hands and 'never again think about the dispute they had about the motions for paying his debts', the Duke was moved.[34]

There were still one or two other divisions in the Whig ranks, notably between Grey and Sheridan over who should become Chancellor of the Exchequer, but the future government was beginning to take shape.

Meanwhile, having reconvened on 20 November – without a Royal Summons, the King being incapable of giving it – Parliament adjourned for two weeks to give the physicians more time to assess the King's situation. On 3 December, the day before Parliament reassembled, they were re-examined by the Privy Council under oath. All except Warren, wrote the Duke of Leeds, 'were clear and distinct in their answers, all five agreeing that the King was at present totally incapable of attending to business; that there certainly from their experience of similar cases appeared a probability of his recovery, but the time which would be necessary to effect his cure was not possibly to be ascertained'.

Warren, on the other hand, was vague and evasive, telling the council that 'he had not and he believed no one else had sufficient data to answer' the question of whether 'he thought it more probable that the

King would or would not recover'. After the four-hour hearing had broken up, Lord Camden whispered to the Duke of Leeds that he thought Warren was 'a damned scoundrel, though I believe him to be a very able Physician'. The implication was clear: he was letting his political bias get the better of his professional opinion.[35]

When Parliament reopened the following day, the report of the examination of the physicians was laid before the two Houses. Four days later, when they reassembled to consider the reports, Pitt and others were dissatisfied and it was agreed that both Houses would appoint a committee to examine the physicians themselves. The Commons' committee sat on Tuesday, 9 December, the Lords' committee the following day. They reported to their respective Houses on 10 and 11 December.

Called first, Warren told the House of Commons' committee that, as 'the majority' of other 'similar cases' had recovered, 'there is a probability that his Majesty may recover likewise'. He could not, however, give any estimate of how long the illness would last. But it was in his assessment of the cause of the illness, and therefore its nature, that Warren was most outspoken. 'I cannot,' he said, 'assign his Majesty's malady to any cause whatever.' The implication was that he was not delirious but insane.

Baker thought that the King's disorder was 'curable' and that his recovery was 'probable', but like Warren he could not say when. He also agreed with Warren on the nature of the illness, telling the House of Lords' committee that none of the King's original symptoms could account for his present illness. Again, the inference was insanity.

In the light of their gloomy evidence, Warren and Baker were dubbed the 'opposition' physicians. The others were more upbeat, particularly Willis who had not been examined before. He had, he told the Commons' committee, 'great hopes of his Majesty's recovery' and his only reservation was that the King's depression might 'retard his cure'. He could not, however, say with any certainty how long the illness would last: other patients similarly afflicted had taken as little as six weeks to recover; the worst cases more than a year and a half. But on average the recovery period in his asylum was about six months. As to the cause of the illness, Willis said that 'weighty business, severe exercise, . . . too great abstemiousness, and little rest' had been 'too much for his constitution'. It was, therefore, a temporary delirium brought on by his position of responsibility and his ascetic lifestyle.

None of the other physicians was able to shed much more light on the King's condition. All were optimistic about his eventual recovery, but none prepared to estimate when that would be. However, like Willis, they did not think that the King was insane. Sir Lucas Pepys, for example, knew 'no evident, or assignable Cause', but was inclined to think that the 'amendment' in the King's general health occurring at the same time as an abatement of his 'particular disorder' suggested that the cause was an underlying bodily disease. Dr Addington also had 'very good grounds of hope' because the King's disorder had not had as 'its forerunner that melancholy which usually precedes a tedious illness of that sort'.

This distinction between insanity and delirium was crucial, according to Macalpine and Hunter:

> 'Original Madness', otherwise mania or insanity, was considered not amenable to art, spontaneous recovery from it was uncommon and its course was therefore prolonged; whereas 'Consequential Madness', delirium and derangement, could be expected to subside with the underlying condition, whether it was a fever or not, rarely leaving an intellectual defect called fatuity or dementia. Willis and Warren, therefore, represented the opposite poles of hopefulness and despair. If Willis was right, then recovery was in sight and a regency might be avoided; if Warren was right, a regency was inevitable and possibly permanent.[36]

During the debate which followed the presentation of the committee's report to the House of Commons on 10 December, Pitt understandably emphasised the positive aspects of the physicians' testimony. The opinions contained within the report, he told the House, 'must fill their minds with a reasonable hope, that a happier moment would arrive than the present, although [the physicians] were still unable to declare the precise time of its arrival'. In the meantime, it was necessary 'to take those intermediate steps which the unfortunate exigency of the moment required'. He therefore moved for the appointment of a committee to search for precedents 'in the case of the personal exercise of the royal authority being prevented or interrupted'.

Regarding this motion as a thinly disguised attempt to delay the Regency for as long as possible, Fox rose to challenge it. Emaciated and pale, yet to recover fully from the effects of his illness and the exertions of his journey, his 'personal appearance' had 'excited a great and general sensation' on his entry to the House. His poor physical condition may, therefore, have been partly responsible for the rashness of his speech:

> The circumstances to be provided for did not depend on their deliberations as a house of parliament; it rested elsewhere. There was then a person in the kingdom different from any other person that any existing precedents could refer to – an heir apparent of full age and capacity to exercise the royal power. It behoved them, therefore, to waste not a moment unnecessarily, but to proceed with all becoming diligence to restore the sovereign power and the exercise of royal authority.

Now that the House was 'in possession of the true state of the King's health,' he continued, 'not a single moment ought to be lost'. For the 'Prince of Wales had as clear, as express a right to exercise the power of sovereignty, during the period of illness and incapacity with which it had pleased God to afflict his Majesty, as in the case of his Majesty having undergone a natural and perfect demise'.

But if Fox's speech seemed to fly in the face of the traditional Whig view that Parliament's role in the constitution was just as important as the Crown's – causing Pitt, during its delivery, to slap his thigh with delight and exclaim, 'I'll un-whig the gentleman for the rest of his life' – Pitt's response was just as injudicious:

> To assert such [an inherent] right in the Prince of Wales, or any one else, independent of the decision of the two Houses of Parliament, was little less than treason to the constitution of the country . . . [In] the case of the interruption of the personal exercise of the royal authority, without any previous lawful provision having been made for carrying on the government, it belonged to the other branches of the legislature, on the part of the nation at large, the body they represented, to provide, according to their discretion, for the temporary exercise of royal authority.

Not content with this extraordinary assertion – little short of espousing the sovereignty of the people – Pitt went on to say that the 'Prince of Wales had no more right (speaking of strict right) to assume the government, than any other individual subject of the country.'

Back came an indignant Fox, rejecting the charge of treason. Parliament could not, he asserted, 'legally deprive the Prince of Wales of the regency during the incapacity of his father . . . or place any restrictions upon him in the exercise of sovereign power'. If 'the crown was by law declared to be hereditary, why should it not be inferred from analogy, that the exercise of the sovereign power was also hereditary?' he asked.

After Edmund Burke had leapt to Fox's defence, charging the Prime Minister with having set himself up as one of the Prince's 'competitors' for the Regency, Pitt responded by saying that he 'knew not one word that he would retract'. To assert that the Prince 'had a claim to the exercise of the sovereign power' during the King's illness *would* be verging on treason to the constitution because such a claim would supersede 'the deliberative power and discretion of the two existing branches of the legislature'.

His motion was then passed and a committee was appointed. The government nominees included Pitt, Henry Dundas, William Grenville, William Windham, Earl Gower, the Lord Advocate of Scotland, and the Attorney- and Solicitor-Generals. The Opposition put forward Burke, Sheridan and William Wilberforce.[37]

The irony of the opposing constitutional stances taken by Fox and Pitt in their speeches was not lost on Lord John Russell, the editor of Fox's papers and a future Prime Minister. He wrote later:

> In a Constitution so regularly poised as ours, it would have been the height of imprudence for the Prince of Wales to have assumed the rights of sovereignty until the Houses of Parliament had acknowledged the necessity of their being exercised by the Prince of Wales. On the other hand, it would have been dangerous in the extreme for the Houses of Parliament to have travelled out of the road of hereditary succession, and have sought elsewhere than in the person of the next heir to the throne a depository of the royal power. The doctrine of Mr. Fox, the popular leader, went far to set aside the constitutional authority of Parliament, while that of Mr. Pitt, the organ of the Crown, tended to shake the stability of the monarchy, and to peril the great rule of hereditary succession.[38]

Government supporters were delighted by Fox's *faux pas*, which they saw as far more politically damaging than Pitt's. 'Only think of Fox's want of judgement to bring himself and them into such a scrape as he has done,' wrote William Grenville on the 11th. Three days later, when the report of the 'precedents' committee was presented to the House of Commons, Fox tried to repair the damage. The Prince undoubtedly had the 'right' to the Regency, but it was not his 'possession', while the 'adjudication' of his right belonged to the two Houses of Parliament. But for all Fox's sophistry, the climb-down was evident.

Pitt, too, was in a conciliatory mood. Though still convinced that all or part of the 'regal power' should not be 'vested in the Prince of

Wales, as a matter of right', he was 'equally ready to say' that it was 'highly desirable' that some form of 'regal power' should be 'vested in a single person', and 'that this person should be the Prince of Wales'. The question was, how much? In his opinion, it should be enough to carry on 'the public business with vigour and dispatch', and to provide 'for the safety and interests of the country'; on the other hand, any authority capable of being 'employed in any way which might tend to embarrass the exercise of the king's lawful authority, when he should be enabled to resume it', should be withheld.[39]

Pitt's motives for proposing a restricted Regency were obvious. On the one hand, by provoking lengthy parliamentary debates, he was playing for time in the hope that the King would recover before the Prince could become Regent; on the other, he was trying to ensure that the Prince would not have sufficient power to effect a permanent change in the balance of power in Parliament by, for example, creating large numbers of Whig peers.

But Fox was confident that the Prince's promise of peerages, offices and pensions would win over enough supporters in Parliament to defeat Pitt's proposal for an amended Regency. 'We shall have several hard fights in the [House of Commons] this week and next,' he wrote to his mistress, Elizabeth Armistead, on 15 December, 'in some of which I fear we shall be beat, but whether we are or not, I think it is certain that in about a fortnight we shall come in.' He continued:

> At any rate the Prince must be Regent and of consequence the ministry must be changed. The manner in which the Prince has behaved throughout the whole has been the most steady, the most friendly, and the handsomest that can be conceived . . . I am sure I cannot . . . advise him to give up anything [from] the full power of a King, to which he is certainly entitled. The King himself (notwithstanding the reports you may possibly hear) is certainly worse and perfectly mad.[40]

The Prince, fretting helplessly at Carlton House, was not so confident that an unrestricted Regency would come about. 'You may easily conceive I am excessively anxious in the event of the day,' he wrote to Sheridan on 15 December, the evening before Pitt introduced his controversial second Resolution (which called for the provision of a temporary Regency 'in such manner as the exigency of the case may appear to require'). 'What are your apprehensions about numbers? For God's sake explain yourself, *who is false*, who is staunch, *who deceives us*, pray remark will you, and for Heaven's sake send me word and relieve my uneasiness.'[41]

The Duchess of Devonshire, whose husband had been offered the Privy Seal, was no less anxious. Despite a headache, she sat up until the early hours of 17 December to hear whether or not the Whigs had managed to pass an amendment to the second Resolution. It was not until 3 a.m., she wrote to her mother, that the Duke of Bedford and her brother, Earl Spencer, 'came like Priam's messengers and told us our defeat'. The government majority was a demoralising 64.[42]

The editorial line taken by newspapers during the so-called Regency Crisis was very much dependent upon which political party was subsidising them. The reason for such a lack of journalistic integrity is that the newspaper industry was still in its infancy and finding it difficult to make ends meet.

When Pitt became Prime Minister in December 1783, Britain had just nine daily newspapers, five of which were advertising journals. An additional ten London papers appeared two or three times a week; the oldest of these was the *London Evening Post*, founded in 1727. Most had been set up by syndicates of printers, booksellers, auctioneers or victuallers who would each subscribe a sum of capital (say £100) in return for free advertisements. Circulation was generally very low – one paper sold daily for every 300 citizens – partly because until 1814 all newspapers were printed by hand (at about 250 sheets an hour), but mainly because of a largely illiterate population, relatively poor communications and heavy taxation in the form of a stamp duty.

Newspapers received more income from advertisements than from their cover price, with the result that fewer than half of their 16 short columns were devoted to news.

But even the revenue from advertisements did not enable them to be entirely self-supporting, and all were 'open' to corruption. The biggest customer, for obvious reasons, was the government, which used secret service funds – allotted to prevent 'treasonable or other dangerous conspiracies against the state – to ensure a favourable press. By 1788, the majority of influential newspapers were being paid government subsidies of up to £600 a year. They included the *Morning Herald*, *Morning Chronicle*, *Morning Post*, *London Evening Post* and St *James's Chronicle*.

It was not therefore surprising that much of the press coverage during December 1788 was hostile to the Prince and his Whig supporters. The *St James's Chronicle*, for example, referring to Fox's injudicious speech of 10 December, commented that the once staunch defender of the Constitution now seemed 'desirous by one stroke to level this most glorious fabric to the dust'. Even *The Times*, founded in 1785 and not then a government-funded paper, was taking a pro-Tory line. Its proprietor, John Walter, was rewarded for his support in January 1789 when Thomas Steele, the Joint Secretary of the Treasury, offered him a subsidy of £300 a year.

But other papers were moving in the opposite direction. The *Morning Herald* and the *Morning Chronicle*, for example, received large sums of money from Carlton House and the Whigs to print antigovernment articles. The *Morning Post* also performed a volte-face, but for different reasons. During December 1788, it printed a paragraph that referred to the Prince's secret marriage to Mrs Fitzherbert. Terrified, the Prince instructed his solicitor to threaten John Benjafield, the author and co-proprietor, with prosecution if he continued his libellous attacks. When Benjafield responded by promising further disclosures, it became obvious that the only way to shut him up would be to buy him out. The result of the negotiations, conducted on the Prince's behalf by Louis Weltje, was that Benjafield sold his half-share for the grossly inflated price of £1,000 guineas and an annuity of

£350. From 2 January 1789, when the agreement was signed, the *Morning Post* became an Opposition paper.[43]

To give the King enough time to recover, Pitt and his ministers skilfully spun out the debates on what form the Regency would take for as long as possible, with the result that the Regency Bill was not introduced to the House of Commons until 3 February 1789. All Opposition attempts to amend the preliminary Resolutions having been defeated, the Prince was forced to accept its four significant restrictions: he would be unable to create peerages except within the Royal Family (and only then if the recipient was 21); he could not grant offices or pensions, except those required by law to be given for life (such as to judges); he was not empowered to dispose of the King's personal property; and, finally, the care of the King and the government of his Household would be entrusted to the Queen.

The Bill also contained a clause which prevented the Regent from marrying a Catholic. Rolle, the Prince's *bête noire*, had proposed an amendment to make the clause retrospective, 'in fact or in law', but it had not been supported, mainly because most M.P.s regarded the Act of Succession and the Royal Marriage Act as adequate safeguards to the Protestant Constitution. On 13 February, having passed its third reading in the Commons the day before, the Bill was sent up to the House of Lords. It passed its second reading on 16 February and was due a third reading three days later, whereupon it would become law and the Regency would come into force. But the final vote never took place because the King was showing signs of rapid improvement.

He had suffered a relapse of his initial illness on 13 December – causing the physicians to apply leeches to his temples and painful blisters to his legs in an effort to divert the morbid humours from his head – but the crisis had passed by the end of the month. By late January, having recovered some of his physical strength, he was capable of increasingly long periods of 'purposeful and consecutive reasoning, although much of it was still founded on irrational notions and beliefs'.

In Dr Willis's opinion, he still needed controlling – and a restraining-chair, dubbed by the King his 'Coronation Chair', was installed at Kew on 24 January – but his confusion and incoherence were gradually receding. On 3 February he shaved himself for the first time in three months; three days later he was allowed to use a knife and fork again. The official bulletin of 10 February announced that he had passed 'the day before in a state of composure, had four hours sleep, and has more recollection than usual this morning'. That same day, Willis refused his request to see the Chancellor on the ground that 'it would lead to conversations of length beyond his present strength'.

'I will not do it till you think fit,' replied the King, 'but I have been ill seventeen weeks and have much to inquire about. I must have lost some friends in that time.'[44]

On 12 February, the daily bulletin announced 'a progressive state of amendment'. Now even the Opposition had to accept the bitter truth. 'The King has been really considerably better the last two days,' wrote Sir Gilbert Elliot (the future Earl of Minto). 'Sir G. Baker says that he conversed rationally and coherently, with a great deal of recollection, for twenty-five minutes . . . he does not consider this amendment an actual convalescence (or as proving anything with regard to a final cure of the disorder), but it is certainly an amendement."[45]

Two days later, William Grenville wrote to his brother:

> I could not refuse myself the pleasure of letting you know that I have been at Kew to-day with Pitt, and that the account which he received from Willis is such as to confirm and strengthen all our hopes . . . His account is confirmed by . . . the other physicians . . . Sir G. Baker told him today, that if it was a case of a common patient whom he was attending, he should not think it necessary to give him any more medicines.[46]

But Fox, who had left for Bath at the end of January to recover from his lengthy illness, was convinced that the positive reports were a Tory stratagem. 'I [have] no belief in the [King's] recovery,' he wrote to Portland, 'but I dare say some of our friends are a good deal alarmed.' To the Prince, on 15 February, he pointed out that 'the report of the great amendment in the King's health' would be used 'by Mr Pitt and his friends to justify the restrictions, and consequently will be much exaggerated'. His advice was for the Prince 'to act precisely as if the King was in the same state as he was a month ago'.[47]

Closer to the centre of events, the Prince knew better. With the Regency Bill just days from becoming law, the King was walking, reading Shakespeare and Pope, playing the flute, working in his hot-houses and conversing with the Queen and the Princesses. On 17 February, the King saw the Lord Chancellor, against the advice of Warren but with the permission of Willis. The Prince and the Duke of York, on the other hand, were refused admittance on the ground that 'such a step might be of the utmost mischief to the King'. A number of subsequent attempts to see the King were also prevented.[48]

Two days later, as the House of Lords met to consider the third and final reading of the Regency Bill, Thurlow stood up and announced that as 'the intelligence from Kew was that day so favourable', he thought it 'would be indecent and improper to go on with the pro-ceedings'. With his fellow-peers in agreement, an adjournment was duly granted.[49]

On 20 February – the day when Lord Thurlow reported that he had never seen 'the King more composed, collected or distinct' – the Prince of Wales wrote to the Queen asking when he and the Duke of York could, like the Lord Chancellor, be 'permitted to throw ourselves at the feet of the King our father, & to pour forth our respectful joy in his Majesty's presence'.

The Queen, naturally angry with her two elder sons for their disloyal behaviour during the period of the King's illness, sent a curt reply, thanking them for their 'affectionate congratulations' which she would pass on to the King as soon as a 'proper opportunity' arose. As to their request to see their father, she would consult with the physicians before giving them an answer the following morning.

This second letter, informing the princes that the King wanted to see Thurlow again before they were admitted to his presence, coincided with a leader in *The Times* strongly censuring those who had abandoned the King for the Whigs:

> Those ungrateful men who turned their backs on their Sovereign in the moment when he most wanted their assistance, are now lamenting their fate. Despised by those to whom they sold their interest, and disdained by him who merited a better return for his bounty, – they must sink into universal contempt, and curse the shallowness of that judgment, which led them from the path of political rectitude, into the road of unprincipled error.

The same article contained a vicious attack on the Dukes of York and Cumberland – both of whom had signed a peers' petition urging the Prince not to accept a restricted Regency – and 'the leaders of the opposition in general':

> [They] affect to join with the friends of our amiable Sovereign, in rejoicing on account of his Majesty's recovery. But the insincerity of their joy is visible. Their late unfeeling conduct will for ever tell against them; and contradict the artful professions they may think it prudent to make.
>
> It argues infinite wisdom in certain persons, to have prevented the Duke of York from rushing into the King's apartment on Wednesday. The rashness, the Germanick severity, and insensibility of this young man, might have proved ruinous to the hopes of a whole nation.[50]

Amidst such open criticism of their behaviour (the Prince, though not mentioned by name, was obviously implicated), the King's eldest sons were understandably nervous when they were finally admitted to their father's presence on 23 February. So too was the King, pausing before the door to the Queen's apartments where they were waiting, saying 'he was not yet able to go in' and 'crying very much'. Having recovered his composure, he entered and 'embraced them both with the greatest tenderness, and shed tears on their faces'. They, in turn, were 'much touched'.

Deliberately avoiding the subject of politics, the King mentioned that he had passed the time by practising his Latin and learning to play piquet. To the Prince he chatted about horses, and to the Duke about his regiment. All the while, the Queen was 'walking to and fro in the room with a countenance and manner of great dissatisfaction, and the King every now and then went to her in a submissive and soothing sort of tone, for she has acquired the same sort of authority over him that Willis and his men have'.[51]

In the opinion of Lord Bulkeley, the manner in which the King received his errant sons was 'proof that his miraculous recovery is not to be shaken'. The princes, on the other hand, were 'quite desperate' and 'endeavour to drown their care, disappointments and internal chagrin in wine and dissipation'.

On 24 February, the King spoke to his Prime Minister for the first time in three months; two days later, the last official bulletin announced: 'There appears this morning to be an entire cessation of His Majesty's illness.' It was signed by Baker, Pepys and Willis, but not Warren. The interregnum was over.[52]

5

———◆———

Rakes and
Revolutionaries

The King's recovery was confirmed on 10 March 1789 by the formal reopening of Parliament and the abandonment of the Regency Bill. The Speech from the Throne, delivered by Lord Chancellor Thurlow, thanked the Members for their 'affectionate attachment to His Person' and asked them to apply themselves, 'with as little delay as possible, to the different objects of national concern which require your attention'. They, in turn, moved for a 'humble address' in answer to the speech, as well as a 'Congratulatory Message to the Queen'.

That evening, in a 'universal exhibition of national loyalty and joy', wrote Wraxall, 'London displayed a blaze of light from one extremity to the other; the illuminations extending . . . from Hampstead and Highgate to Clapham, and even as far as Tooting: while the vast distance between Greenwich and Kensington presented the same dazzling appearance.'

As church bells rang and cannon fired, the Queen and the Princesses drove incognito into London to witness the celebrations, not returning until one in the morning, enchanted by what they had seen. To surprise the King, his wife had arranged for a private illumination of Kew Palace and its courtyard, with the words 'The King – Providence – Health – and Brittania' displayed in 'elegant devises'.[1]

The public goodwill, however, was not extended to the Prince and the Duke of York. When their stationary coach was recognised in a crowded street, the mob surrounded it with shouts of 'God Save the King!' The Prince responded by letting down his window and shouting, 'Long Live the King!' Then came the cry 'Pitt for Ever!', to which the Prince's inevitable retort was 'Fox for Ever!' At this point, 'a man pulled the coach-door open, and the Prince endeavoured to jump out amongst them in order to defend himself; but the Duke of York kept him back with one arm, and with the other struck the man on the head, and called to the coachman to drive on, which he did at great pace, the coach door flapping about as they went'.[2]

The Queen, meanwhile, had yet to forgive her two eldest sons for their callous and self-serving attitude during the King's illness. According to Lord Ailesbury, the Queen held the Duke 'the most blamable . . . as the King had cautioned him before his illness' not to associate with the Prince's friends.[3]

Anxious to be given an opportunity to explain and justify his conduct, the Prince had written to the Queen on 5 March, requesting an audience with the King. He had also enclosed copies of the correspondence between himself and Pitt during the recent 'crisis', asking her to give them to the King as soon as he was fit 'to attend to public business'. When neither request had been granted by 9 March, the Queen explaining that she had *mentioned the* subject of letters to the King but he had not asked to see them, the Prince wrote again, telling the Queen that the contents of her note were of 'too painful a nature' for him 'to return an immediate answer'. His brother and he were not even to be allowed 'to counteract the impressions which our enemies, who have daily access to the King, may have given of the part we took in the late important occurrencies'.

A separate letter, sent to the King, stated that the Prince and his brother would 'have not a moment's ease whilst we have reason to apprehend that all impressions concerning us may be made'.[4]

But the King would not be mollified. He sacked two members of his Household, the Duke of Queensberry and the Earl of Lothian, for opposing the government in the Regency debates. Other parliamentary supporters of the Prince were deprived of their seats – men like William Hamilton, who represented Wilton, the pocket borough of the loyal courtier, the Earl of Pembroke.

To celebrate the King's recovery, a number of royal festivities were held. But when the Prince and the Duke of York expressed a desire to attend a music concert in early April, the Queen's reply was that while they 'would be welcome', she thought they should 'know that the entertainment was intended for those who had supported them . . . on the late occasion'. They turned up, nonetheless, and had to endure the sight of Court ladies dressed in Tory colours and a musical programme littered with party allusions. While the King was polite, the Queen continued 'sour and glum'.[5]

Royal displeasure also extended to Prince William, whose ship docked at Spithead on 28 April. At the request of the Prince of Wales, the Admiralty had ordered him back from the West Indies in February when a Regency looked certain. It was rumoured that the Prince was planning to make him First Lord of the Admiralty. Certainly William expected much of the new regime, telling the Prince in January that he hoped to 'be admitted of the party'.[6]

Three days after Prince William's return, the King wrote to Pitt, castigating his third son for coming home without his permission. He (rightly) blamed the Prince, who was keen to bolster 'the Opposite faction in my own family'. This made him more determined than ever to safeguard his wife and daughters 'from a total dependence on a Successor', and to ensure the continuance of 'Executive Government' should he die or have a relapse.'[7]

In late May, the King wrote what Sir Gilbert Eliot considered to be 'a most harsh and unnatural letter' to Prince William, or the Duke of Clarence as he had recently become (his father commenting sourly that this was another vote 'added to the Opposition'). As well as saying many 'cruel things' about Clarence, it abused him 'for associating with his brothers, and charges them in plain terms with unkindness and misconduct during his illness'. This was, according to the Prince, the 'first intimation' he had received that the King was displeased with his conduct during the recent crisis.[8]

It would not be the last. Also at the end of May, the Duke of York was involved in an 'affair of honour' with Lieutenant-Colonel Charles Lennox of the Coldsteam Guards, the nephew and heir of the third Duke of Richmond, a Cabinet minister. What made the incident particularly unusual was the fact that the Duke of York, as Colonel of the Regiment, was Lennox's superior officer. This meant that they were contravening not only the Articles of War, which forbade duels between brother officers, but also the civil law of the land, which punished the participants in fatal duels with death.

On hearing that Lennox, whose mother was a member of the Queen's Household, had insulted both him and the Prince, the Duke returned the compliment. Lennox then demanded 'satisfaction'. At the subsequent duel on Wimbledon Common, Lennox's first shot narrowly missed the Duke's head, slicing off a curl from his wig in the process. The Duke's response was to fire in the air. 'When the King and Queen heard it,' wrote Fox to Mrs Armistead, 'the first showed very little & the second *no* emotion at all, and both said coldly that they believed it was more Frederick's fault than Lennox's.' He continued:

> As to the poor man he is mad, but the mother seems to me to go beyond the worst woman we ever read of. Lord Winchilsea, a Lord of the Bedchamber, was Lennox's second, and no notice taken of it by the King or Queen. Friend & enemy, excepting only his father & mother, agree in praising the Duke of York to the greatest degree.[9]

A few days later, despite the protests of the Prince, the Queen invited Lennox to a ball at St James's Palace to celebrate the King's 51st birthday, and treated him with 'marked attention'. This was the final straw. On the advice of Fox and the other Opposition leaders, the Prince decided to send a memorial to the King, explaining his conduct and that of other members of the Royal Family during the recent crisis.

The memorial and an introductory letter sent with it, complaining 'in bitter terms' of the way the Queen had treated her sons, were drafted by the Prince's close adviser, Sir Gilbert Elliot. Part of the memorial stated:

> The Prince and the whole Royal Family were left to act for themselves while the whole power of the Crown and all the influence of office in and out of Parliament was in the hands of persons who, from the beginning, the Princes had just reason to apprehend and had afterwards from experience but too good reason to know and feel, did not entertain very favorable dispositions towards them, and who . . . have done everything in their power to alienate from them the minds of your Majesty's people and to heap every sort of indignity on the whole Royal Family without any distinction . . .
>
> In this delicate and critical situation it required the utmost degree of prudence and circumspection in the Prince of Wales to avoid furnishing a pretext for further injuries and insults, and to submit in silence to many things in order to preserve some appearance of legal government in the nation and in order that your Majesty's just authority during your illness should not receive some more dangerous wound.

The memorial concluded with yet another request for an audience so that the Princes would be able to 'lay before your Majesty . . . a full and fair representation of the circumstances in which they have stood and the steps which have been taken on all sides in your Majesty's affairs, public and private, since your illness'.

On the advice of the Duke of Portland and Lord Loughborough, the introductory letter attacking the Queen was not included with the memorial when it was despatched at the end of June. The King, convalescing at Weymouth, did not respond.[10]

Whether the Prince genuinely considered his conduct during the King's illness to be above criticism is a moot point. If that was the case, then he was sadly deluding himself. For no sooner had his father displayed the first signs of delirium, in early November, than he had called in his own physician (a man who was bound to tell him what he wanted to hear), taken over the running of the Royal Household, and begun secret negotiations to replace Pitt's government with his Whig friends.

With a Regency almost in his grasp, it was no wonder that he showed more enthusiasm for those physicians, Warren and Baker, who tended to view the King's 'madness' as permanent. Or that he fought long and hard, and ultimately without success, to obtain an unrestricted Regency which would enable him to settle a few personal and political scores. On the other hand, it is hardly surprising that the well-again King and his Queen found it so difficult to forgive the actions of their sons and of the King's elder brothers – not least because the Prince had so nearly achieved his objective: after his recovery, the King admitted that had the Regency Bill become law, he would have renounced the throne and exiled himself in Hanover.

During the early summer of 1789, in an attempt to repair their tarnished reputations, the Prince and the Duke of York issued Bills of Indictment against John Walter, the Editor of *The Times*, for libellous articles which had appeared in his newspaper in February. The first, published on the 21st, was the piece attacking the 'insincerity', 'rashness' and 'insensibility' of the Duke 'which might have proved ruinous to the hopes and joys of a whole nation'; the second, which appeared five days later, libelled the Duke and the Prince, saying that they had had to endure the rebukes of a justly offended father. The injured parties had wisely waited four months before taking any action in order to allow the public euphoria at the King's recovery to die down.

The case brought by the Duke of York was successfully prosecuted by Sir Thomas Erskine, the Prince's Attorney-General (and a future Lord Chancellor), in the Court of King's Bench on 11 July. Walter was found guilty of libel and sentenced to one year in Newgate Prison and one hour in the pillory at Charing Cross (this last part of the sentence was remitted by the King). He was also fined £50 and ordered to pay £500 as security for his good behaviour for seven years. The Prince's prosecution the following February was also successful, and Walter was sentenced to another year's imprisonment and fined £200.

On 2 March 1790, less than three months after the first jail sentence had taken effect, Walter wrote to Lord Hawkesbury (later 1st Earl of Liverpool), the President of the Board of Trade. He was bitter at the way the Tory government had abandoned him after he − for the relatively small sum of £300 a year − had agreed to support it during the Regency crisis. He had not even written the libellous paragraphs for which he had been prosecuted; they had been supplied by Thomas Steele, the Joint-Secretary of the Treasury. And yet 'it is well known I was offer'd £4,000 for half the Paper,' he told Hawkesbury, 'and could have been appointed Printer to the Regent.'

But the government either could not, or would not, interfere with the court's decision. Walter was eventually released in March 1791, with eight months of his sentence still to serve, having been pardoned by the King 'at the instance of' the Prince of Wales. The only compensation he received from the Treasury was £250, the total amount he had been fined.[11]

Mr Withers, a clergyman, was not so fortunate. Sentenced in November 1789 to twelve months' imprisonment for a libel on Mrs Fitzherbert, he died in Newgate Prison in July the following year. 'Had Mr Withers been committed to the King's Bench Prison, which has for a long series of years been considered the proper place of punishment for offences such as he had committed,' opined *The Times*, 'neither the letter nor the spirit of his sentence would have gone beyond the intention of the law.'[12]

Particularly chilling, in the light of Withers' death, was a letter written by Erskine in February 1790 to Captain Jack Payne, the head of the Prince's Household, advising the Prince not 'to listen . . . to any petition for mercy from Walter'. He concluded: 'By this proper severity we shall get rid of Withers and all the scoundrels; they are damnably affraid of me and I will take care to justify their fears.'[13]

Meanwhile, events of far greater significance were taking place in France. On 5 May 1789, just ten days after the Thanksgiving Service for George III's recovery at St Paul's Cathedral, the Estates-General met at Versailles for the first time since 1614. The equivalent of the French Parliament, it had been summoned by King Louis XVI in response to financial crisis and civil unrest.

Comprised of three orders – the Clergy, the Nobility and the Third Estate (or Commoners) – the Estates-General first had to decide whether to sit in one assembly, and vote by head, or in three separate assemblies, each with one vote. As the members of the Third Estate outnumbered the other two put together, they naturally wanted a single chamber which they could dominate. The majority of the Nobility, on the other hand, were determined to consign them to a separate chamber and – they hoped – a minority of one to two. The outcome depended upon the Clergy. Many were representative of minor clerics, whose grievances were as numerous as those of the Third Estate. They backed the members of the non-privileged order, and they were gradually joined by a number of abbots and bishops.

On 23 June, with the victory of the Third Estate guaranteed, the King tried to intervene. The doors of the Estates-General's meeting-place were locked and the members ordered to sit in separate chambers. Refusing to comply, the majority met in the nearest available building, a tennis court, and there took an oath not to disperse until their work was done. Henceforth, they would call themselves the National Assembly (renamed the Constituent Assembly in early July). The Revolution had begun.

Before long, extremists were forcing the pace of political change. On 14 July, the workers of the Faubourg St Antoine stormed the Bastille, the royal fortress on the east side of Paris which had gained exaggerated notoriety as a state prison by the circulation of revolutionary pamphlets.

Having butchered the garrison (the Governor was decapitated), released the prisoners and secured the arms stored there, the mob razed the fortress to the ground. Within days, the red and blue colours of the city of Paris had been merged with the white of the Bourbons to form the tricolour flag of the new France.

In Britain, the reaction to this initial stage of the Revolution was generally sympathetic, particularly amongst the Whigs. Fox, for example, compared it with Britain's own revolution – the Glorious Revolution of 1688 – when the Whig aristocracy had so effectively limited monarchical power. How apt, then, that the French were following in their footsteps. The fall of the Bastille was, Fox wrote to Fitzpatrick, 'the greatest event . . . that has ever happened in the history of the world'. But not all his colleagues agreed. To Edmund Burke, the Constituent Assembly did not appear to have 'one jot more power than the King'; how could its members exercise 'any function of decided authority', he wrote, 'with a mob of their constituents ready to hang them if they should deviate into moderation?'[14]

Burke had a point. As the summer wore on, the Constituent Assembly issued a number of revolutionary decrees. They included the Abolition of Feudalism on 4 August and the Declaration of the Rights of Man in September, the preface to the new Constitution. Partly modelled on the American Bill of Rights, and heavily influenced by Rousseauist political philosophy, the Declaration was nevertheless an extremely radical document for its time. It declared:

> Men are born free and equal in rights. The aim of every polit-
> ical association is the preservation of the natural and undoubted
> rights of man. These rights are liberty, property, security, and
> resistance to oppression. The principle of all sovereignty resides
> essentially in the nation.

But such fine words could not prevent the price of bread from rising ever higher. Food riots and fears of a royalist counter-revolutionary plot culminated in the 'Bread March of the Women' to Versailles on

5 October to demand the return of the King to Paris. He went, followed by the Constituent Assembly a week or so later. From now on, Paris's control of the Revolution was never seriously challenged.

The Prince saw little of Mrs Fitzherbert during that momentous summer and autumn of 1789. 'He has hardly been three days together at Brighton,' Louis Dutens informed the Duchess of Devonshire in October 1789.[15]

Instead, said Lord Bulkeley, he and the Duke of York chose 'to drown their cares, disappointment and internal chagrin in wine and dissipation'. *The Times* mirrored this sentiment: the Prince could 'drink, wench and swear like a man who at all times would prefer a girl and a bottle to politics and a sermon'. Maybe not 'prefer', but certainly as an alternative to.[16]

Much of his time was spent in the company of notorious rakes like the Dukes of Norfolk and Queensberry. Charles, 11th Duke of Norfolk, may have been 16 years older than the Prince, but he shared his passion for horseracing, women and heavy drinking. He was famous for being able to hold his drink, remaining apparently sober up to the point where he would collapse to the floor and be carried away by four specially trained footmen. The Prince found it difficult to keep up when the Duke came to dinner, having ridden over to Brighton from nearby Arundel Castle, and would devise various stratagems to extricate himself – such as the mock delivery of an important message which needed urgent attention.

A well-known libertine, Norfolk insisted on watching through a glass partition as the mothers of his numerous bastards were paid at the same bank on the same day. 'Blue eyes, Jewish noses, gipsy skins and woolly black hair,' wrote Sir Osbert Sitwell, 'were seen to be grafted on to the unmistakeable Howard features of the infants borne along in their mothers' arms, or of stalwart children now obliged to wheel their mother in a chair.'

Even by the standards of the time, Norfolk was an ill-educated and unhygienic man, whose only exposure to soap and water was when his servants were able to take advantage of his drunkenness. His support for the Prince during the Regency crisis was particularly resented because, coming from a long line of Roman Catholics, his recent conversion to Anglicanism was not taken seriously. 'Remember, once a good Catholic, always one,' declared *The Times*. 'A turn-coat can have absolution!'[17]

The 4th and last Duke of Queensberry was, if anything, even more dissolute. A 65-year-old bachelor and dedicated whoremonger, known as 'Old Q', he was said to have fathered a number of illegitimate children, including Maria Fagniani, the future wife of the 3rd Marquess of Hertford, to whom he left the huge sum of £300,000 when he died in 1810. He was also one of the 'rats', members of the King's Household who deserted to the Prince when it looked certain that he would become Regent. For his disloyalty he was dismissed from his post as Lord of the Bedchamber, though why a man with such a 'low' reputation had ever been appointed to so virtuous a Court is a mystery.

Other disreputable friends included Louis-Philippe, Duke of Orléans, the fantastically rich cousin of King Louis XVI, who made regular visits to England; the Honourable George Hanger, later Baron Coleraine, whom Raikes described as 'a *beau* of the first water' but with 'not much wit or talent', and Wraxall as an 'outcast from decent society'; and Sir John Lade, the inheritor of a brewing fortune who had married the Duke of York's former mistress, Letitia Smith.

Then there was the infamous Barry family: headed by Richard, the young 7th Earl of Barrymore, better known as 'Hellgate', who was 'foremost in every species of dissipation'; his eldest brother, Augustus, a gambling clergyman who was nicknamed 'Newgate' because he was ever on the verge of debtors' prison; the youngest brother, Henry, the future 8th Earl, who was dubbed 'Cripplegate' on account of his club foot; and their sister, Lady Melfort, who was called 'Billingsgate' because of her violent temper and foul vocabulary.[18]

Born in the summer of 1769, Richard Barry was just four when he succeeded to the Irish earldom of Barrymore, two huge estates (one in

Ireland, one in England) and an income of more than £10,000 a year. Over-indulged by his grandmother – he arrived at Eton with £1,000 in his pocket – he never knew the meaning of moderation. Tall and athletic, one of the finest riders in the kingdom, he was particularly fond of juvenile pranks. Driving through Oxford Street in a hackney-coach with friends, he would imitate the voice of a woman in the process of being ravished. 'Murder! Rape! Unhand me, villain!' he would cry. But no sooner had the coach been stopped by law-abiding citizens keen to intervene, than he and his friends would leap out and give them a good thrashing.

Anthony Pasquin, his friend and biographer, describes another prank:

> He made his footman, Frank, put on a coffin, which was buck-led to his body, with the foot-board out; this was carried with great solemnity, by himself and others, who knocked at Mr. P———y's door, on the Steyne, and left the coffin upon the steps; when the maid servant opened the door and saw, as she supposed, the dead body of a man, she shrieked and fainted away; the noise alarming the family, they all rushed out, armed with poker, tongs, and a loaded pistol; Frank, with much diffi-culty, effected his escape, by leaping over some rails, after the pistol had been discharged, and the ball had perforated the coffin but an inch above the poor fellow's head.

The Prince was not averse to such japes, and on another occasion he persuaded Barrymore to ride to the top floor of Mrs Fitzherbert's house in Brighton. But nothing could persuade the horse 'to make the return journey and two blacksmiths were at last called in to get it down by main force, their reward being a bowl of punch at the Castle'.

Barrymore's weakness was his generosity. 'The treasury of Croesus would not have been equal to the completion of his ideas,' wrote Pasquin. During the Ascot Heath races in 1791, he prepared two ban-quets in honour of the Prince at a total cost of 1,700 guineas (£1,785).

But the Prince did not attend either. 'To the first came only Lord Barrymore and Mr. Franco,' wrote Pasquin, 'to the other, Lord Falkland and myself!'

At Wargrave, his estate on the Thames, he spent more than £60,000 on a private playhouse in which he would indulge his passion for drama, regularly performing in roles such as *Scrub*, *Babadil* and *Gregory Gubbins*. In the summer of 1790, a licentious masquerade was held there to celebrate his 21st birthday, attended by the Prince and 'all the beauty and fashion of the surrounding counties'.

Public concern at the Prince's choice of unsuitable friends was articulated in 1792 – albeit in a somewhat extreme form – with the anonymous publication of a scurrilous pamphlet, *The Jockey Club*, or *Sketch of the Manners of the Age*, written by the Radical journalist Charles Pigott. 'Let us enquire who are the . . . confidential intimates of the Prince of Wales?' it asked, before providing the answer: 'They are the very lees of society: . . . The Barrys, Sir J. Lade, and Mr. George Hanger. If a man of the most depraved, the vilest cast, were, from a vicious sympathy, to choose his company, it were impossible for his choice to fix anywhere else.'

Referring to his relationship with Mrs Fitzherbert, the pamphlet said that it would 'one day become a matter of most serious national discussion' and that 'his behaviour to her . . . has not been of the most grateful, delicate, or honourable nature'. Then it turned to the subject of his debts:

> No sooner had parliament voted this money, than decency was set at defiance, public opinion scorned, the turf establishment revived in a more ruinous style than ever, the wide field of dissipation and extravagance enlarged, fresh debts contracted to an enormous amount . . . Had a private individual acted in like manner, he would have become the outcast of his family . . .; but in the case before us, where the example is ten thousand times more contagious, such a flagrant breach of faith . . . has hardly recieved the slightest animadversion.

Having lambasted the Prince, *The Jockey Club* then turned to his cohorts: the Duke of York's 'achievement' since his return was confined to 'the parade in St James's Park', 'the Tennis-Court in James-Street', and 'pretty frequent relaxation among the nymphs of Berkeley Row'; the Duke of Queensberry 'has long shone a splendid meteor on this metropolis of voluptuousness', but it was 'to be lamented, that he now affords only a disgusting instance of extreme folly, in affecting to appear, what is physically impossible for him to practise'; George Hanger was 'an egregious coxcomb' who rarely spoke unless it was 'to entertain the company with some instance . . . of his own folly'; the Earl of Barrymore was 'so notorious' that he needed no elaborate description; and Sir John Lade, setting 'all decency at defiance', had married a 'common prostitute'.[19]

So outraged was the Prince by the pamphlet that he sent a copy of it to the Queen, describing it 'as the most infamous & shocking libellous production that ever disgraced the pen of man' and warning that if it was 'not taken up in *a very serious manner by Government &* prosecuted *as a libel upon the King, yourself, & the constitution*, there will be no end to these atrocious publications'. Such '*damnable doctrines* of the *hellbegotten Jacobines,*' he added, were intended to be 'studiously distributed amongst the common people, as the motives to instigate everyone to adopt the principles of the French Revolution.'[20]

Nothing was done, of course, partly because the pamphlet was anonymous and partly because so many of its criticisms were justified. The author, Pigott, died two years later, by which time the 7th Earl of Barrymore was also dead, accidentally shot by one of his own soldiers in March 1793. At the date of his untimely death, aged just 23, Barrymore had gone through more than £300,000 in five years and was living off a reduced annual income of £2,500.

In January 1790, Lord Sydney reported that the Prince was 'taking all possible pains to form a strong party against the Government'. That may well have been the case, but his efforts were hardly successful. He and the Duke of Clarence supported Lawrence Dundas's failed bid to prevent Pitt and Lord Euston from being elected to represent Cambridge University in June. They also meddled in the election of Scottish Representative Peers to little effect. On the other hand, M.P.s like James Macpherson and the lawyer Adair were beginning to attend the Prince's Levées; and from this time can be dated a lengthy correspondence with the Duke of Northumberland, who controlled four seats in the House of Commons (the most powerful parliamentary patron at this time was the Earl of Lonsdale with seven seats).

The truth is that the Prince and his two eldest brothers were more interested in the dire state of their finances than in politics. Matters came to a head for the Prince in the summer of 1790 when his debtors called in a huge loan for £300,000. York and Clarence were similarly embarrassed, but not to such an extent.

Realising that neither Pitt's government nor the King were likely to come to their aid, the Prince tried to solicit 'loans in Holland and elsewhere, on usurious terms, and to be repaid at the King's death'. 'This has failed, however,' noted Sir Gilbert Eliot, 'and the Duke of Portland is engaged in forming a plan for restoring the Prince's affairs and the Duke of York's to some order; but, as the plan must be executed by the Princes themselves, one cannot feel much confidence in its success.'

As it happened, the plan *was* a success – at least in the short-term. On 26 September 1790, Portland sent a proposal to the Prince on behalf of 'Mr de Wolff' and 'Messrs. Wesbrouck Mellesio & Co. for raising a sum of three hundred thousand pounds by way of loan to your Royal Highness and their Royal Highnesses the Duke of York and the Duke of Clarence'. He continued:

> Your Royal Highness will be pleased to observe that the whole of the sum purported to be advanced will be received by your Royal Highness without any deduction; that you are at liberty to repay it whenever it may be your pleasure, and that you need pay interest only for what is actually paid into your Royal Highness's treasury, and although the interest etc. will exceed

six per cent, the premium of insurance, is a condition which could not be refused under the circumstances of the intended loan, and that the other exceeding is for commission and management, a consideration which is even allowed to the Bank in the case of all public loans.

In addition, the three Princes had just signed bonds to borrow £75,000 from the Duke of Orléans and £30,000 from Nathaniel Forth of Manchester Square. The loans were to be paid back at the rate of £750 a year until one of the princes came into the possession of an income exceeding £200,000, at which time the annual repayments would increase to £17,500 plus interest (this was fixed at 5 per cent).[21]

But the Prince's financial worries were far from over. His expenditure far outstripped his annual income, and by taking out huge loans he was simply adding to the problem. So was the Duke of York, who eventually came to the conclusion that marriage was the simplest solution. In the autumn of 1791, with his parents' permission, he married Princess Frederica, the daughter of King Frederick William II of Prussia. 'I believe and hope she will make him happy,' wrote Lord Malmesbury, the diplomat, who was then in Germany trying to organise loans for the Prince. 'She is far from handsome but lively, sensible and very tractable, and if only one-tenth part of the attachment they now show for each other remains, it will be very sufficient to make an excellent ménage.'[22]

On account of his marriage, the Duke of York was voted an additional parliamentary income of £18,000 a year. This increased his total annual income (including the revenues of the Bishopric of Osnaburgh) to more than £70,000. The Prince, with far more expenses, was living off just £60,000 a year. It would not be long before he too began to consider an official marriage as the key to unlock the public purse.

The one bright spot on this gloomy horizon was the fact that relations with his parents had improved. On 12 August 1790, the King and Queen held a ball to celebrate his 28th birthday at Windsor; the occasion was repeated the following year. 'Perhaps no Heir to the Crown, since the days of Edward the Black Prince, has been more generally admired for his amiable manners than the PRINCE OF WALES,' commented *The Times* after the latter event, 'and the very happy and substantial reconciliation that has taken place between his Royal Highness and his august Parents, contributed in no small degree to add to the pleasure and festivities of the day.'[23]

One of the Prince's chief pleasures at this time was horseracing. Although he had sold his original stud in 1786 as part of his attempt to economise, Parliament's settlement of his debts a year later had enabled him to build up another one at Newmarket. Between 1788 and 1791, his horses won a total of 185 races. Then disaster struck.

On 20 October 1791, the Prince's horse 'Escape', reckoned to be the best then running, was beaten by two rank outsiders at Newmarket. The next day, he ran again and won; only this time, assuming that he was past his best, the punters had bet against him. Suspecting a fix, the press printed a number of allegations: that 'Escape' had been winded by a bucket of water given to him before the first race; that Sam Chifney, the Prince's jockey who had ridden 'Escape' in both races, had made hundreds from the second race; that Warwick Lake, brother of General Gerard Lake and the Prince's racing manager, had made disparaging remarks in public about the horse's performance; and that the Duke of Bedford had publicly remonstrated with the Prince after the second race, demanding Chifney's dismissal.

At the subsequent Jockey Club inquiry, Chifney admitted betting on 'Escape' in the second race, but said that it had made him no *more* than 20 guineas. Lake and Bedford, on the other hand, flatly denied the comments attributed to them, the latter pointing out that he had not even been at Newmarket at the time. The suspicion of wrongdoing remained, however, and Sir Charles Bunbury, a Jockey Club Steward, told the Prince 'that if he allowed Chifney to ride his horses again, no gentleman would start against him'. Incensed by this insinuation, the Prince announced his retirement from the turf. And to confirm his opinion that his jockey was innocent, he said that he would pay Chifney's annual retainer of 200 guineas for life.

Few others were convinced of Chifney's innocence. 'Such a thing has been done by the Prince's people here as, in my opinion, amounts to an absolute cheat,' wrote Charles James Fox, a keen racegoer himself, to Mrs Armistead:

> I hope the P[rince] himself was out of the secret, but those who are not partial to him will not believe it, and all to win about 800 g[uinea]s. I never was more vexed in my life and I consider it as putting an end to amusement here most completely, because there were always people enough inclined to do wrong, and an example of this sort is sure to encourage them . . .

The Prince's stud was sold at Tattersall's in March 1792, for prices ranging from 25 to 270 guineas (it would, in addition, save him £30,000 a year). The main buyers were Lord Grosvenor and the Dukes of Bedford and York. Chifney died in a debtors' prison in 1807, having sold his annuity for £1,260 the year before.[24]

In France, meanwhile, the Revolution was becoming increasingly militant. For some time after the King had been forced to reside in Paris in October 1789, it had seemed as if a constitutional monarchy was possible. The King remained Head of State, and the Constituent Assembly seemed to be more interested in debating the form of the future Constitution than in passing radical reforms.

All this changed in April 1791 with the death of the Comte de Mirabeau, the constitutional monarchist whose oratory had dominated the Assembly. With Mirabeau's moderating influence gone, extremist groups like the Jacobins and the Girondins began to gain ground. This in turn prompted the Royal Family's disastrous attempt to flee from Paris and seek refuge with the still largely royalist army on the eastern frontier of France in June. Intercepted at Varennes and brought back to the capital in disgrace, the King's credibility as a constitutional ruler was in tatters.

At this point, Holy Roman Emperor Leopold II (the brother of Queen Marie Antoinette) and King Frederick William II of Prussia began to show concern for the fate of their fellow monarch. In late August 1791, they issued the Declaration of Pillnitz, appealing for all European rulers to act together in order to find the best way to restore monarchical government in France. A declaration of intent rather than one of war, this led to an inevitable deterioration in relations between France and the rest of Europe. This suited Louis XVI, who was by now relying on foreign interference to restore his political status. At the behest of the Queen, he rejected the advice of constitutional monarchists like Antoine Barnave to work within the limits of the new Constitution which, in September 1791, he had sworn to maintain. Instead, he embarked upon a policy of subterfuge and deception, secretly negotiating with the foreign powers.

When the Girondins took over from the more moderate Feuillant government in March 1792, Louis XVI even encouraged their policy of war against Austria in the hope that military disaster would lead to a restoration of his autocratic power. The Girondins, for their part, were keen to attack the absolutist monarchies of Europe before France itself was attacked. They also believed that war would mean the end of the French monarchy and the fulfilment of their revolutionary aim: the establishment of a republic. On 20 April 1792, therefore, they declared war on Austria (and, by default, her allies, Prussia and the Fürstenbund, the League of German Princes).

The command of the allied German army was given to the liberal Duke of Brunswick, an experienced general who had just turned down a similar offer made by the French. At Coblenz on 25 July, he issued his famous manifesto, threatening to use force unless Louis XVI's legal authority was re-established. But as a tool of propaganda, the Brunswick manifesto backfired because it united the French people against their common enemy – the German invaders. The French King – encouraged by Dumouriez, his Foreign Minister – then made matters worse by dismissing his remaining Girondin ministers. Their reaction was to join with the Jacobins in inciting the

Paris mob – already furious at the publication of the Brunswick manifesto – to invade the Tuileries, the royal palace, on 10 August. The Royal Family was forced to take refuge with the Legislative Assembly (so named since the passing of the Constitution), which promptly suspended the King's authority and imprisoned him and his family in the Temple.

For a time it seemed as if help was at hand. Having crossed the Rhine on 30 July, Brunswick's army took the eastern fortress of Verdun in late August. (When the news reached Paris on 2 September, it prompted a massacre of thousands of people associated with the *ancien régime*.) But on 20 September, Brunswick's 35,000 troops were defeated by a superior French force at Valmy, 40 miles west of Verdun.

Meanwhile, the Girondins and the Jacobins had transformed the Legislative Assembly into a Revolutionary Convention which met for the first time on 21 September. Emboldened by news of the great victory, it abolished the monarchy and proclaimed the first French Republic. Then in November it issued the Compulsory Liberty Decree, which offered military support to all nations who wanted to overthrow their rulers and become republics. The Revolution was about to be exported.

All the while, events in France were being closely monitored back in Britain. In November 1790, Edmund Burke published his *Reflections on the French Revolution*, an eloquent condemnation of the French revolutionaries and their British sympathisers. Four months later, the republican Thomas Paine responded with the first part of *The Rights of Man*, a violent polemic defending the Revolution. Then on 15 April 1791, shortly after Mirabeau's death and during a debate on the Russo-Turkish war, Charles James Fox re-entered the debate. Comparing conditions under the old regime unfavourably with existing ones, and observing that even 'those who detested the principles of the revolution had reason to rejoice its effect', he concluded with the declaration that, 'considered altogether', the revolution was 'the most stupendous and glorious edifice of liberty which has been erected on the foundations of human integrity in any time or country'.

Such comments were starting to worry the more conservative Whigs, particularly the Duke of Portland and Edmund Burke, not to mention the Prince. On 6 May, Burke hit back during a debate on the Quebec Bill (proposing a new Constitution for Canada). Continually interrupted by objections of irrelevancy, heckling and points of order, his opening speech derided the 'spurious' and 'mischievous' rights of man 'imported from a neighbouring country' and warned of plots against the British Constitution.

Burke's speech had done him a 'great injustice', Fox replied. It was clearly trying 'to discover a cause of dispute'. His own belief was that the rights of man underpinned 'every rational constitution' and that the French Revolution was 'one of the most glorious events in the history of mankind'. But Fox went too far when he then referred to the inconsistency of Burke's principles.

Back came Burke, praising monarchy as 'the basis of all good government' and complaining that a 'personal attack had been made upon him from a quarter he never could have expected, after a friendship and intimacy of more than twenty-two years'. He and Fox had disagreed over political questions before, he reminded the House – citing the Royal Marriage Act, parliamentary reform and the attempt to repeal the Test and Corporation Acts – but their friendship had never been in doubt. The threat the French Revolution posed to the British Constitution was different, however.

Hearing this, Fox leaned towards him and whispered that there was 'no loss of friends'.

'Yes, there *was* a loss of friends,' said Burke. He 'knew the price of his conduct – he had done his duty at the price of his friend – their friendship was at an end.'

Fox rose to reply, but was so overcome by Burke's harsh words that 'tears trickled down his cheeks, and he strove in vain to give utterance to feelings that dignified and exalted his nature'. Having recovered, he assured Burke that, despite what had passed, *he* at least did not consider their friendship at an end. He could not, however, refrain from emphasising his joy at the termination of 'a tyranny of the most horrid despotism'. As to the future, he would keep out of Burke's way until time and reflection 'fitted him to think differently on the subject'.

Some hope. Within weeks, Burke had published his *Letter to a Member of the National Assembly*, calling for combined military action to reinstate the old government of France. Three months later, his *An Appeal of the New to the Old Whigs* appeared, charging the radical wing of the party with having abandoned traditional Whig principles. It also confined the concept of the 'sovereignty of the people' to 'great multitudes of people' cooperating in a state under the direction of 'a true, natural aristocracy'. When 'the common sort of men' were separated from 'their natural chieftains', however, you were left not with 'the people', but with 'a disbanded race of deserters and vagabonds'. He was referring not only to the extremists of the French Revolution, but also to the republican-motivated perpetrators of the riots in Birmingham in July.

Fox disagreed with this view, not least because he did not believe that the French aristocracy possessed the same disinterested motives and sense of duty as their British counterparts. He was still convinced that the French Revolution was a legitimate attempt to limit the power of a despotic ruler and a corrupt nobility, but the course it was taking was beginning to alarm him. He did not, therefore, join The Friends of the People, a club formed by the radical wing of the party including Grey, Lauderdale, Sheridan and Erskine. Grey even went so far, in April 1792, as to table a Commons motion for parliamentary reform.

Fox, no democrat but anxious not to fragment the party, managed to tread a delicate middle ground during the subsequent debate. He 'saw nothing in any human institution so very sacred', he told the House, 'as not to admit of being touched or looked at'. 'If the people of the country really wished for a parliamentary reform, they had a right to have it.' But he was careful not to associate himself too closely with Grey who had, he said, 'in his warmth outrun himself'. Paine's *Rights of Man*, he added, was a 'libel on the constitution'. However, this did not prevent the London Corresponding Society, formed in January 1792 by the shoemaker Thomas Hardy to demand universal suffrage, from distributing 500 copies of his speech.[25]

The Prince's stance on the issue of parliamentary reform (and, by extension, the French Revolution) was spelt out in his maiden speech in the House of Lords on 25 May 1792 during a debate on the King's Proclamation against Seditious Writings. Such 'wicked' works, stated the proclamation, had been 'printed, published, and industriously dispersed, tending to excite tumult and disorder, by endeavouring to raise groundless jealousies and discontents in the minds of our faithful and loving subjects, respecting the laws and happy constitution of government'. The proclamation therefore ordered magistrates to 'make diligent inquiry in order to discover the authors and printers of such . . . writings', and to 'take the most immediate and effective care to suppress and prevent all riots, tumults and disorders'.

For the Prince, rising to speak after the motion to consider the proclamation had been seconded by the Earl of Harrington, the 'matter in issue' was 'whether the constitution was or was not to be maintained – whether the wild ideas of theory were to conquer the wholesome maxims of established practice; and whether those laws under which we had flourished for such a series of years were to be subverted by a reform unsanctioned by the people'. It would, he added, 'be treason to the principles of his mind if he did not come forward and declare his disapprobation of those seditious publications which had occasioned the motion'.

Noble sentiments, but tame compared with his concluding peroration. 'I exist by the love, the friendship, and the benevolence of the people,' he said without a hint of irony, 'and their cause I will never forsake so long as I live.' With that he gave his 'most hearty assent to the motion for concurring in this wise and salutary address'.[26]

By this speech, the Prince clearly identified himself with the Portland Whigs; and his antipathy towards Jacobinism, French and English, was merely heightened by the events in Paris during the summer. With the imprisonment of Louis XVI in August and the rise of the republican movement, thousands of aristocrats fled the country. Among them was the young and beautiful Duchesse de Noailles, who landed on Brighton beach in late August disguised as a cabin-boy. The Prince and Mrs Fitzherbert were there to meet her.

'The Prince,' reported the local paper on 29 August, 'with his usual affability escorted the Fair Fugitive to Earl Clermont's, where tea was provided . . . [He] with that humanity and gallantry which so invariably distinguished him, paid every attention to this amiable stranger. She this day rode out with Mrs Fitzherbert.'

The Duchess stayed with Mrs Fitzherbert and even borrowed her gowns. In the small oratory she was able to thank God for her delivery and pray for those left behind in France. Unfortunately her prayers were not answered. Prompted by the advance of the allied army, the September Massacres accounted for many of her family and friends. Particularly shocking for the Prince was the news that the Princesse de Lamballe, who had accompanied him to the Brighton races in 1787, was among those mercilessly butchered.

On 24 September, in a letter to the Queen, the Prince expressed his alarm at reports that the French Revolution was spreading. He had heard from an informant – 'one who, though in a lower sphere of life, yet I can depend upon' – that 'in the small ale houses in and about London, there were a number of French Jacobines who were industriously and strenuously endeavouring to propagate their infernal doctrines . . . by inveighing openly . . . upon the French Revolution and upon the blessings that must come to this country was she alike drenched and deluged with blood as France is.'[27]

If the Prince's fearful imagination was running a little away with him, there was more than a kernel of truth in what he said. But Britain was not France; its political system, though unrepresentative by today's standards with only one man in ten able to vote, was the most enlightened in Europe, with regular parliaments and effective checks to the power of the monarch. Reform was always more likely than revolution.

But there *was* a very real danger of Britain becoming involved in a Continental war, particularly after French forces invaded the Austrian

Netherlands at the end of September 1792. The obvious solution was a government of national unity – a coalition – and to this end Pitt had been conducting negotiations with the Portland Whigs since the previous May. He particularly wanted to replace Lord Thurlow – who had not been forgiven for his duplicity during the Regency crisis, and who had been forced to resign in June – with Lord Loughborough. Loughborough was certainly keen, as were other right-wing Whigs like Burke. But the sticking point for Portland was Fox, who would not serve under Pitt – nor would he be welcome. Yet Portland could not bring himself to desert Fox and fracture the party. Mediators suggested that Pitt and Fox should serve as Secretaries of State under a neutral third party – someone like the Duke of Leeds. But Pitt was not prepared to step down.

The upshot of these negotiations – held without the Prince's knowledge and much to his annoyance – was that, for the meantime, Portland held aloof while his right-wing followers deserted to Pitt one by one. The most prominent defector was Lord Loughborough, who became Lord Chancellor on 28 January 1793. This was a week after the execution of King Louis XVI of France, who had been tried for treason by the Convention after evidence of his secret negotiations with foreign governments had been found in a strong-box in the Tuileries the previous November. Two days after being found guilty by 380 votes to 310, he was guillotined in the Place de la Révolution. (Among the Convention members who voted to execute him was his cousin Philippe Égalité, the former Duke of Orléans and drinking companion of the Prince, who had embraced the democratic principles of the revolution. After his son, the Duke of Chartres, deserted to the Allies, Égalité was arrested and eventually guillotined himself in November 1793).

The news of King Louis's execution reached London on the 23rd, causing the ever sensitive Prince to write to his mother: 'I am not equal to meeting any of you this evening, overpowered with the shocking and horrid events of France and with a species of sentiment towards my *father* which *surpasses all discription.*'

The '*sentiment*' he was referring to was gratitude; the King had just granted his wish to 'act in the military line'. On 26 January, he received official confirmation from Sir George Yonge, Secretary at War, that the King had appointed him Colonel Commandant of the 10th (Prince of Wales's Own) Light Dragoons. A few days later, Yonge told him that his commission had been backdated by the King to 1782 so that he would be the senior colonel in the army.[28]

Raised as a regiment of dragoons in 1715 to help put down the first Jacobite Rebellion, the 10th had since fought with varying degrees of success in the '45 Rebellion and the Seven Years' War. In 1783, it had been one of a number of heavy regiments which were reconstituted as light dragoons, with smaller recruits and lighter arms. It was now back to its full war establishment of six troops, each comprised of an officer, three sergeants, three corporals, a trumpeter and 47 men, all still wearing the regulation military wigs, with 'stiff curls on each side, and a long tail behind, the whole plastered and powdered'.[29]

But the men would not meet their new Colonel Commandant for a few months yet.

Meanwhile, war between Britain and France was imminent. After a meeting of the Privy Council on 24 January, Chauvelin, the French Ambassador, was ordered to leave Britain within a week. He set off the following day. 'The business is now brought to a crisis,' wrote William Grenville, 'and I imagine that the next dispatch . . ., or the next but one, will announce the commencement of hostilities.'[30]

When Chauvelin arrived in Paris on the 29th, there was a public outcry at the news of his expulsion. The commercial treaty with Britain was at once rescinded, an embargo was imposed on British and Dutch shipping, and it was provisionally agreed to order Dumouriez to invade Holland. On 1 February, these decisions by the Executive Council were confirmed when the Convention voted to declare war on Holland and Britain; it also issued a fraternal decree calling on the people of Britain to rise against their rulers.

While the fraternal decree was issued more in hope than expectation, France's military threat to Holland was more tangible. Advancing from Antwerp into western Holland on 16 February, General Dumouriez's troops met with little resistance. Pitt's government responded by sending a Brigade of Guards to assist the Dutch. The 29-year-old Duke of York had already been appointed to lead a corps of Hanoverians on its way to Holland; now he was given overall command of all British and Hanoverian troops in the Low Countries. For a time it seemed as if he might have little to do. In March, the Austrian army won a series of victories over the French in Flanders. The Prussians, too, had reached French soil, while the Hanoverians were approaching from the east. Dumouriez had little option but to retreat to Antwerp.

Meanwhile in Italy Prince Augustus, the sixth son of George III, was about to take a fateful step which would have serious repercussions for his eldest brother. Educated at Göttingen University like his brothers Ernest and Adolphus, he was unable to follow them into the Hanoverian army because of a weak chest. Instead he was forced to spend much of his time in the warmer climes of the Mediterranean. While in Italy, he began a romance with Lady Augusta Murray, the daughter of the 4th Earl of Dunmore. A plain, 'coarse and confident-looking' woman, eleven years his senior, she was ably assisted in her attempt to ensnare a royal prince by her mother. 'The Countess,' wrote the diarist Joseph Farington, 'followed [Prince Augustus] to different places in Italy, and when the danger and impropriety was hinted to her, seemed insensible of it.'

Lady Dunmore's ends were achieved on 4 April 1793 when Prince Augustus and Lady Augusta were secretly married by an Anglican clergyman in Rome. On hearing the news from one of Augustus's attendants, the King ordered his errant son to return home at once. He did so, but brought his pregnant wife with him. And just to be on the safe side, he went through a second marriage service at St George's Church, Hanover Square, on 5 December 1793. The King was beside himself, declaring the marriage null and void under the terms of the Royal Marriage Act, and forbidding Augustus, who had since returned to Italy, to communicate with his 'wife' or his sisters. Henceforth, in the eyes of his father he did not exist.[31]

On 14 April 1793, before his Flanders campaign got under way, the Duke of York received a letter from the Prince congratulating him 'on the happy turn all foreign politics are at present appearing to take'. It continued:

> I have followed with the utmost interest & attention every gradation of success that has attended *our arms* in every quarter (if one may be so allowed to call it) for sure every victory that is obtained over this rabble of scoundrels in any shape we are JUSTLY entitled to call the SUCCESS OF OUR ARMS, for whether a Convention is signed or not, it is *too nice a distinction when the interest, the honor,* THE VERY EXISTENCE OF EVERY PRINCE AT THIS MOMENT IS CONCERNED and DEPENDS UPON THE TOTAL ANNIHILATION OF THIS BANDITTI who are a disgrace to the human species by the atrocities which they have been guilty of . . . When I mention *the cause of Princes* [he added], I am speaking of what not only must affect *you & me, as individuals,* but what under the general name OF THE PEOPLE, under which and in which WE ARE ALL INVOLVED . . ., we are all in the same measure, though in various degrees, equally interested, for the total subversion of all order and civil Society includes every one, at least those who have the smallest regard either to character, probity, property, honor, or justice.[32]

So keen was the Prince to ensure an Allied victory that in June he took the extreme step of writing to the Prince of Saxe-Coburg, the Austrian commander, to ask if he could join his army. The request was passed on to Francis II, who had succeeded his father as Holy Roman Emperor a year earlier; he was not averse to the idea, but George III was. He already had three sons serving at the front: the Duke of York, Prince Ernest (later Duke of Cumberland) and Prince Adolphus (later Duke of Cambridge). He was not about to let the heir-apparent put his life in danger – not least because his over-sensitive, comfort-loving eldest son was hardly cut out for the rigours of campaigning.[33]

In any case, his brother York seemed to have matters well in hand. Having taken Valenciennes in late July, York marched on towards Dunkirk with 6,500 British, 13,000 Hanoverians and 15,000 Dutch troops. But what appeared to be no more than a temporary reverse at Hondschoote was made more serious in October when the Austrians were defeated by General Jourdan at Wattignies. As part of the Allies' general retirement, York was forced to move back to Ostend.

The Prince, meanwhile, was merely playing at soldiers. On 5 August, having managed to squeeze his considerable bulk into the magnificent blue- and gold-embroidered uniform of the 10th Light Dragoons, he joined his regiment in camp near Brighton. It had been conveniently chosen so that the Prince was close to Mrs Fitzherbert and his beloved Pavilion, and the troops well placed to defend the south coast from French invaders. 'The ground is already marked out and the wells dug for the encampment,' reported *The Times*, 'which will be in a delightful spot by the sea-side . . . [His] Royal Highness will dine at the mess every day, and be in actual service in all respects.'

He would not be roughing it though. A 'most superb bed' had been made for the Prince's tent, added *The Times*. It was 'square' with 'hangings of a very delicate chintz', its four corners 'ornamented with the PRINCE's feathers and motto'. The 'State Room' chairs alone had cost £1,000, while 'the rest of the furniture for the tent is in corresponding elegance'.[34]

For a time, the Prince seemed to take his military responsibilities seriously. On 8 August he wrote to the Duke of Richmond, the Master-General of the Ordnance, enclosing the weekly state of his regiment and a request by his subordinate, Lieutenant-Colonel William

Newton, for 'an additional allowance of oats'. His 31st birthday, moreover, was celebrated in the regimental mess. But he quickly realised that the rank of Colonel Commandant was more ceremonial than practical, the day-to-day running of the regiment being Newton's responsibility. With little to do, he was back in the Pavilion within a month.

From there in early October he wrote to Lord Amherst, the Commander-in-Chief, asking to know why his name was not on a list of colonels about to be promoted to major-general. The King's reply, sent through Amherst, was that the 'Prince of Wales ought not to go through the several gradations of General Officers, but should remain the first Colonel at the head of a Regiment.' Amherst concurred: the Prince 'could not with propriety' be promoted; he must either 'remain Colonel or command the Army'. As the latter post was already filled, the *status quo* would have to suffice.

The Prince's response was gracious. Accepting Amherst's reasoning, he added: 'I had much rather remain as I am whilst I am only Colonel Commandant of this Regiment, until either this or some other becomes perfectly my own, especially as the constant occupation and employment . . . are my principal objects.' He did however '*look forward in anxious hopes* that some time hence' his 'zeal for the service' would induce the King to promote him to 'the rank *of full General*'.[35]

6

Caroline of Brunswick

By the winter of 1793, the Prince's relationship with Mrs Fitzherbert was on its last legs. She had long disapproved of his dissolute lifestyle and disreputable friends. 'Few were the happy hours' that Mrs Fitzherbert spent at this time, noted the diarist Thomas Raikes. The Prince was 'young and impetuous and boisterous in his character, and very much addicted to the pleasures of the table'.

A further cause of friction was his mounting debts, which by the summer of 1794 had risen to more than £500,000. So strapped for cash had the Prince become by his overspending that Mrs Fitzherbert often had to lend *him* money from her relatively meagre annuity of £3,000. But the worst tension was caused by his philandering. While the Prince had 'much consideration' for Mrs Fitzherbert, noted the Duke of Cambridge, he found his 'amusements' elsewhere, making her 'jealous and discontented'.[1]

Such 'amusements' did not come cheap. In 'one of those moments when weak men can refuse nothing', wrote Wraxall, he gave Mrs Anna Maria Crouch, a beautiful young singer and actress, 'an engagement under his hand for £10,000'. Yet he only made love to her one more time. When she eventually demanded payment, threatening to make their affair public, the Prince sent 'a confidential friend' (probably Captain Jack Payne) to her Haymarket house to negotiate a settlement. He was 'empowered to offer her three thousand guineas', and the money had been divided into three bags for that purpose. But aware of her desperate need for money, he took only one bag with him, leaving the other two with his footman in the coach. The gamble paid off. In return for just 1,000 guineas, Mrs Crouch handed over the bond for £10,000.[2]

While Mrs Fitzherbert was said to have looked upon the Crouch affair 'with ridicule', she was forced to take his relationship with the Countess of Jersey altogether more seriously. Born Frances Twysden in 1753, the daughter of the Irish Bishop of Raphoe, at 17 she had married the 4th Earl of Jersey, 35, a Lord of the Bedchamber. The Prince had known her since his youth, and had first tried to bed her without success in 1782. 'If he is in love with me,' she commented, 'I cannot help it. It is impossible for anyone to give another less encouragement than I have.'[3]

In 1794 it was different. Though now a 41-year-old grandmother, Lady Jersey was still highly attractive. A tall dark beauty, witty and accomplished, Wraxall referred to her 'irresistable seduction and fascination'. Robert Huish, a contemporary biographer of the Prince, was less generous, describing her as a 'type of serpent – beautiful, bright, and glossy in its exterior – poisonous and pestiferous'.[4]

In an age of such low morals, married to a man 18 years her senior, it was perhaps inevitable that she would take lovers. They included the diplomat William Fawkener, rumoured to be the father of one of her daughters, and the 5th Earl of Carlisle, a politician, poet and occasional playwright. Now she used her considerable womanly wiles to ensnare the Prince. His connection with Mrs Fitzherbert had been a mistake, she told him. Her Roman Catholicism lay behind his unpopularity, and made it impossible for Parliament to vote him an adequate income. Only by marrying a Protestant princess could he hope to solve his financial difficulties.

The Prince was undecided. Whatever their differences, he was still fond of his 'wife' and could not bring himself to abandon her. On the other hand, his crippling debts had to be addressed and an official marriage seemed the only solution. It would also, with a bit of luck, provide him with a legitimate heir. His few remaining qualms were dispelled in the spring of 1794 when the Court of Privileges ruled that the secret marriage of his younger brother, Prince Augustus (later Duke of Sussex) to Lady Augusta Murray was null and void. If a Protestant who claimed descent from Henry VII of England and Charles VII of France was not acceptable as the wife of a royal prince, how much less would a Roman Catholic commoner be? His own marriage to Mrs Fitzherbert was clearly illegal. He was free to remarry.

That summer, while the Prince remained at Brighton, Mrs Fitzherbert spent much of her time at Marble Hill, a small palladian mansion she had rented at Richmond. On the morning of 23 June, while she was making preparations for her evening drive to Bushey Park to dine with the Duke of Clarence and his mistress, the actress Mrs Jordan, she received a letter from the Prince. Addressed to 'My dear love' and signed 'Ever thine', it informed her that he would not be able to join her because he had been called away to Windsor. That evening, however, while she was dining with the Duke, Captain Jack Payne arrived with a message from the Prince that their relationship was over and (in her words) 'he would never enter my house again'.

Later, Mrs Fitzherbert would endorse the earlier letter: 'Lady Jersey's influence.'[5]

On 8 July, the Prince sent Mrs Fitzherbert a long letter of explanation, via Captain Payne. The letter was subsequently destroyed, but the covering note to Payne remains. It reads:

> To tell you what it has cost me to write, and to rip up every and the most distressing feelings of my heart . . . which have so long lodged there is impossible to express. God bless you my friend; whichever way this unpleasant affair now ends I have nothing to reproach myself with. I owe nothing to her family, whatever was due, was due to herself, but in either case this

letter is a final answer to every one. Your affectionate but unhappy friend.[6]

The Prince clearly felt he had no option but to destroy his relationship with Mrs Fitzherbert. It was for her own good, he reasoned, as much as for his. If he had been honest with himself, however, he would have realised that the only beneficiary was likely to be him – but for how long?

London was soon humming with the news. On 10 July 1794, Viscount Wentworth informed his father, the Earl of Denbigh, that 'the Prince & Mrs Fitzherbert are absolutely separated' and the Prince was 'now much with his family but sadly out of spirits'.[7]

Eight days later, however, Lady Stafford told her son, Lord Granville Leveson-Gower (later Earl Granville), that the 'misunderstanding' between the Prince and Mrs Fitzherbert 'is made up'. She continued:

> The story is too long to write, but after he had been persuaded by a certain Lady [Jersey] to give her up, and to write according to that Idea to Mrs. F., he found he could not live without her, and sent Messengers of Peace in Numbers. But Mrs. F. was for some Days *sturdy*; she could not believe that he could continue to love her, when for Months he had given his Time to another, and had behaved to her with the greatest Cruelty. But they are friends now, and the mischief-maker is left to find out another.[8]

But she had been misinformed. While harbouring regrets, the Prince was not about to go back on his decision. He did, however, write to Mrs Fitzherbert at Margate in early August, assuring her that he would ever remain a faithful friend. She in turn replied that 'nothing can be more truly gratifying to me than the continuance of your Friendship and good opinion.'

But their marriage was over. 'I have at last taken my resolution,' the Prince informed Captain Payne on 21 August, 'and all I can say is that

I shall ever be happy to contribute anything that lays in my power to render Mrs. Fitzherbert's situation as comfortable as possible and to testify every sort of attention and kindness to her . . . *mais tout est fini.*[9]

The financial settlement had been announced in *The Times* two weeks earlier. The £3,000 a year allowance which Mrs Fitzherbert had received from the Prince 'two or three years since' would be continued for life (later that year, incredibly, the King agreed to honour the annuity in the event of his son's untimely death). Added to 'her own private fortune of £1800 annually', it would 'make her present income £4800 a year'. 'Unencumbered as she now is,' the article concluded, 'the lady will probably be a happier woman than she has ever been.'[10]

Whether the Prince would be so was another matter. For Lady Jersey had selected as his future bride his first cousin Princess Caroline, the 26-year-old daughter of the Duke of Brunswick-Wolfenbüttel and Princess Augusta, George III's eldest sister. A small north German duchy sandwiched between Hanover and Prussia, Brunswick possessed 'one of the gayest' courts in Germany with little of the 'stiff etiquette' of its neighbours. Because of this, the Princess lacked the social graces and refinement which were *de rigeur* in London and (formerly) Paris; on the contrary, she had acquired the reputation of a wilful flirt.

Years later, the Duke of Wellington told Lady Salisbury that Lady Jersey had deliberately chosen a bride with 'indelicate manners, indifferent character, and not very inviting appearance, from the hope that disgust for the wife would secure constancy to the mistress'.[11]

Wellington may well have been right. When Arthur Paget, the British envoy in Berlin, heard of the match he commented that the Princess's character was held in such low regard that it would be 'inexpedient to commit a sketch of it to paper'. Such a marriage, he said, might well 'draw with it calamities which are unknown or at least forgotten in England'. Lord St Helens, another diplomat, agreed with Paget that there was a 'stain' on the Princess's character and thought it strange that the Prince should plump for a woman he had never met. 'We must endeavour to make the best of it,' he concluded, 'and to hush up all bad stories.' The inference was clear: the Princess was not a virgin.[12]

The King, for one, was unaware of the rumours. On 24 August, while holidaying with the Queen, Prince Ernest and his six daughters at Weymouth, he was visited by the Prince who told him that he had 'broken off all connection with Mrs Fitzherbert' and was anxious to enter 'into a more creditable line of life by marrying' the Princess of Brunswick. The King was only too pleased to give his permission. Pitt, whose government had been strengthened in July by its alliance with the Portland Whigs (the Prince among them), was also relieved. Before long, he was dropping hints that the Prince could expect to receive a married income of at least £100,000 a year.[13]

On 29 August, the Prince informed his brother York that, having been in a 'very uncomfortable situation' for 'some years, but particularly for the latter three or four months', he and Mrs Fitzherbert were *'finally parted, but parted amicably'*. He hoped, given the Duke's knowledge of his 'temper, disposition, and the unvaried attention and affection' he had 'ever treated her with', that his brother would 'not lay the *fault, whatever it may be*' at his 'door'. He continued:

> However tout est fini entre nous and I have obtained the King's consent to my marrying my own cousin Princess Caroline, the Duke of Brunswick's daughter. The King wishes it not to be much talked of at present as he seems rather inclined to have the wedding put off till the spring, but I confess to you *that* neither meets my wishes nor those of his Majesty's Ministers, and we are all working and moving Heaven and earth to immediately send for her over . . . The King told me I made him quite happy, that it was the only proper alliance, and indeed the one in all respects he should have wished for himself . . . I do not say as much for the rest of my family, at least for one person.[14]

He was referring to the Queen. Earlier that summer, with the King about to recommend Princess Caroline as a possible second wife for her brother Charles, the Duke of Mecklenburg-Strelitz, the Queen had intervened. She wrote:

> The fact is, my dear brother, that the King is completely igno-rant of everything concerning the Duke [of Brunswick]'s Family, and that it would be unseemly to speak of him against his niece. But it is not at all unseemly to tell you that a relative of that Family, who is indeed very attached to the Duke, has spoken to me of Princess Caroline with very little respect. They say that her passions are so strong that the Duke himself said that she was not to be allowed even to go from one room to another without her Governess, and that when she dances, this Lady is obliged to follow her for the whole of the dance to prevent her making an exhibition of herself by indecent con-versations with men, . . . and that all amusements have been forbidden her because of her indecent conduct . . . There, dear brother, is a woman I do not recommend at all.[15]

The Queen was the only member of the Royal Family who was aware of Princess Caroline's faults – but she considered it 'unseemly' to speak out. Like the King, her daughters were 'delighted' with the proposed match, telling the Prince 'that it is the event they wished for most'. The Duke of York added his approval from his headquarters in Barleken: 'I have long grieved to see how miserable Mrs Fitzherbert's temper made you,' he assured the Prince. 'I am rejoiced to hear that you are now out of her shackles. As for the Princess, she is a very fine girl and in every respect in my opinion a very proper match for you.'

Anxious to get his hands on a bigger income (not to mention the payment of his debts), the Prince by-passed official channels by sending his own envoy, Major Hislop, to Brunswick in early October with a charming letter for Caroline and a request for her parents to send her over as soon as possible. Hislop arrived back in London on 19 November with letters for the Prince from the Duke and Duchess, and one from Princess Caroline with her portrait enclosed. 'She is in hourly and anxious expectation of being immediately sent for,' he told the Queen, 'so much so that she said if the carriage was ready at the door she would not wait for anybody to hand her into it.'

The Duchess was just as keen. She 'says that the Princess is ready to travel immediately,' added the Prince, 'and desires we will send Lord Malmesbury directly, and the more so, as the season is advancing, and they wish her to set out before the roads grow impossible'.[16]

Malmesbury had in fact already set off for Brunswick. Formerly Sir James Harris, the diplomat who had acted as an intermediary between the government and the Prince in 1785, Malmesbury was not the Prince's first choice as official envoy; he had wanted his ex-Comptroller, Lord Southampton, to be sent. But the King and his ministers insisted on the wily Malmesbury because the mission was as much diplomatic as ceremonial. French victories in May and June over the British and Austrians at Turcoing and Fleurus respectively had resulted in a general retreat of the Allies: the British to Holland and the Austrians to Germany. Pitt and Dundas, the War Secretary, had already decided to recall the Duke of York, ostensibly for talks; in January 1795, as a sop to the King, he would be appointed Commander-in-Chief of the British Army. Malmesbury's task was to induce the Duke of Brunswick to replace York as commander of the British and Hanoverian forces on the Continent.

He arrived in Brunswick, a picturesque medieval city of 20,000 souls, at the end of November, and was put up in the ducal palace, the Grauer Hof, a rambling wooden and stone structure whose rear gardens led down to the River Oker. To the front, across the Bohlweg, the main street, lay the imposing houses of the wool and silk merchants, the St Blasius Cathedral and the Collegium Carolinum, the military academy. West and south of this affluent quarter, hemmed in by a loop of the river, was the rest of the town, a veritable warren of timbered houses and dark narrow streets. On 20 November, Malmesbury was presented to an 'embarrassed' Princess Caroline. He noted in his diary:

Pretty face – not expressive of softness – her figure not graceful
– fine eyes – good hand – tolerable teeth, but going – fair hair
and light eyebrows, good bust – short, with what the French call
'des épaules impertinentes'. Vastly happy with her future expec-
tations. The Duchess full of nothing else – talks incessantly.[17]

A similar description of Caroline was provided many years later by
Lady Charlotte Campbell, one of her ladies-in-waiting:

The Princess was in her early youth a pretty woman; fine light
hair – very delicately formed features, and a fine complexion –
quick, glancing, penetrating eyes, long cut and rather sunk in
the head, which gave them much expression – and a remarkably delicately formed mouth. But her head was always too
large for her body, and her neck too short.[18]

A couple of days after meeting Caroline, Malmesbury recorded a
conversation with her mother who told him that 'all the young German
Princesses . . . had learnt English in the hopes of being Princess of
Wales'. She had not encouraged Caroline, however, because 'the King
had often expressed his dislike to the marriage of cousin-Germans'.[19]

On 3 December, two days after the arrival of Malmesbury's final
instructions, the Duke and Duchess formally consented to 'the demand'
for their daughter's hand. Malmesbury was then taken to see Princess
Caroline, 'who replied in the most graceful and dignified manner to
what I said, although not without some confusion'.[20]

A less welcome event that day was the return of Major Hislop with
a letter from the Prince 'urging' Malmesbury 'to set out with the
Princess Caroline *immediately*. The British envoy was beside himself.
Two days later, having got the signing of the marriage treaty out of the
way on the 4th, Malmesbury wrote to the Duke of Portland:

I am here under the King's immediate command, and cannot
act but by his special orders. Everyone will, I am confident, feel

this but the Prince, and nobody I believe but the Prince would have placed me in the predicament I now stand, by conveying to me his wishes, or rather his orders, without having previously communicated with his Majesty's Ministers, and having it in his power to say to me he wrote under their sanction. If *he* should be displeased with me for a non-compliance with these wishes, I only have to entreat your Grace to justify me . . . I cannot stir from hence but by the King's order.

In his letter to the Prince he was politeness itself, thanking him for the 'very gracious manner' in which he had expressed himself. Everything would be ready by Thursday, 11 December, he told him, 'and on that day we may, and certainly will, set out, providing I receive before that time from Lord Grenville positive intelligence of the certain destination of the Squadron to escort the Princess to England.'[21]

Also during 5 December, the Duke spoke to Malmesbury about his daughter for the first time. 'Elle n'est *pas bête*, mais elle n'a pas de jugement,' he said, 'elle a été élevé sévèrement et *il le faillait.*' He also asked Malmesbury 'to advise her never to show any jealousy of the Prince' and that if she had suspicions she was 'not to notice them'. That evening, Malmesbury sat next to the Princess at dinner. 'Her conversation was very right,' he noted in his diary, 'she entreats me also to guide and direct her. I recommend perfect silence on all subjects for six months after her arrival.'

On 9 December, during another lengthy chat with Caroline, Malmesbury advised her 'never to talk politics or allow them to be talked to her'. She in turn asked him 'about Lady Jersey', whom she seemed to think 'an *intriguante* but not to know of any partiality between her and the Prince'. Malmesbury replied that she should never be 'familiar or too easy' with her ladies, of whom Lady Jersey would be one, but that she could be 'affable without forgetting she was Princess of Wales'.

To learn how to become popular, Malmesbury advised her to take Queen Charlotte as her model. But Caroline was afraid of the Queen, who she felt 'would be jealous of her and do her harm'. All the more reason 'to be attentive to her', said Malmesbury, 'and never to fail in any exterior mark of respect towards her'.

Caroline then changed the subject. 'I am determined never to appear jealous,' she declared. 'I know the Prince is *léger*, and am prepared on this point.' Malmesbury's response was that he did not 'believe she would have any occasion to exercise this very wise resolution', which he 'commended highly'. If, however, she did ever feel jealous, she was not 'to allow it to manifest itself' – 'reproaches and sourness never reclaimed anybody', but 'rather served as an advantageous contrast to the contrary qualities in the rival'. The 'surest way of recovering a tot-tering affection was softness, enduring and caresses'. Malmesbury knew enough about the Prince 'to be quite sure he could not withstand such a conduct, while a contrary one would *probably* make him dis-agreeable and peevish, and certainly force him to be false and dissembling'.

On 16 December, having again sat next to Caroline at dinner, Malmesbury noted that she had 'no *fond*, no fixed character, a light and flighty mind, but meaning well and well disposed; and my eternal theme to her is *to think before she speaks, to recollect herself*'.

But despite the Princess's apparent willingness to be guided, Malmesbury was a worried man. On 20 December, he discussed the Princess with Sir Brooke Boothby, a fellow diplomat who was also in Brunswick to try to persuade the Duke to take command of the Allied forces (he eventually declined). They both regretted 'the apparent facil-ity of Princess Caroline's character – her want of reflection and substance – [and agreed] that with a steady man she would do vastly well, but with one of a different description, there are great risks'.[22]

He did not inform the Prince of his misgivings because, as he told him later, he had not been sent to Brunswick 'on a discretionary mis-sion, but specifically to demand the Princess Caroline in marriage'.[23] On 28 December, the day before Malmesbury and Princess Caroline were due to leave Brunswick, the Duchess received an anonymous letter from 'An Englishman' in London, warning her against Lady Jersey:

She is beautiful, clever, and accomplished, but with all this posseses the spirit of malice and intrigue beyond any other woman. She has repeatedly declared her intention of attaching herself to the young Princess of Wales, and should she succeed in doing so . . . there is no opportunity she will lose, of putting every sort of evil idea into her head. [Although] from what we English hear, the Princess is as near perfect, as a human being can be, yet when absent from her wise mother and this She Devil at her elbow, unless your Royal Highness puts her upon her guard by telling her the sort of woman Lady Jersey is, she may err before she is aware of the danger of listening to such a person.[24]

The obvious implication was that Lady Jersey would encourage the Princess to take lovers. Taking the letter seriously, the Duchess unwisely showed it to her daughter who, quite naturally, became alarmed. To calm her, Malmesbury told her that 'anybody who presumed to *love* her was guilty of *high treason* and punished with *death*, if she was weak enough to listen to him; so also was she.' Malmesbury noted: 'This startled her.' Which presumably was a marginal improvement on her earlier alarm.[25]

On 29 December, as cannon fired a farewell salute from the walls of the ducal castle, the marriage party at last set off from Brunswick. It was an arduous journey in the midst of a severe winter, over poor roads which were clogged with cartloads of refugees from the fighting to the west. But the Princess, travelling in a sprung coach and well wrapped up in furs and cloaks, remained cheerful. Accompanying her were just two maids (the Prince had forbidden her secretary, Mlle Rosenweit, to make the trip) and her unwilling mother, the Duchess, who was worried that marauding French troops might intercept them before they reached the coast. Her fears were justified. At Osnabrück, on New Year's Day 1795, Malmesbury received two conflicting messages: one reported French victories over the Dutch, the other an English advance. He wisely refused to go any further until the situation had clarified itself.

It was just as well. The Royal Navy squadron sent to collect the Princess, commanded by the recently promoted Commodore Jack Payne, had been forced by ice and fog to turn back from Hellevoetsluis. The Princess's party did set off from Osnabrück on 9 January, but retraced its steps after Malmesbury obtained definite news that the French had crossed the Waal River and were astride their route. Only the Princess herself had been keen to go on. Her courage, Malmesbury noted, was one of her few saving graces :

> If her education had been what it ought she might have turned out excellent, but it was that very nonsensical one that most women receive – one of privation, injunction and menace . . . she has quick parts without a sound or distinguishing under-standing . . . a ready conception but no judgement; caught by the first impression, led by the first impulse . . . Some natural but no acquired morality, and no strong innate notions of its value and necessity; warm feelings and nothing to counterbal-ance them . . . In short, the Princess in the hands of a steady and sensible man would probably turn out well, but where it is likely she will find faults perfectly analagous to her own, she will fail. She has no governing powers, although her mind is *physically* strong. She has her father's courage, but it is to her (as to him) of no avail. *He* wants mental decision; *she* character and tact.[26]

After eleven more days at Osnabrück, and with no improvement in the weather or the military situation, the party headed back to Hanover. On 23 January, as they approached the city, Malmesbury had a 'long and serious conversation with the Princess about her conduct at Hanover [of which her future father-in-law was Elector], about the Prince, about herself and about her character'. She expressed her 'uneasiness about the Prince – talked of his being *unlike*, even quite opposite of the King and Queen in his habits and ideas – how to please both!' Malmesbury replied that he 'had seen enough of her to be quite sure her mind and understanding were equal to any exertions, that therefore if she did not do *quite* right, and come up to *everything* that was expected from her, she would have no excuse.'[27]

Two long months were spent in Hanover as the war continued to rage in Holland. Malmesbury used the time to give Caroline some stern advice about her standards of hygiene. 'Argument with the Princess about her toilette,' he noted on 18 February. 'She piques herself on dressing quick; I disapprove this. She maintains her point; I however desire Madame Busche to explain to her that the Prince is very delicate, and that he expects a long and very careful *toilette de propreté*, of which she has no idea. On the contrary, she neglects it sadly, and is offensive from this neglect. Madame Busche executes her commission well, and the princess comes out the next day well washed *all over.*'

But obviously she could not keep it up because, on 6 March, he returned to the subject. He wrote:

> I endeavoured as far as was possible for a *man*, to inculcate the necessity of great and nice attention to every part of dress, as well as to what was hid, as to what was seen. (I knew she wore coarse petticoats, coarse shifts, and thread stockings, and these never well washed, or changed often enough) . . . What I could not say myself on this point, I got said through Madame Busche, and afterwards through Mrs Harcourt. It is remarkable how amazingly on this point her education has been neglected, and how much her mother, although an Englishwoman, was inattentive to it . . . The Princess felt all this, and it made a temporary impression; but in this as on all other subjects, I have had but too many opportunities to observe that her heart is very, *very* light, unsusceptible of strong or lasting feelings.[28]

Towards the end of March, with the French still active in Holland, the naval escort at last arrived in Stade, a Hanoverian port on the Elbe estuary. Having travelled north from the city of Hanover, Malmesbury's party boarded Commodore Payne's flagship, the 50-gun frigate *Jupiter*, on the 28th. The Princess had to share a cabin with Mrs Harcourt, the wife of the British field commander, who had been pressed into service as a lady companion, but this did nothing to dampen her high spirits. 'Impossible to be more cheerful, more *accomondante*, more every thing that is pleasant than the Princess,' wrote Malmesbury. 'No difficulty – no childish fears – all good humour and ease.'

She was 'delighted with the ships', he noted the following day, 'and the officers greatly pleased with her manners and good humours'. Not so encouraging was the Princess's illness as bad weather held up the ships for two days off Great Yarmouth. 'Malaise less sea-sickness than her menstrual complaint,' wrote Malmesbury on 2 April. 'Mrs Harcourt anxious about her desirous of not getting too soon to London.' Presumably so that the squeamish Prince of Wales would not be discouraged from consummating the marriage.[29]

Finally, on the morning of Easter Sunday, 5 April 1795, having spent the previous night at anchor in the Thames, the Princess's party transferred to the royal yacht *Augusta* and was landed at Greenwich. It was a beautiful spring day, and small but enthusiastic crowds lined both river banks. The only hiccup was the absence of Lady Jersey, recently appointed the Princess's lady-in-waiting, who had kept the royal coaches and the escort of 10th Light Dragoons waiting in London. When they did arrive, an hour late, Lady Jersey was 'low and impertinent', criticising the Princess's dress ('though Mrs Harcourt had taken great pains about it') and expressing herself in such 'a tone and manner' that Malmesbury felt obliged 'to speak rather sharply to her and to recommend more respect'.

Ignoring this admonition, the brazen Countess then said that as sitting backwards in the coach 'disagreed with her', she 'hoped she might be allowed to sit forward'. Malmesbury countered by saying that, as she knew this, 'she ought never to have accepted the situation of a Lady of the Bedchamber who never could sit on the same side with her mistress'. He then offered to let her join him in his coach with Lord Claremont, where no one would object to her facing forward, but she refused this downgrading of her equipage and had to put up with sitting next to Mrs Harcourt, and opposite the Princess, for the journey into London.

With 'little crowd and less applause' along the route, the coaches reached St James's Palace, where the Princess was to stay until her wedding, at 2 in the afternoon. No sooner had he been informed of his bride's arrival than the Prince appeared from Carlton House. Their notorious first meeting took place in the apartments of Prince Ernest (the future Duke of Cumberland). Lord Malmesbury was the only witness:

> She very properly, in consequence of my saying to her it was the right mode of proceeding, attempted to kneel to him. He raised her (gracefully enough), and embraced her, said barely one word, turned round, returned to a distant part of the apartment, and calling me to him, said, 'Harris, I am not well; pray get me a glass of brandy.' I said, 'Sir, had you not better have a glass of water?' – upon which he, much out of humour, said with an oath, 'No; I will go directly to the Queen;' and away he went. The Princess, left during this short moment alone, was in a state of astonishment; and, on my joining her, said, '*Mon Dieu! Est ce que le Prince est toujours comme çela? Je le trouve très gros, et nullement aussi beau que son portrait.*' I said His Royal Highness was naturally a good deal affected and flurried at this first interview, but she certainty would find him different at dinner.[30]

She did – but the damage had been done. The Prince's ungallant reception of his future wife was in part due to the fact that she had ignored Malmesbury's advice to wash '*all over*'. She was, in short, smelling riper than a Camembert cheese and his fastidious nose had immediately rebelled. But he was also disappointed with her physical attributes (as she claimed to be with his). He preferred tall, haughty-looking women, the stouter the better. Caroline was short and stocky, with bad teeth to boot; more like a serving wench than a princess.

She retaliated at dinner. 'I was far from satisfied with the Princess's behaviour,' noted Malmesbury, who was present:

> . . . it was flippant, rattling, aiming at sarcasms and vulgar hints about Lady Jersey, who though she did not say a word, *le diable n'en perdait rien*. The Prince was disgusted to a degree he could not conceal, and this ill-fated dinner fixed his dislike, which when left to go alone the Princess had not the talent or powers to remove; lately still observing the same giddy manners and silly attempts at cleverness and coarse joking, increased it, till it became positive hatred, and that not a little [encouraged] by the tricks and artifices of Lady Jersey.[31]

Years later, Caroline told Lady Charlotte Campbell that 'the first moment I saw my *futur* and Lady Jersey together I know how it all was, and I said to myself, "Oh, very well!"' She continued: 'I could be the slave of a man I love; but one whom I love not, and who did not love me, impossible – *c'est autre chose*.'[32]

Meanwhile, the Prince's irritable state of mind was not helped by the fact that he was still at loggerheads with his father over the question of his military employment. In March he had warned Henry Dundas, the War Secretary, that if he was not promoted to the rank of Major-General 'it must lead to a total separation between the King and the Prince of Wales.' Dundas's response was equally threatening. The 'extent' of the Prince's debts would 'undoubtedly . . . produce some disagreeable sensations in the public mind'. Nothing, therefore, could render the settlement of them 'palatable either to Parliament or the public but the anxiety they entertain for the happiness of the royal family'. But if it was 'for a moment supposed that the first fruits of your Royal Highness's establishment were to be a disunion in the royal family', Parliament would not help him out.

Taking the hint, the Prince toned down his letter of complaint to the King, but he could not resist making his point. 'The heroic Edward gave to the inexperienced Prince of Wales the command of the vanguard at

Crécy,' he wrote, 'and the services of the son, not on that day alone but through life, repaid the confidence of the father.'[33]

The King waited until his son's wedding day to tell him that he had no intention of promoting him. His higher-ranking brothers could have no situations in the state 'but what arise from the military lines they have been placed in'. He, on the other hand, had been 'born to a more difficult one, and which I shall be most happy if I find you seriously turn your thoughts to; the happiness of millions depend on it as well as your own. May the Princess's character prove so pleasing to you that your mind may be engrossed with domestic felicity.' Some chance.[34]

A further cause of annoyance for the Prince was the persistent rumour that, even without an open breach between him and the King, Pitt would have problems getting his £40,000 rise in income through Parliament. With the war in France proving both expensive and unsuccessful – the remaining British troops were evacuated from Bremen in March 1795 – there was little public sympathy for a Prince whose outrageous extravagance had run up debts of more than £630,000.

But, worst of all, having met Caroline he was beginning to regret his enforced separation from Mrs Fitzherbert. In November, so the Duchess of Devonshire told Thomas Coutts the banker, he had requested 'all his friends' to show Mrs Fitzherbert 'the same attention as before'. While most were only too happy to comply, those who were particularly fond of Mrs Fitzherbert, like Captain Payne and Lord Hugh Seymour, the younger son of the 2nd Marquess of Hertford, could not forgive the Prince. Nor could he forgive himself. 'It's no use,' he told the Earl of Moira on his way to marry Princess Caroline, 'I shall never love any woman but Fitzherbert.'[35]

The wedding took place during the evening of 8 April 1795 in the Chapel Royal at St James's Palace. Wearing a magnificent dress of silver tissue and lace, and a robe of ermine-lined velvet, Princess Caroline was in fine spirits as she waited at the altar, chatting to the Duke of Clarence. The Prince, attended by the 17-year-old Cornet George (later 'Beau') Brummell, could not have been more of a contrast; the only 'fine spirits' he had had recourse to were of the alcoholic variety. So unsteady was he on his feet that the bachelor Dukes of Bedford and Roxburghe had to help him up the aisle. Lord Melbourne, a member of his household, noted that 'the Prince was like a man doing a thing in desperation; it was like Macheath going to execution; and he was quite drunk.'[36]

He could hardly bring himself to meet his bride's eyes, though he was 'perpetually looking at his favourite Lady Jersey'. At one point during the ceremony, while kneeling for a prayer, he stood up as if to flee. But the King spoke sharply to him and he knelt down again. According to Wraxall, when the Archbishop of Canterbury, John Moore, asked whether there was any lawful impediment to the marriage, 'he laid down the book and looked earnestly for a second or two at the King as well as at the Royal bridegroom.' So affected was the Prince that he cried.[37]

After the service, the Duke of Leeds walked in front of the Prince and Princess of Wales as they made their way to the reception in the Queen's apartments. 'I could not help remarking how little conversation passed between them during the procession,' he wrote, 'and the coolness and indifference apparent in the manner of the Prince towards his amiable bride.'[38]

Little wonder that the wedding night at Carlton House was a fiasco. 'Judge what it was to have a drunken husband on one's wedding day,' Caroline later told Lady Charlotte Campbell, 'and one who passed the greatest part of his bridal-night under the grate, where he fell, and where I left him.'[39]

The details of the first few days of marriage, during which time a child was conceived, were given by the Princess to the Earl of Minto (the former Sir Gilbert Elliot) in 1798. He informed his wife:

It appears that they lived together two or three weeks at first, but not at all afterwards as man and wife. They went to Windsor two days after the marriage, and after a few days residence there they went to Kempshot, where there was no

woman but Lady Jersey, and the men very blackguard companions of the Prince's, who were constantly drunk and filthy,
sleeping and snoring in boots on the sofas, and in other respects
the scene, she says, was more like the Prince of Wales at
Eastcheap in Shakespeare than like any notions she had
acquired of a Prince or a gentleman. Their conversation was
suited to the rest, and the whole resembled a bad brothel much
more than a Palace. You may conceive her surprize with all her
German notions of etiquette and dignity.

Long separated from her husband by this time, the Princess could not
resist a dig at his manhood. 'I fancy the *mutual* disgust broke out at that
time,' added Minto, 'and if I can spell her hums and haws, I take it that
the ground of his antipathy was his own *incapacity*, and the distaste
which a man feels for a woman who *knows* his defects and humilia-
tions.'[40]

Cornet Brummell, who was at Carlton House the day after the
wedding, always insisted that 'the young couple appeared perfectly satisfied with each other, particularly the Princess' who 'was then a very
handsome and desirable-looking woman'.[41]

But in March 1796, the Prince gave Lord Malmesbury a very different version of the wedding night:

> You well recall what I told you the day after my marriage of the
> scars on the Princess's neck and how much I was alarmed and
> disgusted at this appearance of the *evil* in her. She has the same
> on her thighs. But besides this . . . I have every reason to
> believe [that I was not the first], for not only on the first night
> there was no appearance of blood, but her manners were not
> those of a novice. In taking those liberties natural on these
> occasions, she said, '*Ah mon dieu qu'il est gros!*', and how should
> she know this without a previous means of comparison.
> Finding that I had suspicions of her not being *new*, she the next
> night mixed up some tooth powder and water, coloured her

shift with it and . . . in showing these she showed at the same
time such marks of filth both in the fore and *hind* part of
her . . . that she turned my stomach and from that moment I
made a vow *never to touch her again*. I had known her three
times – twice the first and once the second night – it required
no small [effort] to conquer my aversion and overcome the
disgust of her person.[42]

If true, this extraordinary account – discovered in the Malmesbury
Papers at Winchester and never published before – goes a long way to
explaining the Prince's violent antipathy towards his wife. Not only
were Caroline's nether regions filthy and her body scarred, but, worst
of all, she was not a virgin. As a result, the Prince was only able to make
love to her three times before his repulsion got the better of his sense of
duty.

A woman with a high sexual drive, Caroline was frustrated and hurt
by this rejection, and retaliated in the only way she knew how. About
a fortnight after the marriage, Lord Malmesbury was present when she
'behaved very lightly and even improperly' at a Carlton House dinner
to which the Prince of Orange's family had been invited. Malmesbury
wrote:

> It hurt me and I sense still more the Prince who took me into
> his closet, and asked me how I liked that sort of manners and as
> it was not possible for me to conceal my disappointment of
> them, I took this opportunity of repeating in as gentle terms as
> I could the substance of what, at different times, the Duke of
> Brunswick had said to me, that it was expedient . . . that his
> daughter had been brought up very *strictly* and if she was not at
> first *strictly* kept she would from great spirits and little thought
> emancipate too much.

Hearing this, the Prince asked Malmesbury why he had not written as
much from Brunswick. His reply was that he had not considered what

the Duke ('a very . . . anxious father') had said to be 'of sufficient consequence, that it affected neither the moral character or conduct of the
Princess', and he 'conceived it as intended simply as an intimation only
right to notice on a proper occasion'. As for not writing from
Brunswick, again he reminded the Prince that he was 'not sent there on
a discretionary mission, but specifically to demand the Princess Caroline
in marriage'. However, had he 'discovered any notorious glaring
defects, or such as were of a nature to render the union unseemly', he
would have taken it 'as a bounded duty . . . but it must have been *directly
to the King and to no one else*'. Though the Prince appeared to accept the
logic of what Malmesbury had told him, 'it did not please and left a
rankle on his mind.'[43]

In the meantime, as he himself confided to Malmesbury the following March, he wished 'from various motives . . . to keep on terms' with
Caroline. 'But,' he continued, 'I found it necessary to follow the advice
you had given me from the Duke of Brunswick to keep her in order,
lest she should keep me so, and my dear Malmesbury you did not say
half enough for never did there occur in any female mind such a desire
to rule, so much art in so false a character.'[44]

The 'various motives' were money. On 27 April, the King's Message
was presented to the House of Commons, requesting its members to
vote 'such provision as they may judge necessary to enable his majesty
to settle an establishment for the Prince and Princess suited to their
rank and dignity'. It also pointed out 'that the benefit of any settlement . . . cannot be effectually secured to the Prince of Wales without
providing the means of freeing him' from his debts. Just over two weeks
later, Pitt introduced the government's proposals: the Prince's income
from the Civil List would be increased from £60,000 to £125,000, but
£25,000 of this would be appropriated to pay the interest on his huge
debts of £630,000. The debts themselves would be paid off over 27
years by placing the annual Duchy of Cornwall revenue of £13,000
into a sinking fund.[45]

But Pitt had miscalculated. Some of his supporters were aggrieved
that he had taken the Portland Whigs into government in 1794.

Others – and they were not alone in the House – were unhappy that the British public, already burdened with taxes to meet the cost of war, were expected to make further sacrifices to bail out the profligate heir to the throne yet again. In the event, Pitt's proposals met with such 'unreserved marks of disapprobation' from all sides of the House that it was quickly obvious they had no hope of being passed.

Even some of the Prince's former friends were hostile. Stating that 'no reliance could be had that those provisions which might be made with respect to future conduct would be of any avail' (a bitter reference to the Prince's broken promises of 1787), Charles Grey suggested an additional income of £40,000 rather than £65,000. Fox, while supporting the larger increase, proposed paying off the debts by selling the Duchy of Cornwall (a measure the King described as 'insidious and democratical'). Of all the Opposition M.P.s, only the unctuous Sheridan spoke on behalf of the Prince, suggesting that Crown lands should be sold to liquidate the debts. 'He ought not to be seen rolling about the streets in his state-coach as an insolvent prodigal,' argued Sheridan somewhat unconvincingly.[46]

In late May, in danger of being defeated, Pitt changed tack and proposed that a total of £78,000 (£65,000 from his income, plus the Duchy revenue of £13,000) should be put aside from the Prince's income for interest charges and debt redemption. The transformation in the mood of the Commons was immediate, and on 1 June the government won a vote on the Establishment Bill by 266 votes to 52. By the end of the month the Bill was law. To ensure such a state of affairs did not recur, tradesmen were no longer able to recover debts against the Prince after three months had lapsed, debts not claimed at the end of each quarter were said to have lapsed, and any suit for the recovery of debts had to be instituted against those Officers appointed to conduct his financial affairs. In addition, five Commissioners were appointed to manage the Prince's debts: the Speaker of the House of Commons, the Chancellor of the Exchequer, the Master of the Rolls, the Master of the King's Household, and the Surveyor of Crown Lands.

The Prince, needless to say, was furious. The residue of his married income (£60,0000) was actually *less* than he had been receiving as a bachelor (£78,000). 'In the result,' wrote the Earl of Minto, 'he is placed in a worse situation than before he applied for relief, with the addition of having been made the butt of the whole ill humour of both Houses during a period of five years.' Little wonder that in late June he railed against 'the infamous deceit of Pitt'.[47]

The end result was that the Prince was forced to economise by dismissing most of his Household, including Captain Jack Payne and Lord Hugh Seymour. He retained just four gentlemen: the Earl of Cholmondeley as Master of the Household, the Earl of Jersey as Master of the Horse, and Generals Hulse and Lake as equerries. The Princess, in addition, would keep her four Ladies (one of whom was Lady Jersey) and four Women of the Bedchamber.

By midsummer, the Prince and Princess had decamped to Brighton. 'She is extremely delighted with this place which seems to agree with her most perfectly,' wrote the Prince to his mother on 26 June, 'as she is in the best health and spirits possible, excepting at moments a little degree of sickness which is the necessary attendant upon her situation.'[48]

In reality, all was far from well. 'She, poor little creature, is, I am afraid, a most unhappy woman,' wrote Lady Sheffield who dined at the Pavilion in late July. 'Her lively spirits, which she brought over with her, are all gone, and . . . the melancholy and anxiety in her countenance is quite affecting.' Caroline made no bones about her unhappiness that summer in a letter to a friend in Germany: 'I do not know how I shall bear the loneliness, the Queen seldom visits me, and my sisters-in-law show me the same sympathy . . . The Countess [Jersey] is still here. I hate her, and I know she feels the same towards me. My husband is wholly given up to her, so you can easily imagine the rest . . .'[49]

Without even the compensation of improved finances, the Prince's disillusionment with his uncouth wife was complete. To stay with her in the long term was out of the question; but any official separation would have to wait at least until the birth of their child – the sole heir to the throne (the Duke of York, his only married sibling, having no children of his own).

By the autumn of 1795, the King and his government had never been less popular. The suspension of the Habeas Corpus Act and the failed prosecution of radical leaders (including Horne Tooke) for high treason the previous year had caused much resentment. This was compounded by the continuation of an unpopular – not to mention unsuccessful – war and the second poor harvest in two years. The end result was a series of mass meetings by the various reform clubs during the year of the Prince's wedding, one of which was timed to coincide with the opening of Parliament on 29 October. As the King made his way to the House of Lords in his state carriage, 'great quantities' of 'stones and dirt' were thrown by 'an immense mob' shouting 'No War!' and 'Down with Tyrants!' According to the Tory M.P. Charles Abbot (the future Lord Colchester), who heard the story from an eyewitness, the King remained 'uncommonly collected and firm' even when a missile – he suspected it was a bullet – made a 'small circular hole' in one of the coach windows.

This was more than could be said for the King's attendants, Lords Westmorland and Onslow, who became 'extremely agitated' when 'the shot was fired'. The King, however, 'bade them be still' and later added: 'My Lords, you are supposing this and proposing that, but there is One who disposes of all things, and in Him I trust.'

On the return journey the carriage window was again struck. 'That is a stone,' announced the nerveless King. 'You see the difference from a bullet.' When yet another stone lodged in the King's sleeve, he gave it to Lord Onslow and told him to keep it 'as a memorandum of the civilities which we have received'.

Both Pitt and the Duke of York were jostled and jeered as they made their way to the House. The timorous Prince had planned to make an appearance, but put it off until nightfall when he heard of the disturbances.[50]

As a direct result of the attack on the King, Parliament passed two acts to restore order. The Seditious Meetings Act outlawed, for three years, gatherings of more than 50 people unless they had the permission of local magistrates. The Treasonable Practices Act redefined the crime of treason to include those who plotted against the King, intended to help invaders, sought to coerce Parliament and, incredibly, those who dared to attack the Constitution. The latter offence carried a maximum sentence of seven years, but it was rarely implemented. The Duke of Portland, Home Secretary since joining the government in 1794, was a moderate and left much to the discretion of local magistrates. The reform clubs were similarly tentative and kept their meetings to fewer than 50 people.

Gradually revolutionary fervour died away, particularly after Napoleon Bonaparte, a young artillery officer, had helped moderate republicans crush a Parisian uprising in the summer of 1795, leading to the establishment of an executive 'Directory' of five elected leaders a few months later. In 1798, so disillusioned had the London Corresponding Society become with events across the Channel that it debated a motion to form a loyal corps to resist a French invasion.

7

A Royal Separation

Having brought his wife back to Carlton House in late November to prepare for her confinement, the Prince spent little time at home, preferring the diversions of Northington Grange, a shooting-lodge he had rented in Hampshire. He was present for the birth, however, which took place at 9.20 in the morning of 7 January 1796. The Princess, he informed the Queen, 'after a terrible hard labour' lasting more than 12 hours, has been delivered 'of an *immense girl*, and I assure you notwithstanding we might have wished for a boy, I receive her with all the affection possible, and bow with due deference and resignation to the decrees of Providence.'

Writing to congratulate his son, the King said that he had been hoping for a girl (presumably because, in his experience, they gave less trouble than boys and could still ascend the throne). 'You are both young and I trust will have many children, and this newcomer will equally call for the protection of its parents and consequently be a bond of additional union.'[1]

Little chance of that. On 10 January, having convinced himself that he was seriously ill (he was, it transpired, simply tired and over-excited), the Prince wrote his 'last Will and Testament', a long, rambling document of more than 3,000 words. In it he bequeathed all his 'worldly property . . . to *my Maria Fitzherbert, my wife, the wife of my heart & soul,* and though by the laws of the country she *could not avail herself publicly of that name, still such she is in the eyes of Heaven, was, is, and ever will be such in mine'.* He wished to be buried with 'the *picture of my beloved wife, my Maria Fitzherbert . . .* suspended round my neck by a ribbon as I used to wear it when I lived *and placed right upon my heart'.* When she died, he wanted his coffin to be disinterred and placed next to hers.

Turning to his parents, he asked 'forgiveness for any faults I may have ignorantly and unguardedly been guilty of towards them, assuring them that if there have been such, I trust that they will ascribe them to the errors of judgement and youth, and not to any intentional error of my heart'.

His daughter – christened Charlotte Augusta after her two grand-mothers the following day – he left in the care of 'the King, my father' and 'the Queen, my dearest and most excellent mother'. In the event of their death, his brothers William, Edward and Ernest, his sisters Augusta, Sophia and Mary, and his executor Lord Moira would take over.

He was adamant that:

> the mother of this child, called the Princess of Wales, should in *no way either be concerned in the education or care of the child, or have possession of her person,* for though I forgive her the falsehood and treachery of her conduct towards me, *still the convincing and repeated proofs I have received of her entire want of judgement and of feeling, make me [determined]. . . to prevent by all means possible the child's falling into such improper and bad hands as hers.*

As an afterthought, he bequeathed all the Princess's jewels – 'which . . . are mine, having been bought with my own money' – to his daughter, 'and to her who is called the Princess of Wales I leave one shilling'.[2]

Two copies of this extraordinary document were made: one for the

King and one for Lord Moira. They were never delivered. The Prince recovered and the will remained unwitnessed among his private papers for the rest of his life. But while his antipathy towards the Princess of Wales never altered, his noble sentiments of love for Mrs Fitzherbert were more easily subsumed. In late February, as Lady Jersey was playing cards with Princess Augusta and Lady Holdernesse at Buckingham House, the Prince 'repeatedly came up to her table, and publicly squeezed her hand', noted Charles Abbot. 'The King sees and disapproves of the Carlton House system. The Queen is won over to the Prince's wishes by his attentions and presents in jewels.'[3]

The so-called 'Carlton House system' was the Prince's method of keeping Princess Caroline 'in order, lest she should keep me so'. She spent her days 'shut up', as she put it, with Lady Jersey until after dinner – a meal the Prince would often avoid. He and Lady Jersey would then go out, while the Princess went to bed. She was even prevented free access to her daughter. The Prince had told the governess, Lady Dashwood, and the sub-governess, Miss Frances Garth, that his wife was only allowed to see Charlotte once a day, before or after her afternoon airing in the gardens. But Caroline got on well with Miss Garth (whose father, General Garth, was one of the King's equerries) and spent many hours with her daughter in the nursery at the top of Carlton House.

By March, however, the Prince had had enough. On the 18th, in an interview lasting more than three hours, he poured out his complaints to Lord Malmesbury. His wife, who physically repulsed him, had not been a virgin at the time of their marriage. He had made love to her on just three occasions, during one of which 'the child just born was made and it will certainly be the last as I declare I never can or will approach her again, for she never washes or wipes any part of her body'.

His attempts to keep her 'in order' had been futile. For 'never did there occur in any female mind such a desire to rule, so much art in so false a character', not to mention 'levity', 'indiscretion and malice'. The first evidence of this was at Kempshot, while at Brighton 'her character was still worse'. She 'got drunk every day' and even made 'advances to Lord Sackville'. He had, as a consequence, decided to part from her and wanted Malmesbury to convey his reasons for doing so to the Duke and Duchess of Brunswick.[4]

Six days later, in a letter to the Prince, Malmesbury expressed the hope that 'your Royal Highness has, on more mature consideration, entirely dismissed from your thoughts the idea of carrying into effect a step which you then appeared to have nearly resolved upon'. He was convinced, he continued, 'that your parting from . . . the Princess of Wales would, both in its immediate and remote consequences, involve your Royal Highness in difficulties, distresses, and I must add, dangers, to which the uneasinesses you appear to labour under . . . can bear no comparison'.

The Prince replied, somewhat dishonestly, that Malmesbury had 'entirely misunderstood' him. He had not said it was his 'immediate intention to part from the Princess'. Rather that 'whilst things continued quiet and . . . the Princess did not attempt to give false impressions of me to the public', he did 'not wish to expose her to the world', nor to subject himself 'to those discussions which any other man, under similar circumstances to myself in private life, would be certain of making'. He continued:

> I never can wish, as long as the Princess and myself dwell under the same roof, to state to the world her real character, but which I may hereafter be obliged to do in justification of my own, should either she be so ill advised as to force it, or unconquerable circumstances require it . . . I have but to refer to your own correct memory for the other particulars that passed in our late conversation.[5]

A permanent separation was not, however, far off. 'The Princess dines always alone,' noted Lord Colchester on 8 April, 'and sees no company but old people, put on her list by the Queen, Lady Jersey, etc. She goes nowhere but airings in Hyde Park. The Prince uses her unpardonably.'[6]

By 21 April the Princess had had enough. Having received no

answer from an earlier message sent to the Prince via Lord
Cholmondeley, she addressed another directly to him. (It was written in
French because her English was poor, and would remain so for most of
her life.) She had been forced to put pen to paper, she wrote, because
she never had the 'pleasure' of seeing him 'alone'. She knew that he
could not bear to dine with her; could he, then, release her from a similar ordeal – 'to dine alone with a person whom I can neither like nor
respect, and who is your mistress, and to be shut up with her all the
long day'. (Later in the letter she identifies her as 'Lady Jerser'.)

'Forgive me, my dear Prince, if my expressions are too strong,' read
her heart-rending final paragraph, 'believe that it is a heart wounded by
the most acute pain and the most most deadly sorrow which pleads for
your help.'[7]

The Prince was unmoved. Replying the same day – in English
'because it is essential for me to explain myself without any possible
ambiguity upon the . . . groundless and most injurious imputation
which you have thought fit to cast upon me' – he denied any sexual
relationship with her lady-in-waiting:

> What else, Madam, than unconquerable disgust in my mind
> could be the consequence, were it in your power to make me
> meanly and dishonourably sacrifice in the eyes of the public a
> woman whom I declared to you on your arrival not to be *my
> mistress*, as you indecorously term her, but a friend to whom I
> am attached by the strong ties of habitude, esteem and respect.
> Were it otherwise, were my connection with Lady Jersey of a
> different nature, such repugnance at the idea, comes if I may be
> allowed to say so, singularly from you.

He then turned to the complaint that she had been 'forced to keep
company alone' with Lady Jersey:

> You will recollect, Madam, that you have seven Ladies in your
> family besides Lady Jersey, any, or everyone, of whom it is in your

power to summon either for dinner or for company at any hour
of the day . . .; but, Madam, I much fear that the insinuation . . .
was not meant for *me* who must know the total want of founda-
tion for such a representation. I am very apprehensive that you
have been inconsiderate enough to imagine that you might hereafter appeal to the copy of that letter in order to prove to others
not so well informed, the grounds you had for dissatisfaction.

'We have,' he concluded, 'unfortunately been obliged to acknowledge
to each other that we cannot find happiness in our union.
Circumstances of character and education . . . render that impossible. It
then only remains that we should make the situation as little uncomfortable to each other as its nature will allow.'[8]

The die was cast. More recriminations flew back and forth until, on
30 April, the Prince stated the exact terms on which he expected them
to live:

> Our inclinations are not in our power, nor should either of us
> be held answerable to the other because nature has not made us
> suitable to each other. Tranquil and comfortable society is,
> however, in our power; let our intercourse therefore be
> restricted to that, and I will distinctly subscribe to the condition
> which you required through Lady Cholmondeley, that even in
> the event of an accident happening to my daughter . . . I shall
> not infringe the terms of the restriction by proposing, at any
> period, a connection of a more particular nature.[9]

In other words, they would never resume their sexual relationship
(Caroline had insisted on this condition and the Prince was only too
happy to agree).

A week later, while at Petworth in Sussex, the Prince received
Caroline's reply. She would not have bothered to respond, she told the
Prince, if his letter 'had not been so constructed as to leave doubt

whether the arrangement originated from me or from you, and you know that yours is the sole honour'. She had, therefore, sent a copy of his letter, as well as this one, to the King, asking him to intervene.

The Prince was aghast, describing the Princess's letter to the Queen as 'excessively wicked'. He could 'see no drift in it', unless it was to 'make general mischief and noise', and was 'both shocked and hurt to death that the King should be plagued on my account'.[10]

His father was more concerned with saving the marriage. A breach between parents, he told Caroline, would be to 'the ruin of the little one which should be an essential object to both'. Therefore, in 'place of reopening your complaints, do your best to make your home agreeable'. The King also asked his brother, the Duke of Gloucester, to mediate: 'Learn from my son what he expects and bring the Princess to acquiesce to his ideas. Believe me, submission in a woman always secures esteem, she must obtain that before more can be expected.'[11]

So exasperated was the Prince by this time that he even sent his brother, Ernest, to sound out Mrs Fitzherbert on the possibility of a reconciliation. 'She is frightened to death,' came the response on 17 May, 'knows not what to say, as is natural to be assumed as you have come upon her *so* unexpectedly . . . She always owns to this, that *if* she did make it up, you would not agree a fortnight.' Wise words. The Prince was in no position to return to his first wife – not yet, anyway.[12]

By now, the Princess was insisting on the removal of Lady Jersey from her Household as the prerequisite to any future arrangement. The Prince, of course, would not budge. On 24 May, *The Times* made its first mention of a 'SEPARATION IN HIGH LIFE'. The public were in no doubt as to whom the injured party was. When Caroline made an appearance at the opera in Covent Garden on 28 May, noted *The Times*, the 'House seemed as if electrified by her presence, and before she could take her seat, every hand was lifted up to greet her with the loudest plaudits. The gentlemen jumped on the benches and waved their hats, crying out *Huzza!*' After 'repeated curtseying to the audience,' wrote the Duke of Leeds, who joined her in her box, she sat down and said 'she supposed she should be guillotined . . . for what had passed.'[13]

The Princess received another rapturous reception at the opera three days later. Her reaction, according to Charles Abbot who was present, was to tell the Duke that 'she supposed the public had been acquainted with what was only [too true]: that the Prince had not spoken to her for three months . . . and that she had nothing to reproach herself with.'[14] That same day, 31 May, after yet more correspondence between the unhappy couple, the Prince wrote to the King requesting his permission for a 'final separation'. The grounds: 'her attempts to sow the seeds of discord between every branch of us; her odious endeavours to vitiate the principles of my innocent sisters, and the disgusting strain of falsehood in which she constantly indulges herself'. He continued:

> Misled by advisers . . . she has flattered herself she could reduce me to such a situation as would give her a decided political superiority in this country. This was only to be effected by the degradation of my character . . . It was hence their joint view to impress the world with a belief that she suffered the most harsh, the most unjust, and the most ungenerous treatment from me, an insinuation which she has sedulously endeavoured to palm upon the public by theatrical tricks on every occasion . . . The extent to which that erroneous sentiment has gained ground was proved at the Opera House on Saturday night . . .
>
> You must see, Sir, that where tempers are so widely different, education, manners and habits so completely opposite, it would be difficult in the extreme to maintain domestick tranquillity; but when these obstacles are added to the sense of virulent persecution which I have so unjustly suffered, it must be idle to think of real reconciliation, and it is evident that the Princess does not wish it on her part.[15]

On 2 June, in a letter to his mother, he named the ringleaders at the opera as 'Lord Henry Fitzgerald, the bosom friend of Mrs Fitzherbert, Lord Darnley and Colonel Frederick St John, both not only bosom friends of Lord Hugh Seymour but actually governed by him in every respect'. It was, he concluded, a plot by Mrs Fitzherbert's friends – among them Jack Payne and Lord Hugh's wife, Lady Horatia – to blacken his name in revenge for his abandonment of her. His paranoia knew no bounds: 'It is, therefore, from the thorough conviction that not only my humiliation but my total destruction is aimed at, that . . . I have formed the resolution with which the King is acquainted and which I had sooner forfeit my existence than abandon.'

That same day, having received a sympathetic reply from the Queen, he sent another letter, vowing never to give himself up, '*nor those who are solely injured on my account*' (in other words Lady Jersey). 'Oh dearest, dearest, dearest mother,' he added, 'if the King does not now manage to throw some stigma, and one very strong mark of disapprobation upon the Princess, this worthless wretch will prove the ruin of him, of you, of me, of every one of us.' He implored her never to propose that he humiliated himself 'before the vilest wretch this world was ever cursed with, who I cannot feel more disgust for from her personal nastiness than I do from her entire want of all principle. She is a very monster of iniquity.'[16]

The King's reply to his letter of 31 May, written two days later, was to come as a severe disappointment:

> You seem to look on your disunion with the Princess as merely of a private nature, and totally put out of sight that as Heir Apparent of the Crown your marriage is a public act, wherein the Kingdom is concerned; that therefore a separation cannot be brought forward by the mere inference of relations. The Public must be informed of the whole business, and being already certainly not prejudiced in your favour, the auspices in the first outset would not be promising. Parliament could not fail of taking part in the business, and would certainly, as no criminal accusation can be brought against the Princess, think itself obliged to secure out of your income the jointure settled on her in case of your death [£50,000 a year] . . .

I once more call you to look with temper at the evils that may accrue to you by persisting in an idea that may lead to evils without bounds, and if more cannot be effected, have the command on yourself that shall, by keeping up appearances, by degrees render your home more respectable and at the same time less unpleasant.

But the Prince refused to submit. Were he to do so, he told the King on 3 June, his ' situation would be despicable and deplorable indeed, for either with regard to the public or in my own house I should be reduced to the state of an absolute dependent upon her'.[17]

His position had no doubt hardened after the appearance of a vicious article in the *True Briton* the day before. Caroline was the 'amiable and accomplished person who has been the object of so much unmerited ill treatment', while Lady Jersey had 'shown so much aversion to impropriety of conduct in general, and particularly to that which relates to the duties of *conjugal life*, that we are sure nothing but *misrepresentation* could have induced her to have encouraged a contrary conduct'. The most vitriolic criticism was reserved for the Prince:

As to the *gentleman* principally concerned, we are afraid he is incorrigible – a *total disregard* to the opinions of the world seems to mark every part of his conduct . . . We have long looked upon his conduct as favouring the cause of Jacobinism and democracy in this country more than all the speeches of HORNE TOOKE, or all the labours of the *Corresponding Society*.[18]

On 12 June, after yet more negotiations with the Prince, Caroline set out her position in a letter to the King: she could see 'no other true means of permanent reconciliation than the absolute retreat of Lady Jersey' from her 'service and private society'. She was, however, prepared to concede that, were she to hold 'drawing-rooms or grand assemblies' in the future, Lady Jersey would 'be admitted as any other indifferent person, as long as the Queen consents to receive her also'.

When Lord Cholmondeley, at the Princess's request, went to the Prince for an answer, he was told that the Prince 'would rather see toads and vipers crawling over his victuals than sit at the same table with her!!!' While acquiescing in Lady Jersey's dismissal, the Prince told Cholmondeley that he 'would not be dictated to, and was determined to see what company he pleased at any time at Carlton House'.[19]

Finally, on 25 June, after the Prince had given his written consent to Lady Jersey's dismissal, the King advised Caroline to make it clear that she wished for a reconciliation. 'She wrote in consequence,' Lady Stafford noted on the 29th:

> . . . one of the prettiest letters you ever saw, to which she had a
> most formal, cold, stupid answer, to say that he would be at
> Carlton House in the course of Monday [27 June]. His behav-
> iour towards his wife during a late dinner was such that:. . . had
> he behaved so to any other lady the husband must have thought
> that he meant to let her know he never desired to see her again.
> As soon as dinner was over he went to Lady Jersey. He protests
> he will never go to the opera with the Princess, and is entirely
> directed by Lady Jersey. This is called a reconciliation! How
> great a curse is he to the poor King, and to these nations![20]

Soon after, Lady Jersey wrote her letter of resignation. She would, she told the Princess, have left long before – on account of 'the infamous and unjustifiable paragraphs in the public papers' – if the Prince had not advised her that such an action 'would not only be regarded as a confirmation' of those slanders, but would also promote the 'views of those who had been so wickedly labouring to injure [him] in the public mind'. In the opinion of The Times, the letter was 'one of the most disrespectful we ever recollect to have read'.[21]

But the reconciliation was a sham. While Caroline remained in London, the Prince spent much of the summer with Lady Jersey at Brighton, Bognor and Critchell House, his new country estate in Dorset. He even had the nerve to install her and her husband in a residence near Carlton House – formerly earmarked for the out-of-favour Jack Payne – telling an anxious Queen that Lord Jersey, his Master of the Horse, could not be expected to run the stables with the money allotted by Parliament 'unless he was perpetually on the spot'.[22]

This did nothing for the Prince's popularity. Even his allies within the Royal Family felt that his treatment of Caroline had been injudicious. 'My brother has behaved very foolishly,' the Duke of Clarence told Mrs Sutton at a Richmond ball in September. 'To be sure he has married a very foolish, disagreeable person, but he should not have treated her as he has done, but have made the best of a bad bargain, as my father has done. He married a disagreeable woman but has not behaved ill to her.'[23]

1797 was destined to be a black year for Britain. Dissensions in the Cabinet, high prices, a scarcity of food and severe taxation caused much discontent at home. In February, to counteract the drain of bullion from the country in the form of subsidies, and to meet the expenses of war, the Bank of England suspended payments of gold and allowed the provincial banks to issue banknotes. (This in turn led to a gradual depreciation in the paper currency, and a rise in value of precious metals; by 1811, the pound had sunk to 14 shillings, while an ounce of gold had risen from £3 17s. to £5 11s.) In the spring, the Royal Navy – Britain's first line of defence – was shaken by a spate of mutinies in the fleets stationed at Spithead, the Nore and Yarmouth. Most of the mutinous sailors were unhappy with their conditions of service – including low pay, poor living arrangements and draconian punishments – but a few had genuine republican sympathies. Order was eventually restored by a combination of concessions and firm action: eighteen 'republican' ringleaders of the Nore mutiny, for example, were hanged.

Abroad, meanwhile, a series of victories by the French general, Napoleon Bonaparte, in northern Italy in 1796 had crushed Sardinia, driven Naples and the Papacy into neutrality, and forced Austria,

Britain's last ally, to the brink of peace. (In October 1797, Austria signed the Treaty of Campo Formio, giving her Venice and the French the Netherlands, the left bank of the Rhine and the Ionian Islands.) On the credit side, a British fleet of just 15 sail-of-the-line, commanded by Admiral Sir John Jervis and brilliantly led by his deputy, Commodore Horatio Nelson, destroyed a Spanish force almost twice its size off Cape St Vincent in February.

But Ireland was the main cause of concern. In 1791, inspired by the French Revolution, the Irish patriot Wolfe Tone had helped to found the Society of United Irishmen, a predominantly Protestant organisation committed to parliamentary reform – particularly universal suffrage and Catholic emancipation. Pitt appreciated the need to offer concessions to the Irish Catholics and, shortly after the outbreak of war with Revolutionary France in 1793, pressure from his government resulted in the Irish Parliament passing a Catholic Relief Act. As well as allowing papists to sit on juries, to hold minor civil posts and to become junior officers in the army, it gave them the vote on the same basis as Protestants. But they still could not sit in Parliament.

Further concessions seemed likely when Earl Fitzwilliam was appointed Lord Lieutenant of Ireland in January 1795 as part of the deal which brought the Portland Whigs into government. But his immediate sacking of John Beresford, the Head of the Revenue Department and the deputy of the 'pro-English' conservatives, led Irish politicians to assume that a 'new order' was imminent. Henry Grattan, a brilliant orator and leading Whig in the Irish Parliament, promptly introduced a Bill for Catholic emancipation. Although Fitzwilliam refrained from giving it official backing, his personal support was well known. George III was beside himself, declaring that such a measure was 'beyond the decision of a Cabinet of Ministers' on the ground that he was bound by his Coronation oath to resist the entry of Catholics into Parliament. Pitt, who had yet to be convinced of the need for full emancipation, was mindful of the King's determined opposition and forced Fitzwilliam to resign.

But the consequences of Fitzwilliam's brief two-month tenure reached much further. Concluding that the Irish Parliament was a screen for English reactionary control, the United Irishmen now embraced full independence as their main political goal. This could best be achieved, they reasoned, by a general uprising assisted by a French invasion. To this end, Wolfe Tone travelled to Paris in 1796 and was favourably received by the Directory. They eventually agreed to provide him with an invasion fleet. Numbering 43 ships and 14,000 men, it sailed from Brest in December 1796 under the command of a brilliant young French general by the name of Lazare Hoche; Tone, who had recently been commissioned in the French army, was also present. But bad weather dispersed the ships off the west coast of Ireland and the invasion was called off.

In the wake of this near miss, the Prince was persuaded by Grattan and other leadings Whigs in the Irish Parliament that the removal of the remaining Catholic disabilities was the only way to ensure the loyalty of Irish Catholics in the event of a rebellion or a French invasion. They also convinced him that he, in the role of Lord Lieutenant, was the best man to implement such a policy. On 8 February 1797, therefore, he included these proposals in a long memorandum to Pitt.

The 'situation of Ireland', he warned, demanded the 'most serious attention' of ministers 'to prevent *the calamities* that would arise to Great Britain from a *civil war*' in Ireland. Its 'loss or separation would be the most mortal blow that this kingdom could receive'. The French were well aware of this, and their recent expedition, 'fitted out at a prodigious expense and sent in the *depth of winter*,' had shown 'that they consider *no expense too great*, no risk *sufficient* to deter them from the prosecution of their plans'. Though a failure, the attempt had destroyed the assumption 'that they could not attempt invasion without having beat our fleet, and *being masters at sea*'.

There was, he said, 'from the *continuance of the preparations* in their Channel ports, as well as their *avowed declarations*', good reason to assume 'that the *attempt would be renewed*'. The fact that a number of Ulster districts were 'in a *state of insurrection*' was evidence that the French had 'been excited by direct communications from Ireland'.

Whatever 'the *private views*' of the leaders of the rebellion, they had formerly confined themselves to demanding '*Parliamentary Reform*'; in this they had '*acted* artfully' by including '*Roman Catholic claims* in their demands, and thus forming *two* bodies, hitherto opposed, *into one* under the title of *United Irishmen*'.

But 'if the secret object of this union be a *revolution* in the *Government* and *a separation* from *Great Britain*,' as there was every reason to suppose, he continued, 'it is alarming from its *object* and formidable from its *numbers*.' The solution was to 'disunite its members', particularly the Roman Catholics who were not, '*as yet*, to any degree tainted with disaffection, though they may be led, by degrees, to go the *full lengths* with the Presbyterians'. This could best be done by '*repealing every exclusive restriction* and *disqualification* on the *Irish Roman Catholics*'. They were 'naturally loyal and attached to Monarchy' and had 'behaved well . . . on the late threatened invasion'.

In the event of such a measure being adopted, he was willing 'to undertake the Government of Ireland, great and arduous as the task appears under the present circumstances, . . . in the hopes of *more firmly attaching that valuable kingdom to the Crown of Great Britain* and *animating the spirit of that loyal and affectionate people to the most powerful exertions* against *our desperate enemy*'.[24]

It was a brilliantly argued document which, had it been implemented, might well have prevented the rebellion that began the following year. (The fact that the Prince was simply repeating many of the points which had been made to him by others is neither here nor there. All politicians steal ideas: having the courage and determination to follow them through is what makes them great. In this respect, at least, the Prince would prove deficient.)

Pitt's response to the Prince's letter was a flat rejection. Far from offering concessions, the government was planning to subdue Ulster by force. Ironically, the officer given the order to disarm the Presbyterians was none other than General Lake, the Prince's former equerry. With not enough regular troops to subdue the six northern counties, Lake called up the yeomanry and the militia. But these forces were largely Anglican and conservative, and their repressive measures were seen as little short of civil war. 'Murder appears to be the favourite pastime' of the Irish militia, pronounced Lord Cornwallis, the incoming Lord-Lieutenant.[25]

Meanwhile, Pitt's snub had driven the Prince back into the arms of the Opposition. Fox, for one, was in perfect agreement with him over the Irish question. In March 1797, in one of his last major speeches before withdrawing his party from Parliament, he introduced a motion asking the King 'to adopt such healing and lenient measures . . . best calculated to restore tranquillity' to Ireland. Fifteen years earlier, during Rockingham's administration, Fox had forced through the act which gave legislative independence to the Irish Parliament. But this measure had failed to heal the rifts in Irish politics. The greatest stumbling block was the fact that the Anglican élite still held a monopoly of power. When Fitzwilliam tried to break it in 1795; he was sacked for his pains. The hopes of the Irish had been 'disappointed', he told the House, the cup 'dashed from their lips'.

The only solution was to offer the Irish more concessions:

> I know no way of governing mankind but by conciliating them . . . I will therefore adopt the Irish expression, and say that you can only govern Ireland by letting her have her own way . . . If you keep Ireland by force now, what must you do in all future wars? You must in the first place secure her from insurrection. . . My wish is that the whole people of Ireland should have the same principles, the same system, the same operation of government and, though it may be a subordinate consideration, that all classes should have an equal chance of emolument . . . [Only thus] will she be bound to English interests.[26]

Sadly, Fox's enlightened policy towards Ireland was ignored (as the Prince's had been a month earlier). Had it not been, the history of that troubled isle might have been very different.

Shortly after this speech, on 25 March, the Prince gave a dinner at Carlton House for Fox and other prominent opponents of Pitt's government, including the Duke of Norfolk, Sheridan and Erskine. When asked by William Fawkener how he found the Prince, Fox replied: 'Exactly the same as when he left us five years ago.'[27]

By late spring, it seemed as if Pitt's unpopularity in the Commons might lead to a change of government. The likely beneficiary was not Fox, however, but the Earl of Moira. A political general with a reputation for intelligence and decisiveness, Moira would later gain fame as the Governor-General of India (he had, by then, become the Marquess of Hastings). Distinct from both Fox and Pitt, a close friend of the Prince and the Duke of York, he was seen as the ideal compromise candidate.

He had, he told the Duke of Northumberland on 15 May, held conversations with 'a formidable body' of M.P.s. 'They are violent against Pitt, though they vote with him, but they will not bear the Opposition as a party. Their object is to make some effort to save the country from the evident ruin into which it is falling.'[28]

The Prince, probably on account of his recent links with the Opposition, was kept out of the discussions. So too was Fox, although he approved of the plan when he eventually got wind of it; even going so far, on 24 May, as to tell the King that he was prepared to step aside if the ministry was changed. Six days later, Moira was boasting that 'the neutrals' in the House had 'gained ground prodigiously'. By now his political programme was fixed: immediate talks for peace, a 'just and lenient system' in Ireland, 'heavy contributions' to boost finances, and appointments confined to those 'immediately connected with Ministerial function'.

On 2 June, Moira sent an outline of his proposals to George III, enclosing a letter and an Address from five leaders of his supporting group. But while the King was well aware that Pitt had forfeited much goodwill in the Commons, he was not prepared to risk a change of government at such a critical time, not least because his son might benefit. Within a couple of weeks the initiative had collapsed.[29]

By now Fox had come to the conclusion that opposition to the government was futile. During the debate over Charles Grey's motion for parliamentary reform, introduced on 26 May (and subsequently defeated by 256 to 91), he announced that he would not be attending future sessions of the House. Nearly three years would elapse before he and his supporters returned to the Commons on a regular basis.

On 29 May 1797, the Prince turned his attention back to Ireland by sending Pitt an addendum to his earlier proposal. Much to his 'mortification', he wrote, the government had ignored his advice and implemented a 'system of coercion'. He continued:

> Lamenting the adoption of such a system and deploring the consequences it must necessarily produce, I have hitherto . . . preserved silence on the subject that Ministers might give that system a fair trial; but have now done so, and the menacing circumstances increasing every day, I should consider a farther silent acquiescence as betraying the dearest interests of both my King and my country.

His evidence for this was that from December 1796, when the 'system of coercion' first began, to April 1797, when secret papers were 'seized in Belfast', the membership of the Society of United Irishmen in Ulster actually rose from 59,688 to 99,411. The latter figure did not even include the County of Meath, 'one of the most turbulent in the Kingdom'; if it had, 'the numbers would have nearly doubled'. He wrote:

> So alarming an increase can alone be accounted for by the avowal of this system coupled with the declaration of the Irish Ministers . . . that no farther concessions would be made by Government to Irish Catholics, a declaration that I must condemn as unwise and impolitic, and originating in unparalleled ingratitude to a description of men who had shown the greatest zeal, loyalty and sound principles by their distinguished exertions in the public cause when their country was threatened , in . . . December last with a French invasion.

'A strong military force may secure temporary advantages,' the Prince concluded, 'but no force can long coerce a nation of 4 millions of people united in sentiments and interests. I must once more most earnestly recommend conciliatory measures and I adjure you to pause on the awful brink of civil war and to avert its fateful consequences.'[30]

Once again the Prince's advice was rejected. But he was wrong on one point: the coercion of Ulster was working. This in turn encouraged the United Irishmen to act while they still could – but before they could coordinate their efforts with the French. In March 1798, an attempt to assassinate key figures in the Dublin government was thwarted when the perpetrators were arrested. As the authorities began the pacification of Leinster, the rebels came out into the open with attacks on Naas, Carlow and Wexford. By June, a rebel army of 15,000 men had taken Wexford and Enniscorthy.

Lake responded on 21 June by routing the main rebel force at Vinegar Hill, near Enniscorthy. Wexford was retaken and the rebellion in the south soon degenerated into sporadic guerilla warfare. The Ulster rebels, meanwhile, had been separately crushed at Ballinahinch on 12 June. Too late, a French force of 900 regulars under General Humbert landed at Killala, County Mayo, on 22 August. Reinforced by a handful of rebels, it advanced to Castlebar and even managed to inflict a minor defeat on Lake's troops. But after crossing the Shannon, Humbert was caught between Cornwallis at Carrick and Lake at Ballinamuck and forced to surrender. Wolfe Tone had even less success. Entering Lough Swilly, Donegal, with a small French squadron carrying 3,000 men in September, he was intercepted by Commodore Borlase Warren and captured. Condemned to death, he cut his throat with a penknife on the day he was due to be hanged – 12 November – and died a week later. The Great Rebellion of 1798 was over.

Meanwhile, the domestic friction between the Prince and Princess of Wales had come to a head. On 11 October 1797, Admiral Duncan's ships had destroyed the Dutch fleet at Camperdown, removing the last threat of invasion. A Thanksgiving Service in St Paul's Cathedral was planned for 19 December, but Caroline was forbidden by the Prince to attend on the grounds of economy: he lacked the requisite attendants, carriages and horses for the procession.

As if this was not bad enough, the King then confirmed that she could only receive those guests whom her husband approved. This was too much. On 4 December, she demanded and was given a personal interview with the Prince. Speaking in French, she told him that she only had 'two words' to say:

> I have been two and a half years in this house. You have treated me neither as your wife, nor as the mother of your child, nor as the Princess of Wales. I advise you that from this moment I have nothing more to say to you, and that I regard myself as being no longer subject to your orders, or your – rules.

The last word was spoken in English. Asked if that was all she had to say to him, Caroline answered, '*Oui*', upon which the Prince bowed and left the room.[31]

Next day, he wrote to the King, complaining of the Princess's 'extraordinary conduct'. But she refused to retract and on 15 December Lord Cholmondeley presented the Prince's proposal for a separation. She would have 'a house in town', £20,000 a year 'in addition to the five thousand pounds already in trust'. Princess Charlotte would stay with her mother until she was seven, but her governesses would be appointed by the Prince. Caroline's reaction, the Prince informed the King on 24 December, was to express 'her satisfaction and her gratitude for the Prince's liberality'.

The King was not convinced. After consulting Lord Chancellor Loughborough – who felt that the cause of dispute between husband and wife was 'extremely slight' – he authorised him 'to express to the Prince of Wales the impossibility of my consenting to any public separation between him and the Princess of Wales, as incompatible with the religion, laws and government of my kingdom'.[32]

So that was that; a semblance of a marriage, at least, would have to be maintained. Unofficially, however, the Prince and Princess were rarely together. Other than regular visits to Carlton House to see her daughter – and occasionally to change for the opera and for Court – Caroline spent most of her time out of London. First at a house in Charlton, near Blackheath, which she had rented since the spring of 1797; then, from the summer of 1798, at Montague House, near Greenwich Park, which the Prince had originally taken for Princess Charlotte.

A fascinating insight into the appearance and character of the Prince at this time has been left by the M.P. Nathaniel Wraxall:

> His person was undoubtedly cast by nature in an elegant and pleasing mould, of a just height, well-proportioned, and with due regard to symmetry, but it had, nevertheless, something diffused over it indicative of repose or of sloth, rather than of energy or activity . . . There was from head to foot a flaccidity of muscle and a rotundity of outline inimical to our conceptions of masculine strength or beauty. His countenance . . . was handsome and prepossessing and commonly gay, though at times it became suddenly overcast and sullen . . . ; it was a round, not an oval contour of face, destitute of strong expression, though lighted up by much animation, with grey eyes and a fair complexion; add to these corporeal endowments a vast quantity of light brown hair . . . He was never slender, not even at twenty . . .

This last comment was something of an understatement. According to the Old Coffee Mill scales in St James's Street, he weighed 17st 8lb in December 1797.

Wraxall continued:

> His manners were captivating, noble and dignified, yet unaffectedly condescending, if he had only known how to limit his

condescension, which too often degenerated into familiarity . . .

For music he nourished a passion, and displayed a fine taste, being himself not only an admirer but a performer. He sung an excellent song . . .; another talent . . . was mimicry . . . He danced with uncommon grace, nor did he ride with less agility and ease . . .

In conversation he was not only affable and communicative, but most entertaining – full of anecdote which proved an extensive acquaintance with history, and vast powers of recollection in military information relating to the strength of the Continental sovereigns throughout Europe . . .

In personal courage, though it has never been put to the test, I believe the Prince of Wales, like all the individuals of his house, to be in no way deficient . . . But he wanted the King's nerves.[33]

It was also during this period that the Prince came under the spell of that arch-dandy, George 'Beau' Brummell. Born in Downing Street in 1778, the younger son of Lord North's private secretary, Brummell, by his own account, was first 'presented to the heir apparent on the Terrace at Windsor when a boy at Eton'. His 'subsequent intimacy' with the Prince 'grew out of the slight notice with which he was then favoured'.[34]

His father George Brummell, the son of a household servant, had met Lord North in 1767 when he was an Under-Clerk at the Treasury and North was Chancellor of the Exchequer. Impressed by his diligence and discretion, North appointed him his private secretary when he became Prime Minister three years later. During the 12 years of North's administration, Brummell feathered his nest to such an extent that, on his death in March 1794, he was able to leave his two sons and one daughter the huge sum of £20,000 each.

In July 1794, having spent just one term at Oxford, Brummell accepted a cornetcy in the Prince's regiment, the 10th Light Dragoons. He had been in close attendance on the Prince ever since, even accompanying him and the Princess of Wales on their honeymoon. Promoted to Captain in command of a troop in 1796, he spent so little time with his men that he was forced to position one of his dragoons, a man with a blue nose even on the warmest days, in the front rank so that he could recognise his troop. He was eventually caught out when he joined a different troop with a new recruit whose nose was just as blue!

It was no surprise, therefore, when Brummell's military career came to a premature conclusion in March 1798. The occasion was a warning order for the regiment to march north to help put down disturbances among cotton-spinners in Lancashire. Early next morning, Brummell sought an audience with the Prince. 'I have heard that we are ordered to Manchester,' he told him. 'Now you must be aware how disagreeable that would be to *me*.'

The Prince did not answer.

'Think, your Royal Highness, Manchester!'

While the Prince considered the drawbacks of northern garrison life, Brummell played his ace: 'Besides, *you* would not be there. I have therefore, with your Royal Highness's permission, determined to sell out.'

'Oh, by all means, Brummell,' said the Prince. 'Do as you please, do as you please!'[35]

A fine-looking man – tall and fair, with 'particularly well-shaped hands', a high forehead and a rakish broken nose (a fall from a horse having given it a 'quizzical, impertinent, disdainful angle') – Brummell's reputation was founded upon his preoccupation with dress. The cut of his clothes, the fit of his gloves (he was said to employ two glove-makers, one for the thumbs, the other for the palm and fingers), and the shine of his boots were exquisite. The secret, he once told the cour-tesan Harriette Wilson, was 'no perfumes, but very fine linen, plenty of it, and country washing'. If 'John Bull turns round to look after you,' he added, 'you are not well dressed; but either too stiff, too tight, or too fashionable.'[36]

His daily toilet was legendary. Having cleaned his teeth and shaved, he would spend two hours scrubbing his body with a pig-bristle brush and plucking his eyebrows with tweezers. Only then would he embark upon the real challenge of the day – dressing. Mesmerised by the perfection of Brummell's appearance, the Prince set out to emulate it. In July 1798, for example, the sculptor John Rossi, working on a bust of the Prince, was kept waiting for three hours while his subject tried on 'at least forty pair of boots' and conducted 'many trials of patterns and cuttings'.[37]

The novelist William Thackeray, for one, was not impressed. He later wrote of the Prince:

> There is his coat, his star, his wig, his countenance simpering under it . . . I try and take him to pieces, and find silk stockings, padding, stays, a coat with frogs and a fur collar, a star and a blue ribbon, a pocket-handkerchief prodigiously scented, one of Truefitts best nutty brown wigs reeking with oil, a set of teeth and a huge black stock, underwaistcoat, more under-waistcoats, and then nothing.[38]

In the summer of 1798, alienated from his wife and tired of his mistress Lady Jersey, the Prince once more sought a reconciliation with Mrs Fitzherbert. To this end, he sent his confidential servant, Lieutenant-Colonel John McMahon – 'an Irishman of low birth and obsequious manners,' wrote Raikes, '. . . a little man, his face red, covered with pimples, always dressed in the blue and buff uniform, with his hat on one side, copying the air of his master' – to Cheltenham, where Mrs Fitzherbert was staying at the Plough Inn.'[39]

But on 22 August, in a letter to the Prince from Cheltenham, McMahon was forced to admit that Mrs Fitzherbert entertained 'an ill opinion' of him and classed him 'among the particular friends of L[ady] J[ersey]'. Though he had had no 'material conversation' with her, he had taken care to do the Prince 'ample justice by a side wind through one or two ladies with whom she associates'. Furthermore, he had 'reason to think, by what has fallen from a lady of her acquaintance, that your Royal Highness occupies her thoughts a vast deal'.[40]

Temporarily thwarted, the Prince poured out his troubles to his favourite sister, Princess Augusta, during a visit to Windsor Castle . His *'dejected appearance'* had given her and her sisters 'very great concern', she told him in a letter written later that day. Referring to Mrs Fitzherbert, she wrote:

> After such real affection, not to say adoration on your side, and I am confident from all I have heard pretty near the same on *hers*, I am certain it is *nothing* less serious than a *reconciliation*, which would surely make both of you happy . . . . *She* would become again the same respected personage she was formerly, and how much interested should not we *all* and *myself* ('the last not least') be in the happiness and welfare of the object who constitutes your felicity? . . . Oh! if I could but see you really happy with *her* (which I am convinced is the only chance of your *really* being happy) . . ., and why, *if what the world says of the Princess* is true, that she *declares she hopes to hear of her being with you*, why then should she not wish to *make* her *happy situation* be known to all the world; it would proclaim our *mutual constancy* and you would both be admired for it.[41]

Part of the reason why Augusta was so determined her brother would find happiness was because she and her five sisters had been so long denied it. Apart from Princess Charlotte, the eldest, who had had to wait until the age of 31 before being allowed to marry the incredibly fat Hereditary Prince of Württemberg in 1797 (a man of whom Napoleon once remarked that God had created him simply to show how far human skin could stretch without bursting), they were all still living at home. Other than promenading, sewing, drawing and playing music there was little to keep them occupied; evening entertainment was confined to the occasional ball, concert or play. They rarely came into contact with men other than their father, his pages and attendants.

It is hardly surprising, therefore, that a number of them formed attachments with various members of the Royal Household. Princess Augusta, for example, was said to have fallen in love with first Henry Halford, a royal physician, and then Major-General Sir Brent Spencer. Princess Elizabeth, the third eldest, was supposed to have had a liaison with a page; Princess Amelia, the youngest, a long-term affair with General Fitzroy, the King's equerry. But the most persistent rumour – undoubtedly true – was the one which linked Princess Sophia, the second youngest, with Major-General Thomas Garth, another of the King's equerries and a man 33 years her senior.

In August 1800, when she was 22, Sophia is said to have given birth in secret at Weymouth. Some thought that her brother Prince Ernest, by then the Duke of Cumberland, might be the father. But Garth is the more likely candidate, even if his unprepossessing appearance – a large purple birthmark covered part of his forehead and surrounded one eye – was in direct contrast to Sophia's youthful good looks.

Describing Garth as a 'hideous old devil', the diarist Charles Greville went on to explain that 'women fall in love with anything – and opportunity and the accidents of the passions are of more importance than any positive merits of mind or of body . . . [The Princesses] were secluded from the world, mixing with few people – their passions boiling over and ready to fall into the hands of the first man whom circumstances enabled to get at them.'[42] According to Lord Glenbervie, who heard the story from the Princess of Wales, the secret son was christened Thomas Garth and brought up in the home of Major Herbert Taylor, Private Secretary to the Duke of York and later the King. Garth senior, meanwhile, was promoted to full general and given a position in the Household of Princess Charlotte. Presumably for services rendered.[43]

In December 1798, having failed to win back Mrs Fitzherbert, the Prince attempted a reconciliation with the Princess of Wales. On the 12th, he sent her an invitation to dine at Carlton House and stay for the winter. But the Princess would have none of it.

'I told her *she* was wrong [in declining the invitation],' Lord Minto informed his wife three days later, 'and begged her to reflect seriously on any step she might take if similar overtures were renewed, but she said she was a very determined person when she had once formed an opinion, and that her resolution was fixed on this point; that she knew I should think her a very wicked woman, but that I did not know and could not imagine all the circumstances: I might otherwise agree with her.'[44]

She was probably referring to the Prince's efforts to raise money from her cousin, the Landgrave of Hesse-Cassell. 'I told you that the Prince has got £40,000,' wrote Minto to his wife the following December. 'This has probably enabled him to settle with Lady Jersey, who is going abroad, as the Princess says, and all this seems to have some connection with the Prince's late advances to the Princess.'[45]

No sooner had the Princess rebuffed his insincere overtures than the Prince resumed his wooing of Mrs Fitzherbert. In February 1799, he asked the Duchess of Rutland, a mutual friend, to inform Mrs Fitzherbert that 'there *never was an instant*' in which he did not feel for her and that 'everything is finally at an end IN ANOTHER QUAR-TER.' He was referring, of course, to Lady Jersey rather than Princess Caroline.

Just over a week later, the Prince was devastated by a newspaper report that Mrs Fitzherbert had died at Bath. (She had caught a bad cold in December 1798 during a visit to Portsmouth to discuss looking after Mary 'Minney' Seymour, the baby daughter of Lady Horatia Seymour, a consumptive who had been advised to accompany her husband, Lord Hugh, to Madeira for her health.) 'To describe my feelings, to talk even of the subject is totally impossible,' he told the Duchess of Rutland, 'for I could neither feel, think, speak; in short, there was almost an end to my existence.'[46]

When the report turned out to be false, the Prince's attempts to win over Mrs Fitzherbert became increasingly desperate. 'Save me, save me, on my knees I conjure you from myself,' he pleaded in June, in a long rambling letter that took two days to write. 'IF YOU WILL NOT ADHERE TO YOUR PROMISE I WILL *CLAIM YOU AS SUCH,*

PROVE MY MARRIAGE, RELINQUISH EVERYTHING FOR YOU, RANK, SITUATION, BIRTH, & IF THAT IS NOT SUFFICIENT, MY LIFE SHALL GO ALSO.'

With the Prince apparently in terminal decline – taking ever-increasing doses of laudanum, insisting on constant bleeding and telling his sisters 'that he was sure to die if a reconciliation did not take place' – the Queen decided to intervene. According to Lord Glenbervie, she sent Mrs Fitzherbert a letter in her 'own handwriting pressing her to be reconciled with the Prince'. The 'ostensible motive was concern for her son's health', wrote Glenbervie, 'but a different and less amiable motive' was a desire to revenge herself on Princess Caroline for writing letters critical of her to the Duchess of Brunswick. Intercepted by Lady Jersey, they were passed on to the Queen, 'who is believed never to have forgiven her daughter-in-law'.[47]

By mid-July 1799, Mrs Fitzherbert was weakening. After a 'very long tête à tête' with her on the 17th, Prince Edward (recently created the Duke of Kent) informed his elder brother that if he was 'any judge at all of the business', the Prince's 'wishes will ere long be accomplished.' There were certain conditions, however. She would continue to live in a separate house, not as his 'mistress or wife', but as his 'sister'. Furthermore, she would not return to him until the Pope had passed judgement on their marriage. To this end she had already despatched William Nassau, a chaplain of Warwick Street Chapel, to lay her case before His Holiness.'[48]

While waiting for Nassau to return, Mrs Fitzherbert left for the country, taking Minney Seymour with her. Lord Hugh and Lady Horatia Seymour had finally agreed to hand over the youngest of their seven children to her care shortly before their departure to Madeira in early 1799 – but not without certain misgivings. Not least because Mrs Fitzherbert was a Catholic, but also because they knew she might rejoin the Prince, who was hardly an ideal parent. According to Horatia's sister, Lady Euston, her health declined every time Mrs Fitzherbert tried to discuss the possibility of her returning to the Prince.[49]

Eventually Nassau returned with the Pope's pronouncement: in the eyes of the Catholic Church, Mrs Fitzherbert was the Prince's only true wife; as long as he was sincerely penitent for his sins (chief among them bigamy, although the list was endless), she was at liberty to return to him. It was about this time that Mrs St John, a good friend of Mrs Fitzherbert's, heard the Prince say 'at a great assembly at Lady Salisbury's . . . that he thought the Roman Catholic religion the only religion fit for a gentleman'. When Mrs St John expressed her astonishment that not only should he think so, but that he 'should declare' such a dangerous opinion 'openly', he replied: 'My God, it is my opinion and I do not care who knows it.'[50]

By the spring of 1800, the Prince and Mrs Fitzherbert were often seen out together. Unaware of the Pope's sanction, many of her Catholic friends were appalled. 'On Saturday,' wrote Lady Jerningham in mid-March, 'Lady Kenmare tells me, that Mrs Fitzherbert, Mrs Butler and the Prince were in a high box all night in conversation, the Princess at the Opera and also Lady Jersey. I comprehend it no longer for I had thought Mrs Fitzherbert a woman of principle.'[51]

In May, Lady Holland was rightly contemptuous of the hypocrisy displayed by society towards Mrs Fitzherbert. 'Every prude, dowager and maiden visited Mrs. F. before,' she wrote, 'and the decline of her favour scarcely reduced her visitors; but now they all cry out shame for doing that which she did notoriously five years ago. There is a sort of morality I can never comprehend.'[52]

The following month, as a way of announcing their reunion, Mrs Fitzherbert gave a 'public breakfast' for the Prince at her rented villa, Castle Hill in Ealing. Four hundred guests were invited, including most of the fashionable ladies about town. Only a handful – Lady Jerningham among them – made their excuses. The entertainment began at 2 in the afternoon in three marquees which had been erected in the garden. Dinner was taken at 7, and the festivities did not cease until 5 the following morning. Years later, Mrs Fitzherbert spoke to Lord Stourton of her feelings that day. 'She hardly knew how she could summon the resolution to pass that severe ordeal,' he wrote, 'but she thanked God she had the courage to do so. The next eight years were, she said, the happiest of her connection with the Prince.'[53]

Their reconciliation was now official. 'A Gentleman of high rank and MRS. FITZHERBERT are once more *Inseperables*,' announced *The Times* on 4 July 1799. 'Where one is invited, a card to the other is a matter of course.'

8

The Reversionary
Interest

On 5 February 1801, after more than 17 years in power, William Pitt resigned as Prime Minister over the issue of Catholic emancipation. With the suppression of the rebellion in 1798, the government had opted for political union with Ireland as the best way to safeguard it from the threat of republicanism. This in turn had revived hopes that Catholics would be able to sit in the newly unified Westminster Parliament.

Although the Cabinet never actually gave Marquess Cornwallis, the Lord-Lieutenant of Ireland, a categorical assurance that emancipation would follow union, it strongly hinted that such would be the case. By the time the bills for Union were passed by the Irish Parliament in the summer of 1800, therefore, a 'sense of obligation had built up'. But the Cabinet meeting to consider 'the great question', on 1 October, was inconclusive. Lord Grenville, the Foreign Secretary, was the strongest advocate for the measure; Lord Chancellor Loughborough its most vehement opponent. Pitt himself was undecided. While pointing out the likely obstacles – probably from 'the Law', certainly from the Church of England and the King – he was sufficiently impressed by the merits of emancipation to undertake to speak to the King.

But preoccupied with other business – the war with France, a second failed harvest, a relapse in his health – Pitt did not immediately follow up his undertaking. The King, meanwhile, had been informed of the Cabinet's deliberations by Loughborough and the ensuing silence only made him more suspicious. The issue was forced by the Dublin government. With the Act of Irish Union due to come into effect on 1 January 1801, it was anxious to move ahead on the question of emancipation. During the Christmas recess, therefore, Lord Castlereagh, the Irish Chief Secretary, arrived in London and circulated a paper supporting emancipation; Loughborough responded with a counter-document.

With the first Parliament of the new 'United Kingdom' due to open at the end of January, the question of what to include in the King's Speech became ever more pressing. Consequently, a Cabinet meeting was held on 25 January 1801 to make an 'absolute decision' about emancipation. Despite the fact that Loughborough and Liverpool were absent, and a number of dissenting voices were heard, Pitt left the meeting convinced that a majority were in favour of the measure. The following day, he said as much to Lord Castlereagh.

The King had still not been consulted, though Loughborough had kept him informed about the Cabinet's earlier deliberations. When he heard about the latest developments – probably from Westmorland or Clare, the Irish Lord Chancellor – he was understandably incensed. On 28 January, at the weekly Levée, he strode up to Dundas and said 'in a loud voice and agitated Manner, "What is the Question which you are about to force upon me? what is this Catholic Emancipation which *this young Lord, this Irish Secretary* has brought over, that you are going to throw at my Head? I will tell you, that I shall look on every Man as my personal Enemy, who proposes that Question to me," and he added, "I hope *All* my Friends will not desert me." '

On hearing of the King's outburst, Pitt called an emergency Cabinet meeting to sound out opinion. He was now strongly in favour of emancipation and 'declared that he must go out if it was not carried'. But only Grenville, Dundas and Windham were firmly behind him; Loughborough was strongly opposed, Westmorland, Liverpool and Portland moderately so. As a result, the opening of Parliament – scheduled for next day – was postponed until Pitt had consulted with the King. But the King was implacable. On 1 February, in response to Pitt's letter urging that emancipation 'would be attended with no danger' to the Established Church or the Protestant interest in England or Ireland, he emphasised his own 'religious obligation' under the Coronation Oath. The 'fundamental maxims' of the Constitution required that 'those who hold employments in the State must be members' of the Established Church. He was therefore 'prevented from discussing any new proposition tending to destroy this ground', particularly emancipation 'which is no less than the compleat overthrow of the whole fabrick'.[1]

With his position diametrically opposed to that of the King, Pitt had no option but to go. He resigned on the 5th, and in his place the King selected Henry Addington, the 'mad' doctor's son who had been Speaker of the House of Commons since 1793. A modest man well aware of his own limitations, Addington was reluctant to accept. But the King was adamant. 'Lay your hand upon your heart,' he told him, 'and ask yourself where I am to turn for support if *you* do not stand by me.'[2]

Having accepted office on the 5th, Addington was faced with the prospect of forming an administration without the pick of Pitt's supporters – Grenville, Dundas, Windham and Canning. 'When the crew of a vessel is preparing for action,' Sheridan told the Commons on the 16th, 'it is usual to clear the decks by throwing overboard the lumber, but he had never heard of such a manoeuvre as that of throwing their great guns overboard.'[3]

Philip Yorke, Addington's Secretary at War, acknowledged the weakness of the new government in a letter to his mother on 11 February, predicting that it might not last longer than six weeks. But 'it *must* be formed as it is,' he told her, 'or Messrs. Sheridan, Grey and Tierney sent for.'[4]

Before Addington could receive the seals of office, however, the

King suffered a relapse of his 1788–9 illness. On Friday 13th, having caught a cold by remaining too long in church, the old physical symptoms returned: colic, constipation, muscular weakness, sweating, racing pulse and sleeplessness. Six days later, at 'the evening party', Pitt told Rose, 'the King's conversation and conduct' were 'very extravagant' and 'it was evident . . . that his Majesty's mind was not in a proper state'. By Sunday 22nd, he was 'evidently deranged' and his old 'mad doctors', the Willises – Doctors John and Robert, and their brother the Reverend Thomas – were sent for.[5]

The Prince was quick to act. On 23 February, anticipating the King's death, or at the very least a Regency, he sent for Pitt, still the *de facto* Prime Minister. According to Hugh Rose, Pitt's close ally and the former Secretary to the Treasury, the Prime Minister was only too glad to give the Prince 'the best advice and opinions in his power', but only 'on the express condition' that the Prince would no longer consult with 'those who had for a long time acted in direct opposition to his Majesty's Government' – particularly Fox and Sheridan. The Prince 'acquiesced', but added 'he should think himself at liberty to advise occasionally with Lord Moira, which he had long been in the habit of doing'.

At a second interview two days later, Pitt told the Prince that, if necessary, he would introduce a Regency Bill 'with nearly similar provisions' to that of 1789. Furthermore, he had spoken to the Portland Whigs and 'they would not now create any difficulty in passing the Bill'. Reluctant to acquiesce, the Prince replied that he needed time to consider the matter.[6]

Of course he had no intention of restricting his political consultation to Lord Moira. There were, remarked Lord Glenbervie on 13 February, 'great flockings of minor politicians into Carlton House'. As early as 24 February the Prince was holding discreet talks on the formation of a new government. The Duke of Norfolk was offered the Viceroyalty of Ireland, with authority to bring in Catholic emancipation; the Duke of Devonshire was told to take his pick of the Cabinet posts. The Prince also communicated with Addington, Fox, the

Marquess of Buckingham, Sheridan, the Duke of Northumberland and Earl Spencer. But the best advice was given by the Earl of Carlisle, who urged him to accept a restricted Regency and to form a strong administration.

Fox might have expected to be the front-runner for Prime Minister, but Mrs Fitzherbert is said to have vetoed this appointment. He would have to be content with the post of Home Secretary, with Moira as Prime Minister, Sheridan as Chancellor of the Exchequer, Fox as Home Secretary, Shelburne (now the Marquess of Lansdowne) as Foreign Secretary, Grey as Secretary at War, and Thurlow as Lord Chancellor.[7]

But Lord Malmesbury was not impressed. 'His [the King's] eldest son goes about rejoicing at what has happened and may happen,' he wrote. 'I am glad mine does not take after him.' The Duke of York's behaviour, however, could not have been more different from that in 1788–9. He 'remains firm to the King,' remarked Malmesbury, 'and is as discreet in his language as proper in his conduct.' A few days later, he wrote: 'He is their great and only comfort at the Queen's House, and without his manly mind and advice neither the Queen nor Princesses would be able to bear up under the present distress.'[8]

Siding with York was the Duke of Cumberland, a rabid Protestant who feared the consequences of Catholic emancipation; the Dukes of Clarence and Kent, however, were firmly behind the Prince. 'Well, we shall have it all our way now,' Clarence told Lord Cholmondeley. 'He is not only mad, but dying, and I know my brother intends to give you a White Stick.' Cholmondeley's wise reply was 'that having known what it is to be a servant, I am determined never to find myself in that situation again.'

The Prince, complained Mrs Harcourt, only went to the Queen's House when he knew his father would not be well enough to receive him. One such occasion was 2 March. With the King 'so much worse' that the doctors feared for his life, the Prince joined the rest of the Royal Family outside the sick-room. But by evening the crisis was over.

On 5 March, the King was well enough to feed himself. 'The whole day passed with increasing good symptoms,' noted the Willis journal. Two days later, Malmesbury recorded: 'His Majesty recovered in mind, as well as body. Duke of York with him for the first time . . . found him looking pale and ill, but perfectly collected.' The last medical bulletin was issued on the 11th: 'His Majesty free from fever, but it may require some time, as is always necessary after so severe an illness, to complete recovery.'[9]

That same day, the Prince and the Duke of Kent were allowed to see the King for the first time in a month. He was, remarked the Prince, 'thinner and had lost the ruddiness of his complexion', while his 'eyes were a good deal effected' which made him complain of 'the looking glass in his room as faulty in the reflection from it'.

On 14 March, the King was well enough to receive the seals of office from Pitt, who found the occasion 'particularly distressing' as it was being rumoured, notably by the Duke of Cumberland and the Reverend John Willis, that the King's illness had been brought on by the threat of Catholic emancipation. Pitt later authorised Dr John Willis to tell the King that he would never again raise the Catholic question during his reign. 'Now my mind is at peace,' the King is said to have replied.[10]

His eldest son's precipitate politicking – so reminiscent of the Prince's insensitive behaviour during the Regency crisis of 1788–9 – was less easy to forgive. His one consolation was that the Duke of York, his favourite son, had not sided with the Prince for a second time.

'The new government seems to me to want the sufficient proportion of three things – brains, blood and gold, i.e. abilities, family and property,' wrote Lord Glenbervie, himself a member of the Board of Control, on 16 February 1801.[11]

He had a point. While most of Addington's Cabinet were peers, only the Duke of Portland (Home Secretary) could be considered a political grandee. The Earls of Westmorland (Lord Privy Seal), Chatham (Lord

President of the Council) and Liverpool had all served under Pitt, but they were decidedly second-rate compared with Grenville, Dundas, Windham and Spencer.

Nevertheless, Addington's government was representative of the war-weariness which had gradually pervaded the back-benches of the House of Commons. Even Nelson's naval victories over the French fleet at Aboukir Bay (the 'Battle of the Nile') in August 1798 and the Danish fleet at Copenhagen in April 1801 did little to alter the fundamental weakness of Britain's position. With the defeat of the Russians by General Soult in Switzerland in 1799, and that of the Austrians by Napoleon Bonaparte at Marengo in June 1800 and General Moreau at Hohenlinden six months later, the Second Coalition (formed in 1798) had collapsed and Britain was isolated once more.

As if this was not bad enough, the Northern League of Denmark, Sweden, Prussia and Russia then imposed an embargo on British ships, thereby preventing exports into Europe and closing off the sources of corn and wood imports. To make matters worse, the harvest of 1799 had been very bad. Moreover, between 1800 and 1801, Britain paid £23 million to the Continent to cover subsidies, garrison expenses and grain purchases. The Bank of England's gold reserves were nearly exhausted; the pound was in free fall on the foreign exchanges. Britain faced economic ruin. Under the circumstances, a cessation of hostilities was seen as essential.

The lengthy peace negotiations with France (ruled since November 1799 by First Consul Napoleon Bonaparte) were concluded in October 1801, and the actual Treaty of Amiens was signed the following March. Of its imperial conquests, Britain kept only Ceylon and Trinidad. Cochin, the Cape and the Spice Islands were returned to Holland (now the Batavian Republic); the captured Indian and African stations to France, as well as a number of Caribbean islands; Minorca to Spain; Malta to the Knights of St John; and Egypt to Turkey.

France, in return, agreed to compensate the House of Orange – exiled from Holland – and to evacuate Naples and the Papal States. While these concessions were relatively minor, Addington's government believed that its strategic interests had already been met by the terms of the Treaty of Lunéville (February 1801) between France and Austria: in return for the left bank of the Rhine, Napoleon had guaranteed the independence of the fledgling Helvetian (Swiss), Batavian (Dutch), Cisalpine and Ligurian (North Italian) Republics.

With the advent of peace, a number of notable Whigs and their ladies rushed off to Paris to meet the illustrious First Consul and examine the consequences of revolution at first hand. Among them were Mr and Mrs Charles Fox (he had secretly married Mrs Armistead, the Prince's old flame, in 1795), who arrived in the French capital in August. Fox met Bonaparte twice, and was quick to deny the First Consul's claim that Pitt and Windham had arranged to have him assassinated. Another visitor to Paris at this time was Lady Elizabeth Foster, the mistress (and future wife) of the Duke of Devonshire. She noted that the lower orders had grown impertinent, giving the example of a common postilion who dared to peer into the ladies' coach and remark, '*Diable, au moins elles sont jolies.*' 'Very good to hear,' she commented, 'but odd.'[12]

No sooner had the preliminary negotiations for peace been concluded in November than Addington set about strengthening his ministry. In the hope of gaining the support of the Carlton House group, he offered Lord Moira a seat in the Cabinet as the President of the Board of Control. Moira's 'ally', Lord Thurlow, would also enter the Cabinet – but as a minister without portfolio until such time as the Duke of Portland could be removed. There were also hints that Charles Grey and Thomas Erskine, the Prince's former Attorney-General, would be accommodated.

Nothing came of these discussions, partly because Moira would not join a Cabinet which contained the Duke of Portland, and partly because the positions offered were not prestigious enough. A number of Addington's colleagues were mightily relieved. 'I dread a connection with the Prince and his friends,' wrote Charles Yorke, the Secretary at

War. 'No man can serve *two* masters; and then there would be jobs without end.'[13]

In general, however, the Prince got on much better with Addington than he had with Pitt. He approved the terms of the peace treaty, and the M.P.s who made up the Carlton House group were largely supportive of the government. These included Thomas Tyrwhitt, the Prince's Keeper of the Privy Purse, who rose '*a propos* of nothing, to express his perfect confidence in the present Administration'.

This naturally made Addington more approachable with regard to settling the Prince's ever-increasing debts. The ingenious solution proposed by Thomas Manners-Sutton, the Prince's Solicitor-General, was to claim the revenue arrears from the Duchy of Cornwall. Edward III had first granted the Duchy to his son, the 'Black Prince', when he was eight years old. The current Prince, on the other hand, had only received the revenues since the age of 21, whereas he was entitled to them from birth. If the lawyers were right, he was owed more than £230,000.

Towards the end of January 1802, Moira spoke to the Prime Minister about the possibility of government support for the claim. The response was obviously favourable because, two weeks later, Sir John Macpherson informed Addington that what had taken place had had 'the best, the most extensive and the most seasonable political effect'. The Prince, he added, 'feels the happy reaction of his own good wishes to your Administration'. His optimism was noted by Lord Bathurst. 'The Prince,' he wrote on 4 March, 'considers the money as already voted, and was very active at Lady Holdernesse's auction, where everything went for double its reputed worth.'

However, without a sizeable personal following in the House of Commons, Addington was unable to command a majority at will over a non-party issue such as this. The debate took place on 31 March, with Addington and the Crown lawyers supporting a motion for the claim to be settled in the law courts rather than in the House. This was defeated by 160 votes to 103, with a number of independent country gentlemen and some of Canning's friends among the minority, whereas

Grey and his brother-in-law, Samuel Whitbread, voted against the Prince's claim. The King, while surprised at the size of the minority, was 'well pleased that it should not be again discussed in Parliament'.[14]

Nevertheless, a compromise was reached in early 1803. The Prince would abandon his Petition of Right to the Duchy revenue arrears in return for an increased annuity. On 16 February, a Message from the King was read out in the House of Commons, recommending the Prince's financial position to the consideration of Parliament. During the debate a week later, Addington denied that a deal had been struck. The object, he told the House, was to allow the Prince to resume his dignity as heir-apparent by reconstituting his Establishment. He had already paid off £563,000 of the £630,000 debt which he had admitted to in 1795, and the rest would be discharged by the summer of 1806. Was it reasonable to let the Prince live in 'comparative obscurity' for another four years, he asked? His proposal was to give the Prince an additional income of £60,000 for three years to enable him to pay off these outstanding debts.[15]

The House duly agreed to resolve itself into a Committee without a vote. But the issue of additional debts – debts of honour for which the Prince's conscience alone was responsible had also been raised during the debate and required elaboration (more than £170,000 was owed to the Landgrave of Cassell alone, but this figure was never publicly admitted). On 28 February, therefore, Thomas Tyrwhitt told the Commons that these unrevealed debts were so considerable that 'a large sinking fund' was required for their discharge. Until they had been paid in full, the Prince could not resume that 'state and dignity' which was 'essential to his rank and station'.

Four days later, Mr Calcraft, a 'friend' of the Prince, rose to propose a motion that the discharge of these additional debts should also be considered by Parliament. Despite Calcraft's denial that the Prince had put him up to it, the Members were justifiably suspicious and rejected the motion by 184 votes to 139.[16]

Pitt was elated. 'I quite agree with you that any further vote for the Prince ought on every account to be resisted,' he told Rose on

9 March. The proposal was 'highly indecent', founded as it was 'on an admission of debts contracted in the teeth of the last Act of Parliament [1795], and in breach of repeated and positive promises'. The very existence of such a debt could be grounds for a charge 'against the Prince's officers'. 'That Parliament should specifically recognise and pay such a debt,' he concluded, 'is monstrous.'[17]

But Parliament *was* prepared to vote for the Annuity Bill, granting him an extra £60,000 for three years. No sooner had it passed its second reading in the Lords on 14 March than Thomas Erskine, the Prince's Chancellor, rose in the Commons to express his master's satisfaction 'with what Parliament had done'. Now that Britain was once more on the brink of war with France, he added, the Prince 'could not think' of adding to the country's financial 'burdens'.[18]

Meanwhile, Napoleon Bonaparte was busy defying the spirit of the Treaty of Amiens if not its letter. In 1802, having negotiated with Spain to acquire Louisiana, the isle of Elba and the Duchy of Parma, he then accepted the presidency of the Cisalpine Republic. By the end of the year, France had annexed Piedmont and invaded the Helvetian Republic, while Spain, her client state, had confiscated the property of the Knights of St John. In response, Britain postponed the restitution of Malta and France's settlements in India.

With France openly preparing for a renewal of hostilities (the expansion of her navy from 43 ships of the line to 63 was expected to be completed in 1804), Addington got his retaliation in first by declaring war on 17 May 1803. Given the heavy cuts in military spending introduced by his administration (the regular army had been reduced to 95,000 men, and the naval strength by almost a half), he had little option but to fight a defensive conflict. Britain would control the high seas while Napoleon was dominant on the Continent. Napoleon could only gain outright victory by crossing the Channel.

As he had done three times without success in the 1790s, the Prince again put himself forward for promotion. On 18 July, he wrote the first of a series of letters to Addington, the Duke of York and the King, requesting a more responsible military appointment now that there was a very real danger of invasion. 'All I solicit,' he implored Addington, 'is a more ostensible situation than that in which I am at present placed, for situated as I am, as a mere Colonel of a Regiment, the Major General Commanding the Brigade of which such a Regiment must form a part would justly expect and receive the full credit of pre-arrangement and successful enterprize.'[19]

But the King would not budge from his earlier position. 'Though I can applaud your zeal and spirit,' he wrote to his son on 7 August, 'of which I trust no one can suppose any of my family wanting, yet considering the repeated declarations I have made of my determination on your former applications to the same purpose, I had flattered myself to have heard no further on the subject.' He continued:

> Should the implacable enemy so far succeed as to land, you will have an opportunity of showing your zeal at the head of your Regiment. It will be the duty of every man to stand forward on such an occasion, and I shall certainly think it mine to set the example in defence of everything that is dear to me and to my people.[20]

Having failed to move the King, the Prince approached his brother York, the Commander-in-Chief of the Army. 'I hope you know me too well to imagine that idle, inactive rank is in my view,' he wrote on 2 October 1803. 'But in a moment when the danger of the country is thought by Government, so urgent as to call forth the energy of every arm in its defense, I must needs feel myself degraded, both as a Prince and a soldier, if I am not allowed to take a forward and distinguished post in defense of that Empire and Crown . . . To be told I may display this zeal at the head of my Regiment is a degrading mockery.'[21]

The Duke replied on the 6th. 'I trust,' he wrote, 'that you are too well acquainted with my affection for you . . . not be assured of the satisfaction I ever have felt and ever must feel, in forwarding, when in my power, every desire or object of yours, and therefore will believe how much I regret the impossibility there is upon the present occasion of my executing your wishes.' He continued:

> In the year 1795, upon a general promotion taking place, at your instance, I delivered a letter from you to his Majesty, urging your pretensions to promotion in the Army, to which his Majesty was pleased to answer that before ever he had appointed you to the command of the 10th Light Dragoons, he had caused it to be fully explained to you what his sentiments were with respect to the Prince of Wales entering into the Army, and the public grounds upon which he never could admit of your considering it as a profession, or of your being promoted in the service, and his Majesty at the same time added his positive *commands and injunctions* to me, never to mention the subject again to him.[22]

The Prince's lengthy response of the 9th contained an unmistakable threat. 'As it is not at all improbable that every part of this transaction may be publicly canvassed hereafter,' he wrote, 'it is of the utmost importance to my honour, without which I can have no happiness, that my conduct in it shall be fairly represented and correctly understood.'

But the Duke would not be cowed. More letters passed too and fro until the Prince decided enough was enough. 'Feeling,' he wrote on 14 October, 'how useless as well as ungracious controversy is on every occasion, and knowing how fatally it operates on human friendships, I must entreat that our correspondence on *this subject* shall cease here, for nothing could be more distressing to me than to prolong a topic on which it is *now* clear to me, my dear brother, that you and I can never agree.'[23]

On 7 December, when the whole correspondence appeared in several newspapers, it was assumed that the Prince had carried out his threat. He, of course, denied responsibility, but there is no doubt that he welcomed the publicity. Back in August, shortly before the question of his military employment was raised in the Commons, he had sent Pitt an 'extraordinary communication' in an attempt to gain his support. According to George Rose, the letter stated:

> . . . that he wished Mr. Pitt to understand clearly that his Royal Highness had not the slightest disinclination towards him; that he *had* entertained thoughts, whenever power and authority should devolve upon him, of giving his confidence to Lord Moira; and that, indeed, he had at one time intended, in such an event, to call upon Mr. Fox; but he was now satisfied, from those parties themselves, that he could not do so wisely as to determine to employ him (Mr. Pitt), adding many expressions of civility.

But Pitt was too seasoned a political operator to be taken in by the Prince's insincere promise. Sending his reply through a third person, he stressed the 'due respect and proper sense of duty' he entertained for the Prince, but added that 'it would be long before he would have to decide anything on that subject'. Meanwhile the Prince 'could not do better, as far as he might think it right to interfere in political matters, than to give his support to such ministers as the King his father should give his confidence to.'[24]

Fox, on the other hand, was keen for the Prince to take a more active role in politics. In November 1803, shortly after negotiations between the Foxite Whigs, the Carlton House group and Addington had once again foundered, Fox warned Grey that 'by supporting or even sparing Addington for fear of Pitt, we are making ourselves complete Court tools or absolute cyphers'. If only the Prince would 'take a decided part against the present system, he would soon find himself at the head of a great and respectable party . . . and I think it most probable that great numbers even of Pitt's friends would (without entirely breaking with their leader) range under his standard.'[25]

Fox was particularly referring to the Grenvillites – led by Lord Grenville and his brother the Marquess of Buckingham – who, like him, were opposed to Addington's conduct of the war on the one hand, and supportive of Catholic emancipation on the other. However, the Prince's enthusiasm for the latter policy seemed to be waning. 'My opinion [concerning the expediency of introducing a Catholic Relief Bill] is as strong as yours,' Fox informed Earl Fitzwilliam on 29 November . . .

> and if I thought I had Carlton House as much with me on this point as I once thought I had, I would not wait for other opinions; but I suspect Sh[eridan] has been successful in inspiring fears there. It is not that I shall be governed by those fears, but if the Prince is either against the thing or neuter, I must have more preparatory conversations with some friends and more authority to show them than would be otherwise necessary. His name would smooth all.[26]

In the opening months of 1804, military matters were still high on the Prince's agenda. As if the denial of promotion had not been bad enough, his regiment, the 10th Light Dragoons, was then moved from the coastal area around Brighton, where the French might well land, to the Surrey town of Guildford, where he would have less opportunity to distinguish himself at the head of his troops.

The Duke of Northumberland dissuaded him from resigning his command. In a letter to Colonel McMahon, dated 6 January 1804, the Duke advised caution: 'By holding this language, and appearing easy on this subject, should the removal have been ordered to mortify the Prince it will appear as if it had failed in its effect, and his avowed reliance on [the King's] promise will force them to employ [the Prince] should any invasion take place.'

Northumberland blamed the 'ill-advised step of publishing the correspondence' for this latest humiliation. Whoever advised such a course of action 'was certainly no sincere friend of the Prince'. He added: 'I sincerely wish that idea I once suggested had been adopted by H.R.H.

instead of seeking a Commission of General, to have asked leave to place himself at the head of the armed peasantry and yeomanry of the country . . . Three or four hundred thousand British freemen voluntarily following the Standard of the Prince would have placed him in a proud situation.'[27]

For a time, the Prince let it be known that he would never forgive the Duke of York for removing his regiment from the coast, and on more than one occasion in February the Duke was refused admittance to Carlton House. But by 1 March, noted Lord Glenbervie, a reconciliation had taken place thanks to 'the good offices of Sheridan'. Lady Uxbridge, however, credited her eldest son, Lord Paget, who had been thanked 'most cordially' by both the Prince and the Duke of York.[28]

The reason may well have been the King's latest relapse. During the second week in February, when the illness was at its height, he developed a 'high . . . fever' which 'created great apprehensions for his life'. He recovered, but with 'his mind much affected' by 'great agitation and hurries'. On learning from the royal physicians that the King was suffering a recurrence of his old ailment, Addington sent for the Willises. But when they arrived at the Queen's House on Monday, 13 February, 'with the intention of being introduced into the King's apartment to attend him', they found the Dukes of Cumberland and Kent barring their way. With the Royal Dukes refusing to back down – after the last illness, they had given the King a 'solemn promise' never to allow 'anyone of the Willis family' to be 'placed about him' – Addington called in Dr Samuel Simmons, physician to St Luke's Hospital for Lunatics.[29]

In the event, Simmons's methods differed little from those of the Willises, particularly his liberal use of the strait-waistcoat. They also appeared to work. By 20 February, the King was 'recovering fast', having had 'a long interval of reason and composure' the previous day. A month later (22 March), the daily medical bulletin read: 'His Majesty is much better, and in our opinion a short time will perfect his recovery.'[30]

He soon resumed his official duties, but the illness had taken far more out of him than hitherto. 'He was apparently quite himself when talking business, and to his Ministers,' noted Lord Malmesbury. 'He then collected and recollected himself; but in his family and usual society, his manners and conversation were far from steady – fanciful, suspicious, etc.'[31]

Despite the King's recovery, Addington's government was on its last legs. With Pitt voting alongside Fox and the Grenvillites, and the Independent country gentlemen deserting Addington in droves, it was only a matter of time before the government was defeated. Its majority fell from 71 on 15 March (rejecting Pitt's motion on the Navy) to 52 on 23 April (after which vote Charles Yorke, the Home Secretary, admitted that the game was up). The final straw came on Friday 27 April when the government could manage a majority for the Irish Militia Bill of just 21. To avoid the embarrassment of outright defeat, Addington decided to resign at an emergency Cabinet meeting during the evening of Sunday the 29th.

The Prince's part in Addington's downfall was particularly significant. According to Charles Abbot, the Speaker of the House of Commons since 1802, his 'friends' had voted with the government on 15 March (Sheridan and Erskine were still hopeful of ministerial appointments). By the end of April, however, the Prince 'had at last declared openly for the Opposition'. Abbot noted in his diary on 1 May:

> I saw Mr Addington, but not alone; he mentioned that the Prince of Wales, who had it in his power a week ago to have stopped a change of Ministers if he had stood by the King, had thrown himself entirely into the Opposition; that he, Mr Addington had formerly taken, and was now relinquishing his office, upon one and the same principle, that of maintaining the King's peace of mind, and saving him from the outrage of having a Minister forced upon him rudely and violently, to the

degradation of royalty. That even now, the Ministers had proposed to resign before the last extremity, that the King might have the grace of making a new choice without absolute compulsion.'[32]

But if the Prince thought that he could strongly influence the next government, he was to be disappointed. On 7 May, the King told Pitt, his choice as the next Prime Minister, that 'he should consider it as a personal insult if Mr Fox was pressed upon him'. He 'had no objection to Mr Fox's friends having any share in the Government, but could not allow of Mr Fox holding any office which should give occasion for any personal intercourse with him.' During the subsequent meeting at Carlton House to discuss the King's response, Fox urged his followers 'to take their share in the Government, but that they had all resolved not to do so'.[33]

That evening, Lord Grenville's party met at Camelford House, his London residence, and came to the same conclusion. 'At both meetings it was unanimously agreed,' wrote George Rose, 'and positively decided, that no one of the friends of either of the parties, and at [the] Carlton House meeting that no friend of the Prince's, should on any account take any office, unless Mr. Fox should be admitted into the Cabinet directly.'[34]

An additional factor in their refusal was Pitt's determination not to revive the question of Catholic emancipation. For while his 'own conduct' on this was 'fixed', as the King knew, he foresaw that the subject could cause 'great inconvenience and embarrassment' if the country was divided by 'powerful parties'.[35]

Pitt's indignant response to Grenville's rejection was that 'he would teach that proud man that, in the service and with the confidence of the King, he could do without him; though he thought his health such that it might cost him his life.' He was right.[36]

Without the support of Fox, Grenville or the Prince, Pitt had no option but to include a number of Addington's followers in his new Cabinet. The active opposition of the Prince, however, made the new government particularly vulnerable. Rose, now Vice-President of the Board of Trade, wrote:

> The part the Prince of Wales so decidedly takes in the matter, renders the forming of an Administration with little more than some of the late Ministers (whom we have been holding up to ridicule for a long time) a desperate undertaking, not only on account of the number of H.R.H.'s friends in either House, but that a regular standard being set up at Carlton House will have the effect of a rallying place for all discontented men to go to, and it will become a rival Court to that at St. James's. In the event of the King's death or permanent disability, the Government will certainly be put into Mr. Fox's hands, and the recent transaction and intercourse with him will have a considerable effect in lessening the prejudices in the public mind against him.[37]

The influence of the Prince of Wales in Parliament at this time was known as the 'reversionary interest' of the Crown. According to the noted historian Arthur Aspinall, it was natural for 'Hanoverian heirs-apparent' to quarrel 'with their fathers or grandfathers – partly owing to political frustration in an age of monarchical government, partly owing to squabbles over income, and in this case owing to personal friendship between the Prince and Charles Fox. Carlton House therefore became a focal point for the discontented – men who, baulked of employment or income under the Crown, sought either the prospect of office or of pension in the next reign, or the immediate enjoyment of the patronage of the prince's Household.'[38]

While Pitt was planning his ministry in May 1804, his party managers, George Rose and Charles Long, calculated his potential opponents in the House of Commons at about 240. Of these, the Prince's supporters numbered 41 (29 English M.P.s and 12 Irish, not to mention 31 peers), Fox's 79, Grenville's 23, Addington's 68 ('including persons who would oppose from former disappointment'), and 29 of 'doubtful' allegiance. They were 'uncertain' of a further 70 Irish Members and 'many English ones'. If 30 of these were added ('a sanguine estimate'), there would be a grand total of 270 Members opposed to a 'narrow' Ministry at the start.'[39]

As this figure was only 60 short of an outright majority (the total number of M.P.s having risen to 658 with the Act of Union), Pitt's government was extremely vulnerable. It ultimately survived because it retained the support of the Independent country gentlemen and at least some of Addington's former supporters. But for a time it seemed as if an alliance with the Prince was the only way to ensure its continued existence. On 11 November 1804, Henry Dundas (now Lord Melville), the First Lord of the Admiralty, wrote to Pitt:

> . . . In former times, ten or a dozen years ago, the King and the Prince being at variance together, was comparatively of little moment, but the case is now totally changed, and no practicable means ought to be omitted to put the royal family in a state of decorous behaviour to each other . . . Unless a large and powerful party of great property and talents acting under the heir apparent as their head, can be dissolved, it is in vain to look for a strong Government in any beneficial sense of the expression. There is more than one way in which you can with ease make room for Lord Moira in the Cabinet . . . If Lord Moira was speedily placed there, and known to be so with the concurrence of the Prince, the cabal is at an end; and you might at will pick up from the different ingredients in Opposition any parts you pleased.[40]

Pitt was in total agreement. Earlier in the year, he and Moira had encouraged a reconciliation between the Prince and his father, but the meeting set for 22 August had been called off by the Prince at the last moment for two reasons. Firstly, despite Pitt's assurances, the King had shown not the slightest inclination to gratify his demand for military promotion. Secondly, with the Prince having accepted his father's offer to supervise the education of the eight-year-old Princess Charlotte, the King had gone back on his agreement that the Princess of Wales would not be involved. The Prince had it on good authority that the King had had a long conversation with Princess Caroline on 22 August, conferring on her the Rangership of Greenwich Park and assuring her that she was to be consulted in the arrangement of her daughter's establishment. In other words, that the King was proposing to surrender part of what was to have been his 'exclusive' control over Princess Charlotte's education.[41]

Thanks to the tireless efforts of Pitt and Eldon on the one hand, and Moira and Tierney on the other, the cancelled meeting between the King and his son eventually took place on 12 November. It was a frosty occasion, with the King reluctant to extend his hand for the Prince to kiss. The King did most of the talking, gradually working himself up into a paroxysm of rage more violent than any the Prince had previously witnessed. The subject was presumably Princess Charlotte's education, and the fact that the Prince was now steadfastly refusing to cede control to his father.'[42]

Soon after this 'reconciliation', Pitt took Melville's advice by offering Moira a Cabinet post – either Foreign Secretary or Lord Lieutenant of Ireland – with Tierney as the Chief Secretary of Ireland. Mindful of the Prince, Moira insisted that Fox and his friends would have to be included in any arrangement. This was clearly impossible, and the initiative foundered.

'We can do without them,' noted George Canning, the Treasurer of the Navy. He was confident that Pitt could rely on 370 votes in the House of Commons (a number that included the 'King's Friends' and the Independents who thought it their duty to support the King's ministers), while the Foxites and Grenvilles had only 140 votes between them, the Carlton House group just 20, and Addington about 40. The remaining M.P.s were all 'doubtfuls'.[43]

Even so, Pitt was keen to increase his strength in the House and in January he successfully concluded negotiations with Addington, who accepted a peerage (Viscount Sidmouth) and entered the Cabinet as

Lord President of the Council. In addition, Lord Buckinghamshire became Chancellor of the Duchy of Lancashire (with a place in the Cabinet) and four of Addington's closest supporters – brother Hiley, brother-in-law Bragge-Bathurst, Nicholas Vansittart and Nathaniel Bond – were promised junior ministerial appointments in the near future.

In the event, only Vansittart joined the government (as Chief Secretary to Ireland in March 1805). Before the others could be found places, the Pittites fell out with Sidmouth's party over the poor state of the Royal Navy. The Pittites blamed the economies of the previous First Lord of the Admiralty, Earl St Vincent. But when the Committee of Naval Inquiry, set up while Addington was still Prime Minister, reported in February 1805, it made serious allegations against Lord Melville (who had replaced St Vincent) in his former capacity as Treasurer of the Navy.

On 8 April 1805, a censure debate took place in the House of Commons. The charge was not that of negligence, of which Melville was indeed guilty, but malversation (or corruption in a public office), of which he was not. The subsequent motion for impeachment – proposed by Samuel Whitbread, a radical Whig – received 216 votes for and 216 against, with Speaker Abbot giving his casting vote for the motion. So overwhelmed was Pitt by the ruin of his closest political colleague that tears ran down his cheeks. The Prince, who was present during the debate, could not have been more delighted.

He had not been so pleased, however, when Fox and Grenville reintroduced the issue of Catholic emancipation by presenting a petition from the Irish Catholics to the two Houses in the spring of 1805. 'My conviction,' Thomas Grenville told his elder brother, 'is that in persisting you will make the future possessor of the Crown as adverse to it as the present.' He had a point. The closer the Prince came to superseding his ailing 66-year-old father, the further he distanced himself from a measure that was bound to affect his constitutional position. According to the Duke of Northumberland, he was very irritated by Fox and Grenville's initiative, and even considered calling a meeting of the Opposition to ascertain individual opinions. By 9 May, Dr Beche told Speaker Colchester, 'the Duke of Northumberland, Sheridan, Tierney, and several leading persons of the Opposition have declared their decided disapprobation of the Roman Catholic claims.'[44]

Using Sheridan as a go-between, the Prince confined his entreaties to the two Opposition leaders. He had 'so far prevailed with Mr Fox', he told Speaker Abbot on 8 May, 'as not to think of bringing forward the whole claim, but to soften it down to a question for a Committee'. His efforts with Lord Grenville 'had not succeeded quite so easily'. But even this moderated motion – for a review in committee – proved too much for most Members of Parliament, and it was easily defeated in both the Commons and the Lords by 212 and 129 votes respectively.[45]

Meanwhile, the crisis within the government came to a head in early July when Sidmouth's friends voted against the government in favour of a prosecution of Lord Melville rather than an impeachment. Though the motion failed, an irate Pitt took revenge by refusing to implement his promise to find offices for Hiley Addington and Bond, whereupon Sidmouth and Buckinghamshire resigned and the party went into Opposition. But the defection did little immediate harm to Pitt's government because the parliamentary session was due to end on 12 July anyway. As Fox observed, Sidmouth – 'a great fool and one whom experience cannot make wise' – had chosen the worst possible time to leave government because it gave Pitt ample time to renegotiate new allies.[46]

However, his attempt to broaden the base of his administration by offering seats in the Cabinet to the leaders of all the main Opposition parties – including Fox, Grenville, Spencer, Moira, Fitzwilliam, Grey and Windham – foundered on the rock of royal disapproval. There was no need for additional strength, the King told Pitt in August 1805; the government could manage perfectly well. He had, in any case, no confidence in *any* of the Opposition. Furthermore, the fact that the international situation was beginning to improve would make the government's life easier.

Despite his disappointment, Pitt could take solace from the recent turn of events on the Continent. When Napoleon (Emperor of France since May 1804) had himself crowned King of Italy in May 1805, it was the final insult for Austria. She could accept the loss of her influence in Germany or Italy, but not both at the same time. In the interests of self-preservation, therefore, she joined Britain and Russia in the Third Coalition on 9 August. Napoleon responded by telling Talleyrand that he was giving up the invasion of Britain so that he could march against Austria. By the beginning of September, the camps at Boulogne – which until recently had housed 90,000 men earmarked to invade Britain – were deserted.

In Italy, the British and Russians landed in Naples while further north the Austrian Archduke, Charles, assisted by an Italian uprising, forced the French back on the Adige. But General Mack, commanding an Austrian army at Ulm in southern Germany, was not so fortunate. The speed of Napoleon's march through the rain and snow caught him by surprise. By 7 October, 100,000 French troops were astride his line of communication to Vienna. Repeated attempts to break out were thwarted, and on 20 October he surrendered.

Meanwhile the naval war, which had been initiated by Napoleon in an attempt to gain mastery of the sea so that he could invade Britain, was approaching a dramatic conclusion. At the turn of the year, the French had 20 sail-of-the-line in Toulon and five in Rochefort, plus 15 Spanish ships. If these forces could be united, they would present a very real threat to British naval supremacy. In late March 1805, Admiral Villeneuve sailed out of Toulon with 20 French sail-of-the-line and evaded the blockade of British ships. Admiral Lord Nelson, the naval commander in the Mediterranean, gambled that Villeneuve was bound for Jamaica and set off in pursuit. 'If they are not gone to the West Indies,' declared the optically challenged, one-armed admiral (he had lost the sight of his right eye during the siege of Calvi in 1794 and his right limb at Tenerife three years later), 'I shall be blamed: to be burnt in effigy, or Westminster Abbey is my alternative.'

Fortunately, Nelson's gamble paid off and the Channel was not left virtually defenceless. Once Villeneuve learnt that Nelson was on his heels (he took 34 days to cross the Atlantic, to Nelson's 24), he ignored his instructions to wait long enough for all French naval forces to join him, and set sail for Europe. Nelson followed. 'We are all half-starved,' wrote one of his captains, 'and otherwise inconvenienced by being so long away from a port, but our full recompense is that we are with Nelson.'[47]

Once back off the coast of Europe, Nelson again had to guess Villeneuve's destination. He chose the Mediterranean – but this time was wrong. Villeneuve was making for Brest, and it was left to Vice-Admiral Sir Robert Calder to intercept him off Cape Finisterre with an inferior force of 15 ships. During the indecisive action, Villeneuve lost two of his Spanish ships, but fog hampered the pursuit and he was able to retreat to Ferrol. For failing to press home the attack, Calder was relieved of his command and later court-martialled. Though the charge was 'fully proved', he was acquitted of cowardice but severely reprimanded for his error of judgement. 'A most absurd sentence,' commented Speaker Abbot.'[48]

After a brief period of leave – the first time that he had set foot on land for more than two years – Nelson returned to active service in September. He had been given the additional command of Calder's Atlantic fleet and instructions to destroy the main French fleet (now at Cadiz) by any means at his disposal. On 20 October, Villeneuve at last sailed out of Cadiz with a combined French-Spanish force of 33 ships-of-the-line. Next day, Nelson's fleet of 27 ships-of-the-line gave battle off Cape Trafalgar. Advancing in two divisions, Nelson split Villeneuve's crescent-shaped line so that ten of his ships took no real part in the action. Superior British seamanship and gunnery then accounted for the rest. Eighteen of Villeneuve's ships were captured or destroyed, including his flagship *Bucentaure*; none of the remainder ever fought again. French and Spanish casualties were 5,860 killed and wounded, and a further 20,000 taken prisoner. The British losses were just 1,690 – but they included Lord Nelson.

He had been shot by a sniper from the mizzen mast of the French ship *Redoubtable* as he strode across the quarterdeck of his flagship, HMS *Victory,* wearing his four distinctive orders of knighthood. Earlier in the day, Captain Hardy had warned him that the decorations would identify him to enemy sharpshooters. It was too late 'to be shifting a coat' now, replied Nelson. In any case, they were 'military orders and he did not fear to show them to the enemy'.

As Nelson lay dying below deck in the surgeon's quarters, Hardy reported 'a brilliant victory', adding that at least 14 enemy ships had been taken. 'That is well,' responded Nelson, 'but I bargained for twenty.'

His last words were, 'Thank God I have done my duty.' At 4.30 in the afternoon, three hours after receiving the fatal wound, he died.[49]

The news of Nelson's death in victory reached London two weeks later, on 5 November. 'It is an event of wonderful importance,' wrote Lord Moira to Colonel McMahon two days later. 'I wish I could feel it as warmly as I ought: but I really shrink from exultation when I reflect how poor Nelson has been cut off from the enjoyment of a fame he so nobly merited.'[50]

According to Mrs Fitzherbert, the Prince was 'affected most extremely' by Nelson's death. They had never been intimate – the Prince had first provoked Nelson's wrath by ogling his mistress, Lady Hamilton, at a grand dinner given in 1800 to celebrate the Admiral's victory at Aboukir Bay – but he appreciated Nelson's talents and the security his successes had given the country. Towards the end of Nelson's last leave, the Prince had accorded him the honour of cutting short his visit to Weymouth to bid him farewell.[51]

He might have been less attentive had he been aware of Nelson's true feelings for him. On 19 February 1801, for example, while at sea, Nelson had written to Lady Hamilton:

> I feel very much for the unpleasant situation the Prince or rather Sir William [her husband] has unknowingly placed you, for if he knew as much of the P.['s] character as the world does he would rather let the lowest wretch that walks the street dine

at his table than that unprincipalled Lyar. I have heard it reported that he has said he would make you his mistress. Sir William never can admit him into his house nor can any friend advise him to it unless they are determined on your hitherto unimpeached character being ruined. No modest woman would suffer it. He is permitted to visit only people of *notorious ill fame*. For heaven's sake let Sir William pause before he damns your good name.[52]

While the Prince would have deplored the less than complimentary remarks about him, he would surely have been amused by Nelson's reference to Lady Hamilton's 'unimpeached character'. The daughter of a Cheshire blacksmith, she had worked for a time as a household servant before becoming, at the age of 16, the mistress of Sir Harry Fetherstonhaugh. Further affairs with Captain Jack Payne (the Prince's intimate friend) and Charles Greville followed, before she was passed on to Greville's uncle, Sir William Hamilton, whom she eventually married. She first met Nelson in 1793, during her husband's tenure as Envoy to the Kingdom of Naples, and the two became lovers five years later (a daughter, Horatia, was born in 1801). The Hamiltons returned to England in late 1800, and until Sir William's death three years later they all lived together in a bizarre *ménage à trois*.

Now that Nelson was dead, Lady Hamilton was in a difficult financial position. Lady Nelson, the hero's estranged wife, was granted a pension of £2,000 a year, but nothing was done for his mistress. So on 17 December 1805, Nelson's close friend, Alexander Davison, wrote to the Prince, enclosing a copy of Nelson's 'last requests to his King and country in favour of Lady Hamilton', written just hours before the Battle of Trafalgar. Listing the services that she had rendered her country while resident in Naples ('the British Fleet under my command could never have returned the second time to Egypt [to destroy the French fleet at Aboukir Bay] had not Lady Hamilton's influence with the Queen of Naples caused letters to be wrote to the Governor of Syracuse'), Nelson concluded:

Could I have rewarded these services I would not now call upon my country, but as that has not been in my power I leave Emma, Lady Hamilton, therefore, a legacy to my King and country, that they will give her an ample provision to maintain her rank in life.[53]

If it were left to him, the Prince replied, 'there would not be a wish or desire of our ever to be lamented Hero' that he would not consider as 'a solemn obligation upon his friends and Country to fulfill.' But all he could do was pass the letter on to the King's ministers. Well aware that Lady Hamilton had already been amply provided for by her husband, and that Nelson's account of her services was grossly exaggerated, they took no further action. An extravagant woman, she soon ran through her money and died insolvent in Calais ten years later.[54]

Nelson's State Funeral took place in St Paul's Cathedral on 9 January 1806. The Prince had promised Earl Nelson, the deceased's elder brother, that he would attend as chief mourner; but in the event, Admiral of the Fleet Sir Peter Parker filled that honoured role. The Prince had bowed to his father's instructions not to break with family tradition, and he and his brothers attended the funeral in a private capacity only.[55]

Two weeks later, the country was forced to mourn an even greater loss. Already weak from overwork and worry, Pitt's frail constitution had been dealt an additional blow by the news that Napoleon had destroyed an Austro-Russian army at Austerlitz on 2 December 1805, resulting in the collapse of the Third Coalition. On 23 January 1806, at the age of 46, he died.

'Twenty-three years Minister of the country,' noted Charles Abbot in his diary, 'founder of the only effectual sinking fund for the reduction of the debt; deliverer of this country from the horrors of the French Revolution and accomplisher of the Union with Ireland. His transcendant eloquence and talents gave him a complete and easy victory over all his rivals in Parliament, and a popularity throughout the nation which he never condescended to solicit.' As a 'War Minister', however, he had been 'less successful'.[56]

Pitt's death marked the end of his Tory administration. Convinced that they would not be able to command a parliamentary majority without him, his Cabinet colleagues resigned. As in 1783, the King was forced to choose a Prime Minister from the ranks of the Opposition, a course all the more humiliating because the Prince, his disloyal son, was their nominal leader. He approached Lord Grenville – the least objectionable because he had served with Pitt – who accepted on the condition that Lord Chancellor Eldon would be replaced and Fox brought in. 'I know all that,' the King replied, 'have your arrangements ready by Wednesday, and I will come to town for it, reserving to myself the approbation or rejection.'[57]

On 31 January, after consultations with the Prince, Fox and Sidmouth, Grenville gave the King a list of eleven prepared Cabinet ministers. All were eventually approved, including Fox as Foreign Minister, Sidmouth as Lord Privy Seal, Moira as Master-General of the Ordnance and Erskine as Lord Chancellor, although some minor posts were vetoed. This gave the Foxites four Cabinet ministers (Fox, Grey, Fitzwilliam and Lord Henry Petty), the Grenvillites three (Grenville, Spencer and Windham), the Sidmouth party two (Sidmouth and Ellenborough) and the Carlton House group two (Moira and Erskine). Thanks to its combination of ability and experience, the new government was known as the 'Ministry of All the Talents'.

Though only two of the Prince's 'friends' were in the Cabinet, his overall influence was enormous. The disgraced Lord Melville (who would ultimately be acquitted of the charge of embezzlement) even went so far as to declare that the power of the Crown had been in effect transferred to the Prince, who was 'looked up to as the fountain of office, honour and emoluments'. He continued:

> The circumstances in confirmation of the truth of this are innumerable, and universally felt, and it is scarcely necessary in illustration of it, to do more than refer to all the recent creations of Scotch noblemen to the rank of British Peers, and promises of a similar nature made to others . . . If there is any prerogative

of the Crown to which the Constitution teaches us to look up to the King as the fountain of honour, it is the gift of a hereditary title, and yet there is not a person from the one end of the island to the other who does not feel and know that these recent creations, in place of flowing from the favour and munificence of the Crown, have been extorted from him by that usurped authority by which he has been subdued and virtually dethroned.[58]

9

The Delicate
Investigation

The advent of the Fox-Grenville government presented the Prince with the opportunity to settle a few scores; not least with his estranged wife, Princess Caroline, whose behaviour in recent years had become increasingly scandalous.

In 1799, by then living almost exclusively at Montague House in Blackheath, she had spent much time flirting with her father-in-law's ministers, including William Pitt himself, William Windham (Secretary at War), Henry Dundas (Treasurer of the Navy) and Charles Long (a Secretary to the Treasury). While she was not averse to irritating her husband, these senior Tories were keen to cultivate a woman who could conceivably become, in the event of her husband's untimely death, Regent for her daughter Charlotte.

Caroline's particular favourite was George Canning, 29, the talented member of the Board of Control who would one day become Prime Minister. Having met Caroline for the first time in June, he became a regular visitor to Blackheath during the summer of 1799. In August, he wrote to his friend Lord Granville Leveson-Gower, informing him that he had just arrived back from visiting an unnamed lady. 'The keeper [of the Privy Purse, Miss Hayman] left us for a few minutes and the thing is too clear to be doubted. What am I to do? I am perfectly bewildered.'[1]

He wrote again a few weeks later, referring to 'those which I know-not-what feelings – vanity, perhaps, and romance, and a certain sort of lively and grateful interest (but not love)'. Had he not just met Miss Joan Scott (the heiress whom he would marry the following year), he added, 'I know not how I should have resisted, as I ought to do, the abundant and overpowering temptation to the indulgence of passion . . . which must have been dangerous, perhaps ruinous, to her who was the cause of it, and myself.'

In a subsequent letter, however, he admitted that 'the day of the last dinner was not quite so blameless as I promised you it should be.' Also, Canning later told the Duke of Wellington that the Princess had shown him her husband's letter of 30 April 1796, in which he had agreed not to resume 'a connexion of a more particular nature'. Asked how she should interpret the letter, Canning replied that it gave 'her permission to do as they liked, and they took advantage of it on the spot'.[2]

The following February, having discovered that Mrs Crewe had informed the Princess about his passion for Miss Scott, Canning decided to come clean. His explanation, he told friends, 'was received – it is impossible to say *how* kindly! Never, never shall I forget or cease to be grateful for the generous, amiable, disinterested affection, which was shown on that occasion.' The true nature of the Princess's relationship with Canning is difficult to assess. Her most recent biographer thinks that they probably only 'indulged in the prophylactic sport of heavy petting'. But when one takes into account the Princess's hearty sexual appetite – a fact amply borne out by future events – this account is hard to accept; particularly as Canning felt honour bound to offer his resignation from the Cabinet when, years later, the then George IV persuaded his government to prosecute Caroline for adultery.[3]

The Princess's willingness to forgive Canning's inconstancy was typical. She was not one to bear a grudge (except against her husband), and even became godmother to Canning's eldest son. In any case, there were plenty of other young men to occupy her – like Thomas

Lawrence, the portrait painter. Commissioned to paint Caroline and her daughter in the winter of 1800, Lawrence spent several nights at Montague House so as not to waste time when Charlotte arrived in the morning from Shrewsbury House on Shooter's Hill (where she had been living with her governess, Lady Elgin, since autumn the previous year). Five years later, the Princess was accused of having slept with Lawrence by William Cole, a former Page of the Backstairs, whom she had dismissed in 1802.

Next up (so to speak), during the winter of 1801–2, was the 37-year-old Rear-Admiral Sir Sidney Smith, whose gallant defence of Acre three years earlier had thwarted Napoleon's advance through Syria. He was then living in the Blackheath house of Sir John Douglas, a Royal Marine officer knighted for his service at Acre, and his wife, Lady Douglas. As convivial neighbours of the Princess, all three were constant visitors to Montague House. 'She is at present entirely wrapped up in Sir Sidney Smith,' wrote Lord Minto in March 1802, 'who is just the sort of thing that suits her . . . Lady Douglas is now the prima female favourite, and lives entirely with the Princess . . . [She] is a handsome showy woman and seems clever.'[4]

In the autumn of 1802, the gossipmongers were aroused by the mysterious arrival of a three-month-old baby at Montague House. It was later explained that the Princess's maternal feelings were far from satisfied by her weekly visits to and from her daughter, and that she had asked her servants to look out for a baby she could adopt. As luck would have it, a woman by the name of Sophia Austin appeared at Montague House in late October with her recently born son, Willy. She had come to ask the Princess to help her husband, Samuel, who had been dismissed from Deptford Dockyard following the Treaty of Amiens. Stikeman, the page who interviewed her, offered Samuel work at his wife's laundry in Pimlico, and added that the Princess might adopt the child if the mother could bear to part with it. Having returned on 5 November so that the Princess could meet the child, Mrs Austin was told to bring him back and leave him once he had been weaned. This she did ten days later.[5]

But no sooner had the Princess set up young Willy's nursery in her house (with Mrs Gosden, her gardener's wife, as nurse) than Captain Thomas Manby, a handsome young naval officer, arrived in Greenwich to distract her. A Norfolk acquaintance of Lady Townsend, her Mistress of the Robes, Manby was killing time while his frigate, H.M.S. *Africaine*, was fitted out at Deptford. With the Douglases away in Plymouth that Christmas, the Princess welcomed him with (literally) open arms.

During one dinner, so Lady Douglas later told the Prince, Sir Sidney Smith 'observed [the Princess] seek Captain Manby's foot under the table, and, when she had succeeded, put her foot upon Captain Manby's and sat in that manner the whole evening, dealing out *equal attention and politeness above board to them both*; at length she got up and went out of the door, looking at Captain Manby who followed.' They kissed behind the door. 'Sir Sidney saw it and went home immediately.'[6]

Never to return, apparently, having been superseded by Manby. A similar anecdote was told by Lord Glenbervie:

I can never forget my astonishment when on going to dine at Blackheath, some time before the delicate investigation, I found Captain Manby there . . . He certainly was not, from his situation, birth, or manners, a person one could expect to meet in the society of the Princess of Wales. We were only five: her Royal Highness, Lady Glenbervie, Miss Vernon, myself and this captain. She placed him next to her at table, and directed all her *looks*, *words*, and *attentions* to him, at and after dinner, when we went to coffee and when she made him sit very close to her on the same sofa. After a time he withdrew, and the moment he shut the door she started up and said in her broken English, '*Child cry*,' and then hurried into the adjoining room which has a communication with her garden and park. She was absent from us perhaps three quarters of an hour, and to do her justice returned with an air and look of confusion. In about ten minutes we took our leave, having to return to town that night.[7]

Lady Hester Stanhope, one of the Princess's ladies-in-waiting, was horrified by her mistress's loose behaviour. 'How the sea-captains used to colour up when she danced about, exposing herself like an opera girl,' Stanhope recalled. 'I plainly told her it was a hanging matter, that she should mind what she was about.' But sea-captains were not the Princess's only prey. 'There was a handsome footman,' she added, 'who might have been brought into the scrape.'[8]

His frigate refitted, Manby set sail in the spring of 1803, taking two of the Princess's charity boys with him as midshipmen. She in turn had paid for his cabin to be fitted out and had given him a number of gifts, including one of £300. That summer, as Manby was stationed in Dover Roads (the stretch of water just off Dover) she took a house in Ramsgate. Her frequent visits to the ship, wrote one of Manby's officers, 'gave rise to many sayings'.[9]

About this time, according to Lord Glenbervie (who heard the story from Lady Carysfort), the Princess entrusted a packet of letters 'to Admiral Nugent to be delivered to Captain Manby'. Glenbervie wrote:

Admiral Nugent is a very absent man, and left the packet in a hackney-coach, but on missing it advertised the loss and offered a considerable reward for it. The hackney coachman, who had found the packet, upon seeing the advertisement and offer, conceived it must be of importance, opened the letters and found that in them was mention of a *child* of the correspondents. Information of this reached the Prince of Wales, who sent to offer the coachman £1,500 if he would deliver them up to him. The man said he must have £2,000. The Prince's messenger had not authority to go so far, but said he would go to the Prince and would acquaint the coachman next day whether he would give that sum. The Princess in the meantime heard of the business, sent the £2,000 that very evening, and had the whole packet delivered up to her. The man, however, had had copies taken and sold these copies to the Prince, who is now possessed of them.[10]

If true, it is surprising that the Prince never tried to use such explosive material to his advantage. Perhaps he felt that his own indiscretions – issue from a secret marriage to a Roman Catholic widow – were of so serious a nature that it would not do to provoke a woman of uncertain temper who almost certainly knew about them. Years later, Princess Charlotte was in no doubt that her mother and Captain Manby were Willy Austin's parents. '*I am sure of it*,' she told her aunt, Princess Mary.[11]

Towards the end of 1804, rumours about Caroline's unseemly behaviour were rife. 'The Princess of Wales gives great uneasiness by her unguarded conduct,' noted Speaker Abbot. The Prince himself told Lady Bessborough that he knew 'strong facts' against his wife about which he had thus far kept silent. Her advice was for him 'either not to listen to any report at all . . . or at once to accuse her'.[12]

There was more. During the autumn of 1804, having returned to London in August, Sir John and Lady Douglas received three anonymous letters – one with the Princess's seal, they claimed, and all in her handwriting. Two contained obscene sketches entitled 'Sir Sidney Smith, Lady Douglas in an Amorous Sitiation' and 'Sir Sidney Smith doing Lady Douglas your amiable wife'. Douglas went at once to confront Smith, and was assured by his friend that 'the whole was the most audacious and wicked calumny'. Smith added: 'I never said a word to your wife, but what you might have heard; and had I been so base as to attempt anything of the kind under your roof, I should deserve you to shoot me like a mad dog.'[13]

All three then decided to confront the Princess, but their request for an audience was refused. Shortly after, a further anonymous letter was sent to Smith, saying that the author 'wished for no *civil dissensions*, and that there seldom was a difference where, if the parties wished it, they could not arrange matters'. This was undoubtedly from the Princess, and as good as an admission that she had written the previous letters.

One theory is that, having fallen out with Smith and the Douglases, she was attempting to discredit them before they had a chance to do the same to her. The Douglases' knowledge of her affairs with Smith and Manby was particularly dangerous now that the Duke of Sussex – to whom Douglas was a groom of the bedchamber – had returned to Britain and was a regular guest at Carlton House. The motive attributed to her by the Douglases, on the other hand, was the need to keep the existence of her child, Willy Austin, a secret.[14]

A month or two later, Captain Manby received two anonymous letters. The first offered him a large reward for revealing the 'intimacy' of his relationship with the Princess, adding that it could 'be easily proved'. The second repeated the 'offer of a fortune to any amount', and expressed surprise that he had not responded. They had almost certainly been sent from Carlton House at the behest of the Prince.[15]

For a time, he was distracted by the issue of Princess Charlotte's education. After protracted negotiations, he reached a compromise with the King in January 1805: during the time that the Prince was 'usually resident in London' (the summer Season), Charlotte would stay at Warwick House, adjoining Carlton House; for the rest of the year she would live with the King and Queen at Windsor. Her mother would have 'occasional access' to her there, and the right 'to send for her at any time on a visit'.[16]

As part of this settlement, Charlotte's household was reorganised. The Dowager Lady de Clifford, a woman of 'excellent sense and correct conduct', replaced Lady Elgin as governess, while Mrs Alicia Campbell became the sub-governess. Dr John Fisher, the Bishop of Exeter, was appointed to superintend her education, with the Reverend George Nott as sub-preceptor. On relinquishing her position, Lady Elgin declared that she handed over Charlotte to Lady de Clifford and the Bishop 'free from all fault whatever, both in character and disposition; that her mind was pure and innocent, and that her progress in learning had been uncommonly great.'[17]

An attempt to excuse herself in advance for any defects in Charlotte's training which might later be revealed, Lady Elgin's comments could not have been further from the truth. By March 1805, the King was lamenting his grand-daughter's lack of learning. Dr Nott would complain repeatedly about her unwillingness to concentrate, and her tendency to send him written apologies for her failure to prepare her lessons. She hated Latin, she told him when she was ten, and was afraid to write to him in that language because she would make so many errors. Her written English was not much better. One composition – written on 2 May 1805 – contained more than 50 spelling mistakes and several unreadable passages. They were gaffes, he told her, which 'a common servant would have blushed to have committed'. He continued:

> Where, may I ask your Royal Highness, is this to end, or when are we to have the satisfaction of seeing your mind animated with a becoming pride and a generous resolution to improve? More than three months have passed, during which the most unremitting exertions have been employed by those about you, and what is the progress you have made? Let the enclosed paper speak. I shall only add that ignorance is disgraceful in proportion to the rank of the person in whom it is found, and that negligence, when the means of improvement are in our power, is criminal in the sight of the Almighty.

In addition, Charlotte was prone to displays of temper and irritability; but her worst trait, according to Nott, was a 'want of truth and honesty'. On one occasion, her misrepresentations cast a slur on the character of a lady of rank. When questioned by Bishop Fisher, she persisted in her lying statements. Only when Dr Nott spoke to her did she admit her mendacity.[18]

Disappointed by Charlotte's academic progress, the King gained some consolation from the apparent closeness of her relationship with her mother. Caroline frequently visited her at Windsor, much to the King's delight. 'It is quite charming to see the Princess and her child together,' he wrote on 25 February.[19]

That autumn, Lord Minto dined with Caroline at Montague House. 'The King is as fond of her as ever,' he noted, 'and has at last given her the Rangership of Greenwich Park, which I am very glad of. They used to be very shabby and blackguard in refusing her half roods of green under her windows; now the whole is at her disposal.'[20]

One of the Princess's first acts as Ranger was to lease the official house in Greenwich Park to the newly founded Royal Naval School in an effort to relieve her debts. A number of other houses and lodges in the park were also at her disposal, and these she earmarked for various members of her Household and officials of the school. Among the tenants who received notices to quit were Sir John and Lady Douglas. The latter's response was devastating. According to Lady Bessborough, who heard the story from the Prince himself, she sent the Duke of Sussex a deposition 'not only as to the Princess of Wales' general conduct, but her having had a child'. The Duke then informed the Prince, who said that he had heard a similar rumour a year earlier, but 'had forborne taking any notice of it from wishing the subject to be dropped'. His brother replied: 'You may do as you please for yourself, though it is a little hard upon your Daughter; but at any rate we cannot be so passive and run the chance of being cut out by a stranger.'[21]

Only after much persuasion, so the Prince told Lady Bessborough, did he agree to hear Lady Douglas's charge. During the subsequent interview, which took place at Colonel McMahon's house in Charles Street, Mayfair, on 5 November, Lady Douglas repeated her claim that Willy Austin was Princess Caroline's child. In addition, she said that the Princess was prepared to pass the child off as the Prince's because she had slept two nights at Carlton House around the date of conception.

Lady Douglas's allegations could hardly have been more serious: in addition to committing adultery – a crime theoretically punishable by death – the Princess was also accused of plotting to supersede the succession of her own daughter. While the first claim was almost certainly true, the second was ludicrous. The Princess may well have said as much in jest, but she would never have deprived her own daughter of the throne. In any case, there was no need; she had already provided an adequate explanation for Willy Austin's presence.

The Prince's version of events is that he wanted to have 'nothing to do with' the accusation, 'but if his Brothers wished it to be further examined' he would 'leave it to them'. His actions, however, do not bear this statement out. He at once consulted Samuel Romilly, the Whig lawyer, who agreed to look into the matter. In December, the Douglases agreed to put their claims down in writing. Presumably at the request of the Prince, Romilly showed the document to both Lord Thurlow, the former Chancellor, and Thomas Erskine, the Prince's Chancellor. Neither had much faith in the accusations, though Thurlow did put Romilly in touch with Thomas Lowten, a discreet solicitor, who was happy to make further inquiries. Over the next few months, Lowten spoke to a number of people who had been in the service of both the Princess and the Douglases.

Following the death of Pitt and the formation of the Ministry of All the Talents in early 1806 – which included the appointment of Romilly as Solicitor-General – the Prince would have us believe that he 'was particularly anxious not to commence their administration with so unpopular a measure' as the prosecution of the Princess. Lord Erskine, the newly ennobled Lord Chancellor, later confirmed the Prince's unwillingness to proceed in a letter to the King of 25 March 1807. The Prince, he wrote, 'took no steps whatever to make it the subject of public investigation; but manifested on the contrary the greatest desire to avoid it if possible.'[22]

This was simply not true. While secretly pursuing the investigation of the Princess in the hope that it might result, at the very least, in the dissolution of their marriage, he was publicly declaring his impartiality so that natural justice could take its course. To be seen to be interfering would be unpopular with the King and might even provoke the Princess to retaliate. It was an early nineteenth-century version of public relations, with Moira and McMahon playing the role of spin-doctors.

As a result, the Prince simply had to sit back and wait for indignant third parties to force the issue. 'Sir,' replied Lord Thurlow when he was consulted by the Prince, 'if you were a common man, she might sleep with the D—l; I should say, let her alone and hold your tongue. But the Prince of Wales has no right to risk his daughter's crown and his brothers' claims. The Princess of Wales should be like Caesar's wife, not even suspected. For both your sakes the accusation once made must be examined into, but leave it to your Brothers.'[23]

So the Prince 'gave carte blanche', wrote Lady Bessborough, 'and desired to hear no more about it'. (Until, that is, there was something worth hearing.) In the meantime, he had to suffer the shock of losing one of his closest friends when on 30 March 1806 the Duchess of Devonshire died of cirrhosis of the liver after years of heavy drinking. Just 48 years old, she had remained addicted to gambling to the end, and was said to have run up debts of more than £200,000 in her lifetime (dutifully paid off by her husband). The first visitor that Lady Bessborough, her grief-stricken sister, could bring herself to receive in three weeks was the Prince. 'He has been throughout so kind and feeling,' she told her lover, Lord Granville Leveson-Gower, 'that I thought it wrong to persist in refusing to see him, so today he came soon after two and stayed till six!! Nothing ever was kinder or better meant, but this long stay – the first time, too, that I had seen any body – has quite knock'd me up. He gave me a very pretty emerald ring, which he begg'd me to wear, to *bind still stronger the tie of Brotherhood which he has always claimed.*'[24]

Meanwhile, the case against the Princess was gathering momentum. Towards the end of May 1806, a deputation of the Prince's brothers – including the Dukes of York, Sussex and Kent – 'came to him, saying that Romilly as Solicitor had examined' Lowten's evidence 'and thought it so strong that they should be guilty of *misprision of Treason* not to lay it before the Council'. The Prince gave his consent, despite the fact that some of the evidence against the Princess had been contradicted by her two doctors.[25]

On 28 May, Lord Grenville presented Romilly's evidence and opinion to the King. 'Two years ago this would have surprized me,' responded the monarch, 'but not now.' If it had been 'one attachment, and even a child, he would have screened her if he could have done it with safety to the Crown', the Prince told Lady Bessborough, but 'there seemed so much levity and profligacy that she was not worth the screening.' The following day, George III appointed a Secret Commission of Cabinet ministers to examine the witnesses. According to the Prince, the provisional list of members included Grenville, Erskine, Ellenborough (Lord Chief Justice), Fox and Moira; but at his request, the latter pair were 'struck off as too particularly his friends' and Lord Spencer, the Home Secretary, was added. Romilly would advise the Commission. (If the Prince did indeed cause the removal of his 'friends' – and there is no evidence to support such a claim – he would soon regret this show of 'impartiality'.)[26]

The so-called 'Delicate Investigation' began on 1 June with the examination of the Douglases in 10 Downing Street. Lady Douglas's sworn statement, written in December 1805, contained the central allegation that the Princess 'had been pregnant in the year 1802, in consequence of an illicit intercourse, and that she had in the same year been secretly delivered of a male child, which child had ever since that period been brought up by her Royal Highness'. It was up to the four Commissioners to decide whether there was any substance to that accusation.[27]

Lady Douglas told the Commission that she had met the Princess in 1801 and quickly become an intimate friend. In the spring of 1802, she had spent a fortnight in the Round Tower at Montague House, acting as her lady-in-waiting. It was during this time that Caroline had urged her to take Prince William of Gloucester as a lover, expressing her surprise that she could be 'satisfied only with Sir John'. When it was time for her to return to her own house, the Princess had confessed: 'I have the most complaisant husband in the world – I have no one to control me – I see whom I like, I go where I like, I spend what I please, and his Royal Highness pays for all.' The Princess also told her that, during her time at Carlton House, the Prince had encouraged her to 'select some particular gentleman for my friend'. Caroline's next comment was: 'I should have been the man, and he the woman. I am a real Brunswicker, and do not know what the sensation of fear is; but, as to him, he lives in eternal warm water, and delights in it, if he can but have his slippers under any old dowager's table, and sit there scribbling notes; that's his whole delight.'

Soon after, during a visit to Lady Douglas's house, the Princess had admitted that she was 'with child', adding: 'You will be surprised to see how well I manage it, and I am determined to suckle the child myself.' As Lady Douglas herself was expecting a second child in July, 'the Princess often alluded to her situation and to mine, and one day as we were sitting together upon the sofa, she put her hand on her stomach, and said, laughing, "Well, here we sit like Mary and Elizabeth in the Bible."' To conceal her swollen belly the Princess had simply increased the number of cushions behind her. The child's arrival, however, required a more sophisticated stratagem. 'When you hear of my having taken children in baskets from poor people, take no notice,' the Princess told her, 'that is the way I mean to manage; I shall take any that offer, and the one I have will be presented in the same way.'

During a visit to Montague House on 30 October 1802, Lady Douglas had seen the Princess out walking 'dressed in a long Spanish velvet cloak and an enormous muff, but which together could not conceal the state she was in, for I saw directly she was very near her time'. Returning to the house in January 1803, she had found the Princess with 'an infant sleeping on the sofa'. 'Here is the little boy,' explained the Princess, 'I had him two days after I saw you last; is it not a nice little child?' Then Mrs Fitzgerald, the Princess's lady companion, had come in and related the 'whole fable of the child having been brought by a poor woman from Deptford, whose husband had left her'. Lady Douglas, however, had been in no doubt that the child was the Princess's. As to the father, she 'rather suspected' Sir Sidney Smith, 'but only because the Princess was very partial to him'. The Princess had told her 'that Sir Sidney Smith had lain with her; that she believed all men liked a bedfellow, but Sir Sidney better than any body else.'[28]

And so ended Lady Douglas's fanciful testimony. On 6 June, Robert Bidgood, the Princess's former page, was called to give evidence. He confirmed that Sir Sidney Smith had often stayed at Montague House until the early hours of the morning, adding that the Admiral had once been found in the Blue Room at 10 in the morning though no one had let him in. He also voiced his suspicions about Manby: on one occasion he had seen him and the Princess 'kissing each other's lips'; later, while at Southend, the Princess often retired 'alone with Captain Manby'.[29]

William Cole, another of the Princess's former pages, was called next. A long-time servant of the Prince who had since returned to his duties at Carlton House, he was obviously an unreliable witness. He had, he claimed, once seen 'a person wrapped up in a great coat' enter the house from the park at midnight. On another occasion he had walked into the Blue Room to find Sir Sidney Smith 'sitting very close to the Princess on the sofa'; both had appeared 'a little confused' to be so discovered. Two weeks later, he was dismissed from his duties at Blackheath, though he saw the Princess a number of times more that year. In July 1802, he noticed that she 'had grown very large', but was much thinner by the end of the year. Thomas Lawrence, he added, had slept many times at Montague House in late 1801. He had 'often seen him alone with the Princess' late at night, and on one occasion had returned to find 'the Blue Room door locked' and 'whispering' within.[30]

As well as insisting that she had heard Dr Mills, the physician, say 'the Princess was with child, or looked as if she was with child', Fanny Lloyd, the coffee-room woman, told the Commission that a washerwoman by the name of Charlton had discovered 'linen marked with the appearance of a miscarriage or delivery' before William Austin was brought to the house. However, she denied telling Cole that the housemaid Mary Wilson had found a man in the Princess's room in the morning, and that Wilson had been threatened with dismissal 'if she divulged what she had seen'.[31]

The rest of the Princess's servants – when called before the Commission on 7 June – were not of the opinion that she had ever committed adultery or had a bastard child, although she had often been alone with both Sir Sidney Smith and Captain Manby. Her steward, maid and dresser all said that Willy Austin was regularly visited by his mother, the same woman who had handed him over to the Princess in 1802. Mrs Austin herself confirmed this version of events. She had been told to bring the child back when it was weaned; this she did on 15 November 1802. 'I saw the child last Whit-Monday,' she testified, 'and I swear that it is my child.'[32]

Later that month, the Commission obtained a copy of the Brownlow Hospital register which stated that Sophia Austin had indeed given birth to a son, William, on 11 July 1802. But Lady Douglas's version of events had already been fatally undermined by other witnesses. Sir John Douglas admitted that his wife did not tell him about the alleged pregnancy until 1804. Furthermore, his supporting evidence for his wife's story was no more than circumstantial. 'After she had been for some time acquainted with us,' he told the Commission, 'she appeared to me to be with child. One day she leaned on the sofa, and put her hand on her stomach, and said, "Sir John, I shall never be Queen of England." I said, "Not if you don't deserve it."'[33]

Then the maid Mary Wilson denied that she had seen the Princess and Sir Sidney making love; the Princess's physicians, Doctors Mills and Edmeades, refuted ever having told Fanny Lloyd that she was with child; and Mrs Gosden, Willy Austin's nurse, confirmed Mrs Austin's story that the boy had been weaned by the time he arrived at Montague House.

More damaging for the Princess was the testimony given by the washerwoman Betty Towneley, who said that her mistress's sheets had once shown signs of a birth or a miscarriage. Also, on 3 July, the Honourable Mrs Lisle, one of Caroline's Women of the Bedchamber, told the Commission that, while she did not believe the Princess had been pregnant, she was a terrible flirt: 'I should not have thought any married woman would have behaved properly who should have behaved as her Royal Highness behaved to Captain Manby.'[34]

Meanwhile, despite the evidence to the contrary, the Prince had good reason to assume that the Commission would find against his wife. On 23 June, while attending the Bibury Races in Gloucestershire, Lord Moira had written to inform him that there 'is not a doubt of its all terminating rightly, so that your mind may be quite at ease'. As Moira had attended a number of the Commission's examinations, and even suggested lines of questioning, he was in a position to know. He added: 'It is now becoming generally understood that your Royal Highness takes no concern in the matter, and the inference drawn from that circumstance has been in the highest degree important. I rejoice on that account at your absence.'[35]

On 14 July, the Commission presented its report. It concluded:

> We are happy to declare to your Majesty our perfect conviction that there is no foundation whatever for believing that the child now with the Princess is the child of Her Royal Highness, or that she was delivered of any child in the year 1802; nor has anything appeared to us which would warrant the belief that she was pregnant in that year, or at any other period within the compass of our inquiries.

However, it continued, Robert Bidgood, William Cole, Frances Lloyd and Mrs Lisle were all 'witnesses, who cannot, in our judgement, be suspected of any unfavourable bias, and whose veracity, in this respect, we have seen no ground to question'. While 'on the one hand, the facts of pregnancy and delivery are to our minds satisfactorily disproved, so on the other hand we think, that the circumstances to which we now refer, particularly those stated to have passed between her Royal Highness and Captain Manby, must be credited until they receive some decisive contradiction, and if true, are entitled to the most serious con-sideration.'[36]

On the one hand, the Princess had been cleared of giving birth to a bastard; but on the other, she had been declared guilty of adultery until proved innocent. Was this justice? Not in the strictest sense of the word. The Commission was not a court of law (despite the presence of the Lord Chancellor and Lord Chief Justice), yet it had acted like one, imposing oaths and summoning witnesses; the Princess had neither been told the charges nor given a chance to refute them; the witness statements and testimony were largely unreliable, given as they were by people who had either been bribed or had axes to grind. Cole and Bidgood, for example, had served the Prince for 21 and 23 years respectively, and the former had returned to Carlton House after being dismissed by the Princess. Could they really be regarded by the Commission as witnesses with no 'unfavourable bias'?

At the same time, Mary Wilson's denial that she had seen the Princess having sex with Sir Sidney Smith smacks of witness tampering. After all, three separate servants testified to the fact that she had said as much to them. The most likely explanation is that the Princess paid her to stay silent. Years later, when she was letting most of her servants go, the Princess was particularly insistent that Wilson was given a generous pay-off.

Nevertheless, the Commission's verdict was probably not far from the truth. The Brownlow Hospital register and the testimony of Mrs Austin provide compelling proof that Willy Austin was not the Princess's son. She herself later confessed to Henry Brougham's brother, James, that she had 'humbugged . . . the whole lot': Willy was 'not her son', but he was not the Austins' either; he was instead the natural son of Prince Louis Ferdinand of Prussia, the nephew of Frederick the Great (and a man she had once hoped to marry), who had been 'brought over to England in 1803 by a German woman'. The Princess had then substituted him for a child she had got from Mrs Austin, which was 'taken God knows where'. To that day Mrs Austin believed that Willy was her son. The Princess had taken the child in because she 'was always attached to Louis Ferdinand', and for that reason 'she never could love the Prince'. She also 'insinuated' that Prince Louis Ferdinand had been 'in love with her all his life' until, courting death, he was killed at the Battle of Jena in 1806.[37]

On her deathbed, the Princess repeated the gist of this unlikely tale to her lawyer, Dr Stephen Lushington. Willy 'was in truth a son of a brother or friend of Brunswick who was dead' and 'had been clandestinely brought over from the continent'. Corroboration of a sort was then provided by 'a German nobleman or General' who asked to see Willy as he and Lushington travelled to the Princess's funeral in Brunswick. To Lushington's 'great surprize', the German 'repeated in substance' what the Princess had already told him 'respecting W. Austin's birth and parentage', and 'then added that Austin bore a great resemblance to his reputed father'. The Austins, on the other hand, were convinced that Willy looked exactly like his mother and brother Job.[38]

Whoever Willy Austin's parents were, we can be fairly sure that the Princess was not one of them. But this does not preclude the possibility that she had a miscarriage or even a phantom pregnancy in 1802. She adored children, yet was not in a position to have any more of her own. She may even have been indulging her particularly bizarre sense of humour by pretending to be pregnant. What is not in doubt, however, is the fact that she could have become pregnant. For the Commission was surely right when it said that there was compelling evidence to suspect the Princess of adultery. As her footman, Samuel Roberts, once confided to Cole: 'The Princess is very fond of fucking.'[39]

Having received a copy of the Secret Commission's report, the King was in a difficult position. While there was no actual proof of adultery, the circumstantial evidence was compelling. As a result, he told his wife that the Princess would no longer be considered an intimate of the family and all future social intercourse would be confined to 'outward marks of civility'. To decide what action to take, he consulted the Cabinet, and was advised 'in the first instance' to send copies of the report to the Prince and Princess.[40]

But the disappointed Prince had already learnt the gist of the report from Lord Thurlow, who told him that the Commissioners had 'been dilatory in the extreme' and had 'shown in their mode of proceeding too great a degree of lenity to the Princess'. Though 'there might not be' enough evidence 'to try her . . . for high treason', said Thurlow, the 'circumstances of her imprudence, amounting nearly to positive proof', were sufficient for the Commissioners to recommend that an Act of Parliament should be brought in 'to dissolve the marriage'. Anything 'short of this' would 'prove that their conduct has been guided by weakness, irresolution and pusillanimity'.[41]

The Princess, meanwhile, was being advised by a number of prominent Tories who were keen to make political capital out of the issue. Chief among them were Spencer Perceval (Attorney-General during Addington's ministry), Lord Eldon (the former Lord Chancellor), the Duke of Cumberland (who had recently fallen out with his brother) and a number of other prominent lawyers, including Sir Vicary Gibbs, Sir Thomas Plumer and Sir William Grant. On 12 August, the Prince's 44th birthday, they helped to draft the Princess's response to the Commissioners' report. Declaring herself 'innocent' and her 'conduct unquestionable', she implored the King to 'recollect that the whole of the evidence . . . was taken behind my back, without my having any opportunity to contradict or explain any thing, or even to point out those persons who might have been called, to prove the little credit which was due to some of the witnesses, from their connection with Sir John and Lady Douglas; and the absolute falsehood of parts of the evidence'. She yearned, she wrote, for 'that happy moment, when I may be allowed to appear again before your Majesty's eyes, and receive once more the assurance from your Majesty's own mouth that I have your gracious protection'.[42]

But influenced by the Prince, the Cabinet had no intention of letting the Princess off the hook. As a letter from Lord Moira to the Prince, on 4 September, makes clear:

> The Princess considers herself as under an interdict: for she has written to the King to say that she hopes to produce such a refutation of the charges as will allow her to be again received into His Majesty's presence. It appears to Lord Grenville that no ground must be given to have it said that she was interrupted in

this attempt, which is what she would desire, as she can have no means of rebutting such distinct evidence of facts. Indeed, she sinks entirely if she is left where she is.[43]

In any case, the Prince had more pressing worries on his mind. As if the death of the Duchess of Devonshire had not been bad enough, Charles James Fox, his political mentor, was now on his last legs. As Foreign Secretary, he had set himself two main objectives: the abolition of the slave trade and peace with France. The first was set in train on 10 June, his last important speech in the Commons, when the House voted by 114 votes to 15 to proceed 'with all practicable expedition . . . to take effectual measures for abolishing the African slave trade'. The second – if indeed it had been attainable – was interrupted by illness. Pain and swelling in his legs was diagnosed as dropsy, a condition marked by an excess of watery fluid in the body's tissue or cavities.

A number of painful operations were performed to draw off the fluid – one, on 7 August, extracted a full 'sixteen quarts of amber-coloured water' – but the illness persisted. On 8 September, as Fox was being led about the rooms at Chiswick House (lent to him by the Duke of Devonshire) 'to look at the pictures', wrote Lady Holland, 'a *gush* of water burst from the wounds' and he 'fell into a state of alarming weakness'.[44]

The Prince was at Trentham in Nottinghamshire, on a tour of the north, when he received word that Fox was fading fast. 'What is to become of us all if we are to lose our dear Charles?' he wrote to Lord Holland, Fox's nephew, on the 12th. He continued:

His loss will be incalculable to this country and to the interests of Europe at large at the present awful crisis, and irreparable to us his friends . . . Could I be of the smallest use I would fly, but to come merely to see him expire is more than my nature could endure, the blow is too severe; without him I can neither be of use to the country, to my friends nor to myself. He has not only been the friend of my heart, but with his all-powerful mind he has instructed me, and with his hand from the earliest period of my youth he has led me along the path of true patriotism . . . I have neither health nor spirits left to contend without his assistance, and I therefore repeat, that if Fox goes, I consider all gone.

Fox died 'without a struggle' in the early evening of 13 September. His last words were, 'I die happy,' and then to Mrs Fox, who was holding his hand: 'Bless you, I pity you.'[45]

My dearest Holland [wrote the Prince on 14 September], your short note has overwhelmed me with grief . . . My tears fall so thick that I cannot see what I write. As to my distress and my feelings I shall not attempt to say anything, as they are not to be described. If anything is or ought to be done about poor Mrs Fox . . . pray make use of my name; and assure her that through life she will ever find me a true friend, for the sake of him, whose memory will ever live, and be most tenderly recorded in my heart.[46]

To honour Fox's memory, the Prince suggested to Lord Grenville that Lord Holland 'should have his uncle's seals'. Grenville, however, decided that Charles Grey (Viscount Howick since April) should assume Fox's mantle as Foreign Secretary and Leader of the House, with Thomas Grenville as First Lord of the Admiralty, Sidmouth as Lord President, Fitzwilliam as Minister without Portfolio, and Holland as Privy Seal. The Prince took the news with good grace, telling Howick that though the changes 'may not be perhaps quite to the extent of our wishes, still, as the irreparable loss we have sustained will not appear to have shaken in any degree the system laid down by him, and as they appear to embrace all the best abilities of the country, we must feel satisfied and act with cordial unanimity.'[47]

His 'political interest was buried in the grave with Mr Fox', he told Lord Grenville, 'but . . . as it was probable he might at some future time be again forced to public matters, he thought it proper to say that he was ready to give his support to the present administration, on account of the friends he had in it, and that he should always look to the friends of Mr Fox, and particularly to Lord Holland, as his own political friends.'[48]

For a time it seemed as though the Prince was about to follow Fox to the grave. 'The Prince is here and very unwell,' Lord Fitzwilliam informed the Prime Minister from Doncaster on 24 September. 'He was deeply affected with the death of Fox, and has never recovered his spirits since.' Not only was his pulse 'thin, low and weak', but he had 'neither tasted meat nor wine' for a fortnight. Lord Holland, on the other hand, put his illness down to his new passion for Lady Hertford. 'Those,' he wrote, 'who had made a study of his gallantries, recognised his usual system of love-making in these symptoms. He generally, it seems, assailed the hearts which he wished to carry by exciting their commiserations for his sufferings and their apprehensions for his health.'[49]

Meanwhile, the Princess had requested and been sent the original statements placed before the Secret Commission. These were then handed to Spencer Perceval who was drafting her defence to the charges. Presented to the King on 2 October, it was a huge, detailed document (running to 125 pages when printed), arguing, with some justification, that he had 'been advised to pass by the ordinary legal modes of inquiry into such high crimes' in favour of a Commission which, 'having negatived the principal charge', had 'entertained considerations of matters that amounted to no legal offence'. Nor had she been given 'appeal to the laws of the country because the charges, constituting no [crime], cannot be made the ground of a judicial inquiry'.[50]

When the King abrogated responsibility by referring the matter back to the Cabinet, Moira told the Prince that Grenville 'thought nothing more could be done by Ministers, and that your Royal Highness had only to signify to the Princess that her explanations were so unsatisfactory as to make it requisite for her not to revisit Carlton House'. Moira himself had 'urged the unfairness of letting the interdict to the Princess come from you when both had appealed to the King as the only competent judge', adding that 'nothing could satisfy the public but either a publication of the whole evidence, or such a decision on the part of the King as should give the world to understand what had been the bearing of that evidence.'[51]

The Prince was outraged. Grenville's 'proposal', he told Moira on 7 November, 'both astonishes me and revolts me'. Given the 'detailed and strong opinions he individually gave me upon the Report, and accompanied by the strongest assurances and promises of carrying the business through to my complete honour and credit, to make such a proposal now to you, is monstrous in the extreme.' He 'could not have experienced a more entire want of support had the Government been composed of his greatest enemies'. Unless the 'business of the Investigation' was 'brought to an immediate conclusion in the most decided manner', it was his intention, 'together with you and all the rest of my friends to retire, and to have no further concern with this Government, which in the first place have failed in their solemn engagements to me who have been their sheet anchor'.[52]

This threat neither speeded up the process nor produced the desired result. It was not until 23 December 1806 that the Cabinet delivered its ambiguous verdict. Eleven out of its 12 members said that they concurred with the Secret Commission's conclusions – hardly surprising, given that all four Commissioners were still Cabinet members. However, the 'facts of the case' did 'not warrant their advising that any further step should be taken in the business by your Majesty's Government, or any other proceedings instituted upon it', except, perhaps, the prosecution of Lady Douglas for perjury. Furthermore, they did not think it was their place to advise whether or not the Princess should be readmitted to the King's presence. That was for him alone to decide.

The one dissenting member, William Windham, agreed with what he conceived to be the 'opinion of the Cabinet' – that no evidence had been produced to justify 'any legal proceeding' – and added that 'the charge originally brought against Her Royal Highness is as to part directly disproved, and as to the remainder rests on evidence which cannot entitle it to the smallest credit.'[53]

The King, who was far from satisfied by this response, pressed for an 'an explicit answer', which was eventually given on 25 January 1807 in the shape of a Cabinet minute. As 'the facts of the case did not warrant their advising that any further steps should be taken', there was no longer any need for the King to bar the Princess from his presence. At the same time, they thought it 'indispensable that your Majesty should by a serious admonition convey to her Royal Highness your Majesty's expectation that [she] should be more circumspect in her future conduct'.

They even provided a draft letter for the King to send to the Princess, which included the sentence, '. . . even in the answer drawn in the name of the Princess by her legal advisers, there have appeared circumstances of conduct on the part of the Princess which his Majesty never could regard but with concern and disapprobation.' He duly despatched it, merely substituting the words 'serious concern' for 'concern and disapprobation'.[54]

The Princess, who on the advice of Perceval had been threatening to publish all the documents relating to the investigation if she was not readmitted to the King's presence, was mightily relieved. 'Honourably acquitted: but a reprimand,' she told Miss Hayman, her Keeper of the Privy Purse. It could have been a lot worse. 'Are you not glad to see me with my head upon my rump [meaning her neck]?' she had asked a dinner guest shortly after the conclusion of the investigation.[55]

The Prince was now in a quandary. His wife had been chastised for her conduct, but cleared of committing any specific crime. There were, therefore, no grounds for a divorce – unless he could prove adultery in a court of law. So on 1 February 1807, he told Lord Chancellor Erskine that he had discovered a 'degree of misconduct' in the Princess which made it necessary to lay the papers before his own law officers, 'so that

I may not have to charge myself with any possible hazard affecting the interests of my daughter and the succession'. On informing his father, he added the sweetener that he was considering a return to his former neutrality in politics. It worked. On 10 February, the King informed the Princess that he could not receive her until 'the further result of the Prince's intention shall have been made known to him'.[56]

While the Princess remonstrated against her treatment, her husband rejoiced. 'The Prince,' Richard Ryder told his brother, Lord Harrowby, on the 14th, 'has been in the highest spirits since he has gained his point with the King. Does not your blood boil at his conduct? An interval, but that I hope a short one, will be given to consider the case before the Princess publishes. I hear the Prince insists on separation or divorce.'[57]

Ryder was remarkably well informed. On 16 February, in a long letter – drafted by Perceval – to the King, the Princess warned that 'scarce anything, short of a public exposure of all that has passed, can possibly efface' the 'inferences drawn in the public mind' from this 'revocation of your Majesty's gracious purpose'. She added: 'The justice due to me is to be suspended, while the judgement of your Majesty's sworn servants is to be submitted to the revision of my accuser's counsel.' This was a clear reference to the fact that the Prince and his lawyers had been behind the original investigation.[58]

But not all the Princess's advisers approved of her threat to publish. It would be, Lord Eldon told the King in early March, 'an event more deeply to be deplored and deprecated' than anything he could imagine. Not least because the Princess intended to include 'reports or facts of reciprocal crimination'. In other words, she would accuse the Prince of adultery. She may well have got wind of the fact that, in 1805, he had set up Madame de Meyer, a French courtesan, in a house in Duke Street, off Manchester Square, where he used to visit her after dark; not to mention the rumour that he had had a daughter by Mrs Mary Lewis, a boarding-house proprietor he had met in Weymouth.

However, the real danger lay in any public exposure of his relationship with Mrs Fitzherbert – and the fact that they had almost certainly had two, and possibly more, children. To prevent any chance of this happening, Eldon implored the King to receive his daughter-in-law.[59]

As it happened, the crisis disappeared with the fall of the Ministry of All the Talents over the issue of Roman Catholic relief. Well aware that the King (and probably also the Prince) would never agree to full Catholic emancipation, in February Grenville's government had proposed introducing clauses into the annual Mutiny Bill which would extend to any part of the Empire the concessions granted to Roman Catholics by Pitt's Irish Act of 1793: namely, that Catholics could hold commissions in the Irish army below the rank of General on the Staff.

But as well as extending the Irish Act to the Empire, ministers wanted to broaden it by enabling *all* dissenters (not just Catholics) to hold 'any military commission whatever'. Initially opposed, by 12 February the King gave his consent to the measure because he mistakenly assumed it did not go beyond the concessions granted in Ireland in 1793. He realised his error when the new Bill 'for the admission of Dissenters from the Church of England into the Army and Navy' (the idea of tacking the clauses on to the Mutiny Bill having been abandoned) was introduced to the Commons on 5 March. So too did Lord Sidmouth, the Privy Seal, who immediately offered his resignation (he was eventually persuaded to remain in office by Grenville and the King, though he no longer attended Cabinet meetings). Even more fatal to the Bill's chances of success was the withdrawal of support by Lord Erskine and the rest of the Carlton House party. Not only had the Prince become increasingly sceptical of the benefits to be gained by any form of Catholic relief, he was also unable to forgive Grenville's government for its failure to raise the issue of his debts, its unsatisfactory conclusion to the Delicate Investigation, and its 'most marked neglect' of him since the death of Fox. He had, therefore – as he told Lord Moira on 30 March – 'determined to resume my original purpose, sincerely preferred in my own mind upon the death of poor Fox, to *cease to be a party man.*'[60]

With the Cabinet divided, the King vehemently opposed and the Prince on the sidelines, Grenville had no option but to abandon the measure on 15 March. But to save face – and in the absence of the three ministers (Sidmouth, Ellenborough and Erskine) who had opposed the Bill – the Cabinet then informed the King that they reserved the right to propose any measures which might further the well-being of Ireland. When he responded by demanding a written promise that they would never bring in another Catholic Relief Bill, they were forced to resign. On 24 March, the Duke of Portland was invited to form a Tory government, so completing his personal political metamorphosis from Whig to Tory. As the new ministry included a number of the Princess's friends and advisers – 'Lord Eldon as Lord Chancellor, Spencer Perceval as Chancellor of the Exchequer, George Canning as Foreign Secretary, and Sir William Grant as Master of the Rolls – it was thought politically expedient to abandon the threat to publish the papers relating to the Delicate Investigation (known as *The Book*). The new ministers could then work from the inside to secure an acceptable solution to the Princess's predicament.

On 21 April, Portland's Cabinet advised the King to readmit the Princess to his presence. All the 'particulars', they wrote, 'to which the character of criminality can be ascribed, are either satisfactorily contradicted, or rest upon evidence of such a nature, and which was given under such circumstances, as render it . . . undeserving of credit'. The King, no doubt relieved to have seen the back of the 'Talents', accepted this verdict and informed the Princess that he would receive her 'with as little delay as possible'. She would, in addition, be given apartments in Kensington Palace to replace those she had occupied at Carlton House.[61]

The Prince was beside himself. He had, he told his father, been 'arranging some detailed observations' on the new Cabinet's minute when he learnt that the King had agreed to adopt this advice. He continued:

> After this declaration it ceases to become me . . . to engage in controversial discussion either with the legal advisers of the Princess or with the confidential advisers of your Majesty;

characters now so blended as to render the possibility of an equitable decision from them upon this subject rather questionable.[62]

He had a point – but given his own relationship with the previous ministry, it was a bit rich. All that remained was for him to forbid his wife to visit either Carlton or Warwick House, 'there being a communication between that house and mine'. Princess Charlotte could visit her at Blackheath, but not while William Austin – 'the child of a pauper' – was present. It was scant consolation for the loss of a battle which had seemed his for the taking.[63]

10

Minney and Prinny

While the outcome of the Delicate Investigation was not exactly as the Prince would have wished, a quite separate legal issue was concluded to his complete satisfaction during the relatively short existence of the Grenville ministry.

Since the departure of the sickly Lady Horatia Seymour to Madeira in early 1799, Mrs Fitzherbert had been looking after her youngest daughter, Minney. Even when Lady Horatia returned to England in May 1801, she was too ill to do more than receive regular visits from Minney and her benefactor. She died on 12 July, shortly after moving to Clifton in Bristol for the air. Vice-Admiral Lord Hugh Seymour, meanwhile, was unaware of his wife's death. On 23 July he wrote to her from Jamaica (where he was commanding the West Indies Station), giving the reasons why he had forgiven the Prince for his shabby treatment of him in 1795. He, 'a sincere friend', had been 'put away . . . only because he was worthy of that name when endeavouring to prevent [the Prince] committing an act [bigamy] which he would have condemned in another, and which has produced the evil which was sure to be the consequence of it'. He continued:

He mistakes if he supposes that his conduct towards me has ever produced any feeling like that of hatred in my mind, for though I know that he has spoken of me very disrespectfully in accounting for our separation, I have placed that circumstance to the score of his natural want of steadiness . . . I however am glad he shows you attention as it proves that he is sensible of having acted wrong before and that he is willing to atone for it. Mrs. F. only does me justice when she says that I was her true friend.[1]

He wrote again on 15 August, still in the dark as to her death: 'I am not without hopes that little dear beautiful Minny will join [you] when Seymour [their eldest son, a midshipman] reaches England as he, dear little man, has frequently known me dwell upon the prospect of your being surrounded by those whom . . . we love most in the world.'[2]

Within a month Lord Hugh was also dead, the victim of a sudden illness. His will appointed Lord Euston, Lady Horatia's brother-in-law, and Lord Henry Seymour, his brother, as his executors and the children's guardians. Though Minney was not yet born at the time when the will was drawn up, and therefore was not mentioned by name, both executors considered that she came within its terms. At first she was allowed to remain with Mrs Fitzherbert. But in 1802, worried about the long-term consequences of leaving her in the care of a Roman Catholic, Lord Hugh's executors wrote to ask Mrs Fitzherbert to hand her over to Lady Waldegrave, Lady Horatia's sister, who wanted to adopt the two girls.

But Mrs Fitzherbert had become very attached to Minney and was desperate not to lose her. So the Prince, who was also very fond of her, decided to intervene. He wrote to the executors, offering to put aside £10,000 for Minney if she was allowed to remain with Mrs Fitzherbert. His 'ultimate view', he declared, was 'to raise her up as a companion and [he hoped] a bosom friend of his own daughter', who was two years older. Though the executors refused, telling the Prince that Minney had already been provided for and must be brought up by her aunt, he settled the money on her anyway (to be redeemed, with interest, when she reached the age of 21, married, or he died).

So began the long and acrimonious legal battle for Minney's guardianship between the Prince and Mrs Fitzherbert on the one hand, and Lord Hugh's executors on the other. On 16 December 1802, Mrs Fitzherbert put her side of the argument in a letter to Lord Robert Seymour, another of Minney's uncles:

> The misery I have and do experience at the thoughts of having her taken away from me, is more than I can express . . . I could not feel for so young a child of a month or two old anything more than the natural anxiety attending infants of that age and had no other idea than that of returning her to her parents as soon as they came to this country. With this idea, the instant poor Lady Horatia came to England (and I acknowledge I went with a heavy heart) I took my little charge to deliver her up to her mother. Her answer was: Don't think I would be so unfeeling as to take her away from you. You are *more* her Mother than *I am*.
>
> I was very much affected at what passed between us and was going out of the Room when she called me back and begged I would speak to him. I delivered her message and the Prince accordingly went to her. The next day I saw her and she repeated to me the conversation that passed between them, a great deal relative to Lord Hugh's and her own concerns – and then said I have been recommending my little Mary to him and have received his promise to be her friend and protector through life.
>
> About a fortnight after this I received the melancholy account of her death. Immediately the Prince determined to adhere to the promise he made the Mother . . .
>
> From the Mother having left the Child with me so short a time before her death and in a few months after being deprived of her Father, from the attachment and interest I took in the

Child I did flatter myself she might be permitted to remain with me. She is now past four years old. I am perfectly certain that no person can feel for her as I do . . . I fairly own to you that I am so totally wrapped up and devoted to that dear child that if I lose her it will almost break my heart. The whole occupation of my life is centred in her. Judge then how wretched I have been made for some weeks past at the dread of having her taken from me, and how I tremble at Lord Henry [Seymour]'s decision.[3]

A quite different version of events was given by Lady Horatia's two sisters, Ladies Waldegrave and Euston. In a letter to Lord Euston of 12 August 1802, Lady Waldegrave denied that Minney had ever been 'placed by her parents with Mrs Fitzherbert'. Instead, after Lord Hugh and Lady Horatia had left for Madeira, 'unauthorised by them' Mrs Fitzherbert had 'fetched the child from Lord George Seymour's at a moment when Lady George could not resist as she had been brought to bed'. She then quoted a letter to her from her sister, dated 9 July 1800, in which Lady Horatia complains that she has not heard from 'little Mary':

I feel more distressed about her than I can describe, for Mrs Fitzherbert has never written to me since I left Madeira – & it is so very distressing to have my child there – I did write by the Prince of Wales packet to beg she would give her up – but then this new arrangement for the children I am ignorant of seems to preclude little Mary, as Mr Trail names her being likely to remain where she was – every one tells me how fond Mrs. Fitzherbert is of her, but there is an awkwardness in this – dear little soul!

In 'several other letters', continues Lady Waldegrave, her sister 'expresses her anxiety that *all* her children should be together'. Since his return to England, Mr Ward had confided to her that Lord Hugh 'had very frequently told him his uneasiness at Mrs Fitzherbert having got possession of little Mary'. She concluded the letter by responding to Lord Euston's hint that Minney might be placed in her family when she got older:

> You must . . . be aware that it would he a most arduous employment for any one to undertake the care of a child of ten or eleven years old, whose affection would be placed on those who brought her up till then, who either would have *no religion* at all or be a Roman Catholic and whose morals would be corrupted by the society she had till then lived with.[4]

According to Lady Euston, her sister had always had doubts that the Prince was a suitable guardian for Minney. She wanted him to be kind to her children, but felt that to be too much in 'that society' would be dangerous for them. She had not spoken to the Prince since his quarrel with her husband, and had tried to prevent him from visiting her in her sickbed. But he had come anyway. 'He took her by the hand,' stated Lady Euston's affidavit, 'and began to talk as fast as possible . . . She did not speak to him at all, and as she sat with her head turned towards me she once or twice in a low voice expressed a degree of vexation on his volubility – she grew more and more faint.' After the Prince had gone and she had recovered, Lady Horatia smiled and asked Lady Euston 'whether it did not put [her] in mind of former times when he used to go *off* upon some favourite subject till he *talked himself into believing that all he said was true*'.[5]

Lord Robert Seymour was in full agreement with his sisters-in-law. 'Is there a sober man in England,' he asked his co-executor, Lord Euston, in a letter of 29 October 1802, 'who would have his daughter by choice to grow up under Mrs. Fitzherbert's roof. I do not doubt that she would have the utmost care of every kind given to her – but the opinion of the publick would be unanimously against such an education.'[6]

As the legal wrangling dragged on, Minney remained with Mrs

Fitzherbert. They lived for much of the time in Brighton – by 1800 'the most frequented [and] without exception one of the most fashionable towns in the Kingdom' – at Mrs Fitzherbert's Egyptian-style house on the Steine. Along with the rest of society, Mrs Fitzherbert spent the late morning promenading. Tea-parties, card-playing and dancing took place in the afternoon, followed by dinners lasting up to five hours. The main evening entertainments were the theatre and balls, both private and public subscription.[7]

Unlike the Prince, Mrs Fitzherbert never aspired to be a leader of fashion. Her puff-sleeved silken gowns and huge feathered hats were no more than the conventional garb of a gentlewoman. When she strolled on the Steine, often accompanied by the Prince, the men would raise their chimney-pot hats as if she were the Princess of Wales herself. It was this deference, rarely given in London, which made her so fond of Brighton. However, not everyone accepted her position as the Prince's consort. 'I understand,' wrote Lord Glenbervie (a close friend of Princess Caroline), in the autumn of 1801, 'that Mrs Fitzherbert is scarcely visited or taken notice of by the few people of fashion now there.' The following summer, he added:

> There is no company at Brightelmstone but [the Prince] and Mrs Fitzherbert and such divorced ladies as Lady Lucan, and women of the town. Mrs. Walpole, a neighbour at Addiscombe, has been there. She was justifying the Prince and his society till Lord Liverpool says they made her own that there were but two women of character belonging to it when she was there, herself to wit, and one other lady. If certain anecdotes I have heard are true, she was not very well entitled to except herself. She is sister to the late Miss Vanneck, who, being a large masculine woman and a great sycophant to the Prince and therefore of many of his parties, was described by some wit to be a *fellow* of the Royal Society.[8]

Though Mrs Fitzherbert never actually spent a night in the Pavilion, except when the Prince was ill, she often had dinner there. The four-teen or so guests, most of them men, would sit down to extravagant meals of nine or more courses, each washed down with a different wine. After dinner, Mrs Fitzherbert would play cards – usually whist – while the Prince listened to music or chatted to the guests. The Honourable Mrs Calvert, a famous Irish beauty, recorded her impres-sion of Mrs Fitzherbert during one such dinner in 1804:

> She is now I believe about fifty, very fat but with a charming countenance, her features are beautiful, except her mouth which is ugly, having a set of not good false teeth, but her person is too fat and she makes a great display of a very white but not prettily formed bosom, which I often long to throw a handkerchief over.[9]

Lady Bessborough, who stayed at the Pavilion the following year, described the Prince's way of living as 'pleasant enough'. She added:

> Every body meets at dinner, which, par parenthèse, is excellent, with the addition of a few invitations in the evening. Three large rooms, very comfortable, are lit up; whist, backgammon, Chess, trace Madame – every sort of game you can think of in two of them, and Musick in the third. His band is beautiful . . . Mrs. Fitzherbert is ill at present and confined to her bed, so he makes me do the honours.[10]

Behind this homely façade, however, there was the ongoing issue of Minney Seymour's guardianship. The case finally reached the Court of Chancery at the end of 1804. In his affidavit, the Prince repeated his claim that Lady Horatia, on her deathbed, had asked him to 'swear most solemnly' to be the 'father and protector through life, of this dear child' – and how he had done just that. In her affidavit, Mrs Fitzherbert attempted to soothe the court's religious qualms by expressing the opinion that, though she 'was bred in the Roman Catholic faith', 'a child ought to be educated in the religion professed by its parents'. The girl in question was, she added, 'bound to her by as strong ties of affection as she could possibly have been to her natural mother'.[11]

Despite these arguments, the Master in Chancery found against the Prince and Mrs Fitzherbert. So too did Lord Chancellor Eldon when he confirmed, on appeal, the decision of the Master in favour of Lord Euston and Lord Henry Seymour. During the summer of 1805, with the issue still unresolved, Minney was visited a number of times at Mrs Fitzherbert's London home – No. 6 Tilney Street, Mayfair – by the Honourable George Keppel, the six-year-old younger son of the 4th Earl of Albemarle and the grandson of Lady de Clifford, Princess Charlotte's new governess. The same age as Minney, Keppel was a welcome playmate. He recalls:

By my little hostess I had the honour of being presented to the Prince of Wales, afterwards George the Fourth. His appearance and manners were both of a nature to produce a lively impression on the mind of a child – a merry good-humoured man, tall, though somewhat portly in stature, in the prime of life, with laughing eyes, pouting lips, and nose which very slightly turned up, gave a peculiar poignancy to the expression of his face. He wore a well powdered wig, adorned with a profusion of curls – which in my innocence I believed to be his own hair, as I did a very large pigtail appended thereto. His clothes fitted him like a glove, his coat was single-breasted and buttoned up to the chin. His nether garments were leather pantaloons and Hessian boots. Round his throat was a huge white neckcloth of many folds, out of which his chin seemed to be struggling to emerge.

No sooner was his Royal Highness seated in his armchair than my young companion would jump up on one of his knees to which she seemed to claim a prescriptive right. Straightway would arise an animated talk between 'Prinny and Minnie' as they respectively called each other. As my father was in high

favour with the Prince at this time, I was occasionally admitted
to the spare knee and to a share in the conversation, if conversation it could be called in which all were talkers and none
listeners.[12]

And so, as Keppel records, it was thanks to young Minney that the
Prince became known as 'Prinny' (while Keppel was dubbed 'Wiggy').
His relationship with his own daughter, Charlotte, was somewhat less
affectionate – presumably because her wilfulness and art reminded him
of her mother.

With the death of Pitt and the formation of the Ministry of All the
Talents in January 1806, the Prince sensed the opportunity to overturn
the previous judgements against him and Mrs Fitzherbert in the battle
for custody of Minney. Not least because Thomas Erskine, who had
acted for him with Samuel Romilly in the earlier cases, had replaced
the hostile Eldon as Lord Chancellor. (Even his new title, Baron
Erskine of Restormal Castle in Cornwall, was a compliment to the
Prince.)

When the case was brought before the House of Lords – the highest appeal court in the land – in June 1806, the Prince left nothing to
chance. As well as soliciting an assurance from the Marquess of
Hertford, the head of the Seymour family, that he would let Mrs
Fitzherbert keep Minney if *he* was given custody, the Prince also set
about personally canvassing as many peers as he could. By the time
Lord Erskine moved a reversal of Eldon's earlier judgement and the
appointment of Lord Hertford as Minney's guardian on the ground that
he was her nearest relation in blood, the issue was never in doubt.

Sir Samuel Romilly, the Solicitor-General who appeared for the
Prince, would later regret his involvement. Of the last day of the trial,
14 June, he wrote:

> The order of the Lord Chancellor [Eldon] was reversed and
> Lord and Lady Hertford were by the House appointed the
> guardians. Several Peers voted against this, but there was no

division. I counted between eighty and ninety Peers who were present: the Prince, who was as anxious that Mrs. Fitzherbert should continue to have the care of the child as he could have been if the child had been his own, and who knew that Lord and Lady Hertford would not remove her, had earnestly entreated all his friends to attend. I had, on the Prince's account, done every thing that depended on me to prevent this; and which was only to represent to Colonel McMahon what I thought of such a proceeding. The question was certainly one which involved no legal consideration whatever, and which every Peer was as competent to decide as a lawyer could be, but yet to canvass votes for a judicial decision, is that which cannot be too strongly reprobated.[13]

The Prince, of course, was unaffected by such moral and legal qualms. He had shamelessly abused his position and influence to ensure that Minney remained with Mrs Fitzherbert – even if this meant ignoring the wishes of the little girl's deceased parents. For if Lady Horatia's sisters are to be believed, Minney's parents would never have agreed to the Prince and Mrs Fitzherbert becoming her permanent guardians. The case partly hinged on the two different versions of the Prince's final meeting with Lady Horatia: either Lady Euston was lying, or the Prince was. The latter scenario would seem to be the more likely.

Given the Prince's determination that Mrs Fitzherbert would not lose Minney, it was inevitable that some people would assume he was her natural father; he may even have encouraged this belief in an attempt to win support for his case. We can, however, safely discount this possibility. He had not seen Lady Horatia for years when they met for the last time in 1801. Furthermore, the references to Minney in her parents' letters leave no doubt that they, at least, regarded her as their daughter.

A much more likely candidate for daughter of the Prince and Mrs Fitzherbert is Maryanne Smythe, born around 1800 (a date which fits with their reunion) and brought up a Roman Catholic. Maryanne did not join Minney in Mrs Fitzherbert's household until 1817. There is, however, good reason to believe that she was kept out of the way for so long because she was the Prince's daughter. She was always passed off as the daughter of Mrs Fitzherbert's younger brother, Jack Smythe. But the family records of Maryanne's descendants, the Barons Stafford, reject this theory:

> If she was a daughter of John Smythe, she cannot have been legitimate, for John Smythe had no children by his wife, widow of Captain Strickland . . . [Many] indications point with considerable probability to the conclusion that she was a daughter of Mrs Fitzherbert by George IV.[14]

There is, unfortunately, no solid proof that Maryanne was their daughter. Most of the correspondence between the Prince and Mrs Fitzherbert was destroyed by his executors, Sir William Knighton and the Duke of Wellington, after his death; while a number of Mrs Fitzherbert's private papers were also burnt when they were moved from the vault at Coutts Bank to the Royal Archives in 1905. But there is the occasional reference in Mrs Fitzherbert's surviving correspondence to hint at the true relationship between them. Writing to Maryanne in June 1828, shortly after her marriage to the Honourable Edward Jerningham, Mrs Fitzherbert ends the letter: 'Say a thousand kind things from me to my *Son in Law* [her emphasis] and believe me ever most affectionately.'

If Maryanne really was her niece, why would she refer to Maryanne's husband as her '*Son in Law*'? Only her daughter's husband could be described in this way. After all, when writing to Minney, both the Prince and Mrs Fitzherbert were always careful to stress their relationship to her as adoptive parents. In November 1818, for example, the Prince wrote of 'Prayers that never could proceed with more sincerity and fervour from a real and natural Parent', and signed off the letter with 'your ever most affectionate Father by adoption'. Likewise Mrs Fitzherbert, who in August 1825 wrote to Minney: 'No mother, I am certain, ever loved her *own child* more dearly than I have loved you.' Yet nowhere in all the surviving correspondence between Maryanne and Mrs Fitzherbert is there any reference to 'adoption'.[15]

An additional piece of circumstantial evidence is the missing page in the baptismal register of St John the Baptist Church in Brighton – where Mrs Fitzherbert used to worship – for the years 1799 to 1801. The page is said to have been removed by order of the Prince when he became Regent in 1811; any proof that he had married a Catholic would have prevented him from exercising sovereign power.

Mrs Fitzherbert may have won custody of Minney, but the price to be paid was higher than she could have imagined: the loss of her husband to the woman who had made the legal victory possible.

Isabella, Marchioness of Hertford, was an ambitious woman. Born two years before the Prince, the daughter of the 9th Viscount Irvine, she had become the Marquess's second wife when she was just 16. A former Whig who had been converted to Toryism, the King's Master of the Horse from 1804 to 1806, the Marquess was described by Wraxall as 'elegantly formed', 'above the ordinary height', his manners 'noble yet ingratiating'. His wife, 18 years his junior, was tall, handsome and elegant – though a little portly. 'We may reasonably doubt,' wrote Wraxall, 'whether Diana de Poitiers, Ninon de L'Enclos, or Marion de L'Orme, three women who preserved their powers of captivating mankind even in the evening of life, could exhibit at her age finer remains of female grace than the Marchioness of Hertford.'[16]

Lord Holland, who would suffer the consequences of the Prince's gradual estrangement from his old political friends thanks to Lady Hertford's growing influence, was less generous: 'Her character was as timid as her manners were stately, formal and insipid.'[17]

The Prince was particularly fond of the Hertfords' only son, the Earl of Yarmouth. A thoroughly dissolute man whose debauched tastes increased with his age – he appears as the Marquess of Steyne in Thackeray's *Vanity Fair* – he had fallen out with his parents in 1798 by marrying the wealthy heiress Maria Fagniani, the daughter of the Marchese Fagniani and either the Duke of Queensberry ('Old Q') or George Selwyn. Both believed her to be their daughter and left her a fortune.

Yarmouth, who had the ill-fortune to be visiting Paris when the Peace of Amiens broke down in 1803, was promptly imprisoned by Bonaparte in the fortress of Verdun for three years. His release in the summer of 1806 was due in part to the intercession of the Prince, who had put pressure on Fox, the Foreign Secretary, to negotiate his freedom. With Yarmouth back in England, the Prince set about reconciling him to his parents. 'You know that family matters are very delicate ground,' he wrote to Lady Hertford, 'and must be very cautiously trod upon, for obvious reasons, and particularly with a highminded, quick and penetrating disposition which he possesses; at any rate if I can do you no good you may depend that I will do no harm.'[18]

At first, Lady Hertford appeared unmoved by the Prince's attempts to ingratiate himself with her. On 25 October 1806, he chastised her for being 'so very bad a correspondent, still, as I cannot find it in my heart to be *very* angry with you, I cannot resist taking up my pen and writing you a few lines'. The Prince, on the other hand, was already smitten and, as we have seen, Lord Holland attributed his worrying illness in the autumn of 1806 at least in part to this unrequited passion.

On 4 December, still not fully recovered, he wrote another letter to Lady Hertford: 'I deem it absolutely necessary to take up my pen to let you know that there is such a person still in this world as myself . . . The day before yesterday I received a very kind letter from dear Lord Hertford, but in which he neither mentions a word of his health, or of his projects of return to this country . . . P.S. Pray to not be lazy but write soon.'[19]

But unbeknown to the Prince, Lady Hertford had already left for Ireland with her husband. 'It is said my Lord took her off suddenly,' Lady Bessborough informed her lover, Lord Granville Leveson-Gower, on 4 December. 'He arrived at Ragley [Hall, the ancestral home], was shut up with her for seven hours, and at the end of that time announced their immediate departure.'[20]

It seems that the Marquess had begun to suspect his wife and the Prince. But this clumsy attempt to keep them apart simply increased the Prince's ardour – though he would remain on good terms with Mrs Fitzherbert for some time yet. In the spring of 1807 he was still visiting her in the evenings and staying until the early hours of the morning. By the summer, however, he was a regular guest of the Hertfords at Manchester House, their London mansion, and Ragley Hall, the family seat in Warwickshire. So perplexed was Lady Bessborough by the Prince's relentless pursuit of Lady Hertford that, in a letter to Leveson Gower on 23 October, she put it down to his 'father's malady'. She continued:

> He writes day and night almost, and frets himself into a fever, and all to persuade la sua bella *Donnone* [Lady Hertford] *to live with him – publickly!!* A quoi bon, except to make, *if* possible, a greater cry against him? He is now at his country house near the sea, is to be back in London the 2nd, stays till the 8th, and then goes back to Ragley. I should not be surprized if he and the ci devant [Mrs Fitzherbert] were to quarrel . . . during their meeting at Brighton. She has got irritated, and he bored; for this last there is, alas! no cure – the disease is fatal. Irretrievable quarrels may be made up, injuries forgiven, but weariness! – gradual decay of affection from causes too slight for complaint, too numerous for removal – when once this begins all is over.[21]

Lady Bessborough's suspicion that the Prince was suffering from the same affliction as his father was no doubt correct – as we have seen – but that had nothing to do with the manner in which he had gone about wooing Lady Hertford. For, as Lord Holland rightly pointed out, his seduction technique had altered little over the years. Both assaults on Mrs Fitzherbert had also combined persistence with passion, not to mention the implicit threat that his health would suffer unless he got his way.

Once again this seemed to work. Lord Glenbervie noted on 31 December 1807:

> He visits [Lady Hertford] every forenoon when they are both in town, and often dines *en famille* with her and Lord Hertford, and it is said that when absent, and often when they are both in London, he employs a great part of the morning every day in writing to her. What can be the topic of correspondence? She is near fifty and has been a grandmother more than twelve or fourteen years. The Prince is not much younger. Lord Hertford is said to have a revenue of above £70,000. What can be the motive of his connivance at an intercourse almost equally inexplicable whether it be commercial, or, as many people suppose, only sentimental.[22]

So why did the Prince replace one aged companion (Mrs Fitzherbert was now 51) with another almost as old (Lady Hertford was 47)? Lady Bessborough's reference to boredom may be close to the truth. After all, the Prince and Mrs Fitzherbert had never really had much in common beyond physical attraction and mutual respect. While he enjoyed politics, music and rowdy company, she preferred a quiet evening of cards with a few intimates. What he lacked in constancy and moral turpitude, she possessed in abundance; it was this essential 'goodness' that had attracted him in the first place. But the Prince was not a man who could sit still. He was constantly altering the homes that he lived in – both Carlton House and the Brighton Pavilion – and when, late in his life, the alterations were complete, he pulled one down and rarely visited the other. It was the same with women. Once the battle for Minney's custody had been won, he and Mrs Fitzherbert no longer had a common purpose. Their fundamental differences of character, which had first become apparent in the early 1790s, made it impossible for them to stay together.

Lady Hertford, on the other hand, was intelligent and worldly enough to be able both to stimulate him mentally and satisfy him emotionally. It was hinted at the time, by Glenbervie and others, that there may not have been a sexual element to their relationship. The Princess of Wales was certainly of that opinion, telling Lady Charlotte Campbell, her lady-in-waiting, in 1810 'that Lady Hertford is a woman of intact virtue – it is only a *liaison* of vanity on her part with my better half – but it will not last long – she is too formal for him.' However, given the Prince's impressive record of sexual conquest hitherto – he had even managed to make love to Princess Caroline, a woman who revolted him, three times in the space of 24 hours – it seems unlikely that his relationship with Lady Hertford was not physically consummated.

This conclusion is emphasised in the light of his ridiculous attempt to seduce Lady Bessborough in the winter of 1809, when he tried to take advantage of the fact that her long-time lover, Lord Granville Leveson-Gower, was about to marry her late sister's daughter, Lady Harriet Cavendish. 'He has killed me,' she wrote to Leveson-Gower in December, explaining how the Prince had delivered 'the most Vehement Tirade against you for marrying', given 'a list of your inconstancies', and then fallen to his knees. clasped her round the waist and kissed her neck. She continued:

> I screamed with vexation and fright; he continued sometimes struggling with me, sometimes sobbing and crying . . . Then mixing abuse of you, vows of eternal love, entreaties and promises of what he would do – he would break with Mrs F[itzherbert] and Ly. H[ertford], I should *make my own terms!!* I should be his sole confidant, sole adviser – private or public – I should guide his politics, Mr. Canning should be Prime Minister (whether in this reign or the next did not appear); then over and over and over again the same round of complaint, despair, entreaties, and promises, and always Mr. Canning à tout bout de change, and whenever he mentioned him it was in the tenderest accent and attempting some liberty, that really, G., had not my heart been breaking I must have laughed out at the comicality of having [Canning] so coupled and so made use

of – and then that immense, grotesque figure flouncing about
half on the couch, half on the ground.

It took two hours for Lady Bessborough to convince the Prince that she
'never could or would be on any other terms with him than the
acquaintance with which he had always honoured' her. Having arrived
at this 'tolerably friendly making up', the Prince then spent a further two
hours gossiping about Leveson-Gower's love affairs. 'You know I am
humble enough,' declared Lady Bessborough, 'but I really felt revolted
and indignant at his disgusting folly – sad proof of my increasing age.'[23]

If Princess Caroline's assumption that the Prince did not make love
to Lady Hertford is doubtful, her estimation of how long the relationship would last was certainly wide of the mark. It survived for almost 13
years – partly because Lady Hertford was so politically astute. When the
Prince eventually abandoned his Whig principles, she was held responsible; but the truth of the matter is that he had been distancing himself
from the main Whig aspiration – Catholic emancipation – for some
time. Lady Hertford simply accelerated this process by the articulation
with which she espoused the Tory creed.

Mrs Fitzherbert had all but conceded defeat by the time she wrote
the following letter to the Prince in 1808 (the month is undated). 'It
is with the greatest reluctance I take up my pen to address you upon
a subject very painful to my feelings.' Mr Porden, the architect, had
underestimated the cost of her new villa on the Steine at Brighton by
£300 (she had already paid £6,000), and she could not afford to pay
it. 'I feel particularly distressed at this circumstance,' she continued,
'. . . for though we now have been married three-and-twenty years
I never at any period solicited you for assistance.' (He had, however,
recently increased her income to £5,000 per year.) She had 'twice
been threatened with arrests' and would 'feel no degradation in
going to a jail'. She added: 'I thought it my duty to inform you of
these circumstances, for which I hope I shall not incur your displeasure, for as your wife I feel I have still a claim upon your protection,
which I trust is not entirely alienated from me.'[24]

The Prince, who retained his affection for and sense of duty towards his first wife until his death, undoubtedly paid this debt because she was not carted off to a debtors' prison. Notwithstanding his passion for Lady Hertford, he was anxious not to lose all contact with Mrs Fitzherbert – not to mention Minney Seymour and Maryanne Smythe – and regularly sent her invitations to visit the Pavilion. Lady Hertford, too, was happy to see a gradual decline in Mrs Fitzherbert's influence rather than a sudden break. She encouraged the Prince to spend part of his mornings in Brighton at Mrs Fitzherbert's house, but he was not to speak to her at the Pavilion. For a while, to protect her own reputation, she even refused to attend functions at Carlton House unless her rival was present.

However, by December 1809 Mrs Fitzherbert had had enough. She could not, she informed the Prince by letter on the 18th, accept his latest invitation to visit the Pavilion. She explained:

> The very great incivilities I have received these two years just because I obeyed your orders in going there was too visible to everyone present and too poignantly felt by me to admit of my putting myself in a situation of again being treated with such indignity . . . I feel I owe it to myself not to be insulted under your roof with impunity. The influence you are now under, and the conduct of one of your servants [Colonel Bloomfield, his Gentleman Attendant since 1808], I am sorry to say, has the appearance of your sanction and support, and renders my situation in your house . . . impossible any longer to submit to . . . The disappointment to my dear girl mortifies me very much.[25]

The Prince replied the following day. No course of action that she chose to take, he wrote, could ever make him 'deviate from or forget those affectionate feelings' he had 'ever entertained' for her. As for Minney 'and the severe sensation she will naturally experience, nobody can be so great a sufferer as myself'. He consoled himself with the 'reflexion that however I may . . . be prevented from doing all those acts of tenderness to Her which my Heart ever dictates, she never shall . . . experience any alteration from me from that which does not and never can proceed spontaneously from Herself.' He was as good as his word.[26]

Still exerting a major influence over the Prince at this time was Beau Brummell, the undisputed leader of fashion. It was during the 1800s that Brummell introduced the two innovations in dress for which he is best remembered: starched neckcloths and Hessian boots. In the case of neckcloths, Brummell replaced the loose, baggy circle of often grubby material with the finest muslin, standing stiffly under the chin, meticulously tied and symmetrically creased. It was sometimes worn so high, and with so much starch, that the wearer was unable to turn his head – like the young dandy at dinner who, 'when he wanted to speak to a footman, bent his head back until his face became horizontal'.[27]

Brummell brought in Hessians, a tasselled high boot first worn by troops from the Grand Duchy of Hesse, to replace top boots which had fallen out of favour because of their association with French revolutionaries. With the Hessians came pantaloons – tight-fitting leggings – and before long trousers were replacing knee-breeches (the latter having been adopted by Napoleon's court). Brummel solved the tendency for pantaloons to become baggy with unsightly creases by securing the bottom of the leg with straps which passed under the arch of the foot.

Knee-breeches were still worn in the evening with a swallow-tail coat. During the day it was *de rigeur* to don a frock-coat – a long, double-breasted garment – frogged with silk, and trimmed with fur in winter. Brummell had by now managed to discourage the excess of silk and satin, gold lace and multi-coloured embroidery so beloved of the Prince and his friends – though he still approved of fancy waistcoats. One of his less drastic innovations was the use of white leather tops to riding boots instead of brown. Ladies, on the other hand, were beginning to wear knickers beneath their petticoats – so named because they resembled the knee-breeches sketched by the artist George

Cruikshank for Washington Irving's *History of New York by Diedrich Knickerbocker*.

The Prince and Brummell may have shared the same tailors – Schweitzer and Davison in Cork Street, Weston and Meyer in Conduit Street – but only one of them was setting the style. Asked one time what cloth he recommended for a coat, Schweitzer replied: 'Why, sir, the Prince wears superfine, and Mr Brummell the Bath coating; but it is immaterial which you choose. Suppose, sir, we say the Bath coating – I think Mr Brummell has a trifle the preference.'

The Beau was also responsible for introducing the left-hand-only style of opening a snuff-box: pushing up the lid with the thumb, closing it with the index finger, and using the right hand to put a pinch of snuff on the back of the left. The Prince, who was less of a snuff-taker than a snuff-box manipulator, prided himself on the elegance with which he could open a box. He would pretend to convey the snuff to his nose, and then flick away the imaginary residue with his handkerchief. But even he was mystified by the workings of one of Brummell's expensive collection of snuff-boxes with an invisible hinge known as a 'Lawrence Kirk'. He was damned if he could open it, he told the assembled company, and passed it to Lord Liverpool (the future Prime Minister) who set about it with a knife. 'Confound the fellow,' observed Brummell, 'he takes my snuff-box for an oyster.'

As oysters were mainly eaten by the lower echelons of society at this time, the put-down was doubly insulting.[28]

Brummell was the most celebrated member of that exclusive cult of social discrimination known as dandyism. The fact that he himself did not come from the top drawer of society was less important than the clothes he wore. He was aristocratic in everything but his family history, living proof that dandyism embraced both social mobility and rigidity. The dandy was described in the late nineteenth-century play *Beau Austin*, by W.E. Henley and Robert Louis Stevenson, as being 'a private gentleman by birth, but a kind of king by habit and reputation'. Brummell's challenge to the Prince's leadership of high society, and the nicknames of other notable dandies, like 'Prince' Boothby and 'Prince'

Lascelles, tend to indicate that mockery and mimicry of authority was a distinctive trait of dandyism. 'That was his style,' wrote Virginia Woolf of Brummell, 'flickering, sneering, hovering on the edge of insolence, skimming the edge of nonsense, but always keeping within some curious mean.'[29]

With the Prince, however, Brummell had a tendency to go too far, as on the occasion when, out of friendship for Lady Jersey, he called out loudly for '*Mistress* Fitzherbert's carriage'; or when he remarked to Colonel McMahon about the Prince, 'I made him what he is, I can unmake him.' That the two gradually drifted apart was probably less due to the odd indiscreet remark than the fact that, beyond clothes and manners, they had little in common. Where the Prince was an unashamed hedonist, the Beau was curiously ascetic – particularly when it came to matters sexual. The diarist Thomas Raikes wrote:

> Never was there a man who during his career had such unbounded influence and, what is seldom the case, such general popularity in society. Without being a man of intrigue, for I never knew him engaged in what is called a *liaison* in society, he was the idol of women. Happy was she in whose opera-box he would pass an hour, at whose table he would dine, or whose assembly he would honour, and why? Not only because he was a host of amusement in himself with his jokes and his jeers, but because he was such a favourite with the men that were all anxious to join the party.[30]

The obvious inference is that Brummell was homosexual. He certainly enjoyed displaying his naked body to morning callers (including the Prince) and may even have positioned his mirror to give them a better view. At the same time, he gave out clear signals to both sexes that they could look but not touch. He was capable of conducting flirtatious relationships, but they tended to be ritualistic and formal. The typical dandy affected to love all women and be bored by all men – the opposite may have been true for Brummell. Marriage could have saved him from financial ruin, but he professed to be unable to find the ideal partner. One aristocratic candidate was rejected on the spurious ground that she ate cabbage.

It may well have been because of his sexual ambivalence that he felt most at home in the company of courtesans like Harriette Wilson and Julia Johnstone. Such women inhabited the *demi-monde*, but drew their protectors from the *grande monde* of privilege and leisure. Possessed of good looks, character and style, they could command large sums of money, even independence and respect. The basic difference between them and common prostitutes was not so much a question of class as of personality. They provided all the pleasures of companionship without the restrictions of marriage.

Harriette Wilson (née Dubochet), the most sought after courtesan of her time, was born in Mayfair in 1786 to a Swiss watchmaker and the illegitimate daughter of a country squire. Though no beauty, her vitality, wit and willingness to learn, combined with a take-me-or-leave-me attitude, ensured a swift rise to the top of her profession. After becoming the mistress of the Earl of Craven at the age of 15, she was kept at various times by the Honourable Frederick Lamb, the Duke of Argyll, Lord Ponsonby, the Marquess of Worcester and many others besides. But she was never the exclusive possession of any one man, and the Duke of Wellington was among her many partners. When she decided to publish her memoirs in 1825, demanding £200 from her former lovers as the price of omission, the Duke replied famously: 'Publish and be damned.' She did, and made a fortune.

According to Wilson, the Prince was almost one of her conquests. In about 1802, as she was tiring of Craven, she wrote to the heir apparent from Brighton. 'I am told that I am very beautiful,' she began modestly, 'so, perhaps you would like to see me.' Many were 'disposed' to love her, she continued, but she would 'be quite satisfied with one'. In the meantime, her life was 'very dull . . . and worse even than being at home with my father'. She concluded: 'So, if you pity me, and believe you could make me in love with you, write to me, and direct to the post-office here.'

Not one to look a gift horse in the mouth, the Prince replied through one of his equerries, inviting 'Miss Wilson' up to town for 'an interview'. Her tart response read:

> Sir,
>
> To travel fifty-two miles, this bad weather, merely to see a man, with only the given number of legs, arms, fingers, etc., would, you must admit, be madness, in a girl like myself, surrounded by humble admirers, who are ever ready to travel any distance for the honour of kissing the tip of her little finger; but if you can prove to me that you are one bit better than any man who may be ready to attend my bidding, I'll even start for London directly. So, if you can do anything better, in the way of pleasing a lady, than ordinary men, write directly; if not, adieu, Monsieur le Prince.[31]

And there the matter ended – or so Harriette Wilson would have us believe. A more likely scenario is that she did indeed have an affair with the Prince, but kept it quiet when he duly paid up in 1825. Why else would he tell his Private Secretary Sir William Knighton, in January 1828, that Wilson's intention to publish further revelations 'has entirely knocked me up and destroyed almost all the little amount of strength I had'.[32]

The world in which Harriette Wilson plied her trade was an unforgiving one of loose morals, brutal sports, coarse humour and steely wit. The men about town – known as bucks or Corinthians – not only cultivated the manners of the jockeys and prize-fighters whom they patronised; they also rode and boxed like them. One sporting dandy even filed his front teeth so that he could whistle like the stage-coach drivers he so admired. As well as hunting, drinking and cock-fighting, the bucks liked to attend public hangings and bare-knuckle prize-fights.

In his youth, the Prince himself had for a time taken a keen interest in the illegal sport of prize-fighting. These supposedly secret contests would take place in open-air rings, watched by huge crowds of up to

30,000 people. Rules were kept to a minimum. The fighters, wearing just drawers and pumps, were allowed to throw as well as punch. Each round lasted until a man was knocked off his feet; he would then be given 30 seconds to recover before he had to return to the mark. Only when he was unable to do so was his opponent declared the winner. With no time limit as such, a fight could last anything from a matter of minutes to several hours. One of the longest on record was between two Midlanders, Griffiths and Baylis, who fought 213 rounds in four hours and half a minute.

The most controversial fight in the history of prize-fighting took place between Tom Cribb, Champion of England, and Tom Molineaux, an ex-slave from America (and popularly known as 'Black Ajax'), at Copthorne Common in December 1810. It took 34 rounds, and just under an hour, for Cribb to emerge victorious. But in round 31, with both fighters exhausted and their bloody faces unrecognisable, Molineaux had thrown Cribb so heavily that he would never have made the mark in time. He was saved by his second, Joe Ward, who gained him valuable breathing-space by complaining to the umpires that Molineaux had 'bullets' (lead weights) in his fists. In the time it took the umpires to disprove this charge, Cribb managed to recover. According to George Macdonald Fraser, author of *Black Ajax*, the Prince is said to have remarked: 'Molineaux, I maintain, *beat* Cribb! Curse me if he did not!'[33]

In fact, the Prince had long since severed his ties with the prize ring. The first fight he is on record as attending was that between Martin and Humphries at Newmarket on 3 May 1786. A year later – following in the footsteps of his great-uncle, the Duke of Cumberland ('Butcher' Cumberland of Culloden), who had backed the great Jack Broughton, the first Champion of England – the Prince is said to have arranged a fight between his chair man, Tring, and Sam Martin of Bath at Shepherd's Bush. Ironically, the contest was prevented from taking place by the 10th Light Dragoons who, on the orders of the local magistrates, smashed up the stage and dispersed the crowd.

A Gillray print of the epic fight between John 'Gentleman' Jackson and Thomas Fewtrell at Croydon on 9 June 1788 – which Jackson won – depicts the Prince and his disreputable friend, George Hanger, among the spectators. But the Prince's interest in pugilism was brought to an abrupt end the following August when he witnessed the infamous fight at Brighton between Tom Tyne and Earl – the latter dying as a result. He is said to have awarded Earl's widow a pension, and vowed never to attend another contest. Nor did he. When Tring was beaten by Ben Brain in 1789, the Prince was no longer involved as a spectator or a patron.

However, Earl's death did little to discourage the less fastidious members of that well-bred boxing fraternity known as the Fancy. Its numbers included the Dukes of York and Clarence (whose country house, Bushey Park, was near to Moulsey Hurst, the most popular prize-fighting venue of them all); William Windham (Pitt's Secretary at War); Lord Yarmouth; and the Prince's friends, the 7th and 8th Earls of Barrymore. Richard Barry, the 7th Earl (better known as 'Hellgate'), was the patron of Hooper, the 'Tinman', who supplemented his earnings in the ring by acting as Barry's bodyguard. On one occasion, Barry was returning in his phaeton from dinner with the Prince when he got into a disagreement with a gentleman driving a one-horse chaise. By liberal use of his horsewhip, Barry provoked the gentleman into a fight; when it did not go Barry's way, the 'Tinman' stepped in to put an end to it. As Pierce Egan's *Boxiana* (published in 1813) put it: 'His Lordship was fond of *larking*, and whenever he could not come through the piece in style, HOOPER appeared as his bully – whose name overawed, and many a time, he has saved his patron a good *milling*.'[34]

Vast sums were wagered on the outcome of individual fights, and gambling in general was particularly popular in the first decade of the nineteenth century because of the lax system of credit – provincial banks were allowed to print their own banknotes – and the high level of boredom produced by the long war. Faro and macao were the favourite card games in the clubs of St James's. One night at Watiers – dubbed the Dandy's Club by Lord Byron, where fine cuisine and bold play were a matter of course – Brummell came to the rescue of the consumptive Tom Sheridan, son of the dramatist, who was down to his last few counters having lost several hundred pounds at macao. Taking Sheridan's place, Brummell soon transformed his remaining £10 into £1,500. Giving half to Sheridan, he said: 'Now go home Tom and give your wife and brats a supper, and never play again.'[35]

Horses and dazzling carriages were another extravagance. Two-wheeled curricles, open-top britzkas, light-weight tilburys and four-wheeled phaetons skimmed along the streets like so many insects on a pond. Sporting bucks, wont to drive themselves, became renowned for 'tooling the ribbons' or 'coming coachy in prime style'. They liked nothing better than dashing up the Brighton Road in a four- or six-in-hand, horse-whipping the turnpike man out of their way and overturning the slower traffic. Lord Petersham's equipage was all brown, in memory of his unrequited passion for a beautiful widow of that name; Tommy Onslow, the Prince's friend, preferred an all-black rig which looked like a hearse. But none could rival Mr Cope, or the 'Green Man' as he was known. Not only did he wear green clothes and drive a green coach and horses, he powdered his hair green and was never seen to eat anything but spinach.

Most of his contemporaries were not so abstemious; far from it. The sheer quantity and variety of food and drink consumed at this time by those who could afford it was astonishing. Lady Harriet Leveson-Gower, staying at the house of her brother-in-law, the Marquess of Stafford, wrote:

> The dinner for us two was soup, fish, fricasee of chicken, cut-lets, venison, veal, hare, vegetables of all kinds, tart, melon, pineapple, grapes, peaches, nectarines, with wine in propor-tion. Six servants to wait upon us, whom we did not dare dispense with, and a gentleman-in-waiting and a fat old house-keeper hovering round the door to listen, I suppose, if we should express a wish. Before this sumptuous repast was well digested, about four hours later, the doors opened, and in was

pushed a supper of the same proportion, in itself enough to have fed me for a week. I did not know whether to laugh or cry.

Claret was usually offered with the meats (champagne by the vulgar), tokay (a sweet Hungarian wine) with the pudding, and hock, sherry and port or port and water throughout the meal. Brummell did much to alter this latter custom, insisting that this 'hot, intoxicating liquor so much drunk by the lower orders' should wait for the cheese.'[36]

The part of London inhabited by high society was essentially Mayfair, bounded by Bond Street to the east, Park Lane to the west, Grosvenor Square to the north and St James's Park to the south. Fields lay beyond the turnpike at Hyde Park Corner, interrupted only by the villages of Chelsea, Brompton and Kensington. From Oxford Street (then known as Oxford Road) clear views could be had of Hampstead. St Paul's and the City lay outside this exclusive perimeter, home to merchants and lawyers. 'A nobleman,' wrote Robert Southey, 'would not be found by any accident to live in that part which is properly called the City, unless he should be confined for treason or sedition in Newgate or the Tower.'[37]

Entertainment for the well-heeled included balls and dinners, the theatre, the circus and the pleasure-gardens of Vauxhall and Ranelagh. One of the highlights of the Season was the Cyprians' Ball at the Argyle Rooms where the courtesans – the 'Fashionable Impures' – played hostess to their admirers and protectors. But the most popular way for both the *grande* and *demi-monde* to spend the evening was at the opera where Court dress – knee-breeches and *chapeaux bras* (three-cornered flat silk hats) – was *de rigeur*. It was because the opera was the ideal showcase for her charms that Harriette Wilson was prepared to pay 200 guineas a season for a box in the first tier.

Overall, however, London was a noisy, chaotic amalgam of city, town and village. Its two ancient citadels, Westminster and the City, were separated by a densely populated area of stark contrast: on the one hand, elegant squares and opulent thoroughfares; on the other, warrens of dark, dirty alleyways in which a stranger was in danger of losing anything from his pocket-book to his life. In 1807, 13 gas-lamps were installed on the south side of Pall Mall, and five years later the Gas Light and Coke Company established its first gasworks in Westminster. But the process of lighting the common roads of London – as opposed to the main streets of the West End and the City – took more than 20 years to complete.

Often, popular venues were in the midst of seedy districts. Drury Lane and Covent Garden Theatres, for example, were in a notoriously dangerous area, the haunt of murderers, escaped convicts and prostitutes. But the really hard-core 'rookeries' (criminal districts), 'hells' (illegal gambling clubs) and 'flash-houses' (pubs frequented by criminals) were concentrated in Whitechapel, St Giles, Clerkenwell and Southwark.

London had virtually no drainage system. Even the biggest houses were only just beginning to replace chamber-pots with water closets. Outside the smarter areas, slops were slung from windows and refuse accumulated in the gutters. This poor state of hygiene was partly responsible for the high rate of infant mortality: more than 50 per cent of infant deaths were not even reported; many of those which were notified were put down to convulsions. The apothecary still treated most minor ailments, while dentistry was still in its infancy and teeth were either good or bad. When they were bad, most people had them drawn at the street corner by itinerant quacks. False teeth – an expensive luxury – were either made from boxwood or the real thing taken from somebody else's mouth (living and dead).

By 1801, London had grown to just under 1 million inhabitants, more than eleven times the population of any other British city. Its sheer size, allied to a long tradition of lawlessness, encouraged crime on a huge scale. In 1797 Patrick Colquhoun, the Chief Magistrate of Westminster, estimated that no fewer than 115,000 Londoners were engaged in criminal pursuits: there were 52,000 prostitutes and bawdy-house keepers, 8,500 'cheats, swindlers, and gamblers', 8,000 'thieves, pilferers and embezzlers', 3,000 'dissolute Characters' who seduced others 'to intemperance, lewdness, debauchery, gambling, and excess' (Colquhoun did not specify whether the Prince himself was included in this category), and 2,000 'Thieves, Burglars, Highway Robbers, Pick-pockets and River Pirates'.[38]

The City had its watchmen – known as 'charleys' because they were instituted in the reign of Charles II – and Westminster its Bow Street Runners, but the rest of London was in a state of virtual anarchy because the 90 or so parishes and precincts lacked unity and central control. Some headway was made by the Middlesex Justices' Act of 1792, which established seven new Public Offices, each with three stipendiary magistrates and six salaried constables, and the setting up of the Bow Street Horse Patrol in 1805, but there was no unitary police authority until the Metropolitan Police came into being in 1829.

Most convicted criminals were either transported to Australia or sent to the dreaded hulks, former men-of-war moored in the Thames. Conditions were appalling, with unwashed prisoners packed together on three airless decks. At night the hatches were screwed down, leaving the inmates to fight among themselves. Many died of disease; a few at the hands of their fellow prisoners. 'Whatever little remains of innocence or honesty a man might have is sure to be lost there,' wrote one convict. In 1816, more than 2,500 prisoners were aboard five hulks; by 1828, both figures had almost doubled.

Newgate, close to the Old Bailey, the common gaol for both the City and the county of Middlesex, was positively benign in comparison. Its population was mainly made up of prisoners awaiting trial, and those who had been sentenced to transportation and death. Largely left to their own devices, the inmates staged 'prize-fights' and mock trials, aping the language of the courts and awarding harsh 'sentences' to those who transgressed their unwritten code. Riots were commonplace, particularly when a group of convicts was due to be shipped overseas. Public hangings took place outside the gaol or at Tyburn, where huge crowds turned the event into something of a public holiday.

Debtors were kept in three separate prisons: the Fleet, not far from Newgate, the King's Bench at Southwark, and the Marshalsea, also south of the river. Those with money (something of a contradiction in terms) could live there in relative comfort with their families, receiving visitors and sending out for food and drink. At the King's Bench in Southwark, where the gaolers together made more than £800 a year from the sale of beer alone, the prisoners often sub-let rooms to each other.[39]

Perhaps the best contemporary account of London at this time is given in Robert Southey's *Letters from England* (1807), which purport to be the correspondence of a Spanish visitor. This ruse enabled Southey to make general observations that most Britons would take for granted, and also to express particularly frank criticism of their social customs. Of the sights and sounds of the City he wrote:

> When I reached Cheapside the crowd completely astonished me. On each side of the way were two uninterrupted streams of people, one going east, the other west. At first I thought some extraordinary occasion must have collected such a concourse; but I soon perceived it was only the usual course of business . . . [The] rapidity with which they moved was as remarkable as their numbers . . . The carriages were numerous in proportion, and were driven with answerable velocity.
>
> If possible, I was still more astonished at the splendour of the shops: drapers, stationers, confectioners, pastry-cooks, seal-cutters, book-sellers, print-sellers, hosiers, fruiterers, china-sellers – one close to another, without intermission, a shop to every house, street after street, and mile after mile.

London's inhabitants, he observed, were

> . . . divided into two distinct casts, – the Solar and Lunar races, – those who live by day, and those who live by night, antipodes to each other, the one rising just as the others go to

bed. The clatter of the night coaches had scarcely ceased, before that of the morning carts began. The dustman with his bell, and his chant of dust-ho! succeeded to the watchman; then came the porter-house boy for the pewter-pots which had been set out for supper the preceding night; the milkman next, and so on, a succession of cries, each in a different tune.

He also wrote about ballad-sellers peddling news of murders, quack-doctors approaching strangers with their 'never-failing pills', and watchmen calling out the state of the weather every half-hour of the night. London was not for the faint-hearted.[40]

Unlike his elder brother, the Duke of York was not able to keep his liaison with a notorious courtesan from the public eye. His dutiful but unassuming Prussian wife had long since retired to Oatlands Park, their chaotic country house at Weybridge, where she busied herself with an enormous collection of pet dogs, parrots and monkeys. She still saw her husband at week-ends, when he brought boisterous house-parties down from London, but otherwise they led separate lives. 'The Duke and Duchess,' noted Charles Greville, 'live on the best terms; their manner to one another is cordial, and while full of mutual respect and attention, they follow separately their own occupations and amusements without interfering with one another.'[41]

This 'open' marriage – far from unusual at this time – enabled the Duke to take a string of lovers. One such was the remarkable Mrs Mary Anne Clarke, a dark-eyed beauty whom he met in about 1805. Born 29 years earlier, in a humble dwelling off Chancery Lane, Mary Anne had benefited from her mother's remarriage to a typesetter named Farquhar. It was said that she owed her education to the son of her step-father's employer, who fell in love with her and taught her to read. She eventually married Mr Clarke, a well-set-up young stonemason from Golden Lane, and moved with him to the West End where they had two children. But when her husband took to gambling, amassing large debts in the process, she began to entertain gentlemen as the easiest way to supplement her meagre allowance.

Meeting the Duke was like hitting the jackpot. Entranced by his vivacious young lover, he set her up in a house in Gloucester Place, off Portman Square, with a staff of more than 20 servants, including two butlers and six footmen. 'Oh my angel,' he once wrote when called away from town, 'do me justice and be convinced that there never was woman adored as you are . . . Adieu, . . . my sweetest dearest love, till the day after to-morrow and be assured that I shall ever remain yours and yours alone.'[42]

Mrs Clarke embraced this new world of plenty with all the enthusiasm of a pig at a trough, spending her protector's money with gay abandon (including £500 on a dinner service which had belonged to Louis XVI's nephew, the Duc de Berri). After three delightful but expensive years, the Duke tired of his demanding lover and turned for consolation to a Mrs Carey of Fulham, a woman with more modest tastes. But Mrs Clarke would not be fobbed off so easily, and demanded £2,000 to pay off her debts. The Duke, who had already promised her an annual allowance of several hundred pounds, referred the matter to the Prince's Chancellor, William Adam, who kept a friendly eye on his financial affairs. Adam, the M.P. for Kincardineshire and a Scot with a zealous sense of economy, advised against paying either the allowance or the debt.

A furious Mrs Clarke then made repeated threats to disclose details about her relationship with the Duke – but Adam would not budge. So she confided in a former lover, Colonel Gwyllym Wardle, the Radical M.P. for Okehampton, that she had raised money by using her influence with the Duke to secure certain military appointments. Well aware that the allegations were political dynamite – the Opposition in general was looking for every opportunity to accuse the government of mismanaging the conduct of the war – Wardle decided to raise the matter in Parliament.

On 27 January 1809, Wardle shocked the House of Commons by charging the Duke of York with using the patronage at his disposal as Commander-in-Chief for the benefit of his former mistress, Mary Anne Clarke. She had, he claimed, accepted money from officers seeking employment or promotion, and the Duke had not only agreed to her recommendations but shared in the profits. He therefore proposed a committee to investigate the Duke's conduct 'with regard to promotions, exchanges, and appointments to commissions, in the Army and in raising levies for the Army'. Lord Castlereagh, the Secretary for War and the Colonies, responded for the government by declaring his 'unfeigned satisfaction, that, at length, an opportunity was afforded of instituting an effectual inquiry into the grounds of the various calumnies and misrepresentations which had of late been so industriously circulated against that illustrious personage'. Due to the gravity of the charges, however, the inquiry would be conducted by the House of Commons itself.[43]

At first the Prince was firmly behind his brother, telling William Adam 'that he considered an attack upon the Duke as an attack upon himself'. But as the inquiry got under way, and the evidence against the Duke started to build, the Prince began to take a less partial stance. Sensing that the press and public opinion were turning against his brother, he decided 'not to interfere, by his friends or opinions, in the discussion' but to maintain 'a state of neutrality'.[44]

Mrs Clarke was the star witness, telling the House that the Duke was fully complicit in her system of trading commissions for cash. On 'numerous' occasions she had urged him to arrange for Mr X or Lieutenant Y to be appointed to the requisite rank. It had happened so often that she had even taken to pinning the list of names applying for promotion to the bed-curtains at Gloucester Place. Many in the House were swayed by her beauty, courage and saucy wit. In response to detailed questions about her private life, she would reply, 'I cannot tell you because it was indelicate.' At least one member offered her 300 guineas to have supper with him. But many others were sceptical: it was one thing to accept that she might have whispered recommendations to her lover when he was at his most amenable; quite another to believe that he was party to a systematic sale of promotions.

The Duke himself had written to Spencer Perceval, the Leader of the House of Commons, in early February, denying 'not only all corrupt participation in any of the infamous transactions which have appeared in evidence . . ., or any connivance of their existence, but also the slightest knowledge or suspicion that they existed at all'. The majority of the House tended to agree with him, despite the evidence to the contrary – like the testimony of Miss Taylor, a friend of Mrs Clarke's, who claimed to have been present at Gloucester Place when the question of promoting a Colonel French was raised. According to Miss Taylor, the Duke had remarked that Colonel French 'worries me continually about the levy business and is always wanting something more in his favour'.

He then turned to Mrs Clarke and asked, 'How does French behave to darling?'

'Only middling, not very well,' she replied.

'Master French must mind what he is about or I shall cut up him and his levy too.'

While Taylor's evidence was hardly conclusive, one of the Duke's letters to Mrs Clarke was harder to explain away. 'Clavering is mistaken, my angel,' he wrote, 'in thinking that any new regiments are to be raised; it is not intended; only second battalion to the existing corps; you had better therefore tell him so and that you were sure there would be no use in applying for him.'[45]

By the end of February 1809, with the presentation of evidence complete, the Prince was 'worried to death' about the outcome of the inquiry. At the same time, he was highly critical of his brother for promising Mrs Clarke an allowance which had not been paid; in his opinion, if the Duke had kept his word like a gentleman, the inquiry would never have come about. Nevertheless, with his advisers giving conflicting advice – Adam wanted the Prince's friends to attend the crucial debates, Thomas Tyrwhitt did not – he was wavering in his resolution to remain neutral. Lord Temple (later Duke of Buckingham), Lord Grenville's nephew and a junior minister in the previous government, probably clinched matters when he warned the Prince that if he tried to save the Duke he would share his unpopularity.[46]

On 8 March, the day when the House began debating the evidence, the King pleaded with the Prince to abandon a neutrality which was tantamount to condemning his brother; the Queen added that his father's health was in danger of collapsing if the Duke was found guilty. But the Prince – who may even have welcomed the former eventuality – would only partially be swayed. With Tyrwhitt out of town, he told McMahon to vote for the Duke, but would not ask the Dukes of Northumberland and Norfolk to order their M.P.s to do likewise. Further proof, commented William Fremantle, a prominent Grenvillite, 'of his great weakness and indecision'.[47]

In the event, the Prince's equivocation made little difference. On 17 March, Spencer Perceval's resolution that the Duke was innocent both of personal corruption and of connivance was passed by 278 votes to 196 (an earlier amendment – that there were grounds for charging the Duke 'with having knowledge of corruption which has been disclosed by the evidence – having been defeated by 200 votes). However, the relatively small size of the majority, coupled with the revelation that the Commander-in-Chief was in the habit of discussing official business with his mistress, left the Duke no option but to resign.[48]

Whether the Duke's career could have been saved if his elder brother had offered his full support in the Commons is doubtful. The weight of evidence meant that a sizeable minority were always likely to vote against a resolution which did not distinguish between personal corruption and complicity; even if the Duke had not been aware of Mrs Clarke's activities, they must have reasoned, he was certainly guilty of professional misconduct and deserved to lose his post.

Nevertheless, the Prince's failure to stand by his brother was a craven act born partly out of a belief in his (unproven) guilt, partly out of a fear of offending public opinion, and partly as a payback for the Duke's unwillingness to support his own repeated demands for military promotion. Whichever motive was uppermost, the Prince emerges from the affair with little credit.

11

The Restricted Regency

Since the formation of the Portland government in March 1807, the war had not gone well for Britain. Napoleon's victory over the Russians at Friedland in June of that year, and the subsequent Treaty of Tilsit, had transformed Britain's last remaining ally into an aggressive opponent. In return for closing all the ports under her control to British ships, Russia was given a free hand in the Baltic and the Bosphorus.

This enabled the French to complete their subjugation of the Iberian Peninsula. In November 1807, they invaded Portugal and the Regent was forced to escape with his government to Brazil. Five months later, Napoleon deposed the new Spanish king, Ferdinand, and replaced him with his brother, Joseph Bonaparte. But this time he had gone too far and the outraged Spaniards rose in rebellion, as did the Portuguese. Quick to take advantage, the British rushed 10,000 men under Sir Arthur Wellesley to Portugal. But no sooner had Wellesley gained a decisive victory over Marshal Junot's army at Vimieiro on 21 August 1808, than he was superseded first by Sir Hew Dalrymple and then Sir John Moore, who arrived in Portugal with reinforcements in the autumn.

Meanwhile, Napoleon had decided to conduct the Peninsula campaign in person. By early November 1808, at the head of more than

160,000 troops, he had defeated two Spanish armies and taken Madrid. Moore briefly threatened the French line of communication by marching his modest army of 30,000 across northern Spain in the direction of Burgos. But with Marshal Soult's forces blocking his path, and Napoleon hurrying up from Madrid, Moore let discretion take the better part of valour by withdrawing westwards to Corunna and the British fleet. This epic retreat – in which the Prince's regiment, the 10th Hussars (renamed from the Light Dragoons in 1806), distinguished itself – across 250 miles of mountainous country in the depths of winter was achieved despite a partial breakdown in discipline, the hostility of locals who objected to British looting, and constant attacks on the rearguard by Soult's pursuing force. Though 24,000 men were eventually re-embarked at Corunna in January 1809, Moore, who had been mortally wounded in the last rearguard action, was not among them.

Three months later – Napoleon having left the peninsula to deal with a renewed threat from the Austrians – Wellesley returned to Lisbon with 30,000 men. Successive victories against the French on the Douro river in May and at Talavera in eastern Spain two months later (earning him the title Viscount Wellington), were followed by retreat to the frontier fortress of Badajoz as King Joseph brought up the main French army.

Back home, meanwhile, George Canning, the Foreign Secretary, was anxious that Britain should profit from the imminent war between Austria and France by despatching a force either to northern Europe or to the Scheldt. When the War Department claimed in March that it had neither the men nor the materials to undertake either scheme, Canning wrote to Portland, complaining about the inefficiency of his colleagues and threatening to resign unless either Castlereagh was replaced or part of the War Department's business was transferred to his own. Not wanting to lose such an able minister, Portland asked him to keep his views secret until the end of the parliamentary session when a Cabinet reshuffle would not be so disruptive.

With the Austrian defeat of the French at Aspern in May, the plan to send troops to the Scheldt was revived. But even as the expedition got under way in July, Napoleon was gaining revenge for Aspern by trouncing the Austrians at Wagram and forcing them to sue for peace. Undeterred, the British invested Flushing, taking it after a two-week siege. This, however, gave the French time to strengthen Antwerp's defences. By the time the majority of troops were landed on the islands of Walcheren and South Beveland, the British commanders were united in their belief that an assault on Antwerp would be suicidal. Most of the men were re-embarked in mid-September. A strong force was left on Walcheren to keep the River Scheldt open to British trade; but it, too, was evacuated in December after fever on the marshy island had decimated its ranks.

In the wake of the main evacuation, Castlereagh learned from Lord Camden, the Lord President of the Council, of Canning's leading role in the plot to oust him from the War Department. He immediately challenged Canning to a duel, and they met on Putney Heath in the early hours of 21 September. According to the diarist and politician John Croker, Canning's second, Charles Ellis, 'was so nervous for his friend's safety that he could not load his pistols' and Lord Yarmouth (Castlereagh's second) had to do it for him. The protagonists missed with their first shots, but Castlereagh's second struck home, wounding Canning in the fleshy part of his upper thigh.[1]

Both then resigned, and Portland's government collapsed soon after. The Prime Minister, who had been ill for some time, retired to the country to die. He was replaced in early October by Spencer Perceval who became First Lord of the Treasury and Chancellor of the Exchequer, with Lords Bathurst and Liverpool as Foreign and War Secretaries respectively.

A month after the formation of Perceval's ministry, Mirza Abul Hassan Khan, the first Persian ambassador to visit Britain for almost 200 years, arrived in London to secure the ratification of an Anglo-Persian treaty. Kept waiting for more than eight months while ministers and Privy

Counsellors perused every clause, he spent his time riding, sightseeing, shopping and attending social functions. The journal that he kept during this period gives a fascinating insight into the way a non-European viewed the workings of British society.

Aged 34, tall and exceptionally handsome, invariably dressed in sumptuous robes and turbans of silk and brocade, Abul Hassan was much in demand. Of his first meeting with the Prince of Wales at Carlton House on 24 January 1810, he wrote:

> Handsome servants in colourful liveries trimmed with gold braid and pretty bejewelled girls were in attendance. When they saw us, they bowed and curtseyed in the English manner. Red-liveried footmen respectfully conducted us to the upper floor, which is reserved for the Prince of Wales' exclusive use. Here we found the Prince and his brothers and a group of noblemen seated, their heartstrings being plucked by talented musicians playing English tunes.
>
> As I joined the company, I dutifully paid my respects to the Prince who then opened the doors of affability and condescension to me and showed me such extreme kindness that my pen is incapable of describing it . . . It is amazing that, although he is in his 48th year, he looks no more than twenty. His face is marked with pride and dignity and in all my travels I have never encountered a more gracious prince.

Sensing that his Persian visitor was homesick, the Prince told him that if he was ever 'feeling melancholy on a rainy day', he could visit the covered pavilion in the garden of Carlton House to 'relax and banish the sorrow'. Before Abul Hassan took his leave, the Prince promised to send him a clock which needed winding only once every six months. Ten days later, at a dinner in Abul Hassan's honour at Carlton House, the Prince asked him whether he preferred thin women or fat. 'I like a woman as plump and as tall as a Cypress tree,' Hassan replied. 'Thin women do not attract me at all.'

Delighted by Hassan's 'poetic allusion', and admitting that his tastes were similar, the Prince then asked if he had 'found a woman in England'. Though he 'wished it were otherwise', said Hassan, none 'desired' him because of his beard. The Prince replied: 'If indeed they flee from your hairy face, you may at least be thankful to be spared their hairy intellects!'

On 8 February, Hassan recorded his impression of a Queen's Drawing-Room at St James's Palace:

> The guests were lined up on all sides and we tried in vain to make our way through the crowd. Then the Queen entered from another room, followed by ladies-in-waiting, beautiful as the Pleiades, three of the Princesses and a young page, the son of a lord, who carried her long train so that it would not drag on the floor. There must have been 1000 guests. The ladies wore 'hoop' skirts . . . Some wore Phoenix-like feathers in their hair; others wore jewels . . .
>
> The Queen stood on the Royal dais while the ladies brought their daughters forward to be presented individually by the Deputy Master of Ceremonies. Their names and titles were announced as the Queen spoke to each one . . . I learned that young ladies are not presented to the Queen before they reach the age of 17, and that, until they have had that honour, they do not go out in society or attend dinner parties and receptions. No member of a family touched by scandal is received at Court.

Accustomed as he was to the slim, high-waisted and often diaphanous 'Empire' style dresses then in fashion, Hassan was horrified by the tightly boned bodices and hooped skirts which were still being worn at Court (and had been since George III's accession). 'These strange costumes truly depress me,' he told his friend, Sir Gore Ouseley (soon to be appointed British Ambassador to Persia), likening the skirts to 'full-blown tents'. Men's Court clothes were not much better. 'They are immodest and unflattering to the figure,' he wrote, 'especially their trousers which look just like underdrawers.'

On 27 February, Hassan had dinner with the Duke and Duchess of York at their London residence, York House in Stable Yard. Also present were the Prince, Lord Wellesley (the Foreign Secretary since December 1809), Lady Anne Culling Smith, the Duchess's lady-in-waiting, and some of the other Royal Dukes. Hassan recalled:

> The Prince of Wales directed so many jokes and winks at Lord Wellesley that even that serious-minded Minister could not help laughing. And he exchanged such rare anecdotes with his brothers that they too became quite insensible with laughter.
>
> One of his stories was about the huge size of the penis of one of his Royal brothers – a fact which he discovered one night while riding with him in a carriage. His brother had felt the need to relieve himself: when he did so out of the carriage window, the water flowed as if from a fountain and the driver urged the horses forward to escape what he thought was a rainstorm! 'That is how I found out,' said the Prince, 'and I am letting you into his secret too!'

Hassan was particularly fascinated by the 'rules governing entertaining in London'. He recorded:

> A 'dinner' lasts for four hours, from six o'clock until ten o'clock.
>
> A 'ball' is a large gathering attended by the nobility. It begins late in the evening, at ten o'clock, and lasts until five o'clock in the morning – seven hours are spent dancing! Three or four musicians play instruments which resemble the *kamancheh*. When the music begins, each gentleman asks a lady if she wishes to dance; if she says no, he asks another.
>
> Another kind of entertainment is called 'music', which may also mean singing. This also lasts for four hours [10 p.m. to

2 a.m.]. Guests are invited to hear a distinguished musician; and when he appears they become silent out of respect . . .

An 'assembly' is a form of entertainment which I have told my faithful friend Sir Gore Ouseley I think could well be done away with – and he agrees! This lasts for six hours [10 p.m. to 4 a.m.] and resembles nothing so much as the crowd at a ladies' *hammam* or the great gathering of souls at the Last Judgement.

There is one other form of entertainment, which the English call 'breakfast'; this means the morning meal. Guests present themselves at their host's table, partake of some food, and return home.

Night and day, it seems, the English think only of pleasure.

The Prince was obviously under the impression that Hassan thought likewise. When they met at a music party in Devonshire House on 28 May, the Prince mentioned a rumour that Hassan had taken a woman to his house. 'They say,' he continued with a smile, 'that you had sex with her eight times, and would have gone on till twenty if a man had not rushed to her rescue with a naked sword.'

'Lies!' protested Hassan. 'It all comes from people having too much leisure and nothing to do but gossip! These rumours must have been started by that shameless woman who writes to me declaring her love and begging to come with me to Iran. Of course I have replied to none of them – and if she continues to write I shall see that she is punished.'

(This woman, who later accused Hassan of fathering her child, turned out to be the same deluded creature who 'claimed to have had children by all the Royal Princes!')

Three days after the musical evening at Devonshire House, Hassan was shocked to hear the news that the Duke of Cumberland's valet, having narrowly failed to murder his master in the night, had cut his own throat. 'I was very distressed for the Prince,' noted Hassan, 'he has always been very kind and friendly to me – he calls me "Mufti".'[2]

At the inquiry held later that day, the Duke claimed to have been sleeping in his apartments in St James's Palace when he was awoken shortly before 3 in the morning by repeated blows to the head. He was saved from certain death by the thickness of his night-cap and the bed-curtain, which hampered the sabre cuts of his assailant. Shouting for help, the Duke leapt from the bed and was stabbed in the thigh as he opened the door to the ante-room. He was met by his English valet, Cornelius Neale, who had been awakened by his cries of 'Neale! Neale! I am murdered!' Grabbing a poker, Neale rushed into the Duke's bed-room, but it was empty. On the floor he discovered the Duke's bloodstained sword, which had been dropped by the assassin as he made his escape. The Guard was then called, and orders given for the house to be searched.

About 15 minutes later, as servants approached the room of Joseph Sellis, the Duke's Corsican valet, a gurgling sound was heard from within 'like water in a man's throat'. Inside, Sellis was found lying on the bed with his throat cut, the 'blood all in a froth running from his neck'. A white-handled razor lay on the floor nearby. Standing on the table was a basinful of water that 'appeared as if some one had been washing their bloody hands in it'.

Even more conclusive was the discovery by Neale, in a closet adjoin-ing the Duke's bedroom, of 'a pair of black leather slippers with the name Sellis written in each', 'a dark lantern, a bottle of water and the scabbard of the sword'. Furthermore, Neale told the inquiry, 'the key of the closet was in the inside of the door, which was not usual and could have been of no use but for the purpose of locking the door where he supposes the assassin had concealed himself.'

All this evidence pointed to the fact that Sellis had hidden in the closet before trying to kill the Duke. When the attempt failed, he fled to his room, made an effort to wash away some of the incriminating blood, and finally killed himself before he was apprehended. A possible motive – that Sellis was on bad terms with the Duke – was provided by some of the witnesses. Antonio Penzara, the Duke of Sussex's valet, tes-tified that Sellis had frequently mentioned his feud with Neale and the fact 'that he would be glad to leave the service' of the Duke who 'had used him ill by very often speaking sharp to him'. This bad feeling between Sellis on the one hand, and Neale and the Duke on the other, was confirmed by Frederick Greville, the Duke of Cambridge's valet. Sellis had even been heard 'to damn the King and the royal family' and say it was 'a pity they were not done away with'. Neale himself claimed that after Sellis had accused him of theft, and he had been cleared by an investigation, he had been so worried by his fellow valet's 'evil disposition' towards him that he had taken to hanging a pistol at the end of his bed for his own protection.

Mrs Neale said that Sellis 'was very obstinate and quarrelsome and would not bear contradiction, not even from His Royal Highness'. Nevertheless, the Duke was 'very partial' to Sellis, had always 'been very kind to him' and there was 'no reason to believe' that he held any grudge against the Duke. Mrs Sellis added that she had 'never heard' her husband 'make any complaint' of the Duke, 'but felt himself much gratified by the honour which H.R.H. and the Princess Augusta had done him by standing for their last child and for the presents they had made him.' However, during his last illness he had 'frequently complained of a giddiness in his head'.[3]

While the exact motive for the attempted assassination remains a mystery, the jury at the inquest were in no doubt that Sellis was responsible, and that he had then taken his own life. Fears of a cover-up were dispelled when it was discovered that the foreman of the jury was Francis Place, the well-known Charing Cross tailor and Radical politician, who was no friend of the Royal Family.

But not everyone was convinced by the verdict. Henry White, the owner of the Radical *Independent Whig*, made repeated hints that the Duke had murdered Sellis. When, in March 1813, he offered to prove his accusations, he was prosecuted, found guilty and sentenced to 15 months' imprisonment, with a fine of £200. He produced no evidence, and his 'proofs' amounted to little more than an assertion that some of the witnesses had lied at the inquest.

Far more harmful to the Duke of Cumberland's reputation was the memoir written in 1827 by Captain Charles Jones, his former private secretary, who felt 'compelled by some irresistible power' to set down before he died 'a crime which has laid buried in dark mystery for nearly 18 years'. On Christmas Eve 1815, he wrote, the Duke had taken him into the library, locked the door and sworn him to secrecy before confessing: 'You know that miserable business of Sellis's, that wretch, I was forced to destroy him in self defence, the villain threatened to propagate a report and I had no alternative.' Observing Jones's horrified reaction, the Duke said no more and the matter was never raised again during the six years that Jones remained in the Duke's service.[4]

The notebook containing this memoir was eventually discovered in the papers of one of Jones's descendants by Albert Sutton, a Manchester bookseller. In 1899, Sutton presented the notebook to the Royal Archives at Windsor Castle. As legal proof of the Duke's guilt, the document is far from conclusive, however. Written years after the event, it attributes words to the Duke which he may or may not have spoken. Even if the conversation did take place, there is still the possibility that Jones misunderstood the Duke, who was trying to explain that he had driven Sellis to make his assassination attempt, rather than that he was personally responsible for his death.

Any alternative scenario cannot square with the evidence offered at the inquiry – unless Neale and others were in on the plot to murder Sellis and fake the assassination. One theory popular at the time was that Sellis was killed because he was threatening to expose the Duke's homosexuality. The surveillance of gay servicemen, who were seen as a threat to the war effort, had recently been stepped up by the government. One month after Sellis's death, a male brothel (or molly house) in Vere Street was raided. Six men were imprisoned for two years after being violently abused in the public stocks; two others – one a serviceman – were hanged the following March. Mary Crawford's remark in Jane Austen's *Mansfield Park* about the admirals she had met – 'Of *Rears* and *Vices*, I saw enough' – should be read in the context of late Georgian Britain's anxieties about the sexual misconduct of soldiers.[5]

If Sellis's murder was a set-up, the Duke was forced to inflict (or have inflicted) some pretty severe injuries on himself to give his version of events some authority. These included four deep cuts to his head and throat, a partially severed right thumb, and flesh wounds to his left arm and right thigh.

To convalesce, the Duke was taken to Carlton House. Dr Cookson, who attended him there, told Joseph Farington that he was 'in a very nervous state' thanks to the large quantities of laudanum he was taking. 'He suffers much pain,' noted Farington on 13 June, 'and is much afflicted with spasms. One of the servants at *Carlton House* where the Duke now is, told Dr Cookson that the Prince of Wales is much affected by the Duke's illness, "more so," he added, "than either His mother or His sisters appear to be." He went on and said, "when ever any of the Prince's family are indisposed He feels for them." '[6]

On 25 October 1810, the Royal Family gathered at Windsor Castle to celebrate the Golden Anniversary of the King's accession. The occasion was strangely muted: partly because Princess Amelia – the King's youngest and favourite daughter – was seriously ill, and partly because the King himself, aged 72 and virtually blind, was showing symptoms of his earlier disorder. Miss Cornelia Knight, the Queen's companion, noted:

> As he went round the circle as usual, it was easy to perceive the dreadful excitement in his countenance . . . He called to him each of his sons separately, and said things to them equally sublime and instructive, but very unlike what he would have said before so many people had he been conscious of the circumstance.[7]

According to Lord Glenbervie, who heard the story from the Princess of Wales (and she from the Duke of Kent), the King's 'present seizure' had been partly caused by the Princess Amelia's recent confession that 'she had been guilty of great sins and wickedness, greater than his Majesty could believe, and requested that he would pray for her'.

Princess Caroline took this to mean Amelia's relationship with General Fitzroy. The Duke of York had told her that Amelia 'was certainly not privately married to General Fitzroy, but engaged, and that the Prince of Wales had promised to permit the marriage if he came to be King'. She died on 2 November, before her brother could fulfil his pledge.[8]

Spencer Perceval, who saw the King four days before Princess Amelia's death, noted that 'his conversation was prodigiously hurried . . . and extremely diffuse, explicit, and indiscreet.' On 1 November, Lord Chancellor Eldon found him 'quite incompetent to sign the Commission' to prorogue Parliament until the end of the month. Both Houses therefore adjourned for a fortnight.

With the first sign of this new attack, the King had extracted a promise from his Household physicians – Sir Henry Halford, Matthew Baillie and William Heberden junior – that 'he should never be left entirely alone with any medical person specially engaged in the department of insanity'. They kept their word, causing Dr Samuel Simmons, the first mad-doctor sent for, to walk out in protest.

The other mad-doctors were not so insistent on sole management of the patient. By 3 November, Henry Reynolds, John Meadows and P.G. Briand (who kept a private mad-house in Kensington) were all in attendance under the overall authority of the royal physicians. Next day, the strait-waistcoat was applied for the first time. On 6 November, at the Prime Minister's request, the mad-doctors were joined by Dr Robert Willis, much to the dismay of the physicians and the irritation of the Royal Princes.

Between 7 and 15 November the King began to show signs of improvement. On the 12th he was well enough to have the restraint taken off; two days later, the extra evening bulletin announced 'a progressive state of amendment' which enabled Perceval to secure a two-week extension to the adjournment of Parliament next day. But during the night of the 16th, the King became feverish, his pulse rose above 100 and the strait-waistcoat had to be reapplied. This latest relapse would last until the second week of December.[9]

The Prince, meanwhile – according to Lady Holland – was

conducting 'himself with very unusual discretion'. On hearing of his father's illness, he had hurried down to Windsor and remained for some time in his apartments at the Lower Lodge, avoiding all contact with Opposition politicians. When Cabinet ministers approached him, he told them that 'they must be the best judges of the line of conduct they ought to pursue'. He has 'conducted himself with . . . great caution, great dignity and real feeling,' noted Lord Holland, putting his exemplary behaviour down to the fact that he had been so 'deeply affected' by the illness and death of Princess Amelia.[10]

However, by late November, with the likelihood of the King's recovery ever more distant, he began to sound out the reaction of ministers to a Regency. 'The Duke of Cumberland called here and sat an hour,' wrote George Rose, the Treasurer of the Navy, on 23 November. 'He was full of commendation of the Prince of Wales for his prudent and temperate conduct; said he had seen none of the Opposition; that he had no objection to the present Ministers, and insinuated very strongly that his conduct, in the event of a regency, would depend upon theirs towards him; alluding evidently to the restrictions in the Regency Bill, if one should be brought in.'[11]

The Princess of Wales told Lord Glenbervie that the Duke 'now entirely governs the Prince' and 'it is by his persuasion (others say by Lord and Lady Hertford's) that he has determined to make no changes, except probably giving the Presidency of the Council or some other great office to Lord Moira.' In truth, the Prince had been moving in the direction of the Tories for some time, not least because of their determination to continue prosecuting the war against Napoleon with vigour; the Whigs, on the other hand, were beginning to make noises about a negotiated peace.[12]

Nevertheless, Perceval was understandably cautious. The Prince still had many friends in Opposition, and there was every reason to suspect that his reassuring words were designed to encourage the government to introduce a Regency with unrestricted powers, at which point he would turn to the Whigs. One option for the government was to delay the Regency for as long as possible – as Pitt had done in 1788 – to give the King time to make a full recovery. But given the King's age and general state of health, there was no guarantee that this would happen. Furthermore, time was not on the government's side, as it had been in 1788; Britain was engaged in a brutal struggle for national survival, and the many naval and military operations had to be paid for and supervised. If the King did not recover, a Regency Bill would have to be passed before the end of January 1811, to give enough time to push through certain finance Bills by the middle of February.

On 19 December, therefore – with the doctors having told Select Committees of both Houses that they believed the King would recover, but they could not say when – Spencer Perceval wrote to inform the Prince that the government intended to introduce a Regency Bill with restrictions similar to those proposed in 1789. But unlike Pitt's Bill, which had imposed no time limit, the new restrictions would apply for just one year: the Prince would not be able to create peers (except as a reward for some outstanding naval or military achievement); he could only grant pensions and make appointments to public offices for the duration of the Regency 'and subject, as to their further continuance, to the subsequent pleasure' of the King; the 'custody of his Majesty's royal person' and the management of the Royal Household would be entrusted to the Queen, the former 'during the whole period of his Majesty's indisposition' and the latter for just the 12 months; the King's personal property would be vested in trustees to be appointed by the Bill and to include the Prince and the Queen.[13]

Disappointed that his condition for retaining the present ministry – an unrestricted Regency – had not been heeded, the Prince sent a terse reply that evening, advising Perceval that his reasons for opposing a restricted Regency were exactly the same as those expressed in his answer to Pitt's letter of 30 December 1788. Meanwhile, he had summoned his six brothers and his cousin William, now Duke of Gloucester, to a meeting at Carlton House. At midnight, these seven Royal Dukes signed a letter, written by the Duke of York, protesting 'against measures that we consider as perfectly unconstitutional, and contrary to and subversive of the principles which seated our family upon the throne of these realms'.

They were, in effect, calling for the Prince to be appointed Regent without restrictions by the Address of both Houses of Parliament. Most of the Opposition supported this method, including Lord Grey who described it as 'the plainest, the most direct and the only constitutional mode of supplying the deficiency'. But the Independent country gentlemen and public opinion were mostly opposed. 'The indignation against [the Royal Dukes] is very general out of doors,' noted Richard Ryder, the Home Secretary, 'and we may have some difficulty in preventing their Protest from being taken serious notice of in our House.'[14]

The Prince's 'friends' were now instructed to oppose the government's proposals. But this could not prevent Perceval's motion that the Regency should proceed by Bill rather than Address from passing the House of Commons by 269 votes to 157 on 20 December. Eight days later, the same motion was carried in the Lords by 26 votes. On 31 December, Perceval moved the five Resolutions on which the Regency Bill was to be based. The first three – empowering the Prince to exercise the Royal authority with limitations, precluding him from creating peers, and restricting his right to grant pensions and offices – were passed by small majorities ranging from 24 to 16. The fourth, putting the King's private property in the hands of trustees, was non-controversial and carried without a division.

But on 1 January 1811, an Opposition amendment to the fifth Resolution – which gave the Queen care of the King's person and control over the entire Royal Household – was supported by Castlereagh and Canning, and passed by 226 votes to 213. By stating that the Queen should have 'such direction of his Household as may be suitable for the care of his Majesty's Royal person', the amendment was an attempt to prevent undue political power from being transferred to the Queen. Complete control over the Royal Household would have given the Queen a fund of patronage which she could have used to oppose the Prince. In Canning's opinion, the best way to prevent this was by giving the Regent control of those Officers of State whose appointments were more political than domestic: the Lord Chamberlain, the Master of the Horse, the two Gold Sticks and the Lord Steward. Whereas the King's personal servants – including the Master of the Robes, the Keeper of the Privy Purse, and the Lords and Grooms of the Bedchamber – would remain in place throughout his illness. Though a reasonable compromise, it was not adopted because the Whigs opposed any restriction of the Regent's power.[15]

On 4 January, when the Resolutions were debated in the Lords, the Whigs passed an amendment to omit all reference to restrictions in the Bill (though not the restrictions themselves) by 105 votes to 102. However, Lord Grenville – who had vigorously supported restrictions in 1789 – then voted for the Second Resolution which limited the Regent's right to create peers, thereby helping the government to a wafer-thin majority of six. By 8 January the Resolutions had been accepted by both Houses and an Address sent by deputation to the Prince.

His response, in the form of an Answer drafted by Sheridan and delivered on the 11th, was to accept the Regency whilst restating his objection to the restrictions. The initial draft, more conciliatory, had been composed by Lords Grenville and Grey, the two leaders of the Opposition, but rejected on the advice of Sheridan. They responded to this rebuff by expressing their 'deep concern' that 'their humble endeavours' had been 'submitted to the judgement of another person by whose advice your Royal Highness has been guided in your final decision'. The implication was that Sheridan should not have been consulted because he was not constitutionally responsible for the advice he had given; they, on the other hand, were because they were ministers in waiting.[16]

There was some truth in this, for the Prince had already consulted Grenville and Grey about the formation of a Whig government. Though no longer an adherent of the party's main policies, particularly Catholic emancipation, he was still smarting from Perceval's imposition of a restricted Regency and anxious to keep his options open. His dilemma, he told Grenville on 6 January, was that while he did not want to keep ministers in whom he had no confidence, he could not very well dismiss them if the King was likely to make a speedy recovery. If, however, he did make a change, he would have no objection to Canning being brought in, despite his close connection with the Princess of Wales. He was, in addition, determined to reinstate the Duke of York as Commander-in-Chief.

Both Grenville and Grey, to whom the Prince spoke on the 9th, objected to the latter condition on the ground that the Whig rank-and-file would not agree. This circumstance alone was enough to make a Whig ministry extremely unlikely, and Grey made it even more so by ruling out an approach to Canning. Ever 'artless, open and manly', according to Lord Holland, Grey 'exposed the impolicy of weakening an attachment of old friends by a precarious connection with new or doubtful ones'. He regarded Canning as a political adventurer who had done irreparable harm to the Catholic cause by serving under the Duke of Portland between 1807 and 1809. He might command a dozen votes, but he would alienate far more Whigs if he was brought in.[17]

Despite these strictures, the Prince continued to give the impression that he would appoint a Whig ministry at the earliest opportunity. On 22 January, Grey informed the Prince that a list of provisional Cabinet members was ready for his inspection. It nominated Grenville as Prime Minister, Grey as Foreign Secretary, Holland as Home Secretary, Lansdowne as President of the Board of Trade, George Tierney as Chancellor of the Exchequer, Erskine as Lord Chancellor, and Samuel Whitbread as First Lord of the Admiralty.

But with the King showing signs of improvement, the Prince began to voice his doubts about changing the ministry. Even Grey and Grenville advised him on 21 January that he was right to be wary about dismissing Perceval if there was a good chance that the King would recover in the near future. At the same time, they were convinced that such an eventuality would not come about. On 25 January, to put his mind at rest, they persuaded the nervous Prince to consult his father's doctors at Windsor the following day. In the event, the Prince cried off, citing ill-health as the reason. 'I do not believe,' commented Grey, 'he will have the nerves to take the manly and decisive measures which alone can enable him to conduct the Government with effect, and I am persuaded, if the present reports of the King's improved state continue, that he will not dare to make any change in the Administration.'

Grey's fears were well founded. On 26 January, Perceval and Eldon spoke to the King for almost two hours, informing him of the progress of the Regency Bill. The King's first reaction was to state his intention to retire to Hanover with a favourite lady; he came to his senses when Perceval reminded him of his religious and public duties, and offered to resume his sovereignty immediately. But when Perceval told him that his doctors did not consider him well enough, he seemed irritated and his conversation began to ramble. 'When you are tired of the Prince,' he remarked, 'you will perhaps send for me again.'

The King was more rational when Perceval saw him three days later, expressing his satisfaction with everything the government had done. He was particularly pleased when the Prime Minister told him that the Prince had behaved 'very respectfully towards your Majesty, and very properly in every respect as far as I know'. Though he was thin, Perceval thought him in good health and well on the way to a full mental recovery.

Shortly after Perceval's second visit, the Prince received a brief note from the Queen, informing him that the King had given 'perfect attention' to the Prime Minister's report on 'the state of public business pending in the two Houses of Parliament'. 'His Majesty,' she added, '. . . was particularly desirous to know how you had conducted yourself, which Mr Perceval answered to have been in the most respectful, most prudent & affectionate manner.'

The Whig leaders, however, suspected that the Queen was not the real author. 'The letter,' wrote Lord Grey:

> is evidently written in concert with Perceval, appears indeed to
> be of his dictation, and is evidently part of a plan in which I

think there can be no doubt that the greatest of all villains, the D[uke] of Cumberland, has had an active part, to intimidate the Prince by the expectation of the King's immediate recovery, from changing the Administration. So bare-faced a plot . . . ought to have a directly contrary effect. But *I believe it will be successful.*[18]

The Prince may well, in Lady Holland's words, have 'ridiculed the artifice, which was too gross to escape detection. What woman, he said, ever used the Westminster Hall term of *pending the business*?' But this knowledge did not lessen the impact of the letter's words; nor did it nullify the unwritten threat that a change of government could jeopardise the King's recovery. Such an insinuation, the Whigs believed, had been made more than once by Sir Henry Halford, the royal physician. He 'had frequent audiences of the Prince,' wrote Lady Holland, 'in which he worked upon his imagination and fears by drawing the picture of the King agitated and thrown into an exa-tion [*sic*] which might end fatally; their removing his confidential servants would inevitably produce that effect.'[19]

No sooner had he received the Queen's letter than the Prince sent for William Adam, his Chancellor, and 'announced his intention of not changing the Ministry'. The communication from the Queen, wrote Adam, 'was the immediate cause of the P[rince]'s resolution'. Though the doctors were more pessimistic than Perceval about the King's early recovery when they were interviewed at Carlton House on the 30th – Robert Willis could 'not look with any degree of confidence to his Majesty's complete recovery within any limited time; Halford and Heberden thought it would take up to three months – the Prince's mind was made up.

During the night of 1 February, Lord Hutchinson and William Adam told Grey and Grenville that the Prince had decided not to change the government. The Prince confirmed this in person on the 3rd. 'It is, I confess, a great relief to me,' wrote Grey. 'I am now exempted from the difficulty and danger of taking any part in the

Government, and by no fault of my own. What has passed has given me such an insight into the probable state of things under a new Government that I much doubt whether any circumstances could ever induce me to take a share in it.'

On 4 February, Perceval received a letter from the Prince informing him that he would remain in office. The sole reason given was 'the irresistable impulse of filial duty' which caused him 'to dread that any act of the Regent might in the smallest degree have the affect of interfering with the progress of his Sovereign's recovery'.[20]

While the Prince was undoubtedly genuine in his desire to avoid harming his father's chances of recuperation, not to mention the embarrassment which a change of government would present if the King made a speedy recovery, his decision not to bring in the Whigs probably had more to do with the fact that he opposed many of their central policies – particularly Catholic emancipation and a lukewarm approach to the prosecution of the war. The final straw may well have been when Grey and Grenville ruled out the reappointment of the Duke of York and an alliance with the Canningites, rather than when the Prince received the Queen's letter. After all, the Prince was heavily influenced by the Marchioness of Hertford and the Duke of Cumberland, both staunch Tories, and was not intending to sack Perceval *until* he declared his preference for a restricted Regency.

On 5 February 1811, the Regency Bill became law when it was passed by Commission in the House of Lords. Next day, shortly before 2 in the afternoon, the Privy Counsellors began to arrive at Carlton House for the ceremony to swear in the Prince as Regent, while the band of the Grenadier Guards played 'God Save the King – there being no alternative anthem to herald the start of a Regent's reign – in the courtyard. Inside, Yeomen of the Guard, Life Guards and liveried servants lined the splendid entrance hall and the double staircase which led to the state apartments.

After keeping the 90 or so Privy Counsellors waiting for almost an hour and a half in the 'long gilt saloon' next to the garden, the Prince appeared in the gorgeous blue and gold uniform of the 10th Hussars. Preceded by his six brothers and the officers of his Household, he passed through the saloon and the circular drawing-room beyond it to the grand saloon, where he took his place at the head of an immensely long table. One by one, in order of precedence, the Privy Counsellors entered the room and bowed to the Prince as they passed the lower end of the table. When all were seated and the doors shut, the Prince spoke: 'My lords, understanding that the law requires me to take certain oaths, I am now here ready to take them.'

Earl Camden, the Lord President of the Council, then rose to read the first of the oaths for the Prince to repeat. He did so standing, as were the rest of the Council. At the end of each oath the Clerk of the Council knelt and proffered the Bible for the Prince to kiss. When the oaths had all been taken, the Privy Counsellors approached the Prince in turn, knelt and kissed his hand. He was very gracious to some, speaking a few words; but rude to others, like Perceval and Speaker Abbot, turning his head away as they took his hand. He left with his officers, having put his name to the Regency document, leaving the Counsellors to follow suit. The whole ceremony had lasted just half an hour.

On 19 June 1811, with the King showing no signs of recovery, the Prince held a grand fête at Carlton House to celebrate the inauguration of the Regency. Heading the huge list of 2,000 guests were the members of the exiled French Royal Family, including the Comtes de Provence and d'Artois (the future Louis XVIII and Charles X respectively), the Ducs de Berri and de Bourbon, and Louis XVI's sole surviving child, the Duchesse d'Angoulême. Notable absentees included Queen Charlotte and her daughters, on account of the King's illness; Mrs Fitzherbert, because she had not been given a seat at the Prince Regent's table of the 200 most honoured guests (though he had sent her a dress to wear); the Princess of Wales, for obvious reasons; and Princess Charlotte, because she was too young.

Another surprising omission, according to the diarist Joseph Farington, was 'Lady W———h, wife to one of the Lords of the Bedchamber'. On hearing her complain, some wag commented that the invitations must have run out before they reached the letter 'W'. 'That could not be,' she replied, 'for half the Ws (whores) in town were invited.'[21]

Dressed in the gaudy uniform of a field-marshal – a rank so long denied him – the Prince made his appearance at 9 in the evening to greet the French Royal Family in a room hung with blue silk and white fleur-de-lis. After receiving the Comte de Provence, Louis XVI's eldest brother, 'as *King*' he 'released his French Majesty from all further ceremony, and conducted him as a private person with the rest of the French Court, through the different apartments'.[22]

'Nothing was ever half so magnificent,' wrote Tom Moore, the lyricist and poet, who stayed until 6 in the morning:

> It was in *reality* all that they try to imitate in the gorgeous scenery of the theatre; and I really sat for three quarters of an hour in the Prince 's room after supper, silently looking at the spectacle, and feeding my eyes with the assemblage of beauty, splendour, and profuse magnificence which it presented . . . The Prince spoke to me, as he always does, with the cordial familiarity of an old acquaintance.[23]

At 2.30 in the morning, the favoured guests sat down to dinner at a huge table which extended the whole length of the Gothic conservatory. The Duchesse d'Angoulême was in pride of place on the Regent's right, the Duchess of York to his left. 'Along the centre of the table,' noted the *Gentleman's Magazine*, 'about six inches above the surface, a canal of pure water continued flowing from a silver fountain, beautifully constructed at the head of the table.' The account continued:

> Its banks were covered with green moss and aquatic flowers; gold and silver fish swam and sported through the bubbling

current, which produced a pleasing murmur where it fell, and formed a cascade at the outlet. At the head of the table, above the fountain, sat his Royal Highness . . . on a plain mahogany chair with a feather back. The most particular friends of the Prince were arranged on each side. They were attended by sixty *servitors*; seven waited on the Prince, besides six of the King's and six of the Queen's footmen, in their state liveries, *with one man in a complete suit of ancient armour*. At the back of the Prince's seat appeared aureola tables, covered with crimson drapery, constructed to exhibit with the greatest effect, a pro-fusion of the most exquisitely wrought silver-gilt plate, consisting of fountains, tripods, épergnes, dishes, and other ornaments . . .[24]

But not everyone was impressed by the opulence of the occasion. 'It is said,' wrote the poet Shelley, 'that this entertainment will cost £120,000. Nor will it be the last bauble which the nation must buy to amuse this overgrown bantling of Regency.' Sir Samuel Romilly, who was present, contrasted its 'great expense' with 'the misery of the starv-ing weavers of Lancashire and Glasgow'.[25]

Such criticism was understandable at a time when the disruption of war was causing severe economic hardship. Towards the end of 1811, in an effort to stop the production of inferior stockings by unskilled labourers using wide frames, the framework-knitters of the East Midlands began the systematic smashing of machines which came to be known as Luddism, after their mythical leader 'General Ludd'. As the movement spread into the woollen industry of Yorkshire, it assumed a simpler anti-technology stance, with croppers destroying the shearing-frames and finishing-machinery which threatened them with redundancy. In Lancashire, where cotton workers had been petitioning in vain for a minimum wage, the breaking of steam-looms was more overtly political. But though some contact was made with under-ground radical groups, there was no national revolutionary network. The government's draconian response was to move troops to the affected districts and make machine-breaking a capital offence. In January 1813, 17 men were executed at York and a further six transported. Luddism broke out again on a smaller scale in 1814 and 1816–17, but by then most of its potential supporters had abandoned violent protest and joined the radical Hampden Clubs to demand parliamentary reform.

Meanwhile, the Regent was finding the post of stand-in sovereign more onerous than he had expected. By early August – with Parliament in recess – he was believed to have put his signature to more than 14,000 documents. He sits 'at a table,' wrote Farington, 'with General Turner on one hand, and Colonel McMahon on the other, the one placing a paper before him for signature, and the other drawing it away. Lord Dundas, who attends much upon the Prince, happened to be there when He came out after having done much of this business. The Prince said to Him "Playing at King is no sinecure." '[26]

There were some consolations, nevertheless. In May, following the timely resignation of General Sir David Dundas, the Cabinet unanimously agreed to the reappointment of the Duke of York as Commander-in-Chief. The Regent's nomination of General Lord Harcourt for the appointment as Military Governor of Portsmouth was also successful, despite Perceval's preference for Wellington. So too was his demand that Colonel McMahon, his faithful servant, be given the lucrative sinecure of Paymaster of Widows Pensions, worth £2,700 a year, though the Prime Minister had put forward an alternative candidate. When, in February 1812, the sinecure was abolished by a narrow vote in the House of Commons – 115 votes to 112 – the Regent responded by appointing McMahon as his Private Secretary with a salary of £2,000 a year.

Less successful was his sponsorship of Lord Leitrim as the vacant Irish Representative Peer and William Adam as President of the Scottish Court of Judiciary. In the former case, Lord Gosford, the Prime Minister's choice, was appointed instead; in the latter, Adam knew of the Cabinet's objections and was sensible enough not to accept. These collisions did not, however, make the Regent any more likely to invite the Whigs to form a government when the period of the restricted Regency ended in February 1812. An invitation for some of the leading Whigs to join the existing administration was the most he was prepared to offer, not least because 40 rank-and-file Whigs had voted for Lord Milton's motion in the House of Commons condemning his brother's reappointment as Commander-in-Chief.

But the Regent was never one for confrontations – and as the date for a final decision drew nearer, his anxiety increased. It was almost a blessing in disguise when, during a visit to Oatlands in mid-November, he badly damaged two tendons in his right ankle as he demonstrated the 'Highland Fling' to his daughter, Princess Charlotte. 'This took place ten days ago,' wrote William Fremantle to the Marquess of Buckingham on the 28th, 'since which he has *never been out of his* bed.' He continued:

> He complained of violent pain and spasmodic affection; for which he prescribed for himself, and took a hundred drops of laudanum every three hours. When Farquhar and the other medical men came down, they saw him, under the influence of this laudanum, so enervated and hurt, that they immediately prescribed to him the strongest dose of castor oil, which of course relieved him; but he still perseveres in his laudanum, which, he says, relieves him from pain: and lays *constantly on his stomach* in bed. He will sign nothing, and converse with no one on business . . .; and you may imagine, therefore, the distress and difficulty in which the Ministers are placed. The Duke of Cumberland is going about saying it is all a sham, and that he could get up, and would be perfectly well if he pleased. I protest, I think he is worried and perplexed by all the prospect before him, and by the necessity which now arises of his taking a definite step, that it has harassed his mind, and rendered him totally incapable, for want of nerves, of doing anything; and in order to shun the necessity, he encourages the illness, and continues in his bed . . .

In a letter to the Marquess, his brother, on 6 January 1812, Lord Grenville was in no doubt as to the Regent's intentions:

> The Prince is still very unwell, and it is much believed that the attack in his arm is paralytic. The language of his Court is that he has taken no decision, and is to take none till the 18th. This is only to put off the evil day . . .
>
> I suspect the pretence about the Catholics is to be that it will be *indelicate* to do anything for them, so long as the King lives. That is very possibly, and not improbably, for fifteen or twenty years more. Will the rest of the world stand still for him? and will Ireland be as easy to be settled then, as it would even now . . .
>
> I shall take an early opportunity, probably to-morrow, of protesting against one hour's more delay in that business.
>
> That will do my business at Carlton House, if, indeed, that remained to be done. But, in fact, that was done five years ago, when I recalled Lord Yarmouth from Paris [thereby gaining the enmity of the Hertford family].
>
> I am, therefore, God be thanked, out of the question. There is no misery I should dread, like that of undertaking in such a state of the court and country, any share in the government of either.[27]

Ominous signs for the Opposition were there for all to see. On 16 January, shortly after the reopening of Parliament, Perceval moved a Bill to establish a permanent Royal Household for the Regent at a cost of £180,000, with an additional grant of £100,000 for the expense he had incurred since taking up the reins of government. It passed without a division. The Members were not to know that the Regent had initially asked for larger sums, not to mention an assurance from Perceval that the question of his debts – now a staggering £552,000 – would be raised in Parliament. The Cabinet rejected this last proposal outright, safe in the knowledge that neither House would have agreed to pay such a huge sum.

Perceval had good reason to feel that his government was secure. Lord Wellington's recent run of success in the Peninsula – culminating in the capture of Ciudad Rodrigo on 19 January, for which he was made an earl – had convinced the Regent that the campaign had to be supported to its conclusion. He had not always been so supportive. When, following his great victory over the French at Bussaco in September 1810, Wellington made a tactical withdrawal into the heartland of Portugal, the then Prince of Wales told his brother, Lord Wellesley, that he was sorry to hear of 'poor Arthur's retreat', adding: 'Massena has quite outgeneralled him.' (In this he could not have been further from the truth.)[28]

Many Whigs, however, were still questioning the future of an enterprise which they saw as financially ruinous and bound to end in failure. Grenville, for one, spoke of the 'desperate and hopeless character' of the struggle; while Lord Holland, who had personal knowledge of Spain, was unconvinced that the French would ever be driven over the Pyrenees.

The Regent also supported the government's determination not to restore the gold standard until the war was over; whereas the Opposition blamed the sharp depreciation in the value of the pound on the introduction of banknotes in 1797, and favoured an early resumption of cash payments. But the issue which really set the Prince apart from his former friends was Catholic emancipation; particularly when the Whigs tried, in William Adam's words, to 'take him by storm' by introducing a motion to consider the Catholic question in the Lords on 31 January and the Commons four days later (defeated by 162 votes to 79 and 229 to 135 respectively).[29]

However, the determination of Lord Wellesley, the Foreign Secretary, to resign from Perceval's government meant that the Regent was not in a position to abandon his plan to form a Coalition with at least some of the leading Whigs. In any case, he did not want to leave himself open to the charge of betrayal. On 13 February – five days before the restricted Regency was due to expire – he wrote a letter to the Duke of York, authorising him to communicate its contents to

Lord Grey (who, he had no doubt, would 'make them known to Lord Grenville'). 'At a moment of unexampled difficulty and danger,' he wrote, 'I was called upon to make a selection of persons to whom I should entrust the functions of Executive Government. My sense of duty to our royal father solely decided that choice, and every private feeling gave way to considerations which admitted of no doubt or hesitation.' He continued:

> A new era is now arrived and I cannot but reflect with satisfaction on the events which have distinguished the short period of my restricted Regency. Instead of suffering any loss of her possessions by the gigantic force which has been employed against them, Great Britain has added most important acquisitions to her Empire . . . In the critical situation of the war in the Peninsula I shall be most anxious to avoid any measure which can lead my allies to suppose that I mean to depart from the present system. Perseverance alone can achieve the great object in question, and I cannot withhold my approbation from those who have honourably distinguished themselves in support of it. . . .
>
> . . . I cannot conclude without expressing the gratification I should feel if some of those persons with whom the early habits of my life were formed, would strengthen my hands and constitute a part of my Government. With such support, and aided by a vigorous and united Administration formed on the most liberal basis, I shall look with additional confidence to a prosperous issue of the most arduous contest in which Great Britain was ever engaged.[30]

Grenville was appalled when Grey passed on the news that he had been approached by the Duke of York, on behalf of the Regent, to join a Coalition government. This stratagem, Grenville informed Buckingham on the 13th, was the same one George III had used 'to disunite Lord Rockingham and Lord Shelburne; viz., the sending for the latter in preference to the former, though he was the avowed head of the party then in Opposition'. But far from 'creating jealousy between Grey and me', it would strengthen his determination ' to keep out of this *maudite galère*, in which no good could be done but by the co-operation of the whole crew, instead of having . . . the whole efforts of the *master* against them.' He had been 'betrayed once by the King' and had 'no taste for affording his son the same opportunity'. Grey, he thought, was of the same opinion. 'The whole will end, I doubt not, in the continuance of Perceval, with Castlereagh and Sidmouth to help him.'

The choice of the Duke of York as a go-between was, Thomas Grenville told Buckingham on the 14th, a strong indication that the Regent did not intend 'a successful issue to it' because he 'would certainly not have employed the Duke to form any administration'. Nor could he have selected anyone 'whose opinions were more decidedly hostile to the Catholic Question'.

That same day, having seen the text of the Regent's letter, Lord Grenville denounced it to Buckingham as 'more offensive than I could have believed'. He added: 'It is most occupied in the praise of the great things that he and his Ministers have achieved in this year; and then adds, as it were, in a postscript, his wish that *some of the friends of his early public life* would strengthen his hands, and form a part of his Government.' As Grenville had been a supporter of Pitt during this period, it was clearly meant to exclude him.

He wrote again to Buckingham the following day:

> There has not been, indeed there could not be, one moment's difference of opinion between Grey and myself, in this business. He is still more incensed than I am at the unworthy trick of attempting to separate us; indeed he has more reason to be so, because it could succeed only by his acting in an unworthy manner. The answer, such as we deliver it, is not very courtly. Had he and I followed our own course it would have been still less so, but we softened it in compliance with the wishes of all the few persons which it was fit to consult on such an occasion.

Later that day, Grenville and Grey delivered their joint response to the Duke of York. They could not unite with the 'present government' because their 'differences of opinion' were 'too many and too important', embracing as they did 'all the leading features of the present policy of empire', the Irish question in particular. 'We are,' they wrote, 'firmly persuaded of the necessity of a total change of the present system of government in that country, and of the immediate repeal of all those civil disabilities under which so large a portion of his Majesty's subjects still labour, on account of their religious opinions.' To recommend such a measure would be their first priority.[31]

Even when the Duke told them that the Regent did not necessarily intend them to join the existing government – 'His idea was to form an administration upon a broad basis by a union of different parties of which he should consider himself a keystone' – it made little difference. Grey could not be parted from Grenville, and neither would agree to drop the issue of Catholic emancipation. This left the Regent free to confirm Perceval as Prime Minister (an option he had probably preferred all along, although he paid lip-service to Lord Wellesley's offer to form a Coalition government).

The only sour note was Wellesley's determination not to serve under Perceval, whom he saw as incompetent. To replace him and strengthen the government, the Prime Minister had proposed Castlereagh as Foreign Secretary and Lord Sidmouth as Lord President of the Council. While the Regent had no objection to the former appointment – describing Castlereagh as 'a man of honour and of talents, I believe' – the latter filled him with horror. He blamed Sidmouth not only for his earlier failure to secure military promotion, but also for the break-up of the 'Talents' in 1807. 'That damned scoundrel, that fool,' he is said to have responded. 'No! anyone else. Strengthen yourself as you will from any other quarter, but not the Doctor, if you please.' But there was no one else, and the Regent was forced to give way.'[32]

On a personal level, the Regent's retention of the Tories was a disaster. Of his close friends and allies, only Sheridan and the Duke of Northumberland were able to forgive his final betrayal of the Whigs.

The biggest loss was Lord Moira, a faithful adviser for more than 20 years. On 28 February, he wrote:

> It grieves me to tell you, Sir, that the general astonishment at the step which you have taken is only equalled by a dreadful augury for your future security. It is not the dissatisfaction of disappointed expectants to which I allude. A disinterested public views with wonder your unqualified and unexplained departure from all those principles which you have so long professed. It observes with a still more uneasy sensation your abandonment of all those persons for whom you had hitherto proclaimed esteem, whose adherence you had spontaneously solicited, and of whose services (rendered at the expense of foregoing their private advantages) you had for years availed yourself.[33]

'Lord Moira has behaved in the handsomest and most direct manner,' wrote Lord Grenville to his brother Buckingham. 'He represented in strong terms against the letter (which, however, he did not see till it was actually sent), and told the Premier he had nothing left for it, but to withdraw from public life; which he should immediately do.' According to Thomas Grenville, the Regent tried to get him to change his mind by offering him the Order of the Garter, but he refused. 'This is very manly and very honourable.'

During dinner at Carlton House on 22 February – attended by Princess Charlotte, the Duke of York, Lords Erskine and Lauderdale, Sheridan, Adam and others – the Prince defended his actions by making a 'furious and unmeasured attack' on Grey and Grenville. 'This went on some time,' Thomas Grenville informed Buckingham. 'The Princess Charlotte rose to make her first appearance at the Opera, but rose *in tears*, and expressed herself strongly to Sheridan, as he led her out, upon the distress which she had felt in hearing her father's language. Nor should it be forgot that, at the Opera, seeing Lord Grey in the box opposite to her, she got up, and kissed her hand to him repeatedly, in the sight of the whole Opera.'[34]

If the Regent resented his daughter's display of emotion, he had only himself to blame; it was he who had brought her up to admire Whig principles, in particular the 'political conduct' of his 'most revered and lamented friend, Mr Fox'.[35]

Lord Byron's lyrical response, published anonymously in the *Morning Chronicle*, was entitled 'Lines to a Lady Weeping':

> Weep, daughter of a royal line,
> A sire's disgrace, a realm's decay;
> Ah, happy! if each tear of thine
> Could wash a father's fault away.

> Weep – for thy tears are virtue's tears –
> Auspicious to these suffering isles;
> And be each drop in future years
> Repaid by thy people's smiles.[36]

Grey blamed Lady Hertford for the Regent's conversion to Toryism, referring to her in the House of Lords on 19 March as 'an unseen and separate influence which lurked behind the throne . . . an influence of odious character, leading to consequences the most pestilent and disgusting'.[37]

Just as vitriolic – but without the protection of Parliamentary privilege – were the attacks made on the Regent in March by Leigh Hunt, the editor of the *Examiner*. On 15 March, Hunt printed Charles Lamb's anonymous poem entitled the 'Prince of Whales'. Part of it read:

> Not a fatter fish than he
> Flounders round the polar sea.
> See his blubbers – at his gills
> What a world of drink he swills . . .
> Every fish of generous kind
> Scuds aside or shrinks behind;
> But about his presence keep
> All the monsters of the deep . . .

The *Morning Post*, by now a Tory paper, hit back three days later by portraying the Regent as 'the Glory of the People' and 'the Protector of the Arts'. 'Wherever you appear, you conquer all hearts, wipe away tears, excite desire and love, and win beauty towards you. You breathe eloquence. You inspire the Graces, you are an Adonis of loveliness.'

Hunt was incensed:

> What person [he asked his readers on 19 March], unacquainted with the true state of the case would imagine, in reading these astounding eulogies, that the Glory of the People was the subject of millions of shrugs and reproaches! That this Adonis of loveliness was *a corpulent gentleman* of fifty! In short, that this delightful, blissful, wise, pleasurable, honourable, virtuous, true *and* immortal PRINCE [was] *a violator of his word, a libertine over head and ears in debt and disgrace, a despiser of domestic ties, the companion of gamblers and demireps, a man who has just closed half a century without one single claim on the gratitude of this country or the respect of posterity.*

But Hunt had gone too far this time. The Regent brought libel proceedings against him and his brother John, the publisher, and in December 1812 they were found guilty, fined £500 each and sentenced to two years' imprisonment. Henceforth, the more outspoken criticism of the Regent tended to be anonymous – like Tom Moore's *Intercepted Letters* or the *Twopenny Post-Bag*, a collection of political squibs published in March 1813.

Though most literary luminaries – including Moore, Shelley and Keats – were quick to condemn the Regent for his abandonment of the Whigs and his treatment of the Hunts, some, like Lord Byron, were still susceptible to his charm. Shortly after the publication of his epic poem *Childe Harolde* in March 1812, at the height of his fame, the 24-year-old Byron was presented at a ball to the man he had so recently lampooned in his anonymous verse, 'To a Lady Weeping'. He later gave an account of their conversation to his fellow poet, Walter Scott:

[After] some sayings peculiarly pleasing from royal lips, as to my own attempts, he talked to me of you and your immortalities: he preferred you to every bard past and present . . . He spoke alternately of Homer and yourself, and seemed well acquainted with both; so that (with the exception of the Turks and your humble servant) you were in very good company. I defy [John] Murray [their publisher] to have exaggerated his royal highness's opinion of your powers, nor can I pretend to ennumerate all he said on the subject; but it may give you pleasure to hear that it was conveyed in language which would only suffer by my attempting to transcribe it, and with a tone and taste which gave me a very high idea of his abilities and accomplishments, which I had hitherto considered as confined to *manners*, certainly superior to those of any living gentleman.[38]

Byron may have seen something of himself in the Regent. As well as poetry, they shared a passion for wine and women; though even the Regent at his dissolute worst was unable to compete with Byron's seduction of his half-sister, Augusta, and the alleged birth of a daughter, Elizabeth Medora. His brief but tumultuous affair in 1812 with Lady Caroline Lamb, the daughter of Lady Bessborough and the wife of William Lamb (who later became Lord Melbourne, Queen Victoria's first Prime Minister), was only marginally less scandalous. Described by her lover at the height of their passion as the 'cleverest, most agreeable, absurd, amiable, perplexing, dangerous, fascinating being that lives,' Caro Lamb responded yet more famously, calling Byron 'mad, bad and dangerous to know'. Her pursuit of Byron continued long after he had tired of her, culminating in a feeble suicide attempt when she slashed her wrist at Lady Heathcote's ball in the summer of 1813.[39]

Byron's admiration for the Prince was similarly short-lived. In January 1814, he instructed John Murray, his publisher, to republish 'Lines to a Lady Weeping' with his latest poem, 'The Corsair'. 'I care nothing for consequence, on this point,' he added. 'My politics are to me like a young mistress to an old man – the worse they grow, the fonder I become of them.'

Predictably, the re-publication of 'Lines to a Lady Weeping' under Byron's name in early February caused a storm in the Tory press. 'You can have no conception,' Byron told Tom Moore on the 10th, 'of the uproar the eight lines on the little Royalty's weeping . . . have occasioned. The Regent, who had always thought them *yours*, chose – God knows why – on discovering them to be mine, to be *affected* "in sorrow rather than anger". The Morning Post, Sun, Herald, Courier, have all been in hysterics ever since . . . I feel a little compunctious as to [the] Regent's *regret*; – "would he have been only angry! but I fear him not".'[40]

——•——

12

The Two Princesses

The news that Wellington's troops had successfully stormed the Spanish fortress of Badojoz provoked a bout of wild rejoicing when it reached London towards the end of April 1812. But the capital's celebrations were soon given over to mourning. On 11 May, shortly before 5 o'clock in the evening, Spencer Perceval was shot and killed in the lobby of the House of Commons by John Bellingham, a bankrupt Liverpool commercial agent who held the Prime Minister personally responsible for his failure. Though clearly insane, Bellingham was found guilty of murder and publicly hanged at Newgate Prison on the 18th (Byron was among the onlookers).

Two days after the assassination – Parliament having agreed to the Regent's request that £50,000 be given to the Perceval children and £2,000 a year to Mrs Perceval for life – the Cabinet expressed its willingness to 'carry on the administration . . . under any' of its members that the Regent 'might think proper to select'. He duly nominated the Earl of Liverpool, the War Secretary, as the new Prime Minister, and encouraged him to strengthen his administration by approaching Canning and Wellesley, the leaders of the only two Tory groups not in government. Canning was offered the Foreign Secretaryship, but refused when Liverpool made it clear that Castlereagh, his rival, would be the Leader of the House of Commons; Wellesley would not consider joining without Canning unless he was offered the premiership. Both gave the Cabinet's opposition to Catholic emancipation as the ostensible reason for their refusal.[1]

Forced to soldier on without reinforcements, Liverpool's government came temporarily unstuck when Stuart Wortley, an Independent M.P. who admired Canning, proposed a motion of no confidence on 21 May; it was carried, and Liverpool resigned the following day. In desperation, the Regent authorised first Wellesley, then Moira, to form a Coalition government of Tories and Whigs. 'This is capital,' wrote the Whig gossip Creevey, 'two fellows without an acre between them . . . condescend to offer to Earl Grey of spotless character, followed by the Russells and Cavendishes, by all the ancient nobility and all the great property of the realm and by an unshaken phalanx of 150 of the best men in Parliament . . . four seats in the Cabinet to him and his friends.'[2]

In fact, the main sticking points were Catholic emancipation, the presence of the Marquess of Hertford and his son, Lord Yarmouth – Chamberlain and Vice-Chamberlain respectively – in the Regent's Household (dubbed the 'Carlton House Cabinet' by the Whigs), and the mutual antipathy which the Whig leaders and the Regent now felt for each other. Finally, after two weeks of fruitless negotiation – during which time he soothed his shredded nerves by imbibing equally large quantities of alcohol and laudanum – the Regent reappointed Liverpool and his original Cabinet. He was able to return to his first choice because many of the backbenchers who had supported the original vote of no confidence now saw Liverpool as the only politician who was prepared to put the national interest ahead of particular projects. It was a reputation that would sustain him in power for the next 15 years.

The greatest casualty was Lord Moira. Having failed in his attempt to form a Coalition government, he was vilified by the Whigs for taking the Regent's side. Even his good friend Tom Moore was suspicious, telling James Corry that he did not 'know what to make of . . . Moira's conduct', adding: 'A sword when put into the water will look crooked, and the weak medium of Carlton House may produce an *appearance* of *obliquity* even in Lord M. But both the sword and he, I trust, are as bright and straight as ever.'

Moore was less understanding when he discovered that the Regent had 'rewarded' Moira's years of faithful service by giving him the Order of the Garter and appointing him Governor-General and Commander-in-Chief of India. 'Poor Lord Moira!' he sneered in a letter to a friend in November, 'his good qualities have been the ruin of him . . . They must keep him out of the reach of all Indian *princes* or the Company's rights will be in a bad way. A shake *by* the hand from a *tawny* prince-regent, and a plume of *heron's feathers* to wear upon birthdays, would go near to endanger our empire in India. This is too severe, but it is *wrung* from me by his criminal gullibility to such a ———— as the Prince.'[3]

In fact Moore's fears proved groundless. Moira, who became the Marquess of Hastings in 1817, remained in India for nine years, building a reputation as one of the great Governor-Generals.

After the strain of the recent Cabinet crisis, the good news from Spain was particularly welcome for the Regent: Wellington's army had entered Madrid on 12 August, having defeated the French (in the shape of Marshal Marmont) at Salamanca three weeks earlier. Not to be outdone by the Spanish Cortes – which had appointed Wellington Generalissimo of all their forces, with an estate near Granada – the Regent made him a marquess and Parliament approved a grant of £100,000 towards his future home.

Just as gratifying was the report from Russia that Napoleon was in difficulty. He had invaded Russia in June 1812, following Tsar Alexander's withdrawal from the Continental System. But as his *Grande Armée* of 500,000 men (less than half of whom were French) advanced, the Russian armies withdrew, destroying crops and supplies as they went. They gave battle only twice: at Smolensk, where they were defeated, and at Borodino (to the west of Moscow), a bloody engagement that neither side could claim as a victory. As the withdrawal continued, the French entered Moscow in September. But the Tsar's refusal to sue for peace, and the problems of supply caused by his 'scorched earth' policy, left Napoleon no option but to retreat. Assailed by hunger, the cold and Russian cavalry, the once *Grande Armée* wasted away. By the time Napoleon abandoned it to its fate in Poland – arriving back in Paris on 5 December – it numbered fewer than 10,000 men under arms.

Back home, however, domestic disputes were threatening to sour this turning point in the war. In December, Lady de Clifford gave notice of her intention to resign as Princess Charlotte's governess. Her explanation to the Queen was that she 'felt she had lost Charlotte's confidence'. But when Princess Charlotte discovered that the Regent intended to replace Lady de Clifford with the Dowager Duchess of Leeds, she rebelled. 'Charlotte . . . gave me to understand,' Princess Mary told her brother on 10 January, 'that she was ready to receive any body you appointed as Lady of the Bed Chamber but never would *submit to obey any body* in the capacity of Governess.'[4]

Now 17, and on the verge of womanhood, Charlotte was chafing against the strict regime that her father had imposed. Whig opinions were banned at Court after February 1812 and the doors of Warwick House were closed to those friends, like Mercer Elphinstone (the daughter of Lord Keith), who shared Charlotte's views. The Regent even forbade her from writing to Miss Elphinstone, though she carried on a secret correspondence via her mother and her mother's lady-in-waiting, Lady Charlotte Lindsay, regardless. From June 1812, however, she was only allowed to see the Princess of Wales once a fortnight, on account of the unsuitable company that her mother kept at Blackheath. Among the guests were Jane Harley, Countess of Oxford, a supporter of the Hampden Clubs and a conquest of Lord Byron's, whose children by various fathers were known as the Harleian Miscellany (after a famous collection of 17th-century manuscripts); Lord Henry Fitzgerald, the disreputable son of the first Duke of Leinster; Sir William Drummond, the scholarly diplomat, who assured Charlotte that the Bible was 'an allegory' and priests 'the most corrupt and contemptible of mankind'; and Henry Brougham, the lawyer and Whig M.P., who had agreed to champion the Princess of Wales's cause against her husband.[5]

Charlotte spent the summer of 1812 in the Lower Lodge at Windsor, but found it 'dreadfully dull to be shut up for 5 hours' in the evening with her grandmother, the Queen, and her four maiden aunts as they practised their needlework in silence. Windsor, she once wrote, was 'an abominable and infamous place', its inhabitants a 'pack of devils'. But not all the time that she spent at Windsor was objectionable. During the autumn, when out riding, she met Captain Charles Hesse, a hand-some young officer whose regiment, the 18th Light Dragoons, was stationed nearby. Because Hesse was reputed to be the illegitimate son of the Duke of York, and therefore Charlotte's cousin, Lady de Clifford 'allowed him to ride by the side of the open carriage, morning and evening, for six weeks' before she reprimanded her young charge's conduct. 'They then came to high words, and Lady de Clifford, find-ing she had no power over Princess Charlotte and had lost her confidence, resigned.[6]'

She had good reason to do so. For Charlotte had fallen in love with Hesse and remained in secret contact with him for some months. She later confessed to her father 'that she always met him at her mother's at Kensington, and had private interviews with him'. Her mother, she explained, would 'let him into her own apartment by a door that opens into Kensington Gardens' and then 'leave them together in her own bed room', with the parting words, 'amuse yourselves'.[7]

Charlotte was by now an attractive, well-developed young lady with many accomplishments, though her deportment and manners some-times left a little to be desired. Mary Berry, who had dinner with her and her mother at Blackheath in May 1812, thought she had 'grown and improved' since she had last seen her the previous November, and 'with rouge she would be really striking'. She was 'gay' and 'talkative', with great musical talent – 'after dinner she played all sorts of things upon the piano' – but 'very ill brought up.[8]

The impression gained of her a year earlier by Lady Charlotte

Campbell, another of her mother's ladies-in-waiting and a noted beauty, was just as ambivalent :

> Princess Charlotte [she noted in her diary] is above the middle height, extremely spread for her age; her bosom full, but finely shaped; her shoulders large, and her whole person voluptuous; but a nature to become soon spoiled, and without much care and exercise she will shortly lose all beauty in fat and clumsiness. Her skin is white, but not a transparent white; there is little or no shade in her face; but her features are very fine. Their expression . . . is noble. Her feet are rather small, and her hands and arms are finely moulded. She has a hesitation in her speech, amounting almost to a stammer; an additional proof, if any were wanting, of her being her father's own child; but in everything she is his very image. Her voice is flexible, and its tones dulcet, except when she laughs; then it becomes too loud, but is never unmusical . . . I fear that she is capricious, self-willed, and obstinate. I think she is kind-hearted, clever, and enthusiastic. Her faults have evidently never been checked, nor her virtues fostered.[9]

Campbell's perceptive comments were spot on. But then Charlotte could hardly be blamed for her shortcomings. Forcefully separated from her mother and largely neglected by her father – she saw through his occasional 'sugary' letters 'which, after all, were but *des phrases, without* any meaning' – she grew up without a parent's guiding hand. Was it any wonder that she rebelled when, in her eighteenth year, her sometime father appointed the Dowager Duchess of Leeds to replace Lady de Clifford as her governess?

On 10 January 1813, she wrote to her father from Windsor, informing him that while she had no '*personal objection*' to the Duchess of Leeds, and would not protest if she was appointed her 'Lady', she could not 'accept or submit' to her 'or anyone else' taking Lady de Clifford's place. When the Regent discovered that Charlotte had sent a copy of this letter to Lord Liverpool, he rushed down to Windsor to confront her, taking Lord Chancellor Eldon with him. What did she mean by refusing to have a governess? he asked her in the presence of the Queen and the Chancellor. According to Lady Charlotte Campbell (who heard the details from the Princess of Wales), 'she referred him entirely to her letter – upon which the Queen and her father abused her, as being an obstinate, perverse, headstrong girl. "Besides," said the Prince, "I know all that passed in Windsor Park [between you and Captain Hesse]; and if it were not for my clemency I would have shut you up for life. Depend upon it, as long as I live you shall never have an establishment, unless you marry." '[10]

Lord Eldon then explained the authority the Regent had over his daughter, at which point the Regent asked him what he would have done as her father. 'If she had been my daughter,' he replied, 'I would have locked her up.' Charlotte endured these insults in silence; but later, in Princess Mary's room, she burst into tears, exclaiming, 'What would the King say if he could know that his grand-daughter had been compared to the grand-daughter of a collier?' (Eldon's grandfather, William Scott, had risen from humble beginnings in Newcastle-upon-Tyne to make a fortune transporting coal).[11]

The upshot of all this was that the Duchess of Leeds became governess as planned, with Miss Cornelia Knight and Miss Rawdon appointed lady companions to soften the blow. 'Nothing could more perfectly resemble a convent' than Warwick House, noted Miss Knight on entering Charlotte's service, 'but it was a seat of happiness to [the Princess] compared with the Lower Lodge at Windsor and she was anxiously desirous to remain in Town as much as possible. It was announced to us that we were to be one week in Town and one at Windsor; that when in Town we were to dine at Carlton House, go to the Play and Opera, and to have a party at Warwick House, despite balls and great parties at Carlton House.'

This was as far as the Regent's attempts at reconciliation went. When Charlotte dined with him, noted Miss Knight, he 'talked but little' to her and 'not with the manner or voice of affection'. With the Princess

showing signs of forming her own political judgement, 'every consideration was to be sacrificed to the plan of keeping' her 'as long as
possible a *child*'. As if this was not bad enough, in mid-February she had
to endure the distressing news from her father 'that an investigation was
being made with respect to the conduct of her mother, on the result of
which depended her ever being allowed to visit her again, and that in
the mean while her usual visits must be suspended'.[12]

On the advice of Henry Brougham, Princess Caroline had written to
the Regent on 19 January, complaining about the number of times she
was allowed to see her daughter. The letter, which was returned
unopened, was eventually published in the Whig *Morning Chronicle* on
10 February. (Caroline protested her innocence, but she and Brougham
were almost certainly responsible.) Jane Austen voiced the disgust
which most people now felt towards the Regent for his unpardonable
treatment of his wife in a letter to an acquaintance on the 16th. 'Poor
woman,' she wrote of Caroline, 'I shall support her as long as I can,
because she is a Woman, and because I hate her Husband . . . [If] I must
give up the Princess, I am resolved at least always to think that she
would have been respectable, if the Prince had behaved tolerably by her
at first.'[13]

Aware that he was some way behind his wife in the popularity stakes,
the Regent initiated a review of the papers relating to the 'Delicate
Investigation' in an attempt to regain the moral high ground. A
Committee of 23 Privy Councillors – including the 12 members of the
Cabinet, the Archbishops of Canterbury and York, a number of senior
judges and the Speaker of the House of Commons – was appointed to
decide 'whether it was fit and proper that the intercourse between . . .
Princess Charlotte and the Princess of Wales should continue under
restriction and regulation'.[14]

On 26 February, the Committee presented its report to the Regent.
Having examined 'all the documents', they were unanimous in the opinion that it was 'highly fit and proper . . . that the intercourse between . . .
the Princess of Wales . . . and . . . Princess Charlotte should continue to
be subject to regulation and restraint'. In other words, Princess Caroline

was not, in their estimation, a sufficiently fit enough mother to be granted unrestricted access to her daughter.[15]

To highlight the hypocrisy of those Committee members – like Lord Eldon and Sir William Grant – who had defended the Princess in 1806, Brougham arranged for the publication of *The Book* (which Perceval had suppressed on becoming Chancellor of the Exchequer in 1807). The Regent responded by printing his Law Officers' Report of 1807, which contained the depositions taken against her. But he was still losing the publicity war which had been raging in the newspapers for many months. In an effort to turn the tide, Charles Arbuthnot, the Secretary to the Treasury, had for some time been trying to influence newspapers loyal to the Princess with Secret Service money. So, too, had Colonel McMahon, using a combination of bribery and threats. According to Lady Charlotte Lindsay, Mayne, the proprietor of the *Star*, was offered £300 a year in March 1813 to turn against the Princess. But he rejected the offer, and was refused admission to the Strangers' Gallery in the House of Commons as a result.[16]

Sensing the chance to make political capital, the Lord Mayor, Aldermen and Liverymen of the City of London – most of whom were Radicals – were fully supportive of Princess Caroline. On 12 April, accompanied by a huge crowd, they proceeded to Kensington Palace to present her with an Address which expressed the 'indignation and abhorrence' with which the Livery of London viewed 'the foul conspiracy against the honour and life of her Royal Highness, and their admiration at her moderation, frankness and magnanimity under her long persecution'.

After the deputation had departed – the Lord Mayor proceeding down the Haymarket; Alderman Wood, the man who had proposed the Address, taking his party along St James's to hiss at Carlton House as they passed –'the crowd outside,' wrote Mary Berry, 'called so loudly for the Princess, that her ladies begged of her to show herself at the middle window, and then at the doors, and then at the two ends of the apartment: this she did, accompanied by her ladies and conducted by her chamberlain, and, having curtsied to the people, immediately

retired. I never saw a crowd that better deserved to have its wishes gratified, for it was not a common mob, but workmen, small tradespeople,
mixed with well-dressed people, and conducting themselves perfectly.'[17]

Only the favourable course of the war could provide the Regent with
any relief from his domestic worries. In February 1813, the Prussians
had joined the victorious Russians and declared war on their former
allies, the French. Despite successive defeats by a resurgent Napoleon at
Lützen and Bautzen, the Allies were kept in the field by subsidies of
£2 million from Britain. The turning point came in August when
Napoleon rejected peace overtures and Austria joined the Coalition.
Two months later, a combined army defeated Napoleon at Leipzig, the
'Battle of the Nations'.

Wellington, meanwhile, was trouncing the French at Vittoria on 21
June, capturing King Joseph's sword and Marshal Jourdan's baton in the
process. These he sent back as gifts for the Regent, who replied: 'You
have sent me among the trophies of your unrivalled fame, the staff of a
French Marshal, and I send you in return that of England.' The Regent
had personally designed Wellington's field-marshal's baton, the first of
its kind, adorning it with lions instead of eagles. 'I can,' replied
Wellington, 'evince my Gratitude for your Royal Highness's repeated
favours only by devoting my life to your service.'[18]

Public rejoicing at the news of Wellington's latest success was
untrammelled. The Regent sponsored a huge fête at Vauxhall
Gardens – the most 'splendid and magnificent' ever held in England,
according to William Wellesley-Pole, one of the organisers – to which
8,500 were invited and 1,200 sat down to a grand dinner. The Regent
was not among them; he had decided not to attend when he heard that
his wife would be present.

Instead, he held his own victory fête in the gardens of Carlton
House. At 3 in the afternoon, wrote the diarist Captain Gronow, then
a 19-year-old ensign in the 1st Foot Guards, 'the *élite* of London society . . . began to arrive, all in full dress, the ladies particularly displaying

their diamonds and pearls, as if they were going to a drawing-room, the men, of course, in full dress, wearing knee-breeches and buckles.' He added:

> This was the first day that . . . Princess Charlotte appeared in public. She was a young lady of more than ordinary personal attractions; her features were regular, and her complexion fair, with the rich bloom of youthful beauty; her eyes were blue and very expressive, and her hair was abundant, and of that peculiar light brown which merges into the golden . . . In figure her Royal Highness was somewhat over the ordinary height of women, but finely proportioned and well developed. Her manners were remarkable for a simplicity and good-nature . . . She created universal admiration, and I may say a feeling of national pride, amongst all who attended the ball.

Princess Charlotte took to the floor twice, once with the Duke of Devonshire and once with the Earl of Aboyne, entering 'so much into the spirit of the *fête* as to ask for the then fashionable Scotch dances'. The Prince, who was 'dressed in the Windsor uniform, and wore the garter and star', made 'himself very amiable, and conversed much with the Ladies Hertford, Cholmondeley, and Montford'.[19]

July 1813 also saw the final breach between the Regent and his old friend Beau Brummell. Temperamentally unsuited, they had been drifting apart for some years – not least because Brummell was in the habit of reacting to the latest example of the Regent's inconstancy with a typically injudicious remark: as when he threatened to 'bring the old King back into fashion'. The grand fête to celebrate the inauguration of the Regency in June 1811 was the last time when Brummell had been invited to Carlton House. In revenge, Brummell insisted on omitting the Regent from the guest list to a ball which he and three fellow dandies – Lord Alvanley, Henry Pierrepoint and Henry Mildmay – were holding at the Argyle Rooms in July 1813. But when the Regent wrote to announce that he would attend, the organisers had no option but to send him an invitation.

On the evening of the ball, the Regent was met at the door by his four hosts. Bowing to Pierrepoint on one side, he turned to the other, saw Brummell, and ignored him by turning back to Alvanley who was next to Pierrepoint. The shocked silence that followed was broken by Brummell's angry rejoinder: 'Ah, Alvanley, who is your fat friend?'

Some of those present regarded it as 'a witty retort to a provocation, rather than an unmannerly insult'; but it was clear that the Prince had been 'cut to the quick by the aptness of the satire'. He could not forgive Brummell and they never spoke again.

In late 1827, twelve years after Brummell had been forced to flee his debtors to France, Alvanley persuaded the Duke of Wellington to approach the then King George IV with the idea of appointing the impoverished Beau as the next Consul at Calais. At first, so Wellington told Greville in 1829, the King 'made objections, abusing Brummell' and saying 'that he was a damned fellow and had behaved very ill to him'. But 'having let him run out of his tether of abuse', the Duke gained his consent. Brummell's appointment seemed inevitable when Wellington became Prime Minister in January 1828, but his Foreign Secretary, Lord Aberdeen, disapproved of the scheme and nothing was done until Charles Greville, having met Brummell while passing through Calais, asked Wellington 'to do what he could for him' in March 1830. This time the King agreed to appoint Brummell to the vacant Consulship at Caen. He was, however, prevented by his debtors at Calais from taking up the post until September 1830, three months after George IV's death. Brummell himself died in a Caen lunatic asylum ten years later.[20]

The plan to marry Princess Charlotte to William, the Hereditary Prince of Orange – first proposed by the government in the spring of 1812 – was designed to strengthen the alliance between Great Britain and the Netherlands. For the Regent, it had the additional attraction of removing a rebellious young woman from the harmful influence of her mother.

But when the first hints of the intended union reached Charlotte herself in February 1813, she was determined to oppose it. 'Silly Billy', as he was known, had grown up in exile in England, been educated at Oxford University and joined Wellington's staff in the Peninsula in 1811. Charlotte had not seen him for many years, but he was known to be amiable if not handsome. Writing to Mercer Elphinstone on 16 February, she asked:

> Can you and do you really think that the character you give of him is sufficient to make him likeable or desirable? The qualities of the head and heart there must be, or all the rest is nothing. We may have a scene, but only one I think, as a *positive* declaration of refusal must, I should think, *amply satisfy. Force* will never do anything with me, nor intrigue . . . They *well know my disinclination*, for I have taken care to throw out things occasionally. Besides all this, I should not want to make the [Princess of Wales] *unhappy*, which I should *undoubtedly* do if I was fool enough to chain myself in this way . . .; and it is a family she detested always for being intriguant and violent.

Charlotte's objections would not last – partly because her respect for her mother evaporated after the publication of *The Book* and the Law Officers' Report in March 1813. 'It really came upon me with *such a blow* and it *staggered* me so terribly,' she admitted to Miss Elphinstone the following September, 'that I *never have* and shall *not ever recover* [from] it, because it sinks her so very low in my opinion.'

In addition, her incentive to marry was considerable. It would not only free her from her father's control, but provide her with her own establishment and financial independence (no small advantage given that her debts now amounted to £22,000). On 8 December 1813, therefore – with Prince William's father, the Prince of Orange, only recently re-established on the throne in Holland – Charlotte informed

Miss Elphinstone that she had '*agreed without any demur* to see the young
P[rince] when he comes'. She added:

> The account I have had of him is . . . that he is tall and exces-
> sivly thin with a good figure, excessive light hair and white
> eyebrows, blue eyes, a short nose but good teeth. That he has
> good manners and is very manly, shy, but not awkward or for-
> ward, but master of the subjects you talk to him upon. This I
> fancy to be true as it is from eyewitnesses, and that he is lively
> and likes fun and amusement . . .
>
> As heiress presumptive to the Crown it *is certain* that I could
> not quit this country, as Queen of England *still less*. Therefore
> the P[rince] of O[range] *must visit his frogs solo*, and a few
> months in the year I suppose would satisfy . . . I *will not* be per-
> suaded by any party, but *judge* and *act* . . . *for myself* impartially.

The Regent was delighted and arranged a dinner at Carlton House
for the two to meet on 11 December, extracting a promise from
Charlotte that she would give her 'fair and undisguised opinion' of
Prince William. '*My answer*,' she informed Miss Elphinstone, 'must be
decided that night one way or the other with no *hezitation*.'

During the dinner, Charlotte found the Prince 'shy' and very 'plain',
but 'so lively and animated that it quite went off'. When the meal was
over, the Regent took his daughter into another room and asked her for
her opinion. She hesitated for a moment, causing her father to cry out,
'Then it will not do!' To which she replied that he was 'mistaken', for
she 'approved' of what she had seen. 'You make me the happiest person
in the world,' exclaimed her relieved father.

Three days later, however, Charlotte was distraught to learn from her
fiancé that she would be expected to live for part of the year in
Holland. 'My soul is wrung out to the bottom,' she told Miss
Elphinstone. 'Altogether the idea of even quitting England for a short
time (as it will be) is unpleasant, but the pain is lessened greatly by the
prospect of taking over or having some of my friends there.'[21]

The Princess of Wales, meanwhile, had rented out her house in Blackheath and moved to one in Connaught Place, at the top of Oxford Street. There her regular guests included the well-travelled archaeologist Sir William Gell, the author 'Monk' Lewis, her former lover Sir Sydney Smith, Lady Oxford, Lord Byron and her current paramour, Pietro Sapio, a handsome Italian musician.

But she had lost her looks by now – Farington described her as 'very large, and coarse', her appearance exhibiting 'nothing of feminine grace or dignity' – and was prone to depression when she dwelt upon the future. 'I reckon that I shall remain in this purgatory at least ten years longer,' she told Miss Hayman in October 1813. Presumably she was referring to the length of time it would take the Regent to die. To speed up the process, she took to sticking pins into wax effigies of her husband before burning them.[22]

In early April 1814 came the joyous news that the Allies had taken Paris, forcing Napoleon to abdicate. Wellington's hard-fought victory at Toulouse on the 10th – for which he was made a Duke – was simply gilding the lily. On 24 April, the Comte de Provence returned to France to become Louis XVIII; four days later, Napoleon was exiled to the isle of Elba. The subsequent Treaty of Paris confined France to her pre-1792 frontiers (with the addition of a piece of Savoy), and gave Belgium to Holland, thereby enlarging the principality which one day would be ruled by Princess Charlotte's fiancé.

On 7 June, Tsar Alexander I of Russia, King Frederick William III of Prussia and their respective commanders, Prince Platoff and Marshal Blücher, arrived in London for three weeks of victory celebrations. Much to the Regent's irritation, the Tsar spurned the offer of rooms at St James's Palace and joined his recently widowed sister, the Grand Duchess of Oldenburg, in the Pulteney Hotel in Piccadilly. Since arriving in England in March, the Grand Duchess had done everything she could to infuriate the Regent: first she had received various leading Whigs; then she had offered to visit the Princess of Wales, though Count Lieven, the Russian ambassador, had stopped her by threatening to resign. In an attempt to repair the damage, the Regent had given a dinner in her honour at Carlton House. But she had taken the opportunity to criticise his treatment of his daughter, causing him to reply caustically: 'When she is married, Madam, she will do as her husband pleases. For the present she does as I wish.'

'Your Highness is right,' retorted the Grand Duchess. 'Between husband and wife there can only be one will.'

Temporarily speechless, the Regent turned to Countess Lieven, the Russian ambassador's beautiful wife, and whispered: 'This is intolerable.'

The Grand Duchess thought so too. 'Handsome as he is,' she told her brother on his arrival, 'he is a man visibly used up by dissipation and rather disgusting. His much boasted affability is the most licentious, I may even say obscene, strain I have ever listened to . . . [He has] a brazen way of looking where eyes should not go.'[23]

As it turned out, the Regent got on as badly with the Tsar as he did with his sister. It did not help that the Tsar had 'a fine, tall, manly figure', 'a clear complexion' and 'a good open countenance', and was loudly cheered wherever he went. The Regent, on the other hand, was as likely to be jeered as applauded, which was hardly surprising. 'Among all these fighting chieftains,' observed Tom Moore, 'he seems particularly to distinguish himself in what is called *fighting shy*.'[24]

In addition, the British public could not forgive his harsh treatment of the Princess of Wales. Though barred from all the official engagements, on 11 June she appeared at the same Covent Garden opera that the Regent and his fellow sovereigns were attending. As she entered, dressed in a black wig and dripping with diamonds, the audience rose to applaud her, some calling out, 'Three hearty cheers for an *injured* woman.' Assuming the applause was for him, the Regent rose and bowed to the audience. 'This', wrote Lady Charlotte Campbell, was unfortunately 'construed as a bow to the Princess', who was criticised for not returning it. In fact, 'the Prince *took the applause* to himself; and his friends, or rather his *toadies . . .,* to save him from the imputation of this ridiculous vanity, chose to say that he did the most beautiful and elegant thing in the world, and bowed to his wife!!'

As the Princess passed Carlton House on her way back from the opera, her carriage was surrounded by a cheering mob. Some even opened the door and asked her if they should burn the Prince's residence. 'No, my good people,' she replied, presumably with regret, 'be quite quiet – let me pass, and go home to your beds.' Lady Charlotte had never seen 'her look so well or behave with so much dignity'.[25]

But such displays of public support were scant consolation for the increasingly restricted lifestyle which she was expected to lead. As recently as 23 May, the Queen had written to inform her that, in view of the Regent's 'fixed and ulalterable determination' never to set eyes on her again, she could not be received at her Drawing-Rooms. This was too much. On 31 May, she told Lady Charlotte Campbell of 'her intention of going abroad as soon as possible, saying she thought she was more likely to be able to escape now than she had ever been':

> For that she hoped, and had reason to believe, the Emperor of Russia would be friendly towards her – that she meant to ask [him] to bear her request to the Prince that she might leave this country. 'I will tell you, my dear ———, what I expect he is to answer – that we are parted from *incompatibilité d'humeur* – that I am to have fifty thousand a year, and may come and go as I choose.'[26]

As it turned out, the Tsar was no help at all; anxious to avoid interfering in the Regent's domestic arrangements, he did not reply to the Princess's letter until he was on the point of leaving the country. It made no difference. She was determined to go, and wrote to her brother on 9 June asking if she could visit him in Brunswick, the duchy having recently been restored under the terms of the Treaty of Paris.

Aware that Princess Caroline was planning to live abroad, Henry Brougham was desperate to prevent her daughter from doing likewise. He and the Opposition in general had high hopes that Charlotte, like her father before her, would build up a 'reversionary interest' in Parliament which might enable them to return to power. But if she married Prince William of Orange, and was forced to live part of the year in Holland, these hopes would be dashed. Brougham therefore sought an urgent interview with Charlotte, at which he explained that if she went abroad, as she was bound to do by the terms of her marriage contract, her mother would follow suit. But if the Princess of Wales left England, as she was 'always threatening to do from her ill usage in this country', then a divorce would 'inevitably take place, a second marriage follow, and the young Princess's title to the throne [would] be gone'. This argument, commented Thomas Creevey, a close friend of Brougham's, 'had an effect upon the young one almost magical!'[27]

Charlotte had been having second thoughts about the marriage for some time, and had recently demanded the insertion of a clause in the marriage contract stating she would never be forced to leave the country against her will. Brougham's argument provided her with the perfect excuse to call it off. On 16 June, she asked Prince William to visit her in Warwick House. Lady Charlotte Lindsay, who was in attendance, later gave Brougham an account of the meeting:

> While we were talking the Prince of Orange was announced: she went to him and desired that I should remain where I was to hear the result of their conference, which has ended in her *positive declaration* that she *will not leave England now*, but will avail herself of the discretionary power promised in her contract; and gave as her reason the situation of the Princess of Wales, whom she thought herself bound in duty not to leave under the present circumstances. He appeared to be very unhappy, but seemed to admit that if Princess Charlotte adhered to this resolution the marriage must be off.[28]

That evening, Charlotte wrote to inform Prince William that she considered their engagement 'to be *totally and for ever* at an end'. She explained: 'I am fully convinced that my interest is materially connected with that of my mother, and that my residence out of this kingdom would be equally prejudicial to her welfare as to my own.' The duty of telling her father, she added, would be left to him.

Prince William did not reply for two days, and only then to inform Charlotte that he had told his own family but not the Regent. She was distressed 'beyond all measure' by 'this last cowardly act', telling Miss Elphinstone that the delay would 'add doubly' to her father's 'rage'. In the event, his response was uncharacteristically restrained. He had received her letters 'with astonishment, grief and concern', he told her on the 18th, but declined from 'entering into any particulars'.[29]

The Regent was probably hoping that a period of reflection would encourage his daughter to change her mind. He would not have been so understanding had he been aware of the additional reason why the marriage could not go ahead. For Charlotte had fallen hopelessly in love with Prince Frederick, the King of Prussia's 19-year-old nephew, who was accompanying his sovereign on his visit to England. Having been introduced to him at a dinner party at Carlton House, she had arranged – with the help of Miss Cornelia Knight, one of her lady companions – a number of follow-up meetings at her own home. After his return to Berlin, they kept up a secret correspondence until January 1815 when he sent back her portrait with the unwelcome revelation that he had formed another attachment.

The Regent never discovered the truth about Prince Frederick, but he did hear rumours that Frederick's disreputable cousin, the 35-year-old Prince Augustus of Prussia, had secretly visited Charlotte at Warwick House. On top of her refusal to marry Prince William and her predilection for Whig politicians (she was being advised by Lord Grey), these latest revelations were the final straw. On 12 July, he informed his daughter that her servants were to be dismissed and her ladies, principally the Duchess of Leeds and Miss Knight, replaced by the Countesses of Ilchester and Rosslyn. Henceforth, she would be confined to Cranbourne Lodge in Windsor Great Park, where she would see no one but the Queen.

That evening, a horrified Charlotte fled to her mother's house in Connaught Place; but when Brougham, whom she had summoned, explained to her that the Regent had absolute authority over her until she was 21, she was forced to submit to her uncle, the Duke of York, who escorted her to Carlton House. She was bitterly upset with the Princess of Wales for not being more supportive; what she did not know, but would soon find out, was that her mother was still determined to live abroad.

At the end of June, to speed the Princess on her way, the Regent had agreed to the government's suggestion that her income should be raised from £22,000 to £50,000. She had accepted – much to the annoyance of her Whig advisers, Brougham and Samuel Whitbread, who felt that her compliance with such an 'insidious offer' would be seen as an abrogation of her rights as the Princess of Wales. Though she later took Whitbread's advice to accept a reduced amount of £35,000 a year, she would not abandon her intention to live on the Continent. Lord Liverpool, having received the Princess's formal request for permission to leave the country on 25 July, replied that the Regent had no wish to 'interfere in any plan which may be formed by your Royal Highness for your present or future residence'. She duly sailed from Lancing in the frigate *Jason* on 8 August 1814, accompanied by a motley crew of ladies-in-waiting, gentlemen attendants, a doctor, servants, couriers and her adopted son William Austin, 14, 'a sickly looking child with fair hair and blue eyes'.[30]

Charlotte was understandably distraught. To Mercer Elphinstone, her best friend, she complained: 'She decidedly deserts me. After all if a *mother* has not *feeling* for her child or children are they to *teach it to her* or can they *expect to be listened to* with any *hopes of success.*'[31]

The Regent, on the other hand, could not have been more delighted. At a party held the evening before her departure, he is said to have offered the toast: 'To the Princess of Wales's damnation, and may she never return to England.'[32]

According to Captain Gronow, the 'seventh heaven of the fashionable world' in 1814 was Almack's Assembly Rooms in King's Street, St

James's. Entrance through its celebrated portals was strictly controlled by seven lady patronesses: the Countesses of Jersey (the daughter-in-law of the Regent's discarded mistress), Cowper, Sefton and Lieven, Viscountess Castlereagh (the wife of the Foreign Secretary), Princess Esterhazy (the wife of the Austrian ambassador) and Mrs Drummond Burrell.

> The most popular [wrote Gronow] . . . was unquestionably Lady Cowper, now Lady Palmerston. Lady Jersey's bearing, on the contrary, was that of a theatrical tragedy queen; and whilst attempting the sublime, she frequently made herself simply ridiculous, being inconceivably rude, and in her manner ill-bred. Lady Sefton was kind and amiable, Madame de Lieven haughty and exclusive, Princess Esterhazy was a *bon enfant*, Lady Castlereagh and Mrs Burrell *de très grandes dames*. Very often persons whose rank and fortunes entitled them to the *entrée* anywhere, were excluded by the cliqueism of the lady patronesses.

Gronow himself – a handsome young ensign who claimed descent from Sir Tudor ap Gronow, the great-great-grandfather of Henry VIII – was among the half-dozen of so Guards officers (out of a total of more than 300) who were fortunate enough to be 'honoured with vouchers of admission to this exclusive temple of the *beau monde*'.[33]

Similarly honoured, according to George Macdonald Fraser, was Captain Buckley Flashman of the 23rd Light Dragoons, the father of the celebrated 'Flash Harry', who had distinguished himself at Talavera. He was presented to Lady Jersey – 'still in her twenties, devilish handsome and mistress of forty thousand pounds a year, but renowned as the most . . . downright uncivil woman in England' – by Colonel 'Kangaroo' Cooke, aide-de-camp to the Duke of York.

'I am told that they call you Mad Buck, Mr Flashman,' she is said to have drawled. 'I wonder why?'

'I am told that they call your ladyship Sweet Sally, marm,' he replied with a grin. 'But I don't wonder at all.' He added hastily: 'There, marm – now you know why they call me Mad Buck.'[34]

Even the great Duke of Wellington, who made an appearance at Almack's during his triumphant return to England in the summer of 1814, was turned away because he was wearing trousers rather than the Court dress – knee-breeches, white cravat and *chapeau bras* – decreed by the patronesses. On being informed that he could not be admitted, 'the Duke, who had a great respect for orders and regulations, quietly walked away'.[35]

The Prince Regent was also a stickler for proper dress. He took great exception when Gronow appeared at one of Lady Hertford's parties at Manchester House in 1816 dressed '*à la Française* . . . with white neckcloth and waistcoat, and black shoes and silk stockings'. Having been told of the Regent's displeasure that he was not wearing knee-breeches, Gronow beat a hasty retreat; only to discover, less than a month later, that the Regent had appeared at Lady Cholmondeley's ball 'dressed exactly' as Gronow had been at Lady Hertford's 'in black trousers and shoes'.[36]

On Christmas Day 1814, in an attempt to improve relations with his daughter, the Regent justified his harsh treatment of her over many years on the ground that he was trying to protect her from the corrupting influence of her mother. Princess Caroline, he implied, was only interested in the welfare of her adopted son, William Austin, who 'might prove to be a very serious misfortune' to Princess Charlotte, 'as well as to the country', if the Prince died suddenly.

Seemingly convinced by this argument – and still angry with her mother for deserting her – Charlotte confirmed that 'the boy had always been greatly preferred before her'. She also gave her father a full account of her relationship with Captain Hesse. When he reacted with horror to the news that Princess Caroline had locked the young lovers in her bedroom with the parting words, '*amusez vous*', Charlotte added: 'I can tell you what is more, that my mother carried on a correspondence for us, and all the letters backwards and forwards went through her hands until I spoke to *one person* [probably Mercer Elphinstone] who advised me to break off this correspondence.'

Upon learning that Captain Hesse had joined her mother in Brunswick as an equerry, Charlotte had written to him demanding the return of her letters and presents. That these had not been sent gave her an additional reason to 'throw herself upon her father's mercy' (before they could be used to blackmail her). 'God knows what would have become of me if he had not behaved with so much respect to me,' she remarked.

'My dear child,' replied the Regent, 'it is Providence alone that has saved you.'

Charlotte then denied that she had mentioned any of this to her uncle, the Duke of Brunswick, though 'he has often put me on my guard on the subject of my mother's conduct and told me he was sure that boy [Austin] was her child.' On the subject of her 'mother's favourites', she told the Regent that she looked upon Keppel Craven, who had accompanied Princess Caroline abroad as one of her Vice-Chamberlains, 'as the present lover', with 'young Sappio' and Sir William Gell, her other Vice-Chamberlain, as his predecessors. She concluded the conversation 'by saying she never could make out whether Captain Hesse was her lover or her mother's, and that she supposed the Princess's object was to draw her into this scrape to bring the boy [Austin] forwards'.

Four days later, hoping to capitalise on his daughter's gullibility, the Regent spoke of 'the dreadful situation in which she had been placed' and said 'that his object must be . . . to prevent the possibility of such a thing ever happening again'. The solution he proposed was for her to renew her engagement with Prince William of Orange, but she would have none of it. Since Prince Frederick of Prussia had made it clear that his affections lay elsewhere, she had pinned her hopes upon marrying Prince Leopold, the handsome third son of the Duke of Saxe-Coburg-Saalfeld. Leopold had made no secret of his admiration for Charlotte when, as an officer in the Russian army, he had accompanied the Tsar during his summer visit. She was now in a position to reciprocate his feelings.[37]

When Leopold had not returned to England by March 1815, Charlotte persuaded Mercer Elphinstone to sound out his intentions. But on 10 March, as Charlotte eagerly awaited his response, the momentous news reached Britain that Napoleon Bonaparte had escaped from the isle of Elba and landed in the south of France. 'The whole Town is thrown into extreme amazement,' noted Charles Greville, Lord Bathurst's well-informed private secretary. 'Some laugh at the news, others are alarmed, but the utmost confusion, astonishment and curiosity are excited.'

For two weeks, London nervously awaited the outcome of Napoleon's audacious move; every scrap of information, official and unofficial, was eagerly devoured. On 12 March, dispatches arrived from Lord Fitzroy Somerset in Paris to the effect that 'Bonaparte had not advanced further than Gap, and had not received any assistance'. Four days later, Somerset was forced to correct himself: 'Bonaparte had been joined by all the troops which had been sent against him, and . . . had entered Grenoble, and afterwards Lyons on the 10th.'

Somerset was more upbeat on the 18th. Napoleon, whose 'whole force did not amount to 9,000 men', had 'not advanced beyond Lyons', Paris 'was quite quiet' and the marshals 'were all firm in their allegiance' to Louis XVIII. This misguided optimism was further boosted by an unofficial report, two days later, that Napoleon's rearguard 'had been defeated with great loss by Marshal Ney'. But normal service was resumed on the 22nd when a King's Messenger confirmed that the French King had left Paris and retired to Abbeville. The following day, word reached London that Napoleon had entered Paris on the 20th. Greville noted: 'No . . . dispatches have arrived, but it appears that the Troops everywhere joined him, and that he marched to the capital without the slightest opposition, or a shot having been fired since his landing at Cannes.'[38]

The immediate reaction from senior British politicians was surprisingly mixed. Lord Grey, Samuel Whitbread and a significant proportion of the Whigs were all for recognising Bonaparte's new régime. So, too, was Lord Wellesley, Wellington's brother. But Liverpool's government, backed up by a sizeable parliamentary majority – all the Tories, most of the Independent M.P.s and Lord Grenville's Whigs – was determined to crush Napoleon once and for all. Britain's three European allies – Prussia, Austria and Russia – were similarly resolute. Each country agreed to provide 150,000 men for the purpose of suppressing Napoleon, with Britain pledging an additional £5 million in subsidies to make up for its shortfall in troops. In April, the Duke of Wellington took command of the British and Dutch-Belgian forces in Flanders. He was joined there in May by Marshal Blucher's Prussians; the Austrians and the Russians, meanwhile, were making more leisurely progress towards the French frontier.

Napoleon's only hope was to deal with the British and Prussians before the other armies could intervene. Initially, everything went to plan. Having left Paris on 12 June, he engaged the Prussians at Ligny four days later, driving them back 18 miles to the rear. Wellington, whose own army had been hard pressed at Quatre Bras on the 16th, was also forced to retire to a strong position near the village of Waterloo on the main road to Brussels. Napoleon attacked on the morning of the 18th, hoping to destroy Wellington's force while Blücher was at a distance.

With the French artillery bogged down by the heavy ground, the first serious assault – by d'Erlon's infantry corps against the left centre of Wellington's line – did not take place until 1 in the afternoon. D'Erlon's four columns, 16,000 strong, met with immediate success, isolating the fortified farmhouse of La Haye Sainte and taking the key outworks of Papelotte and La Haye. As the French advance continued up the slope towards Wellington's main position, a Dutch-Belgian infantry brigade fell back in disorder, leaving a dangerous gap in the Allied centre. This was filled by two British infantry brigades, led on by their commander, Sir Thomas Picton, who was killed in the action. But his men managed to hold d'Erlon's troops long enough for Lord Uxbridge to come to the rescue with the Union and Household

Brigades of heavy cavalry. Taken utterly by surprise, more than 15,000 French infantrymen were soon fleeing before these 2,000 gallant horsemen. Unfortunately, Uxbridge was unable to check the wild charge which continued on towards the heart of Napoleon's position, and many of the survivors were cut down by French cavalry as they tried to retire.

Shortly before 4 p.m., after yet another intense bombardment, Marshal Ney led the first of a number of assaults on the British-held crest by 5,000 heavy cavalry. Wellington's infantry responded by forming squares, the front rank kneeling so that a double row of muskets and bayonets could be presented. Though the British squares took a terrible pounding from the French artillery, Ney's cavalry were unable to find a way in.

At 6.30 in the evening, Napoleon's one fleeting chance of victory presented itself when his infantry at last captured La Haye Sainte. But instead of using his remaining reserves to attack the dangerously weak Allied centre, as Ney urgently requested, he sent troops to guard against the expected Prussian intervention. In the crucial half hour which it took Napoleon to make up his mind about launching one last massive assault, using the untouched Imperial Guard and the remnants of d'Erlon's and Reille's corps, 15,000 men in all, Wellington was able to shore up his weak points. Met by musket fire from front and flank, this final attack stuttered and then disintegrated, the Imperial Guard fleeing for the first time in their illustrious history.

By 7.30 in the evening, with Blücher's Prussians engaging the right and rear of the French position, the battle was as good as won. Taking off his hat and waving it three times towards the French, Wellington ordered a general advance.

News of the great victory was carried to London by a messenger in the pay of the Rothschild banking family. But so confused was his version of events that Lord Liverpool became 'increasingly sceptical' and John Croker, the Secretary to the Admiralty and a former lawyer, was given the task of questioning him. How, asked Croker, had King Louis XVIII in Brussels reacted to the news? 'His Majesty embraced me, and kissed me!' replied the messenger.

'How did the King kiss you?'

'On both cheeks,' came the response.

This was enough for Croker. 'My Lord, it is true,' he exclaimed. 'His news is genuine.'[39]

The Prince Regent was attending a party given by Mrs Boehm in St James's Square when Major the Honourable Henry Percy, still blood-stained and dusty from the battlefield, arrived with Wellington's official despatch. As it contained details of the casualties, the Regent asked the ladies to leave the room before it was read out aloud by Lord Liverpool. When he had finished, the Regent turned to Major Percy and said, 'I congratulate you, *Colonel* Percy.'

But his joy was mixed with sadness, and as he reflected upon the huge number of dead and wounded – more than 15,000 in Wellington's army alone – tears began to course down his fleshy cheeks. 'It is a glorious victory, and we must rejoice at it,' he commented, 'but the loss of life has been fearful, and *I* have lost many friends.'[40]

One of the Regent's first acts of compassion was to put the royal yacht at the disposal of Lady Uxbridge, whose husband had had his right leg amputated after a piece of grape-shot had shattered the knee joint. From one of the last French cannon to be fired that day, the shot had narrowly missed Wellington, passing over the neck of his horse before striking Uxbridge. 'By God, sir,' exclaimed the wounded officer, 'I've lost my leg!'

'By God, sir, so you have!' replied Wellington, taking the telescope from his eye.

Having accompanied his wife back across the Channel in the royal yacht, the one-legged Earl was greeted by joyous crowds when he entered London on 9 July. The following day he was visited by the Regent, who told him 'that he *loved* him . . . that he was his best officer and subject', and that he was going to make him a marquess' (he duly became the Marquess of Anglesey).[41]

Wellington's reward for saving Europe from Napoleon was the Royal Hanoverian Guelphic Order – the Regent had no other honours left to give him.

No one was more delighted by the victory at Waterloo than Princess Charlotte: not only had Napoleon been defeated, but the war had ended before Prince Leopold could enter the fray. As recently as 2 June, he had written to tell Mercer Elphinstone that to die on the battlefield would be preferable to the knowledge that Charlotte did not care for him. The opposite was of course true, and Mercer hinted as much when she replied that he would receive a satisfactory explanation as to Charlotte's feelings when he returned to England. He finally did so in January 1816, by which time the marriage of Prince William of Orange to Grand Duchess Anna – the Tsar of Russia's sister – and the advocacy of the Duke of York and Lord Castlereagh, had made the Prince Regent more favourable towards such a politically insignificant son-in-law. Charlotte, too, had been working on her father, assuring him in December 1815 that 'no one will be more steady or consistent in this their present and last engagement than myself'.[42]

By the time the marriage was formally announced in Parliament on 14 March, the whole Royal Family had come to the conclusion that Leopold was an ideal match for Charlotte. 'Everybody is pleased with him,' Charlotte reported to Mercer from Brighton on 1 March. She added:

> Certainly his manners and appearance strike amazingly. The P[rince] R[egent] told me it would be [my] *own* fault if I was not happy, as from the little he had seen and could say of him, he thought he had every qualification to make a woman happy . . . With the Q[ueen] he is wonderfully in favour . . . They had two conversations together, and she told the P.R. that this was of all marriages the only marriage for me, and now that the other was over she would say that it was infinitely better.

As for herself, Charlotte delighted in Leopold and was '*quite satisfied he is really*, truly, and sincerely attached *to me,* and very much so desirous . . . to [do] all in his power to make me happy'.[43]

On 15 March, Nicholas Vansittart, the Chancellor of the Exchequer, announced the financial settlement to the House of Commons. The couple would jointly receive £50,000 a year (to be continued in the event of either of them dying), with an extra £10,000 going to Charlotte's Privy Purse to pay for her Household. As well as Camelford House in London, they would be given a country seat (Lord Clive's former home, Claremont Park in Surrey, was subsequently bought for £69,000) and a capital sum of £60,000 to pay for furniture, plate, jewels and clothes.

Originally planned for early April, the marriage had to be postponed because of the Regent's ill-health. It finally took place at Carlton House on 2 May 1816, the Princess wearing a gown of glittering silver and a wreath of diamond roses, Prince Leopold resplendent in full dress uniform. There was one moment of levity: as Leopold repeated the words, 'With all my worldly goods I thee endow', Charlotte 'was observed to laugh'.[44]

Only her husband failed to see the joke. One of his few failings was that he lacked a sense of humour; this, and his reputation as a pious adventurer, earned him the nickname of 'Humbug' in some Whig circles. Shortly after the wedding, an anonymous print appeared (its artist was probably the young William Heath), entitled 'The Contrast! or the Ci-devant German Captain in Good Quarters'. Its two halves parody the startling change in Leopold's circumstances: the first half, 'A Single Life on the Continent starving on SOUR KROUT!', shows him sitting on a stool in a decrepit room, with holes in his boots, eating sauerkraut off a broken plate; in the second, 'Comes to England, Is made a General, Marry's a Lady of £60,000 per annum', he is sitting at a table with Princess Charlotte, dressed in the uniform of a British general, and surrounded by the trappings of luxurious living.[45]

13

The Milan Commission

In early 1815, despite the fact that his debts still amounted to £339,000, the Prince Regent commissioned the architect John Nash to rebuild the Marine Pavilion in Brighton. Born in 1752, the son of a Lambeth millwright, Nash had risen to prominence late in life: a failed builder of stucco-fronted houses, he did not set up his own architectural business until 1795. Thereafter his reputation grew quickly, bringing him to the attention of the then Prince of Wales.

His first major commission came in 1811 when he was chosen by the Regent to design a new metropolitan thoroughfare, Regent Street, that would link Carlton House in Pall Mall with an extensive development of Marylebone Park (to be known as Regent's Park), a large stretch of open land which had recently reverted to Crown ownership. By combining the features of Bath – crescents and terraces – with his new doctrines of movement and the use of grass and trees, Nash produced a brilliant blend of the formal and the picturesque. Regent Street, begun in 1813, was particularly admired for the elegance of its curve.

Many of Nash's contemporaries, however, were not as impressed as the Regent with the finished product. Maria Edgeworth was 'properly surprised by the new . . . town built in Regent's Park – and indignant at plaister statues and horrid useless *domes* and pediments crowded with mock sculpture figures which damp and smoke must destroy in a season or two'. Others decried the fretting of straight exteriors and the addition of balconies and trellises (often in metals cheapened by the Industrial Revolution) as fanciful decoration which distorted the basic simplicity of the classical design.[1]

Undeterred, the Regent also used Nash to design a new set of Corinthian rooms at Carlton House (including a golden drawing-room) and the Royal Lodge in Windsor Great Park. The latter project involved converting the modest dwelling originally occupied by the Deputy Ranger into a huge Gothic *cottage orné*, complete with thatched roof, mullioned windows and coloured plaster. By 1814 the work had already cost £52,000, and it was still ongoing at the time of George IV's death in 1830. Countess Lieven, a frequent visitor to the 'Cottage' (as it was then known), was not an admirer. 'The place is very low and damp,' she wrote in 1823. '. . . The Suite we are using is a little beneath the level of the garden, and the field-mice come in boldly and run about the rooms.'[2]

But Nash is best remembered for his transformation of Henry Holland's neo-classical Marine Pavilion into the magnificent Indian-style Royal Pavilion which still stands today. Begun in 1815, it took eight years and cost £155,000 to complete. Among the new rooms added were the Great Kitchen, two State Rooms, the Music Room and the Banqueting Room. The latter pair, both domed and 60 by 40 feet in dimension, were the most extravagant. In the opinion of John Croker, who visited the Pavilion in December 1818, the Music Room, with its nine lotus-shaped chandeliers and walls adorned with hand-painted Chinese scenes, was 'the most splendid'; while the lav-ishly decorated Banqueting Room, which could accommodate up to 36 people, was the 'handsomer'. Both, however, were 'too handsome for Brighton'. Comparing the exterior with 'the Kremlin in Moscow', Croker concluded that the whole structure was 'an absurd waste of money, and will be a ruin in half a century or sooner'.[3]

Needless to say, the Regent's patronage was not confined to architecture. He knighted Thomas Lawrence in April 1815, after the portrait painter had brilliantly executed his commission to portray the various Allied monarchs, ministers and generals who had had a hand in Napoleon's first downfall. (Lawrence's improper relationship with the Princess of Wales was now long forgotten.) He also restored the Royal Collection of pictures to the pre-eminent position it had held before the depredations of the Commonwealth in the seventeenth century. But his greatest achievement in the field of fine art was, when King, to urge the government to form a national collection which would rival those of Italy and France. Taking his advice, they bought the 38 magnificent pictures of his good friend John Julius Angerstein, who died in 1823, for £57,000. To these they added another 16 pictures which had been donated by Sir George Beaumont, and the whole collection was displayed in Angerstein's house in Pall Mall until the National Portrait Gallery was completed on the north side of Trafalgar Square in 1828.

The Regent's appreciation of art in general was highly developed, as the sculptor Richard Westmacott discovered when he was unpacking some statues of the group of Niobe which had been sent to London by the Grand Duke of Tuscany. One of the casts, commented the watching Regent, was not of the group. 'The Prince's remarks,' Westmacott told Lawrence, '. . . were not only judicious but expressed with a feeling and in a language of art that I was not aware he was master of.'[4]

The Regent's 'fine taste, sound judgment, and extensive information' also impressed the famous Italian sculptor, Antonio Canova, whose huge marble statue of Napoleon was bought by the Regent in 1816 for £3,000 and presented to the Duke of Wellington. Canova – who completed a number of works for the Regent, including the marble group of Mars and Venus which stands today in Buckingham Palace – was particularly impressed by the Regent's support for the nation's purchase of the Elgin Marbles at a time when many were questioning their artistic significance. Recovered from the neglected Acropolis in Athens by the 7th Earl of Elgin between 1801 and 1803, these marble sculptures and friezes were bought by the British Museum in 1816.

Like his father before him, the Regent was for many years a patron of the Royal Academy, constituted in 1768 as a 'society for promoting the Arts and Design'. As well as donating works of art and a chain of office bearing his likeness to the president, he regularly attended the annual dinner in Somerset House for the 40 painters, sculptors and architects who comprised the Academy. In April 1811, at his first annual dinner as Regent, he spoke of the 'pride and satisfaction' that he felt sitting in a room full of art which would 'have done honour to any country'. Others 'might be more able to judge of the excellence of works of art', but they 'could not exceed him in his love of arts' or his 'wishes for their prosperity'. The speech was 'delivered in a manly and graceful manner,' wrote the academician Joseph Farington, 'and it made a very strong impression.'[5]

Literature, as Byron discovered in 1812, was another of the Regent's passions. Next to Walter Scott, his favourite novelist was probably Jane Austen, who was given a guided tour of Carlton House in November 1815 by the Royal librarian, James Stanier Clarke. Having told her that the Regent read all her books, and kept copies in all of his houses, Clarke hinted that the dedication of any future book to his royal master would be favourably received. Though Austen had little respect for the Regent – and had even gone so far as to express hatred for him in his treatment of his wife – she had little option but to comply. When *Emma* was first published in 1816, it was 'most respectfully dedicated' to the Prince Regent 'by His Royal Highness's dutiful and obedient humble servant, the Author'.

That the dedication should be read in an ironic light is indicated by Austen's thinly veiled criticism of the Regent in her third novel, *Mansfield Park*, published in 1814. The book contains its own regency crisis when Sir Thomas Bertram has to visit his plantations in the West Indies. Tom, his eldest son, who takes over the regency from his brother Edmund, has much in common with the real Regent: he, too, loves to gamble, live well and run up debts; when he becomes regent, he prefers the ceremonial to the practical aspects of government. Austen's subversive conclusion is that the younger son is a more suitable regent than the legal heir, while the poor female relation (Fanny Price) is preferable to them both.[6]

The Regent, who was apparently delighted with the 'handsome' copy of *Emma* sent by Austen's publishers, remained an enthusiastic promoter of literature for the rest of his life. In 1823, by then King George IV, he donated his father's magnificent book collection of more than 65,000 volumes to the British Museum Library (66 years after his great-grandfather, George II, had given it the Royal Library of the Kings of England). Three years later, he provided the fledgling Royal Society of Literature with a Charter of Incorporation and an annual subscription of 1,100 guineas; this was discontinued when his lowbrow brother, the Duke of Clarence, succeeded him as King William IV in 1830.

In the field of science, too, the Regent was a source of encouragement and generosity: he was President of the Royal Institution; endowed readerships in geology and minerology at Oxford University; knighted Humphry Davy, the chemist who later invented the safety-lamp for miners, and William Herschel, the astronomer; and championed William Congreve, the inventor of the Congreve rocket, at a time when many saw him as a figure of ridicule.

Among those musicians who benefited from the Prince's patronage was George Bridgtower, the son of a Barbadian negro who had come to Europe and married a German woman in the 1770s. George's remarkable musical gifts were obvious from a young age, and it is possible that he was taught by Franz Joseph Haydn, who was resident composer at the summer palace of Prince Miklos Esterhazy at the same time as George's father, Friedrich, was employed there as a page. In 1789 at the age of nine, having made his professional début as a solo violinist in Paris a few months earlier, George was brought to England by his father to perform in front of the King and Queen. He 'played to perfection', noted Charlotte Papendiek, 'with a clear, good tone, spirit, pathos, and good taste'.[7]

Highly successful concerts in London, Bath and Bristol followed. But Bridgtower senior soon fell out of favour and in January 1791, following rumours that he had maltreated his son and squandered the money he had earned, the Prince sent him £25 and an order to 'leave the kingdom immediately'. George, however, remained under the protection of the Prince, who provided him with tutors and eminent musicians to teach him musical theory. For 14 years, young Bridgtower held the position of first violinist in the Prince's private orchestra, which divided its time between Carlton House and the Marine Pavilion; during this period he also performed in more than 50 concerts as soloist or principal violinist at venues such as Covent Garden and Drury Lane.

In 1803, Bridgtower was given leave of absence for a concert tour of Germany and Austria. While in Vienna, he met Ludwig van Beethoven, who was quick to appreciate his talent – describing him in a letter of introduction to a nobleman as 'a very able virtuoso and an absolute master of his instrument'. Had the two not fallen out over a woman, the 'Kreuzer' sonata would almost certainly have been named after Bridgtower; Beethoven wrote it for him, dedicating the rough score to 'the mulatto Brishdauer, the great mulatto idiot and composer'. Bridgtower even had the confidence – when giving the sonata's first performance, with the composer at the piano, in Vienna in 1803 – to alter a brief passage in the first movement, making the violin echo a preceding piano flourish. Whereupon Beethoven leapt up and hugged him, exclaiming: 'Once more, my dear fellow!' But then came their quarrel and the subsequent bestowal of the dedication upon Rodolphe Kreuzer. Bridgtower eventually returned to England – though not to the Prince's orchestra – and gained the degree of Bachelor of Music at Cambridge in 1811. The man whom Samuel Wesley ranked 'with the very first Masters of the Violin' was to outlive his royal patron by almost 30 years.[8]

When Gioacchino Rossini, the great Neapolitan composer, visited London as a young man after the Battle of Waterloo, he was given a lavish welcome by the music-loving Prince Regent who insisted that they play together. Though a competent cellist, the Regent was unable to keep time with the maestro and eventually had to apologise. 'There are few in your Royal Highness's position who could play so well,' was Rossini's generous reply.[9]

The final defeat of Napoleon at Waterloo – and his subsequent exile to the South Atlantic island of St Helena – may have removed the military threat to Britain, but it also ushered in an uncomfortable period of economic distress and political unrest.

A major cause of discontent was the passing of the Corn Law – which excluded the import of foreign wheat until the price had reached 80 shillings a bushel – in March 1815. A measure designed to stem the fall in the price of corn which had resulted from the end of the Continental blockade, it infuriated the urban poor who had to pay more for their bread. Serious riots took place in London on the 6th and 7th, with the mob attacking the houses of a number of M.P.s and ministers who had spoken in favour of the Bill. Most of the furniture in the Burlington Street house of Mr Robinson, who had introduced the Bill, was destroyed.

Assuming that the Regent was among the Bill's supporters – he was not – a large crowd left a bloodstained loaf on the parapet of Carlton House; but an actual assault was discouraged because of the large number of troops present. In the midst of this turmoil, however, the Regent remained uncharacteristically calm:

> The depradations of last night [he wrote to the Queen on 8 March] . . . were not as great, as might have been expected from the timely precautions that had been taken, although the disposition towards mischief and riot, and the violence of the tone and expressions of the mobility were . . . as vehement as ever . . . The principal objects of their greatest inveteracy appears to be directed against Lord Darnley's, and the wreck of Robinson, but in every instance they immediately flew without

any attempt at resistance, the moment the military . . . approached them. In the latter instance (Robinson's house) some soldiers being placed as a guard in it, upon their coming to it with the intention of pulling it down . . ., the soldiers then fired upon them, and killed two, a man and a woman, *et tant mieux* (God forgive me for saying so). At present there is an immense crowd all the way from the Horse Guards, to and about the two Houses of Parliament, but as to what they may intend in particular to do, or to attempt, it is impossible to cal-culate upon, perhaps something of magnitude, and possibly nothing at all.[10]

The ugly mood in the country generally was not helped by the fall in demand for British manufactured goods, and the subsequent rise in unemployment, which coincided with the end of the war. There were riots by labourers on the verge of starvation, particularly in the eastern counties; Luddite violence flared up for the last time in Nottinghamshire. But most alarming for the government was the revival of the Hampden Clubs. Founded as a middle-class movement devoted to parliamentary reform, their membership was now open to working men able to afford a penny a week. Two mass meetings were held in Spa Fields at the end of 1816; the main speaker at both was Henry 'Orator' Hunt, a well-to-do farmer with a gift for rabble-rousing. At the first meeting he arrived with an escort carrying the tricolour flag and a revolutionary cap on a pike; at the second he delib-erately arrived late, by which time part of the crowd had broken into a gunsmith's shop and marched towards the City, where they were dis-persed by troops. So alarmed was the Regent that he asked Sir Thomas Lawrence to supervise the valuation and insurance of his picture coll-ection in Carlton House.

He had good reason to be cautious. On 28 January 1817, his carriage was attacked as he returned to Carlton House from the State Opening of Parliament. Lord James Murray, who was accompanying the Regent, spoke of 'two small holes made by a sharp blow of some sort within one inch of each other, through an uncommonly thick plate glass window'. He was convinced that they had been made by someone firing an air-gun, though 'no bullets were found in the coach, nor was any person in it hurt'. [11]

Captain Gronow, who was marching his squad of 1st Foot Guards across St James's Park at the time, was of the opinion that a genuine assassination attempt had been made. 'It was,' he wrote, 'anything but pleasant to get through the mob of blackguards who were ripe for mischief. The Life Guards, who escorted the Prince Regent, evinced great want of energy on that occasion. The officer commanding the troop, when he saw the danger, should have commanded his men to charge and clear the way.' He added: 'I can speak from personal knowledge that a shot was fired, and it was aimed at the royal carriage.'[12]

Queen Charlotte, whose relations with her son had improved of late, wrote to congratulate him on his escape from 'so vile an attempt as that of yesterday upon your life'. Her 'affection' for him, she continued without the slightest trace of irony, was 'too deeply rooted' in her heart and 'too well known . . . to leave any doubt of its being very sincere'. She concluded: 'God grant that this time the law may for once prove more than insanity against the perpetrators, for . . . unless some example is made I fear that with the present disposition of the mobility much mischief may arise.'[13]

In the event, no one was arrested for the attack, but the Cabinet was able to present secret committees of the two Houses with evidence of a revolutionary plot to seize the Bank of England and the Tower. Though the evidence was based on the hearsay of informers, Parliament agreed to pass legislation which suspended the Habeas Corpus Act, outlawed the holding of seditious meetings and cracked down heavily on attempts to weaken the loyalty of troops.

Princess Charlotte, meanwhile, was blissfully happy with her husband Leopold. The only clouds to pass over her horizon were two early miscarriages – but when she became pregnant for a third time in January 1817, and stayed pregnant, the outlook was decidedly fine. Just to be on the safe side, Sir Richard Croft, the leading *accoucheur* of the day, was brought in to assist her regular physician, Dr Matthew Baillie. During the early months of her pregnancy, as Charlotte began to display 'a morbid excess of animal spirits', Croft thought them serious enough to require repeated bleedings and other 'lowering' measures such as a mainly liquid, vegetarian diet. As the pregnancy continued, however, these states of excitement became less frequent.[14]

However, they were replaced by bouts of depression. On 10 October, with the birth expected in eight or nine days, Charlotte voiced her forebodings in a letter to her mother which began full of hope. 'United to a man,' she wrote, 'whose whole attentions are directed to the promotion of my happiness, I cannot but feel pleasure in the anticipation of that hour of perilous hope which shall enable me to present him a new tie of connubial love, and to the nation a new and abundant source of consolation and future promise.'

But she could not suppress her unease:

> When I look to the dark probabilities which may put a period to the claim of hope, even shadows shake my courage, and I feel myself the victim of terrors which reason would almost demonstrate absurd, at such a trying moment. Why am I debarred from the soothing voice of maternal affection? Why is not my mother allowed to pour cheerfulness into the sinking heart of her inexperienced and trembling child? I have no friend, no relation near me, whose advice may guide, or whose admonitions may check my conduct. Surrounded by strangers, with a single exception [her husband Leopold], my heart feels itself alone, and should the protection of Heaven leave me and I fall, the presence of a mother would assuredly impart a serenity and resignation to the mind which would soothe the pillow of her dying head and prevent her distracted soul from sinking in the hour of her severest trial.

Her parting words were particularly prescient: 'Should it be the pleasure of Providence that I survive the hour of approaching danger, I may at some future period be embued with power to restore you to that situation you were formed to embellish. But if an allwise decree should summon me from this sphere of anxious apprehension, not for myself but for my mother a pang of terror shoots across my bewildered brain.'[15]

The expected birth date came and went – but the doctors at Claremont did not seem unduly concerned. Her Royal Highness 'has occasionally suffered a little from headache', stated the bulletin of 22 October, but repeated bleedings had afforded her 'great relief'.[16]

Charlotte's labour began at last in the evening of 3 November. 'Nothing can be going on better,' announced Sir Richard Croft to the waiting dignitaries – who included Lord Sidmouth, the Home Secretary, Earl Bathurst, the Secretary for War, Lord Chancellor Eldon and the Archbishop of Canterbury – at 3 in the afternoon of 4 November. But Sir Robert Gardiner, Prince Leopold's equerry, was not so confident. 'It is impossible for us not to feel anxious even under his assurances,' he wrote two and a half hours later to Sir Benjamin Bloomfield, the Regent's Private Secretary since the death of Colonel McMahon earlier that year.

At 10 in the evening Gardiner wrote again, this time to the Prince Regent who was staying with the Hertfords at Sudbourne in Suffolk. Though her Royal Highness had already been in labour 'for twenty seven hours', he stated, the pains were 'slight' and the 'exertions of the womb . . . less vigorous than they ought to be'. The doctors had assured him that the labour 'will go on successfully – but they begin to doubt, whether some artificial assistance might not become necessary'.[17]

Meanwhile, Croft had summoned Dr John Sims, another eminent *accoucheur*, from London to assist him. At 8.15 in the morning of 5 November, they signed a joint letter to the Cabinet: 'Princess Charlotte has made a considerable, though very gradual progress throughout the night.' There was, therefore, a good chance that the child could be born 'without artificial assistance', but they could not say when.

After a labour lasting almost two days, the child was finally delivered at 9 o'clock that evening. Unfortunately, the infant – 'male and well formed' – was stillborn. Having informed the Regent by letter, Lord Bathurst added by way of consolation: 'Princess Charlotte is going on well.'[18]

In point of fact, she was far from well and at midnight, having woken from a sleeping-draught-induced slumber, she started to vomit and was unable to hold down the gruel she was given by her nurse. An hour later, she began to complain of acute stomach pains. When the doctors appeared, having been called from their beds, they found her pulse rapid and irregular; she soon drifted into restlessness and even convulsions. At last these stopped, and Croft was able to administer brandy and wine. 'Is there any danger?' the Princess is said to have asked.

'Not if you will lay still and compose yourself,' replied Croft.

She did as she was told, recalled Lady John Thynne, one of her ladies-in-waiting, 'and almost immediately expired'. It was a little after 4 in the morning of 7 November 1817.[19]

The Regent, who had set off for London shortly after receiving Gardiner's note stating that the labour had already lasted 27 hours, reached Carlton House at about this time to be told of his grandson's death. Charlotte, on the other hand, was 'doing extremely well'. He went to bed exhausted, but was roused soon afterwards by the Duke of York and Lord Bathurst who gave him the terrible news that his daughter, too, was dead. His anguished response was to strike 'his forehead violently with both hands', before falling into his brother's arms. Only after being heavily bled did he feel up to travelling down to Claremont to pay his last respects.[20]

Unlike Prince Leopold, who remained 'completely calm and composed' in his grief, the Regent was for a time inconsolable. 'He sees nobody,' John Croker informed Lord Whitworth on 14 November, 'but his own attendants, the Royal Family, and such of the Ministers as have business with him, and all his thoughts and conversation turn upon the late sad event. He never stirs out of his room, and goes to bed sometimes at eight or nine o'clock, wearied out, and yet not composed enough for rest.' However, by the 18th he was 'better', wrote Croker. 'The necessity of giving orders about the funeral has acted like a blister, and has given employment to his mind.'[21]

Princess Caroline is said to have received the news of her daughter's death 'with a composure which it was hard to distinguish from indifference'. A more likely version of events is the one given by her most recent biographer: that the callous Regent left the task of informing Charlotte's mother of her death to Prince Leopold; but he delayed and the Princess heard the dreadful tidings by chance, from a courier destined for the Pope, whereupon she fainted with shock.[22]

Back home, so Croker informed Robert Peel (Chief Secretary to Ireland) on 15 November, 'the people continue exceedingly afflicted by the loss of the Princess and her child; but that which was at first mere grief takes, I am sorry to tell you, a very *sour* turn.' He added:

The Prince's absence, above all, the absence of the Queen, are subjects of very *bitter* regret with all those who do not know that the Princess would *not* have the assistance of her Majesty, nor the attendance of any one but those named by herself, and who do not recollect that a father is on such occasions worse than useless. Fortunate it was for the Prince . . . that he did come up with such rapidity when the alarming express reached him; his anxiety and alacrity in that moment has preserved him from the most dreadful weight of unpopularity . . .

It is also said, and I think with some justice, that no fancy of the poor Princess's nor any confidence of Dr Croft's ought to have induced the Government to leave her fate in the hands of a single man at the distance of seventeen miles from any assistance . . . [And] was it right that when the crisis should occur, they should have to send off to London for another doctor to consult with? . . . I am satisfied that nothing could have saved her, nor even the child, but in an affair of such vital importance to herself, to her offspring, to her family, to the nation, and to Europe, surely precautions should have been taken which you

or I in our private families would have thought necessary if our
wives were to lie in at a great distance from immediate assistance or additional advice.[23]

Inevitably, the lion's share of the blame was directed towards the doctors, particularly Sir Richard Croft for leaving the Princess unattended
after such an arduous labour. Though the Regent personally exoner-
ated Croft – thanking him on 8 November for the 'zealous care and
indefatigable attention' that he had displayed 'towards his beloved
daughter during her late eventful confinement', and expressing his
'entire confidence in the medical skill and ability which he displayed' –
the celebrated *accoucheur* never recovered from the criticism. In
February 1818, while attending a woman whose complications in
labour replicated Charlotte's, he took a gun from the wall and shot
himself.[24]

In fact, there was very little that Croft or the other doctors could
have done to save Charlotte. According to the *London Medical and
Physical Journal* of that year, her death was not due to exhaustion, since
'a labour much longer protracted has often ended happily for mother
and child'. Nor was there an excessive loss of blood. 'During the whole
period,' they noted, 'and for some time after, no unfavourable symptoms occurred, excepting that her Royal Highness was less exhausted
than might have been expected by so tedious a labour . . . [There
seemed] no apparent danger, excepting what arose from the almost
unnatural composure, not to say cheerfulness, of Her Royal Highness.'

The explanation provided by the psychiatrists Ida Macalpine and
Richard Hunter, authors of *George III and the Mad-Business,* is that
'already during labour she had suffered a degree of lightheadedness
which impaired her insight and clouded her consciousness.' This is
why, they say, 'she was never heard to complain or even utter a sigh' –
a fortitude which Dr Baillie put down to her 'Brunswick heart'.[25]

'What was the link,' ask Macalpine and Hunter, 'connecting her
impaired mental state during labour with the periods of excitability . . .
she had shown before? Was it the same disease process which when

mild irritated her nervous system and produced excitement or a manic state, and when more severe impaired her faculties and lowered her awareness, and when at its height caused convulsions and led to paralysis of vital functions and so to death?' In other words porphyria – they certainly think so, and their argument is compelling.[26]

Charlotte – who could have inherited the disorder from either of her parents (they were first cousins) – displayed many of the symptoms connected with porphyria throughout her short life: particularly a tendency to abdominal pain, excitability and lowness of spirits. When she was 18, for example, and had been sent to Weymouth because of ill-health, Dr Baillie reported to her father: 'Her pulse is still too frequent . . . [She] complains of distensions of the stomach from indigestion, but has much less of the feeling of restriction in her chest.' She herself wrote: 'Last night I had a slight nervous attack again, which always affects my spirits as well as my side . . . At times I laugh and talk away as *fast* that you would think I had no cares at all.'[27]

Then there were the findings of the post-mortem ordered by the Prince Regent: not only 'loss of uterine control', but a general 'atony of the viscera' (in other words the stomach contained three pints of water and the large bowel was blown out with air). 'These findings,' wrote Macalpine and Hunter, 'indicate a general paralysis . . . of the autonomic system, and are consistent with the diagnosis of porphyria.'[28]

The deaths of Princess Charlotte and her son robbed the country of two heirs-apparent at a stroke, and left the insensible George III without a legitimate grandson. Only two of the Regent's six brothers were legally married – the Dukes of York and Cumberland (who had become the third husband of the Princess of Solms-Braunfel in 1815) – and neither had produced a child. Now the race was on to provide a successor to the throne.

Determined that he would at least get to the start line, the Regent was anxious to divorce his wife and remarry – but there were many obstacles. '*Jealousies* have already begun to be felt in the Royal

Family,' Croker told Peel in his letter of 15 November, 'and you may depend upon it they will not diminish. The Princess of Wales and the divorce occupy many thoughts, but nobody speaks about them. The Prince is anxious for it, the Ministers strong against it; the public only waiting to see the Prince take a part to take one against him. In short, my dear Peel, I never looked into a blacker political horizon than is now around us.'[29]

The other runners were the Regent's three unmarried brothers: the Dukes of Clarence, Kent and Cambridge. Their chances of success, however, depended upon the selection of the right mount. First out of the stalls was the 43-year-old Duke of Cambridge, Governor of Hanover and the Regent's youngest surviving brother, who sent off his marriage proposal to Princess Augusta, the youngest daughter of the Electoral Prince of Hesse-Cassel, before his niece had been dead ten days.

This stung the Duke of Kent, seven years Cambridge's senior, into action. For two years he had been on the lookout for a suitable wife, calculating that the increase in income from Parliament would help to alleviate his debts. Since late 1816, his preferred choice had been the Dowager Princess Victoire of Leiningen (née Saxe-Coburg), Prince Leopold's sister. With Charlotte's death, he pressed the Princess to give him an answer.

The Duke of Clarence had also long sought a wife as the solution to his financial worries. Having separated from Mrs Jordan, the mother of his ten illegitimate children, in 1811, he had variously proposed to Catherine Tylney-Pole, worth £40,000 a year, the equally rich Miss Mercer Elphinstone, Lady Charlotte Lindsay, the Dowager Lady Downshire and even the Tsar of Russia's sister, the Grand Duchess of Oldenburg. But all had turned him down, and recently he had settled upon Princess Caroline of Hesse-Cassel, Augusta's elder sister.

Liverpool's government, meanwhile, was considering the financial implications of all these putative marriages:

> *Apropos* of royal matches [wrote Croker to Peel on 26 November], I hear that Ministers have been a little puzzled

how to deal with the avowed readiness of the Duke of Kent to sacrifice himself and jump into the matrimonial gulf for the good of his country, but they have hit upon a scheme which seems politic. They propose to marry the Duke of Clarence, as the eldest unmarried Prince, and he who has a right to the first chance; and also to marry the Duke of Cambridge, the youngest unmarried Prince, from whom the country has the best chance; and having thus resolved to burn the candle at both ends, Vansittart [the Chancellor of the Exchequer] discovers that he cannot afford to burn it in the middle too, and therefore Kent . . . cannot have the wedding establishment . . . suited to [his] rank.[30]

The Duke of Kent – who was duly married on 29 May 1818 in Coburg – had been hoping for an increase of £25,000 a year, with a grant of £12,000 to pay for his 'outfit' and marriage expenses. Instead, the House of Commons voted him £6,000 a year and nothing for an 'outfit', Lord Althorp commenting that it might be desirable for the country to enable some of the Royal Family to marry, but not all of them. 'By God,' exclaimed the Duke of Wellington on hearing the outcome, 'they [the Royal Dukes] are the damnedest millstone about the necks of any government that can be imagined. They have insulted – *personally* insulted – two thirds of the gentlemen of England, and how can it be wondered at that they take their revenge upon them when they get them in the House of Commons? It is their only opportunity, and I think, by God, they are quite right to use it.'[31]

All three Royal Dukes were married by the summer of 1818, though Clarence had switched mounts at the last minute to the plain but good-natured Princess Adelaide, the 25-year-old daughter of the Duke of Saxe-Coburg-Meiningen. The subsequent race to produce an heir was narrowly won by the Duke of Cambridge, whose wife gave birth to a healthy son – christened George – in Hanover on 26 March 1819. But Prince George would only become King if neither of his father's elder brothers produced a child of either sex; for Salic law, which prohibits a female from inheriting the throne, is not applicable in England.

In the event, the Clarences had two daughters, but neither of them survived infancy: the first, born on 27 March 1819, lived for just seven hours; the second, Princess Elizabeth, born in December 1820, died three months later from an 'entanglement of the bowels'. The Kents were more successful. On 24 May 1819, the Duchess gave birth to 'a pretty little Princess, as plump as a partridge'. Though the Prince Regent insisted she be christened Alexandrina in honour of the Russian Tsar, she was always known by her second name Victoria. As the child of the Duke of Kent, George III's fourth son, she would ascend the throne ahead of Prince William, whose father was the seventh son. By such a tiny margin was the destiny of Queen Victoria, the longest-reigning monarch in British history, decided.'[32]

The Prince Regent, meanwhile, had not given up all hope that he himself might one day father another legitimate child. Since the autumn of 1814, when the first reports of his wife's outrageous conduct in Europe had begun to reach Britain, he had been weighing up the possibility of a divorce: the grounds for such an action seemed to be numerous.

Bored after just a few days in Brunswick, the Princess had set off for Italy in September 1814, and was 'most imprudent' during a brief stay in Lausanne, according to the writer of an anonymous letter which was later discovered in the archives of the French Foreign Ministry. It read:

> She learned on her arrival that a little ball was in progress at a house opposite the 'Golden Lion', and she asked for an invitation. After dancing with everybody and anybody, she finished up by dancing a Savoyard dance called a 'fricasée' with a nobody. Madame de Corsal, who blushed and wept for the rest of the company, declares that it has made her ill, and that she feels that the honour of England has been compromised.[33]

At Geneva she was said to have had an affair with Carlo Sismondi, the illustrious Swiss historian. But it was with Bartolomeo Pergami, 32, the scion of a well-to-do Crema family whom she met in Milan in October, that the Princess committed her greatest indiscretions. A strikingly handsome man, tall and well built with curly black hair and dark eyes, Pergami had the additional attraction of being separated from his wife. He had been a quartermaster in the Austrian Viceregal army, serving in the Russian campaign of 1812 as a courier on the staff of General Pino; but now he was unemployed, having killed a higher-ranking officer in a duel it was said. The Princess, who needed an Italian courier to accompany her on her journey south, took Pino's advice and hired him. By the time she reached Rome, members of her entourage were already beginning to resent her familiarity towards Pergami. Her behaviour in public was hardly more discreet. Invited to a ball in her honour, given by the banker Torlonia, she shocked the Roman ladies by appearing in a simple embroidered dress that fastened beneath the bosom, with a diaphanous shawl which did little to protect her modesty.

But what the Prince Regent needed was hard evidence, not salacious stories. To this end Baron Ompteda, the Hanoverian envoy to the Vatican, was employed in late October 1814 to spy on Princess Caroline. 'The Baron,' his instructions read, 'is to approach as near as he can to the Princess, and write an exact account of her conduct. If that conduct is not as it ought to be, it is extremely important to obtain sufficient proofs to legitimate the fact.'[34]

Ompteda caught up with the Princess in Naples, where she was enjoying the hospitality, if not the bed, of the wily King Joachim Murat, Napoleon's brother-in-law. 'He was raped by the Princess,' reported Ompteda, 'it is impossible to find another word to describe the excess of her extravagance.' At first, the Hanoverian envoy was uncertain about Pergami's relationship with the Princess (the courier had by now been promoted to equerry), partly because of a rumour that a war wound had 'wholly deprived him of the means of satisfying a woman'. Though soon disabused of that notion, he lacked proof that they were having sexual relations. Nevertheless, he was able to report on 1 March: 'Her unguarded conduct, especially towards men, exposes her to scandalous suspicions . . . in a town where chastity has never had much of a ministry.'[35]

When news of Napoleon's escape from Elba reached Britain in early March, Liverpool's government decided that it was too dangerous for the Princess to remain in a kingdom which every day was expected to declare for Bonaparte. A frigate, the *Clorinde*, was sent to transport her to British-protected Genoa; but by the time she embarked from Civitavecchia in late March, her original Household had been reduced to just Lady Charlotte Lindsay (and she too would soon depart). Captain Hesse had returned to his regiment; Sir William Gell, Keppel Craven and Lady Elizabeth Forbes had all decided to take their chances in Naples rather than continue in the service of such an increasingly outrageous mistress.

Lady Charlotte Campbell took over from Lindsay in Genoa; but in June she too parted company with the Princess. She stated the reasons for her departure in a letter to Lady Charlotte Lindsay, who passed on the bad news to Henry Brougham, the principal trustee for the Princess's parliamentary annuity. 'I enclose a letter,' she wrote on 4 August 1815, 'just received from Lady C.C. Nothing can be worse than the state of things described in it, but yet I do not see what can be done more than we have done . . . Perhaps a strong letter advising extreme caution of conduct from a certainty of her being watched, and watchful particularly in regard to this domestic bird [Pergami] might be advisable.'[36]

Brougham wrote accordingly – but it made little difference. By the time the Princess moved into the Villa del Garrovo (soon to be renamed the Villa d'Este after the Guelph family from which she was descended) on Lake Como in late August, her Household was dominated by members of the Pergami family: Bartolomeo himself was now her Chamberlain in all but name; his brother Luigi and his cousin Bernardo had become her steward and her accountant respectively; and his sister, the Countess of Oldi, had succeeded Campbell as her lady-in-waiting. Pergami's four-year-old daughter, Vittorine, was also in residence; Livia, his mother, would move in before too long. The only Britons left were William Austin and Lieutenant Joseph Hownham R.N., the son of her former page who had gone to sea as a boy with Captain Manby; Hownham had recently arrived from England to act as her private secretary.

In November 1815, while alterations were being made to the villa (shades of her husband), the Princess decided to go travelling. Enthused by those acquaintances who had been to far-off places – Gell, Keppel Craven, Byron and Sir Sidney Smith – she was, she wrote, determined to journey to Sicily, 'to Malta, to Sardinia and then to Tunis to deliver the poor slaves which are now retained there'. She added: 'Jerusalem is my great ambition, to see Jan [St Jean] d'Acre, and Cairo.'[37]

Accompanied by Pergami, Hownham, Austin, the Countess of Oldi, and a number of servants and attendants including Louise Demont, the Countess's Swiss maid, she set off from Genoa on 14 November in the Royal Navy frigate *Leviathan*. At Messina in Sicily, having fallen out with Captain Pechell, on whose frigate *Clorinde* they were due to continue their journey (Pechell objected to Pergami joining them at meals), she hired a polacca – a three-masted trading ship – to transport them east instead.

Brougham was shocked when the news reached London. 'The accounts of the Princess of Wales are worse and worse,' he wrote to Lord Grey on 7 December:

> She embarked on the 17th of November for Palermo, courier and all . . . On her daughter's account I hope that she may not be got rid of, and it may be said that bad treatment drove her to it originally. My opinion is that they will be afraid to touch her, at least until they have evidence of *English witnesses*, for no Italian would be believed; but the voyage may supply this defect in their case.[38]

He was right to be worried. While the Princess's polacca was being fitted out, she was busy buying Pergami an estate in the south of the island which came with a barony so that she could appoint him her chamberlain: by the strict rules of Court etiquette, only a nobleman could fill this exalted position. Henceforth, he was known as Barone Pergami della Franchina. She eventually set sail for Tunis in the refurbished polacca – renamed the *Royal Charlotte* for the occasion – on April Fools' Day 1816 (an apt date). It was the first leg of an extraordinary journey which was to take her via Tunis, Athens, and Constantinople to Acre and the Holy Land. At Jerusalem, having entered on an ass like some modern-day Messiah, she proceeded to found the Order of St Caroline, with Pergami as its Grand Master, Austin its most honoured Knight, and '*Honi soit qui mal y pense*' as its motto. On 17 July, she left Jerusalem for Jaffa where she re-embarked aboard the *Royal Charlotte*; Capo d'Anzio, south of Rome, was finally reached on 10 September, and the Villa d'Este six days later.

Meanwhile, the operation to gather evidence against the Princess had yielded little fruit. Ompteda's detailed reports, full of hearsay, were of little use in an English court of law. What was needed were witnesses and signed depositions; to this end John Leach, the ambitious Chancellor of the Duchy of Cornwall who was overseeing the spying operation, sent out an English lawyer to advise Ompteda. But little had been accomplished by the time of Princess Charlotte's death in November 1817. It was this tragedy which caused Leach – soon to be knighted and appointed Vice-Chancellor – to redouble his efforts: for if the Prince Regent was to take part in the race to produce a new heir to the throne, he needed to divorce Caroline – and fast.

On New Year's Day 1818, the evidence that Leach had accumulated so far was presented to the Cabinet as grounds for a divorce; but it was rejected because much of it was inadmissible in court and none of it provided conclusive proof of the Princess's adultery. Leach's subsequent proposal in March, to send an official commission of lawyers to Italy to gather the requisite evidence, was also opposed by ministers who feared the disapproval of public opinion. Only when the Regent offered to send out his own commissioners did Lord Liverpool's government reluctantly consent to bankroll it from the Secret Service Fund; and on one condition: 'that, whatever might be the nature of the evidence obtained, however decisive as to criminality, the question of the expediency of any proceeding must always be considered as an open question.'[39]

The Regent's so-called Milan Commission – named after the city in which it was based – comprised three men: William Cooke, a barrister, John Powell, a solicitor, and Major James Browne, an Italian-speaking military attaché seconded from the British Embassy in Vienna. They received their final instructions from Leach on 8 August 1818:

> By command of His Royal Highness the Prince Regent, and with the approbation of the Lord High Chancellor and the Earl of Liverpool you are hereby authorized to proceed forthwith to Milan, and from thence to all other places at your discretion for the purpose of making enquiries into the conduct of Her Royal Highness the Princess of Wales since she quitted England in the month of August 1814. And for the better prosecution of those enquiries you are to engage all such assistance either legal or otherwise as in your judgement shall be expedient; and for defraying the expences incident upon these inquiries, you are to draw in your own names upon the firm of Messrs Thomas Coutts.[40]

In March 1819, as the Commission's work was drawing to a close, James Brougham, Henry's brother, arrived in Italy: ostensibly to make an evaluation of the Princess's financial affairs for her trustees in London; but more importantly to report to his brother Henry on the state of the Princess's domestic arrangements – and her intentions for the future. 'She says she has no ambition to be Queen *and never had*,' he wrote to his brother in mid-March. 'That the only thing which *ever would have taken her to England* would be, if the Duke of York was King she might go for a few weeks to pay him and her a visit as she likes them both.'

As for Pergami – 'the Baron' – 'they are to all appearances man and wife, never was anything so obvious. *His room* is close to hers, and his *bed room* the only one in that part of the house. The whole thing is apparent to every one, though perhaps there might be difficulty in proving the fact to find her guilty of high treason, yet I should think all the circumstances being stated would completely ruin her in the opinion of the people of England, that once done, the P[rince] might get a divorce, or at any rate prevent her being Queen if she wished it.'

Under the circumstances, the best course of action would be to 'make a good bargain *for her*, as to money, and come to terms about a divorce or separation with the P[rince]'. He added: 'I do assure you she seriously wishes for this. She said she would take 100,000 and give up her annuity and everything. This of course would be madness, not *three years income*! but she does not know the value of money. *We* can arrange all that, and the more she gets the more she will be obliged to you and me.'[41]

Brougham was quick to take his brother's advice. If the Princess could not be defended successfully, then it made sense to keep her out of England while he negotiated the best possible terms for her with the Regent and his government (a service for which he expected to be suitably rewarded). To this end, he eventually wrote to Lord Hutchinson, a close friend of the Regent's but also a Whig, on 14 June, informing him that he was in a position 'to advise the Princess' to accede to the following 'arrangment':

> That she shall agree to a formal separation to be ratified by the Act of Parliament . . . that she shall renounce the right to be crowned . . . and shall henceforth take some other style and title, as that of Duchess of Cornwall, that she shall renounce the jointure to which she is entitled should she survive the Prince Regent, and that her annuity shall be granted for her life, instead of ceasing on the demise of the Crown. My firm belief is that although the Princess can have nothing to dread from the result of any proceedings, she will be more comfortable after

such arrangement, since the Princess Charlotte's death has in all probability removed any desire of returning to England.[42]

Two days later, the Regent conceded that there were certain advantages to be gained by such a proposal: not least a divorce 'by arrangement' rather than court action. Unfortunately the Cabinet did not agree. A divorce 'never could be accomplished by arrangement', they advised the Regent on 17 June, 'nor obtained except upon proof of adultery, to be substantiated by evidence before some tribunal in this country', which would, in such unsettled times, present a 'serious hazard to the interests and peace of the kingdom'. Therefore a separation 'by some arrangement upon the principles suggested' would be preferable. But the Regent would not drop his demand for a divorce. The Milan Commissioners' Report was almost ready, and he was convinced that it would convert the ministers to his point of view.[43]

Brougham, meanwhile, had told the Princess nothing of this proposal. Instead, on 11 June, in an attempt to frighten her into agreeing to such a settlement, his brother James had written to warn her that she would probably have to stand trial in November.[44]

On 13 July 1819, the Milan Commissioners finally presented their report. Having interviewed more than 80 witnesses – everyone from servants to sailors, innkeepers to postilions – they were in a position to state that: 'From this comparison of evidence and from the cool, clear, and distinct manner in which these persons delivered their testimony, we should give credit to the truth of what they have said. We are under the necessity, therefore, of humbly stating that in our opinion this great body of evidence established the fact of a continued adulterous intercourse' between the Princess of Wales and Pergami.[45]

Among the more damaging depositions were those provided by Giuseppe Sacchini, Teodoro Majocchi and Louise Demont. Sacchini, a former cavalry officer, had served the Princess for nine months as a courier and three as an equerry, before being sacked in November 1817 for stealing gold coins from the Princess's strong-box. During his service he had frequently seen Pergami, who was in the habit of calling his mistress '*mon coeur*' and '*mon amour*', enter her room late at night. They often used to travel in the same carriage at night; and on at least two or three occasions Sacchi had discovered them asleep with their hands on each other. 'Once Bergami [his name was sometimes spelt this way] had his breeches loosened and the Princess's hand was upon that part.' Majocchi, a former postilion in Murat's service, had joined the Princess's Household as a domestic servant in March 1815, but had been sacked just over two years later for quarrelling with the other servants. He, too, had often seen Pergami entering the Princess's room at night. But his most devastating evidence referred to the voyage east in the polacca: not only had Pergami slept with the Princess in a tent she had had constructed on deck to keep cool, he was also in the habit of joining her in her cabin when she had a bath (which, if her normal routine was anything to go by, cannot have been that often). Mlle Demont, who had been dismissed as the Princess's maid and secretary in November 1817 for being an accomplice to Sacchini's theft, confirmed that Pergami and her former mistress had been lovers.[46]

But the Cabinet, having considered the Commissioners' Report on 24 July 1819, could not concur with its conclusions. In their opinion, the evidence was not strong enough to guarantee that the Princess would be found guilty of adultery in a court of law. They were, in addition, worried that the Princess's lawyers would present counter-evidence of the Regent's own infidelities. But the Regent had to be let down gently; so they agreed that Cooke and Powell would interview a few more witnesses – Captain Pechell in particular – while the Commission's papers were reviewed by the law officers of both the Crown and the Regent. A final decision would then be taken.

As the Prince Regent strove to sever all ties with his estranged wife, the death of his 74-year-old mother, Queen Charlotte, on 19 November 1818 was understandably upsetting. 'The Prince was extremely affected,' wrote Croker, 'and they were obliged to give him some cordial to prevent his fainting.' Their frosty relationship had thawed considerably since 1812, when the Regent had marked the start of his unrestricted rule by retaining the Tory ministry. But now she was gone, along with his daughter and grandson, leaving the deranged 80-year-old King – blind, deaf and sporting a long white beard – as the only remaining member of his immediate family. Of course he had illegitimate children, including two by Mrs Fitzherbert, but he never saw them.

Nor did he ever see his first wife Mrs Fitzherbert, now 62, though he still paid her annuity of £6,000 (it would be increased to £10,000 after he became King). 'To her presence is attributed the Prince's never going abroad at Brighton,' noted Croker on 7 December 1818. 'I have known H.R.H. here seven or eight years, and never saw or heard of his being on foot out of the limits of the Pavilion, and in general he avoids even riding through the principal streets.' In fact, as Croker soon discovered, the Regent's 'great size and weight make him nervous, and he is afraid to ride'. Asked by Croker why he did not get out more, the Regent replied: 'Why should I? I never had better spirits, appetite, and health than when I stay within, and I am not so well when I go abroad.'[47]

The truth of the matter was that the Regent was becoming increasingly reclusive: partly because his physical size and frequent ailments made it more difficult to get about, but mainly because he was more likely to be received with derision than enthusiasm in public. This in turn provoked a paranoid belief that *all* his subjects saw him as a figure of fun (when the true proportion cannot have been more than 75 per cent!). Captain Gronow was on guard duty at Carlton House when he heard the Regent exclaim: 'I will not allow these maid-servants to look at me when I go in and out; and if I find they do so again, I will have them discharged.' Gronow was astonished 'that a man born to the highest rank could take umbrage at such pardonable curiosity'.[48]

The Regent was even beginning to tire of his current mistress, Lady Hertford, now 58. Though not in the habit of remaining with any one woman for more than ten years at a time – Mrs Fitzherbert had had two such terms – he had extended Lady Hertford's tenure while he searched for a suitable replacement. His choice eventually fell on another grand-mother, the 48-year-old Marchioness of Conyngham. Born Elizabeth Denison in 1770, the daughter of a self-made merchant banker, she had married Viscount Conyngham, an Irish peer four years her senior, when she was 24. Solid Tories, though not particularly active in poli-tics, the Conynghams were friends of the Hertfords and had been part of the Regent's inner circle since 1812; four years later, in return for their loyalty, the Regent had raised Conyngham to the rank of mar-quess.

A beautiful, shrewd, greedy woman whose figure mirrored the Regent's own, Lady Conyngham had a history of infidelity. In the 1790s she began a long affair with the Honourable John (and future Lord) Ponsonby, the 'handsomest man of his time', who was saved from being hanged from a lamp-post in Paris during the Revolution by the intervention of women who considered him too attractive to kill. More affairs followed, including a brief liaison with the future Tsar Nicholas I of Russia during his visit to London as a Grand Duke in 1816. But to satisfy her insatiable demand for expensive clothes and jewellery, not to mention her ambitions for her four grown-up chil-dren, she needed a rich and influential British lover: who better than the Prince Regent, the future King of England?

Towards the end of February 1819, Lady Charlotte Campbell was told on good authority that 'Lady Conyngham is now the reigning favourite of the Regent', while 'Lady Hertford's influence is quite at an end'. This was not yet strictly true, though it would be by December of that year. 'I never saw anyone in such high spirits as [the Regent] was at St Carlos's Ball,' wrote Lady Cowper on Christmas Day, 'quite merry and good-humoured as in old times – the scowl quite gone and all sun-shine and prosperity, and this I am told is the present disposition – all powerful Love again rules his destiny . . . Lady Conyngham has carried the day completely, and they say the other is quite dished.'[49]

The voluptuous Lady Conyngham was just the tonic the Regent needed to forget the turmoil of the summer. On 16 August 1819, 60,000 men, women and children had gathered at St Peter's Field,

Manchester, to listen to various radical speakers demanding parliamentary reform. But when Henry 'Orator' Hunt took the platform, William Hulton, the young chief magistrate, ordered his arrest. The Manchester Yeomanry moved forward with their swords drawn, but so dense was the crowd that they could make little headway. It did not help that the yeomanry were mainly members of the employing class and had little sympathy for the kind of reform being demanded. With the situation getting out of hand, Hulton sent in the 15th Hussars, a regular unit which had fought at Waterloo, to clear the field. They, at least, acted without bad feeling and brutality; but the huge crowd panicked in its desperation to escape, leaving nine men and two women dead, and several hundred injured.

The so-called 'Peterloo Massacre' divided the nation. Many ordinary people were outraged that British troops could have caused the deaths of their own countrymen; their anger was intensified by the publication of a letter from Lord Sidmouth, the Home Secretary, to the commander of the yeomanry and the Manchester magistrates. Written five days after the tragedy, it assured them of 'the great satisfaction derived by his Royal Highness from their prompt, decisive and efficient measures for the preservation of the public tranquility'.[50]

For the Prince Regent to have approved this form of congratulation was entirely in character; the worst depredations of the French Revolution had made him extremely fearful of any form of public disorder. But the wording of Sidmouth's insensitive letter showed that he and his government had become entirely out of touch with public opinion. (He must have suspected as much when he was hissed by a large crowd as he returned to London from Cowes at the end of the month.)

The leaders of the Whig Opposition were certainly under no illusions. 'Nothing could be more unjustifiable,' wrote Lord Grey to Henry Brougham on 25 August, 'than the conduct of the magistrates in employing the military as they did.' Unless there was something like general agreement on that point, he continued, 'the consequences may prove most fatal to the freedom of the country'. But he was also conscious of the danger of encouraging extreme radicals like Hunt, and felt that the 'Whigs should reserve action until Parliament met'.[51]

However, not all the leading Whigs were of this opinion: Brougham felt it was time for the party to embrace some limited form of parliamentary reform; Earl Fitzwilliam organised a county meeting in Yorkshire to demand an official investigation into the massacre (the government replaced him as Lord Lieutenant of the county for his pains). The call for an inquiry was again ignored when Parliament reopened in November. Instead the government passed the Six Acts, emergency measures designed to keep order: three were directed against seditious publications and meetings, two against the unlawful stockpiling and use of arms, and one speeded up the trials of wrongdoers. But the upsurge of popular unrest caused by Peterloo and the Six Acts would not reach its peak until the following year.

14

The Queen's Trial

The new decade was marred by two royal deaths in quick succession: first, on 23 January 1820, the Duke of Cambridge, 52, 'the strongest of the strong', died in Devonshire after catching a cold while out walking in bad weather; six days later his father, the 82-year-old King, took his last breath. The Regent – said to have been 'extremely shocked and upset when he heard of his father's death' – was George IV at last.[1]

But for a time it seemed as if the longest reign in history was about to be followed by the shortest. 'The King has been very unwell with an inflammation of the chest,' noted John Croker, the Secretary to the Admiralty, on 30 January, 'but he got up to receive the [Privy] Council.' As the 30th was the anniversary of Charles I's execution, an inauspicious date, the official proclamation of the new reign did not take place until noon the following day in the courtyard of Carlton House. By evening, however, the 'hurry and agitation of all these great affairs' had left the King's health worse than ever. 'The King is very ill,' wrote Countess Lieven on 2 February, 'he has got an inflammation of the lungs. Heavens, if he should die! Shakespeare's tragedies would pale before such a catastrophe. Father and son, in the past, have been buried together. But two kings! I hope this one will recover.'[2]

He did – but no thanks to his physicians, Sir William Halford and Sir Matthew Tierney, who drew from him more than 150 ounces of blood. By 6 February, he was well enough to raise with his ministers the issue of his divorce. 'They would sooner resign than have to deal with it,' commented Countess Lieven, 'but, at the same time, they realise that something must be done. They are going to propose a separation, to deprive her of a coronation and of the public honours to which a queen is entitled.' In particular, the King wanted to remove Queen Caroline's name from the Liturgy of the Church of England. Since their marriage in 1796, 'their Royal Highnesses George, Prince of Wales, and the Princess of Wales' had been prayed for by church congregations across the land. Now that he had become King, he was determined to prevent any reference in the Liturgy to 'our most gracious Queen'. Of particular assistance to him was John Croker's argument that 'if she is fit to be introduced to the Almighty, she is fit to be received by men, and if we are to pray for her in Church we may surely bow to her at Court'.[3]

The Cabinet were divided over the issue, with Canning (the President of the Board of Control since 1816) arguing that such an action would prejudice any future proceedings against the Queen. On purely religious grounds, Dr Charles Manners-Sutton, the Archbishop of Canterbury, was also opposed. Nevertheless, on 10 February the Cabinet agreed to omit the Queen from the Liturgy, justifying their decision on the ground that she was adequately covered by the expression 'all the royal family'. The real reason for this concession, however, was that the members of the Cabinet were keen to make a stand on the connected issue of the King's divorce. Having seen the additional evidence collected by the Milan Commission since the summer of 1819, they were still unconvinced that it was sufficient to prove a charge of adultery. Furthermore, the Queen would be able to offer recriminatory evidence, while the publicity of a parliamentary investigation would have a bad effect on public morals. Surely it was preferable, they advised the King on the 10th, to offer 'the Princess' money on condition that she stayed abroad.[4] The King 'is furious', noted Croker on the 13th, 'and says they have decieved him . . . Sir John Leach . . . suggests, it is said, a new administration, and it is reported has authority to sound Lord Wellesley, if not the Opposition. The Cabinet offer all but a divorce; the King will have a divorce or nothing. His agitation is extreme and alarming; it not only retards his recovery, but threatens a relapse. He eats hardly anything – a bit of dry toast and a little claret and water.'[5]

But for all his posturing – 'it is said,' wrote Greville, 'that he treated Lord Liverpool very coarsely, and ordered him out of the room' – the King was not in a position to sack his government because there was no viable alternative: Wellesley could not have commanded a sufficient majority in the House of Commons; the Whigs were divided over the issue of parliamentary reform (and their support for Catholic emancipation was still unacceptable to the King). On 14 February, therefore, to enable the King to save face, the Cabinet suggested a compromise: they were prepared to institute proceedings for a divorce – but only if the Queen was unwise enough to return to England. They were willing to do this because they did not believe for a minute that she would actually return. The King, who was not so sure, grudgingly agreed.[6]

Caroline was at Leghorn when she received word from Henry Brougham that George III was dead and she was Queen of England. The letter urged her to set off at once for Brussels, Paris or even Calais, and then demand a yacht to take her across the Channel. But far from actually wanting her to return home, Brougham was simply hoping to frighten the King and his government into agreeing to the most favourable terms of separation possible. 'All now depends on her coming to Brussels or some near and handy spot,' wrote Brougham to Lady Charlotte Lindsay on 18 February. 'If she arrives plump on you at Paris, make her either stay there or at Calais till I come out to her. It would be *frightfully dangerous* for her to come here all at once.'[7]

Caroline herself had no intention of setting off immediately. Having acceded to Brougham's request that he and Thomas Denman be appointed her Attorney- and Solicitor-Generals, she headed for Rome to collect her quarterly pension. But the frosty manner in which she was received by the Papal authorities – who had been told by Baron Reden, Ompteda's successor as Hanoverian minister, that the Queen was about to be stripped of her title – and the news that her name had been removed from the Liturgy, soon altered her priorities. In mid-March, she wrote to inform Brougham that she was on her way to England. It is just possible that George IV, in his guise as the King of Hanover, deliberately goaded his wife into returning so that he could institute proceedings against her. After all, Reden's actions had not been – and would not have been – authorised by Liverpool's government.

On 1 June the Queen arrived at St Omer, accompanied by Pergami, Austin and various members of her Italian suite. Also in attendance were Alderman Matthew Wood, the Radical M.P., for the City of London, and Lady Anne Hamilton, her former lady-in-waiting (also Radical in her politics), who had travelled out from England to encourage her to return home. Wood's political agenda depended upon the Queen's presence in London, where she could act as a focal point for popular unrest.

Meanwhile the Cabinet, in consultation with the King, had decided to make the Queen a final offer: her annuity, which had lapsed on the death of George III, would be continued at the increased rate of £50,000 a year if she agreed to stay away from 'any part of British dominions', take 'some other name or title than that of Queen', and accept that the rights and privileges of a Queen Consort were not to be exercised by her with respect to the appointment of law officers 'or to any proceedings in courts of justice'. If she violated any part of this agreement, she would lose her annuity.[8]

Armed with this offer, Brougham reached St Omer on 3 June; he was accompanied by Lord Hutchinson, who was to act as a supplementary negotiator. During the next 24 hours, they had a number of separate discussions with the Queen – but neither specified the exact terms of the proposal. Brougham, the chief negotiator, was keen to discover the minimum terms she would accept before playing his hand. Unfortunately the Queen ran out of patience. During a meeting with Hutchinson in the afternoon of the 4th, she demanded to know the terms; he recalled from memory that one of them was the renunciation of all royal titles – though in fact it only referred to the title of Queen – and then repeated the error in writing. Before Brougham had a chance to correct Hutchinson's mistake, not that it would have made any difference, she had left for Calais – and England. Pergami and most of her Italian attendants, meanwhile, had set off back to Italy.

At 1 o'clock in the afternoon of 5 June, having crossed the Channel in the common packet *Prince Leopold,* the Queen and her remaining entourage arrived in Dover to an enthusiastic welcome from the local tradesmen and fishermen. 'God bless Queen Caroline!' they cried as she attempted to walk from the pier to the Ship Hotel. Hemmed in by the cheering crowds, she took refuge in the nearer York Hotel, prompting the proprietor of its rival to send an open carriage to collect her. Even then, the local populace insisted on taking the horses from their traces and dragging the carriage themselves.

London was abuzz at the astonishing news that the Queen had returned :

> Neither at the landing of William the Conqueror, nor at that of the Earl of Richmond, nor of William III [read the *Times* editorial of 6 June] were the people's bosoms of this metropolis so much agitated as they were last night, when it was known that Her Majesty, the Queen of England, had once again – bravely, we will say – set her foot on British ground. The most important Parliamentary questions were adjourned, the King's Ministers fled to the council-chamber, the streets were crowded, everyone was inquiring 'When did she land? Where will she sleep? Where will she reside? How will she enter London?'

The answer to the last question was supplied that very day. Charles Greville, who rode as far as Greenwich to witness her arrival, noted:

The road was thronged with an immense multitude the whole way from Westminster Bridge to Greenwich. Carriages, carts, and horsemen followed, preceded, and surrounded her coach the whole way. She was everywhere received with the greatest enthusiasm. Women waved pocket handkerchiefs, and men shouted . . . She travelled in an open landau, Alderman Wood sitting by her side and Lady Anne Hamilton and another woman opposite. Everybody was disgusted at the vulgarity of Wood in sitting in the place of honour, while the D[uke] of Hamilton's sister was sitting backwards in the carriage. She [the Queen] looked exactly as she did before she left England, and seemed neither dispirited nor dismayed. As she passed by White's she bowed and smiled to the men who were in the window.[9]

That night, and the next, the Queen slept at Alderman Wood's house in South Audley Street as the mob kept up a constant attendance, shouting 'Long Live the Queen!', pelting those who would not take off their hats as they passed Wood's door, and smashing the windows of houses which refused to illuminate in her honour. Among the houses targeted were those owned by Lady Hertford, the King's former mistress, and Lord Sidmouth, the Home Secretary – though Lord Exmouth, who was having dinner in the latter residence, managed to drive away the mob by rushing outside with a pistol and a sword.

Meanwhile, the King was said to be in 'the most excellent spirits'. In the early evening of 6 June, as the Queen was entering London, John Powell had deposited two green barristers' brief bags – each containing copies of the Milan Commission evidence, along with the papers relating to the investigations of 1806 and 1813 – in both Houses of Parliament. With the evidence in place, Lord Liverpool had then delivered the King's message to the House of Lords. The return of the Queen, he said, had made it necessary 'to communicate to the House of Lords certain papers respecting the conduct of her Majesty since her departure from this kingdom'. The government would therefore be referring the evidence to a Secret Committee which would recommend the most suitable course of action.[10]

The King's victory over his government was sweet. 'He has laid a nice burden on the shoulders of his Ministers,' commented Countess Lieven, 'and now he says, "Let them get on with it."' But Greville could see trouble ahead for everyone. 'Her business,' he noted on the 7th, '. . . will in all probability raise such a tempest as [the ministers] will find it beyond their powers to appease; and for all [the King's] unconcern . . . the day of her arrival in England may be such an anniversary to him as he will have no cause to celebrate.'[11]

Greville's fears seemed to be justified when, on 15 June, nine men from the 1st Battalion, Scots Guards, refused to give up their ammunition after coming off duty. Their dissatisfaction was mainly with conditions of service, though a general sympathy for the Queen's cause had pervaded the ranks. The response of the Duke of York, Commander-in-Chief, was to order the battalion to march to Portsmouth. One wing left early the next morning, the other the following day, 'having been shut up in the Mews the whole of Friday' with 'a considerable mob' threatening to break down the gates to free it. Even during the march, the men 'have betrayed instances of indiscipline,' noted Henry Cam Hobhouse, the Under-Secretary of State for the Home Department, 'and have used expressions in derogation of the King and approbation of the Queen.' So alarmed was Greville with the level of 'military dissatisfaction' that he doubted how far the Guards 'could be counted upon in any case of disturbance arising out of this subject'. Henry Luttrell, the well-known wit, was more succinct. 'The extinguisher,' he announced, 'is taking fire.'[12]

For a brief moment it looked as if a settlement with the Queen might be possible. From 14 to 19 June, negotiations took place between Brougham and Denman, the law officers of the Queen, on the one hand, and Lord Castlereagh and the Duke of Wellington on the other. But they foundered on the King's determination not to include the Queen's name in the Liturgy. 'You might as easily move Carlton House,' commented Castlereagh. In addition, the government would only agree to designate her Queen of Great Britain to the government of the country she chose to reside in.[13]

The Secret Committee – which included the Archbishop of Canterbury, the Lord Chancellor and various members of the Cabinet – finally presented its report to the House of Lords on 4 July. They had, it stated, examined documents which contained 'allegations supported by the concurrent testimony of a great number of persons . . . which deeply affect the honour of the queen, charging her majesty with an adulterous connection with a foreigner, originally in her service in a menial capacity'. So potentially damaging were these charges to 'the honour of the Queen, . . . the dignity of the Crown, and the moral feeling and honour of the country', that the Committee had no hesitation in recommending a 'solemn inquiry' in the form of a 'legislative proceeding'.[14]

In layman's terms, this meant a parliamentary Bill of Pains and Penalties whereby an individual could be punished without resorting to a court of law. Introduced into the House of Lords by the Prime Minister on 5 July, the Bill sought 'to deprive her Majesty Caroline Amelia Elizabeth of the title, prerogatives, rights, privileges and exemptions of Queen Consort of this Realm, and to dissolve the Marriage between his Majesty and the said [Queen] Caroline'. Though technically a private Bill in which the law officers of the Crown were acting for an unnamed person, nobody was in any doubt that the individual concerned was the King. (The offence of high treason was not applicable, the law officers of the Crown had concluded in January, because the alleged offence had taken place abroad with the Queen's full complicity. In any case, the public would not have stood for it.)[15]

For the Bill to become law, the allegations in its preamble – that the Queen had 'carried on a licentious, disgraceful and adulterous intercourse' with Bartolomeo Pergami – would have to be proved in the eyes of both Houses of Parliament. Consequently, the second reading in the Lords would resemble a trial, with cross-examination of witnesses by counsel and peers. 'Everybody thinks the charges will be proved and that the King will be divorced,' recorded Greville on the 6th.

Lady Charlotte Lindsay was not so sure. 'I have little doubt of this Bill passing in the House of Lords,' she wrote to Mary Berry in Italy on 11 July, 'but I think it by no means likely to pass in the Commons – and, if so, the sentiment in the country against the decision of the Peers will be violent indeed. Not only the common people, but the middle ranks, and also many of the upper class, who live retired in the country, are all warmly interested in the Queen.'[16]

To leave time for the necessary witnesses to be summoned – many of them from Italy – the second reading of the Bill did not take place in the House of Lords until 17 August. George Keppel, who was present that day as the Duke of Sussex's equerry, had 'never beheld so dense a crowd as that which assembled between Pall Mall and Westminster Abbey'. He recalled:

> The Household Cavalry, the City Light Horse, and the Horse Police, patrolled the streets; a regiment of Guards were posted in Westminster Hall and the avenues of the Law Courts, and the approach to the Houses of Parliament was lined with infantry. The mob seemed to make a shrewd guess at the manner in which almost every Peer would vote, and received with groans or cheers the supposed supporters or opponents of the Ministerial measure. The Duke of Sussex met with a most enthusiastic greeting from them.[17]

Shortly after 10 a.m., as the 258 peers liable to attend – the remaining 109 had been excused on the grounds of age, sickness, bereavement or absence from the country – were still being called into the chamber that would serve as a court, loud cheers from outside signalled the arrival of the Queen. The triumphant procession, from the house she had taken for the duration of the trial in St James's Square, had been led by a man on horseback holding a green bag on a pole. Next came Alderman Wood's carriage; then the Queen herself, attended by Lady Anne Hamilton, in a handsome coach-and-six; another containing her vice-chamberlains, Gell and Keppel Craven, who had just arrived from

Naples; and finally one carrying William Austin, Colonel Vassalli, and Lord and Lady Hood (her Italian courier, Chamberlain and Mistress of the Robes respectively). So excited were the crowds when the Queen's coach reached Palace Yard that they broke down the barriers and accompanied it all the way to the doors of Westminster Hall.

There the Queen was met by Sir Thomas Tyrwhitt, dressed in the black and silver costume of the Usher of the Black Rod. 'Well, Sir Thomas,' she is reported to have asked, 'what is your master trying me for? Is it for intermarrying with a man whose first wife I knew to be alive?' Tyrwhitt did not reply.

The peers rose as the Queen entered the crowded chamber from the door behind the throne and took her seat in a crimson and gilt chair in front of those reserved for her five counsel and two solicitors. She was wearing a 'richly twilled black sarsenet dress' and a white veil wound many times about her head and bosom. Creevey, who was sitting among his fellow M.P.s nearby, likened her appearance to that of a Dutch doll. Then, when all 258 peers had been crammed into the benches and temporary galleries, the Duke of Leinster rose to move that the order for the second reading of the Bill should be rescinded. He was supported by just 41 peers, most of them Whigs opposed to the hypocrisy of the proceedings. None of the leading Whig peers was among them: they were convinced that the Bill would fail (probably in the Commons) and bring down Liverpool's government with it; in the meantime, they would treat it on its merits and try not to become aligned with the popular party.[18]

Following the defeat of Leinster's motion, the counsel were called in and the trial began. Opening for the Queen was her Attorney-General, Henry Brougham, who had briefly considered resigning after the fiasco at St Omer. But his desire to be at the centre of events had got the better of his private belief that the Queen was indeed guilty of adultery. His speech was a brilliant assault on the hypocrisy of the trial. 'I will not now advert to any topic of recrimination,' he began. '. . . I dismiss for the present all . . . questions respecting the conduct or connections of any parties previous to the marriage.' But, he warned, he would address such a subject if it was necessary, whatever the consequences. 'Are we arrived in this age at that highest pitch of polish in society when we shall be afraid to call things by their proper names yet shall not scruple to punish by express laws an offence in the weaker sex which has been passed over in the stronger?' he asked.

For had not the Duke of York escaped impeachment in 1809 after admitting adultery with Mrs Clarke? And was not the King under the influence of Lady Hertford during the period when the Queen's offences were alleged to have been committed? The Bill, he concluded, was not only *ex parte*, odious and unjust, it was also unnecessary because the succession to the throne was no longer in doubt.[19]

During the next two days, Thomas Denman, the Queen's Solicitor-General, continued the attack on the principle of the Bill, while Sir John Copley, the King's Solicitor-General, and Sir Robert Gifford, his Attorney-General, replied for the government. Like Brougham, Denman was a skilful orator though his knowledge of the law was not as comprehensive as it might have been. Gifford was competent, but the most gifted prosecution counsel was Copley, his junior. Though not a great speaker, he was always master of his material and brilliant in cross-examination. 'He possessed,' wrote Brougham, 'the gift of unfolding the subject in such a manner as to carry conviction by mere strength of exposition.'[20]

Even Gifford could not fail to impress when he outlined the heads of the charges on 19 August. The then Princess of Wales was accused of committing her first adulterous act with Pergami in Naples in November 1814: the imprints of two bodies were seen on her bed in the morning. At a New Year's Eve ball she had appeared indecently attired, and it was Pergami who had dressed her. Then there was her pilgrimage to Jerusalem, when she and Pergami had slept together in the tent on the polacca, and he had joined her when she bathed in her cabin.[21]

The country was astonished. 'What horrors in the newspapers!' wrote Countess Lieven to her lover Prince Metternich, the Austrian Foreign Minister. 'I read the speech for the prosecution; I have not had the heart to read the evidence; it is too disgusting. Is the Queen really a woman? And how can the House of Lords, uniting as it does all that is most dignified and most exalted in the greatest nation in the world, lower itself by listening to such vile trash?'[22]

Next it was the turn of the 60 or so prosecution witnesses, the majority of whom were Italian. These foreigners were being housed for their own safety in the Cotton Garden, a large building situated between the two Houses of Parliament. George Keppel likened it to a 'prison', for its inhabitants 'would have been torn in pieces by the populace if they had ventured beyond its precincts'. He explained:

> The side facing Westminster Bridge was shut out from the public by a wall run up for the express purpose . . . Thus the only access was by the river . . . The street side was guarded by a strong military force, the water side by gun-boats. An ample supply of provisions was stealthily (for fear of the mob) introduced into the building; a bevy of royal cooks were sent to see that the food was of good quality, and to render it as palatable as their art could make it. About this building, in which the witnesses were immured from August till November, the London mob would hover like a cat round the cage of a canary.[23]

The first witness to emerge to give evidence was Teodoro Majocchi on Monday, 21 August. The Queen's immediate reaction at the bar was one of horror. '[She] stood up,' noted Lady Granville, 'threw her head back, . . . put both her arms akimbo, and looked at him for some time with a countenance which those who saw it said was quite terrific. She then exclaimed, 'Ah, Theodore', and trundled out of the House.[24]

Lady Charlotte Lindsay, who was due to appear as a witness for the defence, was not convinced by the Queen's histrionics. 'I cannot make out the meaning of this exhibition,' she wrote to Mary Berry, 'for it must have been done to produce stage effect, as she knew before . . . that Theodore Majocchi was to be examined as a witness against her;

but whatever was the intention, the effect was not favourable, as it gave the impression of her being much alarmed at his evidence.'[25]

Caroline had good reason to be alarmed. Through the interpreter Marchese Spineto – the assistant to a Cambridge professor, whose wild gesticulations provided the peers with much entertainment – Majocchi repeated the evidence he had given to the Milan Commission. Pergami's bedroom was always situated close to the Princess's, with the rest of the household much more distant; twice in a week at Naples he had seen the Princess enter Pergami's room at night, staying for 'between 15 and 18 minutes'. And he had often observed Pergami dining with the Princess, walking with her arm in arm, and even holding her hand while she rode a donkey. At Aum in Syria, the Princess and Pergami had spent 'the whole time that was allotted for sleep' in the same tent; and during the return voyage in the polacca, they had slept 'every night' in the tent on deck, while Pergami 'assisted' the Princess when she had a bath in her cabin.[26]

As a result of Majocchi's evidence, the following epigram became immensely popular:

> The Grand Master of St Caroline
> has found promotion's path
> He is made both Night Companion
> and Commander of the *Bath*.[27]

Majocchi's testimony made a great impression on the peers. He was, noted Lady Granville, whose husband was in daily attendance, 'a very shrewd, intelligent man, perfectly undaunted', who had given 'his strong evidence without embarrassment or hesitation'. So worried were Denman and Thomas Wilde (one of the Queen's junior counsel) that they woke up Brougham twice that night with further suggestions for his cross-examination. The Queen, meanwhile, was so distressed that she had to be 'copiously bled'. Next day, when she took her seat in the House of Lords, her 'face was pale, her eyelids a little sunken, her eyes fixed on the ground'.[28]

Brougham's cross-examination was about to come to the rescue. To his seventh question – Did not Sir William Gell's servant also sit, like Pergami, at the table of the gentlemen? – Majocchi answered, '*Non mi recordo,*' 'I do not remember.' Then a few questions later, when he was asked where William Austin slept in the Princess's house at Naples, he gave the same answer. Brougham sensed an opening. During the course of his two-day cross-examination, Majocchi answered '*Non mi recordo*' to an incredible 87 questions. Some he could not have known the answer to, and Brougham had thrown these in for good measure. But others he was deliberately evading: as when he was asked whether the Princess had had any British ladies in attendance after she left Naples (she had had at least three); and whether he had asked to be taken back into the Princess's service after being dismissed. So bewildered did Majocchi become at one point that the interpreter was forced to complain: 'He does not understand the most common words, he is frightened out of his wits.'[29]

Though much of his testimony was undoubtedly true, Majocchi's credibility had been severely dented by Brougham's brilliantly executed cross-examination. His oft-repeated phrase, however, would not be forgotten. 'The Italian witnesses are supplying not only the Press but even Society with all its jokes,' wrote Countess Lieven on 27 August. 'Everyone is using the catchword "*Non mi ricordo*".'[30]

And so it went on, with a procession of witnesses offering evidence more or less damaging to the reputation of the Queen (who had been advised by Brougham to stay away unless her presence was specifically required). In the former category was the testimony of Gaetarno Paturzo, Captain Briggs, Captain Pechell and Barbara Kress. Paturzo, the mate of the polacca, confirmed that Pergami had slept with the Princess in the tent on deck; he had also seen them embrace. Briggs, the captain of the *Leviathan* which had transported Caroline from Genoa to Sicily, said that the Princess had altered the sleeping arrangements so that Pergami was in a cabin next to her own. Pechell, the captain of the frigate *Clorinde*, related how he had refused to sit at table with Pergami during the second voyage because the Italian had been a common servant when he had last seen him. Kress, a Karlsruhe cellarmaid, recalled seeing the Princess sitting on Pergami's bed with her arm around his neck.

Less harmful was the evidence given by the other prosecution star witness, Louise Demont, the Swiss maid. As with Majocchi, Brougham and his fellow counsel managed to elicit a number of defensive responses: '*Je ne me rappelle pas*', in her case. But the clincher came when they produced Demont's letters to the Queen written after her dismissal in 1817, asking to be reinstated, and to her sister in which she referred to the Queen in glowing terms. Demont's feeble defence was that they were '*double entendre*'.

Then, after a host of minor characters had been examined, came the final prosecution witness Giuseppe Sacchini, the Princess's equerry who had been dismissed with Demont. He repeated what he had told the Milan Commission: how, on a journey from Senigallia to Pesaro, he had opened the curtains of the Princess's carriage and found her and Pergami asleep, her hand resting on his genitals.[31]

On 8 September, Copley regained much of the ground lost by the prosecution during the cross-examinations of Majocchi and Demont in a brilliant summing-up. After it, Mrs Arbuthnot noted that 'nothing could appear stronger than the fact of the Queen's infamy as stated by [Copley] and sworn to by the witnesses.' Many of the leading Whig peers, like Grey and Fitzwilliam, were similarly convinced that she was guilty. Even Brougham was prepared to admit to Countess Lieven, on 6 September, that he could 'believe in any folly on the part of that woman'. But a belief in the Queen's guilt did not necessarily mean unqualified support for the Bill. The Archbishop of York, for example, told Lieven that none of the peers spiritual could vote for the divorce clause 'without dishonouring their calling'. Even Tory peers like Morley and Granville, according to the latter's wife, were 'anxious to have the thing knocked up in the Upper House'. She added:

> They think that without the divorce clause the proceeding is nonsense, with it quite unallowable. Ministers hold a different

language. 'What is to be proved if this is not? What would you have more, no two witnesses contradicting each other? The Queen, the disgrace of her sex . . .' etc. The fallacy of all this is that what we want is not belief, but proof; witnesses, but credible ones – ten Englishmen instead of a hundred Italians.[32]

So worried was Lord Liverpool that he had requested the King's permission to abandon the divorce clause even before the prosecution evidence was over.

The evidence in support of the preamble of the Bill is nearly closed [he wrote to the King on 1 September]. It is difficult to speculate upon the effect of it taken altogether. Some parts of it have made a considerable impression upon the minds of the peers against the Queen. Two of the most material witnesses [Majocchi and Demont] have, however, been shaken in their credit and character. The facts to which they have sworn have in other respects been strongly confirmed, and the conclusion might not be doubtful if we could be sure that those facts would not be repelled by evidence on the part of the Queen.

Furthermore, he added, it had become obvious that the Opposition were 'determined to make a party question of the whole business', and that they would 'strain every nerve and raise every doubt, however futile, to acquit the Queen'.

As if that was not bad enough, he had had 'an extensive personal communication with the Peers, ecclesiastical and lay, as well as with other persons', and had come to the conclusion that there was 'scarcely a chance' of the divorce clause 'passing the House of Lords', let alone the House of Commons. Then there was the danger of recrimination. 'Under all these circumstances,' concluded Liverpool, it would be better 'to give up the part of the Bill relative to divorce before the defence is commenced.'

Having spoken to Liverpool and other members of the Cabinet at the 'Cottage' in Windsor Great Park, where he was living during the trial, the King reluctantly agreed to follow his Prime Minister's advice. He then changed his mind: the Bill would proceed in its entirety.[33]

The general populace was still solidly behind the Queen. Enthusiastic crowds greeted her every time she ventured out; addresses of support arrived from all over the country. 'There is no denying it,' wrote Lady Cowper, 'the feeling of the people is almost everywhere in favour of the Queen, not merely the rabble, but the respectable middle ranks. All their prejudices are in her favour. They hate the King, disapprove of his moral conduct and think all foreigners are liars and villains.'[34]

On 3 October, after a lengthy adjournment, Brougham opened the case for the defence. In a speech spanning two days, he repeated his threat of recrimination, accused the prosecution of promising its Italian witnesses huge sums of money, and pointed out that nearly all the witnesses had perjured themselves by denying that they had received either money or promises. He also made the obvious point that they had not provided all the evidence which the Attorney-General had said they would do in his opening speech, the inference being that many of them had lied to the Milan Commission, and only the less serious falsehoods had been repeated in London.

'My lords,' he concluded:

> You are standing upon the brink of a precipice. It will go forth on your judgement, if it goes against the Queen. But it will be the only judgement you will ever pronounce which will fail in its object, and return upon those who give it. Save the country, my lords, from the horror of this catastrophe – . . . rescue that country, of which you are the ornament, but in which you could flourish no longer, when severed from the people, than the blossom when cut off from the root and the stem of the tree. Save the country, that you may continue to adorn it – save the Crown, which is in jeopardy – the aristocracy which is shaken – the altar itself . . . You have said, my lords, you have

willed – the Church and the King have willed – that the Queen should be deprived of its solemn service. She has indeed, instead of that solemnity, the heartfelt prayers of the people. She wants no prayers of mine. But I do here pour forth my supplications at the throne of mercy, that that mercy may be poured down upon the people, in a larger measure than the merits of its rulers may deserve, and that your hearts may be turned to justice.[35]

Brougham sat down to complete silence. So stunned were his listeners that nobody moved or spoke for at least 30 seconds. Denman described it as 'one of the most powerful orations that ever proceeded from human lips'; it was, wrote Lady Charlotte Lindsay, 'a most strikingly beautiful piece of eloquence'. Even Brougham's more violent opponents, like the Tory Lord Lonsdale, 'were struck with admiration and astonishment'. Charles Greville thought it was 'the most magnificent display of argument and oratory that has been heard for years'; while Earl Fitzwilliam, who had formerly been convinced of the Queen's guilt, was of the opinion that Brougham had 'shown incontestibly that one and all of the Italian witnesses' were perjured.[36]

On 5 October, the first witnesses for the defence were examined: Lord Guilford (formerly Frederick North, who had succeeded his brother in 1817), his sister Lady Charlotte Lindsay, Lord Glenbervie, Sir William Gell and Keppel Craven. All former or present members of the Queen's Household and circle, they dutifully claimed that they had witnessed no improprieties during their time in Italy. Guilford, however, was prepared to admit that he had advised his sister to resign her position as Lady of the Bedchamber in 1817, while Lady Charlotte explained that she would have done so earlier had she and her husband not needed the money. She also conceded that, while she 'had not seen any thing improper in her Royal Highness's service', she had heard a number of reports of 'so unpleasant and degrading a nature' that they had made her want to resign.[37]

The King was suitably dismissive of this evidence: 'I never thought,' he wrote to his brother, the Duke of York, on 7 October, 'that I should have lived to witness so much prevarication, so much lying, and so much wilfull and convenient forgetfulness, as, I am sorry to say, both Lord Guilford and Lady Charlotte Lindsay, have displayed in their late examinations.'[38]

The defence case received a welcome boost when Carlo Fortis claimed that he, and not Sacchini, had been the equerry during the Princess's journey from Pesaro to Senigallia. Moreover, the carriage was equipped with sprung blinds, not curtains, and had contained Contessa Oldi and young Vittorine as well as Pergami and the Princess.

But 7 October was not such a good day for the Queen. The witnesses responsible for this change of fortune were Lieutenants Flynn and Hownham, both officers in the Royal Navy. Flynn, who had been in nominal command of the polacca (with Gargiulo the working captain), told the court that he had no reason to believe Pergami had slept under the tent with the Princess. Where, then, had Pergami slept? he was asked. He did not know. Eventually, under persistent cross-examination from Copley, he fainted and had to be taken away, his credibility in tatters.

Hownham, the Princess's former private secretary, also tried to deny any knowledge of Pergami's sleeping arrangements. He, too, cracked under cross-examination:

Q. You have said that you did not know where Pergami slept; upon your oath do you not believe he slept under the tent?
A. I have heard he did sleep under the tent.
Q. I do not wish to know what you have heard.
A. And I believe he did sleep under the tent.
...

Q. Do you say that you see no impropriety . . . in a male and female sleeping so placed in a tent?
A. I do not conceive there was any impropriety in the thing, because I must have felt it, and I did not feel it; I have seen so many situations

that her Royal Highness has been placed in, in the course of her travels, that I do not look upon it as improper.[39]

The King was delighted. 'We seem . . . to have made up our ground today,' he informed his brother York. Greville agreed: since Hownham's admission that Pergami had slept under the tent with the Queen, 'all unprejudiced men seem to think the adultery sufficiently proved,' Among them was the Duke of Portland, who had been 'violently against the Bill'. He was 'so satisfied by Hownham's evidence,' wrote Greville, that he 'thought all further proceedings useless . . . as the fact was proved.' This would 'not, however, induce him to vote for the Bill, because he thinks that upon the ground of expediency it ought not to pass.' When Portland put this view to the Duke of Wellington, pointing out 'the disgrace it would entail upon the K[ing] by the recriminations that would ensue' in the House of Commons, Wellington replied 'that the King was degraded as low as could be already'.[40]

The case turned again on 13 October when Brougham requested a re-examination of Giuseppe Restelli, the Queen's former groom, who had served the Milan Commission as a courier. After giving evidence, Restelli had been sent back to Italy by John Powell to reassure the families of the other Italian witnesses that they were safe in England. He had still not returned. Brougham, meanwhile, claimed to have proof that Restelli had been an agent as well as a witness for the Crown, and that he had bribed other witnesses to give evidence. Restelli's absence, therefore, was a godsend for Brougham because it seemed to confirm this conspiracy theory.

When Powell was then called to the bar to explain why Restelli had been sent back to Italy, Brougham used the opportunity to taunt him about the identity of his 'client or employer in this case'. Everyone knew that it was the King – but his identity had never been specified. 'I know nothing about . . . this retiring phantom, this uncertain shape,' said Brougham, before illustrating his point with a quotation from Milton's *Paradise Lost*:

If shape it might be called that shape had none
Distinguishable in member, joint or limb,
Or substance might be called that shadow seemed;
For each seemed either . . .
    What seem'd his head
The likeness of a kingly crown had on.

The King is said to have responded: 'He might have left my shape alone.'[41]

On 24 October, Denman began to sum up the case for the defence. Having somewhat clumsily compared the King with Nero – with the result that the mob began to refer to Carlton House as 'Nero's Hotel' – he then quoted in Greek the reply given by Empress Octavia's servant to an agent who wanted her to give evidence against her mistress: 'My mistress's vagina is purer than your mouth.' Denman had of course been referring to Restelli; when it was taken to apply to the King himself, he was forced to apologise. Even his concluding words, a quotation from Christ to the adulterous woman, were ill advised: 'If no accuser can come forward to condemn thee, neither do I condemn thee: go, and sin no more.' He had meant to imply that in the Queen's case, where there was no guilt, they should exercise the same justice. But it had not come out like that.[42]

On 6 November, the House passed the second reading of the Bill by 123 votes to 95 – a majority of just 28. Most of the bishops had only voted for the Bill on the understanding that the divorce clause would be dropped before the third reading. The Whig lords, on the other hand, voted solidly against the Bill. Many felt that the evidence created suspicion but not overwhelming proof of the Queen's guilt; others disapproved of this type of legislation *per se*. They were joined by a number of Tory peers who, though they believed the Queen to be guilty (as did many of the Whigs), did not consider it prudent to proceed with the measure. Among them were some of the King's closest associates, including two of his Lords of the Bedchamber. 'In short,' wrote Charles Arbuthnot, 'the King's friends deserted him.'

The government was delighted with the outcome – not because it thought for a minute that the Bill would now become law, but because it had salvaged its reputation. 'Only 28 majority,' wrote Charles Arbuthnot to his wife. 'But still we are in high spirits; for her guilt has been pronounced most forcibly by many who voted against the Bill. In short, her character is blasted forever.' He added:

> I have been with Lord Liverpool and Lord Castlereagh since the division, and their minds are in a most comfortable state, the guilt having been pronounced much more conclusively than we had ever anticipated. I am sure the Government now, as to stability, stands much firmer than I had expected, and whatever may be the fate of the Bill, the King and his Administration have been fully justified for the enquiry into her conduct. She *is blasted*, and that is sufficient . . . Between ourselves, I now expect that the Bill will not come to the Commons.[43]

Two days later, in what was taken to be a last-ditch effort to save the Bill, the government introduced a motion to delete the divorce clause. But the Whig peers were determined to defeat the whole Bill (and bring down the government if possible), and they voted against it, as did a sizeable number of Tories who wanted the entire measure to succeed. This unholy alliance produced a large majority against the motion, and the divorce clause remained. 'Morality and the peace of the country go for nothing,' commented a disgusted Countess Lieven, 'thirst for power is the only thing that counts.'[44]

By now, the government was pinning its hopes on winning the vote for a third reading by such a small majority that it would provide an excuse to drop the Bill. The ministers particularly feared the consequences of it going to the lower chamber, where Brougham intended to bring direct recrimination against the King. He had managed to get hold of a copy of the will the King had made in 1796, in which Mrs Fitzherbert is referred to as his 'dear wife', and was threatening to produce it as evidence that George IV had forfeited his right to the throne. (Brougham said later that, though he believed he was right in point of law, he was throwing out hints merely to frighten). He had also tracked down several witnesses prepared to testify that the King had had sexual relations with a number of women: Madame de Meyer, the French courtesan; Mrs Mary Lewis, the boarding-house keeper he had met in Weymouth; Mrs Crowe, of Charles Street, St James's Square, with whom he was said to have had a son; the daughters of a turnpike collector called Hyfield; even a common prostitute.[45]

The government was duly granted its wish on 10 November when the third reading of the Bill received a majority of just nine votes (108 to 99). Whereupon Lord Liverpool rose to his feet and announced that the government was abandoning the whole measure. Brougham broke the news to the Queen in her robing-room, which adjoined the main chamber. 'She did not evince the satisfaction which might have been expected,' wrote Lady Charlotte Campbell, her former lady-in-waiting. 'She appeared worn-out in mind and body. The desolateness of her private existence seemed to make her very sorrowful: she appeared to feel the loss of her daughter more than at any previous moment, and she wept incessantly.'[46]

However, the Queen's depressed spirits did not seem to affect her supporters. Lady Charlotte Lindsay hugged Denman 'in a paroxysm of delight'; Brougham was carried head-high to Brook's Club by a cheering crowd. As the news of the Queen's 'acquittal' spread across the country, bonfires were lit and church bells rang out. The wild celebrations in London continued for days. 'There is a terrific burst of firing in the street,' wrote Countess Lieven to Prince Metternich on the evening of the 13th. 'That is the English way of rejoicing. They fire off cannons and muskets . . . The whole city is illuminated, but we have held out, as well as our windows; I can see that the mob is pleased at the victory of the Queen only because it gives an excuse for all this tomfoolery. She will soon be forgotten.'[47]

And so she was – but her trial had served a useful purpose by providing a release for the revolutionary pressure which had been building up in the country since the end of the Napoleonic Wars. 'Radicalism has taken the shape of affection for the Queen, and has deserted its old form,' wrote Bootle Wilbraham to Lord Colchester in mid-September 1820, 'for we are all as quiet as lambs in this part of England, and you would not imagine that this would have been a disturbed county twelve months ago.' Henceforth, radical change would be sought through the legitimate medium of an increasingly liberal Whig party.[48]

In the short term, however, the abandonment of the Bill seemed to represent a victory for the mob. The King was outraged, and even considered 'retiring to Hanover, and leaving his kingdom to the Duke of York'. He also mulled over the possibility of replacing his government. On 13 November, having received 'a letter from the Chancellor giving a most unsatisfactory account of his conversation with the King', Liverpool noted that he and his ministers were 'in a sea of troubles, and God only knows how we are to get out of them'.[49]

But get out of them they did: partly by refusing the Queen's demand to be given a royal palace (and therefore pleasing the King); but mainly because, as before, there was no viable alternative to Liverpool's government. If the Whigs had been unpalatable to the King before the Queen's Trial, how much more so were they now. Only Lord Grenville had emerged with his reputation intact, and he could not hope to secure a working majority in both Houses. A year later, alienated by the Whigs' adoption of parliamentary reform, Grenville's remaining supporters went over to the Tories.

But was the Queen innocent of adultery with Pergami? And did she deserve to be 'acquitted'? The answer to the first question is surely no. She had had a number of affairs since separating from her husband, and there is every reason to believe that her relationship with Pergami was sexual – not least because the prosecution evidence at her trial was so compelling. It would have been even more so if Iacinto Greco, a Sicilian who had cooked for the Queen at Syracuse in 1816, had come forward sooner. Shortly after the Bill was abandoned, he confessed to a British lieutenant – who had been sent by the Foreign Office to southern Italy to gather more evidence – that he had caught the then Princess of Wales and Pergami in *flagrante delicto*. He had opened the door and seen:

> . . . the Princess on the sofa at the further end of the saloon – Pergami was standing between her legs which were in his arms – his breeches were down, and his back towards the door . . . I saw the Princess's thighs quite naked – Pergami was moving backwards and forwards in the very act with the Princess.[50]

But Greco's presence had been noticed, and he was given his marching orders the following day.

As to whether the Queen deserved to be acquitted – the answer has to be yes. Not just because her husband was a worse adulterer than even she, though that would have been reason enough, but also because his unforgivable treatment of her since their first meeting in 1795 had surely driven her to behave so immorally.

15

Blackguard or Gentleman?

Shortly after the end of the trial, the Queen replied to a letter from Lady Charlotte Campbell congratulating her on its successful outcome. She wrote:

> I do indeed feel thankful at having put my enemies to confusion, and received the justice my conduct and character deserved. *Mais, hélas!* it comes too late, dear Charlotte. Her who would have rejoiced with me at her moder's triumph is losset to me; but she is in a much better world dan de present, and we shall meet soon, I trust, for, to tell you de truth, I cannot expect much comfort nowhere so long as I shall live . . . Dat cruel personage will never let me have peace so long as I stay in dis country: his *rancune* is boundless against me.[1]

She knew her husband only too well. Towards the end of November, while discussing the possible formation of a new government, the King asked Lord Grenville if he would be prepared to publish the memorandum written by Princess Charlotte in 1814, detailing her mother's connivance in the Captain Hesse affair. It would, the King hoped, provide a basis for refusing to reinstate the Queen's name in the Liturgy, as well as a ground for reinstituting divorce proceedings. But Grenville refused.

The King got his way on the issue of the Liturgy nonetheless. By authorising an increase in the Queen's annuity to £50,000 – announced in the King's Speech at the reopening of Parliament on 23 January 1821 – he took the wind out of the Opposition's sails. Three days later, Lord Archibald Hamilton's motion in the House of Commons that the removal of the Queen's name from the Liturgy was 'ill advised and inexpedient' was defeated by an incredible 310 votes.[2]

His final act of revenge was to ban the Queen from taking part in his Coronation at Westminster Abbey on 19 July. She turned up nonetheless, accompanied by Lady Anne Hamilton, Lord and Lady Hood, and Keppel Craven, but was prevented from entering by prize-fighters dressed as pages who had been hired to guard the entrances. In desperation, she tried to gain access to Westminster Hall, but was turned away by the door-keeper because she did not have a ticket. 'This is your Queen,' Lord Hood implored. 'She is entitled to admission without such a form.'

'Yes, I am your Queen,' Caroline added. 'Will you not admit me?'

'My orders are specific, and I feel myself bound to obey them,' came the inflexible reply.

At this juncture Sir Robert Inglis, one of the Gold Staffs, made an appearance. 'Madam,' he said, 'it is my duty to inform your Majesty that there is no place for your Majesty in the Royal box.'

'I am sorry for it,' the Queen replied, before admitting defeat and leaving.[3]

The King, meanwhile, was thoroughly enjoying the day. His splendid Coronation robes – including a crimson velvet train with golden stars that was 27 feet long – had cost £24,000 alone; another fortune had been spent hiring the 12,314 diamonds which made up his Coronation Crown. There had been 'one attempt to raise a hiss, and a cry of "Queen" at the corner of a street', recorded Mr Bootle Wilbraham, 'but it totally failed, and the voices were overpowered by bursts of loyalty'.[4]

Following the five-hour ceremony in the Abbey, a banquet was held in Westminster Hall. 'The King behaved very indecently,' noted Mrs Arbuthnot, 'he was continually nodding and winking at Lady Conyngham and sighing and making eyes at her. At one time in the Abbey he took a diamond brooch from his breast and, looking at her, kissed it, on which she took off her glove and kissed the ring she had on!!! Any body who could have seen this disgusting figure, with a wig the curls of which hung down his back, & quite bending beneath the weight of his robes & his *60* years would have been quite sick.'[5]

During the journey back to Carlton House in the evening, the King's cortège was blocked by two overturned carriages. It was decided, therefore, to take a back route through the slums of Westminster. 'The King,' wrote George Keppel, 'was horribly nervous, and kept constantly calling to the officers of the escort to keep well up to the carriage windows.'

According to Lady Lyttelton, who heard the story second-hand from Lord St Helens, the procession eventually came to 'a broad deep canal, full of water and mud, over which lay an old wooden bridge, stopped up at its entrance by strong barricadoes'. Afraid to return the way they had come, the King's attendants ordered the guards to demolish the barricades so that the carriages could cross. As they did so, the 'planks cracked, shook, bent, and were all in great holes'. But the carriages all got over safely. No sooner had they done so than the owner of the bridge appeared; observing what had occurred, he nearly fainted with shock. 'The bridge,' wrote Lady Lyttelton, 'had been *for many years condemned as impassably dangerous*, surveyors having so reported it, and no workman with a wheelbarrow had been permitted to pass over it since the decree was passed . . . Never was a monarch so lucky certainly. He must have been drowned if the bridge had given way.'[6]

On 7 August 1821, less than three weeks after her humiliating rebuffal at the doors of Westminster Abbey, Queen Caroline died of 'an obstruction of the bowels, attended with inflammation'. The most likely explanation for the blockage was a tumour, though it was suggested by some that she had been poisoned. The King was on board the royal yacht in Holyhead harbour, waiting for a favourable wind so that he could continue on his state visit to Ireland, when he received the news that his wife was dead. Contrary to expectation, he 'reacted as we could have wished,' noted the Marquess of Londonderry (formerly Lord Castlereagh), 'and since has not been unreasonable to any of the observances recommended for his sanction.' John Croker heard a similar report: 'The King was uncommonly well during his passage and gayer than it might be proper to tell; but he did not appear upon deck after he heard of the Queen's death, and, though it would be absurd to think he was afflicted, he certainly was affected at the first accounts of this event.' But not enough to order a period of general mourning – three weeks of Court mourning were considered adequate.'[7]

The King never remarried: partly because the succession to the throne was no longer an issue; and partly because Lady Conyngham, the new love of his life, already had a husband. (Lord Conyngham was rewarded for his forbearance by being appointed Lord Steward of the King's Household in 1821.) He retained a Tory ministry until the end, though Wellington's support for Catholic emancipation – on the ground that it was the only way to prevent civil war – almost caused him to abdicate in 1829. Royal patronage had been steadily eroded, and the days when monarchs could make or break ministries at will had gone for ever.

Much of the last two years of the King's life were spent at Windsor Castle, which he had had rebuilt by Sir Jeffry Wyatville at vast expense. He had vacated Carlton House in 1823 because he considered it too small and antiquated to serve as the residence of a King. It was pulled down three years later to make way for a terrace of houses. Buckingham House, its replacement, was still in the process of being transformed into a palace by John Nash at the time of his death.

Of this latter period at Windsor, the diarist Thomas Raikes wrote:

He very seldom went out, even in his favourite low phaeton and ponies . . . His more general habit was to remain in his *robe de chambre* all the morning, and never dress till the hour of dinner. In this *dishabille* he received his ministers, inspected the arrangement of all the curiosities which now adorn the gallery in the Castle, . . . amused himself with mimicking Jack Radford, the stud groom, who came to receive orders, or lectured Davison, the tailor, on the cut of the last new coat. I have been told by those about him . . . that a plain coat, from its repeated alterations, would often cost £300 before it met his approbation.[8]

According to Captain Gronow, the King 'abstained from eating animal food' during his final months, 'and lived on vegetables and pastry, for which he had a great liking'. Gronow added:

> His conduct, from being that of a sensual, greedy old man, became that of a spoilt child; and the way he spent his time was frivolous in the extreme. He was very fond of punch, made from a recipe by his maître d'hôtel, Mr Maddison, and which he drank after dinner; that was the only time he was agreeable, and on these occasions he would sing songs, relate anecdotes of his youth, and play on the violoncello: afterwards going to bed in a 'comfortable' state. But a nervous disorder which affected him prevented his sleeping well, and he invariably rose in the morning in the most unamiable of tempers. Poor man, he was greatly to be pitied; for he was surrounded by a set of harpies, only intent on what they could get out of him, among the most prominent of whom was Lady C[onyngham], the 'English Pompadour'.[9]

Lady Conyngham was still the royal favourite in the spring of 1830, when the King first began to show signs of rapid physical decline. Regular attacks of breathlessness, legs swollen by dropsy and severe bladder pains made it difficult for him to sleep – even when large doses of laudanum were administered. His mind remained alert, however, and he refused to rule out the possibility of a recovery. 'No man clung to life with greater eagerness than George IV,' wrote Raikes.[10]

The end came, nonetheless, during the early hours of 26 June. Having fallen asleep in his chair as usual, the King awoke just before 3 a.m. and asked the pages to bring in his night-chair (his bed being too uncomfortable to sleep in). While this was being done Sir Wathen Waller, the physician who was sitting up with him, administered a purgative. 'I do not think all is right,' commented the King, before asking: 'What shall we do next?'

'Return as soon as possible to your chair,' replied Waller.

He did so, but felt faint and asked for the windows to be opened. Waller then tried without success to get him to drink some sal volatile – at which point Sir Henry Halford, the senior royal physician, was sent for. Gripping Waller's hand 'more strongly than usual', the King turned to him with 'an eager eye' and exclaimed: 'My dear boy! This is death!'

Halford arrived just as he lay back in his chair and closed his eyes. 'His Majesty gave him his hand,' wrote Waller, but never spoke afterwards and, with a very few short breathings, expired exactly as the clock struck the quarter after three.'[11]

According to the post-mortem conducted by Sir Astley Cooper, the King's primary and mortal disorder was 'an ossification of the vessels of the heart' (better known today as arteriosclerosis). Cooper had never seen a heart so 'enveloped in masses of fat'. He also discovered a small stone in the bladder – which accounted for the pain in that region. But the immediate cause of death was put down to a ruptured blood vessel in the King's stomach, the result of a 'violent fit of coughing' on 24 June. Had it not been for this, his 'struggle against death' would only have been 'prolonged for three or four weeks'.[12]

The funeral took place at Windsor on 15 July. In keeping with the character of the new reign – George IV was succeeded not by the formal Duke of York, who had died in 1827, but by the down-to-earth Duke of Clarence, who became William IV, the 'Sailor King' – it was a muddled affair. 'We never saw so motley, so rude, so ill-managed a body of persons,' reported *The Times*. 'Those who first entered [St

George's Chapel] not only seized the best places, but prevented others from taking any.'[13]

In accordance with his dying wishes, George IV was buried in his nightshirt. Around his neck, 'attached to a very dirty and faded piece of black riband', was a diamond locket containing a miniature portrait of Mrs Fitzherbert. And so, wrote George Keppel, 'he carried with him to the grave the image of her, who was perhaps the only woman he had respected as well as loved.'[14]

'There never was an individual less regretted by his fellow-creatures than this deceased King,' read *The Times* leader the day after the funeral. It continued:

> What eye has wept for him? What heart has heaved one throb of unmercenary sorrow? Was there at any time a gorgeous pageant on the stage more completely forgotten than he has been, even from the day on which the herald proclaimed his successor? Has not that successor gained more upon the English tastes and prepossessions of his subjects, by the blunt and unaffected – even should it be the grotesque – cordiality of his demeanour, within a few short weeks, than George IV, – that Leviathan of the *haut ton* – ever did during 68 years of his existance. If George IV ever had a friend – a devoted friend – in any rank of life, we protest that the name of him or her has not yet reached us. An inveterate voluptuary, especially if he be an artificial person, is of all known beings the most selfish. Selfishness is the true repellant of human sympathy. Selfishness feels no attachment, and invites none; it is the charnel-house of our affections.[15]

The Times, it should be mentioned, had had little time for the King – or the Tory government, for that matter – since Lord Sidmouth had conveyed his congratulations to the Manchester Yeomanry and magistrates for their prompt action at Peterloo. But it had a point: the King was not popular and his passing was not greeted with much sorrow.

So what are we to make of his life? That it was one of unfulfilled promise there is no doubt. Born shortly before the onset of an Industrial Revolution which would alter the economic and political landscape for ever, he had the intellectual potential to become one of the great reforming monarchs. But the horrors of the French Revolution, which he learned at first hand from refugees, blunted his liberal instincts and eventually drove him into the arms of the Tories, the one party which promised to retain the *status quo* in Church and State. Only towards the end of his reign, when even the leading Tories had come to the conclusion that it was the only way to prevent civil war in Ireland, did he reluctantly consent to Catholic emancipation, a measure he had championed as a young man.

It is for this reason, and for his final abandonment of the Whigs in 1812, that George IV has often been accused of political inconsistency. But this is to ignore the fact that his guiding mantra was opportunity rather than principle (as you would expect from a man whose main pursuit was pleasure). After all, his early preference for the Whigs had more to do with creating, in the words of *The Times*, 'an ostensible rallying point of Parliamentary opposition to his father's Government' (much as his grandfather had done) than any firm political conviction.[16]

If he felt any sense of political loyalty, it was towards Fox personally rather than the Whigs as a group. And even this attachment was partly severed during the early 1790s, when Fox displayed too much enthusiasm for the French Revolution and the left wing of the party began to raise the issue of parliamentary reform. For a time the Prince withdrew from politics, though his sympathies lay with the Portland Whigs who threw in their lot with Pitt's Tory government.

He was reunited with Fox in 1797 because of the threat to Ireland. Grattan and other leading Irish Whigs had convinced him that Catholic emancipation was the only way to ensure the loyalty of Irish Catholics in the event of a rebellion or a French invasion. But with the suppression of the Great Rebellion in 1798, and the final removal of the French threat by Nelson's victory at Trafalgar in 1805, he no longer saw the need for a measure which would, he allowed himself to be convinced, weaken his own authority as a Protestant monarch. Catholic emancipation was for him a policy of necessity rather than principle; once the necessity had gone, the policy could be shelved.

Fox's death in 1806 made it possible for him to ignore the Whigs at the outset of the Regency with only the slightest pang of nostalgic regret. Often given as an example of his moral cowardice, this was in fact one of the few occasions when he put his country first. After his death, even *The Times* was prepared to admit this:

> If the choice of Mr. Perceval and his colleagues for Ministers . . . has been made a reproach to his Royal Highness on the score of personal consistency, we must acknowledge that the REGENT appears to have acted from higher and more extensive views. England was at war with NAPOLEON for her existence. [With] MR. PERCEVAL and his party the war had been carried – feebly, perhaps – . . . but with a conviction, shared by the great body of the people of England, that the country must go through, or perish.[17]

In truth, he had long had more in common with the Tories than the Whigs; but Pitt's parsimonious approach to public finance – and therefore the Prince of Wales's debts – and the fact that he was the King's minister, meant that the two rarely saw eye to eye. The two exceptions were during the years 1794–5, when Pitt assured the Prince that he would receive a generous marriage settlement, and 1801–4, when Pitt was in Opposition. Contrary to appearances, therefore, the Prince's retention of the Tories in 1811–12 was wholly consistent with his political development (if it could be called that). Only in the 1820s, with the King a virtual recluse and out of touch with political reality, did his innate political conservatism seriously clash with the national interest over the issue of Catholic emancipation. But thanks to the unselfish sponsorship of the Duke of Wellington, hitherto so staunch in his support for the Established Church, the measure became law.

On a personal level, his character was shaped by an austere upbringing. A bright and precocious child, he longed to escape from the cloying atmosphere of restraint and duty. But the more rebellious he became, the tighter the restrictions his parents imposed upon him. It did not help that he possessed those self-same hedonistic traits which his father had so successfully repressed; or that he was particularly impressionable, and easily led astray.

On the surface, his insatiable appetite for women was mere sexual gratification, but at a deeper level it was probably a manifestation of his search for a 'mother' figure. Queen Charlotte was a distant, formal woman, and it is probably no coincidence that his longer-lasting relationships were formed with matronly ladies like Mrs Fitzherbert and the Marchionesses of Hertford and Conyngham (the last two were both grandmothers when he took up with them). He, in turn, repeated the mistakes his parents had made with his own daughter – and for the same reason. Their relationship was never close, and it is telling that her last thoughts were for her absent mother.

Mrs Fitzherbert has always been considered the love of his life. That he was reckless enough to jeopardise his chances of succeeding to the throne by secretly marrying her in 1785 could be taken as proof of this. It could also be seen as the wilful act of a selfish man who was determined to get what he wanted – without regard for the long-term consequences to himself, his wife or his country. In that he was capable of loving any woman, he loved Mrs Fitzherbert. But this did not prevent him from abandoning her twice – the second time for good. She may have been amply provided for – he was never less than generous with his money – but this could hardly compensate for the loss of her husband *and* her reputation.

His treatment of his second wife was even more unforgivable. Having sacrificed Mrs Fitzherbert for money, he then allowed his scheming mistress, Lady Jersey, to choose for him an official wife who, because of certain character defects, would not threaten her own position of influence. This unfortunate Princess – grossly insulted by the Prince's ungracious behaviour at their first meeting – was then forced to endure the humiliation of having his mistress as her lady-in-waiting. She retaliated in the only way she knew how: with sarcasm and vulgarity. This in turn alienated the Prince further – as did his discovery on the wedding night that his new wife was not a virgin. The disastrous consequences of a Prince of Wales marrying for reasons of duty (not to mention financial gain) when his heart had already been given to another are there for all to see. Unfortunately it was an historical lesson that was not heeded by our current heir to the throne. Like his recently departed wife, Princess Caroline would not 'go quietly' either. She too became the darling of the people, a propaganda tool with which the press could attack an increasingly hidebound monarchy. She too would die prematurely amidst suspicions – however groundless – of foul play.

George was also vindictive: his hounding of his second wife and his ruthless prosecution of those newspaper editors foolish enough to publish libels of him is proof enough of this. As also is the speed with which he was prepared to discard close friends if they ever crossed him: Beau Brummell, Jack Payne and Lord Hugh Seymour all suffered in this way. At the same time, he could be tremendously generous to those people who kept in with him. But he was never loyal in the true sense of the word – through thick and thin – which explains why so few people mourned his passing.

It is often assumed that he lacked the physical courage of his forebears, particularly his father, and there is some truth in this. He certainly had a pathological fear of the mob – a legacy of the French Revolution – and took care to avoid angry crowds. On the other hand, he was keen to see active service during the Napoleonic Wars – possibly in the knowledge that it would be denied him – and behaved with great *sang froid* when an unruly multitude surrounded his carriage shortly after the 1788–9 Regency crisis (and before the French Revolution had begun). Nor did he particularly fear pain; in 1821, for example, he endured a dangerous operation to remove a tumour from the top of his head without anaesthetic.

And so we return to the popular image of George IV as 'Prinny', the overweight, overdressed and oversexed buffoon waiting for his periodically deranged father to be declared unfit to rule. There is of course much truth in this caricature – yet it fails to acknowledge either his personal qualities or his lasting achievements. He was, after all, a man capable of impressing the poet Lord Byron – formerly so critical – with his 'abilities and accomplishments', not to mention his 'manners' which were 'certainly superior to those of any living *gentleman*'.[18]

He was also a member of the triumvirate of Allied monarchs (albeit in his acting capacity) who did so much to bring about the fall of Napoleon – his determination to continue the war when he became Regent in 1811 being a major factor in his decision not to replace Perceval's Tory government with his 'friends' the Whigs (who were less committed to fighting).

But it is for his contribution to 'civilisation' that George IV deserves the most credit. A highly intelligent, well-read man, a lover of music and art, he spent an inordinate amount of time and money on cultural pursuits. Regency architecture, the purchase of the Elgin Marbles, the founding of the Royal Society of Literature, the donation of George III's magnificent collection of books to the British Library, the restoration of the Royal Collection of pictures and the inauguration of the National Portrait Gallery: all were – directly or indirectly – due to him. He also sponsored individual artists, scientists and musicians, was a patron of the Royal Academy and a President of the Royal Institution. Surely no member of the Royal Family – other than Prince Albert (Queen Victoria's husband) – has ever come close to matching these cultural achievements.

So the Bishop of Coventry was right: his 15-year-old charge did become an 'admixture' of the 'most polished gentleman' and 'the most accomplished blackguard in Europe'. The King's last Prime Minister, the Duke of Wellington, would certainly have agreed. Two years after George's death, the Duke described him as 'the most extraordinary compound of talent, wit, buffoonery, obstinacy, and good feeling – in short a medley of the most opposite qualities, with a great preponderance of good – that I ever saw in any character in my life'.[19]

The last word should perhaps go to the composer Dr Charles Burney. Having dined with the Prince at Carlton House in July 1805, he wrote the following letter to his daughter Fanny, the celebrated novelist:

> I was astonished to find him amidst much constant dissipation, possessed of so much learning, wit, knowledge of books in general, discrimination of character, as well as original humour. He quoted Homer in Greek to my son as readily as if the beauties of Dryden or Pope had been under consideration. And as to music, he is an excellent critic; has an enlarged taste – admiring what is good in its kind, of whatever age or country the composers or performers may be; without, however, being insensible to the superior genius and learning necessary to some kinds of music more than others . . . [He] may with truth be said to have as much wit as Charles II, with much more learning – for his merry majesty could spell no better than the *bourgeois gentil-homme*.[20]

Chapter Notes

Abbreviations: principal archives

British Library, London: BL
Egerton Papers (EGERTON)
Francis Papers (FRANCIS)
Hastings Papers (HASTINGS)
Leeds Papers (LEEDS)
Liverpool Papers (LIVERPL)
Miscellaneous Papers (MISC)
The Correspondence of Richard Brinsley Sheridan (SHERIDAN)

Hampshire Record Office, Winchester: HRO
Malmesbury Papers (MALMES)

Royal Archives, Windsor Castle: RA

Warwickshire Record Office, Warwick: WRO
Denbigh Papers (DENBIGH)
Seymour Papers (SEYMOUR)

Private Papers
Dr William Wheeler Papers (WHEELER)
Cynthia Campbell Papers (CAMPBELL)

As the following sources are frequently used, they are abbreviated as shown. Full descriptions are contained in the bibliography.

C/Corr.	Aspinall (ed.), *Letters of the Princess Charlotte 1811–1817.*
Cobbett	*Cobbett's Parliamentary Papers.*
Fraser	Flora Fraser, *The Unruly Queen.*
Gronow	Rees Howell Gronow, *The Reminiscences of Captain Gronow.*
GIII/Corr.	Aspinall (ed.), *The Later Correspondence of George III.*
GIV/P	Christopher Hibbert, *George IV: Prince of Wales 1762–1811.*
GIV/K	Christopher Hibbert, *George IV: Regent and King 1811–1830.*
Hansard	*Hansard's Parliamentary Proceedings.*
K/Corr.	Aspinall (ed.), *The Letters of King George IV, 1812–1830.*
Macalpine	Ida Macalpine and Richard Hunter, *George III and the Mad-Business.*
P/Corr.	Aspinall (ed.), *The Correspondence of George, Prince of Wales, 1770–1812.*
Wraxall	Nathaniel Wraxall, *Memoirs.*

Prologue

1 MALMES, Malmesbury Diary, 5 April 1795, 9M73/G2008, HRO.
2 Ibid., 18 Feb and 6 March 1795.
3 MALMES, *Detailed Account by Malmesbury of what he was told by the Prince of Wales about the Princess's character and behaviour, their wedding night, etc,* 9M73/G2031, HRO.
4 Leslie, *George the Fourth,* 19.

1 – A Dissipated Youth

1 *Northumberland Diaries,* 47–8.
2 *Papendiek Journals,* I, 27.
3 Williams, *Life in Georgian England,* 41.
4 Ibid., 33.
5 *Walpole Journals,* I, 125.
6 *Northumberland Diaries,* 51.
7 Palmer, *George IV,* 16.
8 *Farington Diary,* VII, 191–2.
9 P/Corr., I, 5–6.
10 *Papendiek Journals,* I, 50, 94.

11   *Walpole Correspondence*, XXVI, 191; *Walpole Journals*, I, 108.

12   P/Corr., I, 6.

13   MISC, George III to Holdernesse, 16 July 1772, Add. MS 40730.f.60.

14   GIV/P, 5.

15   Ibid., 6; P/Corr., I, 35.

16   GIV/P, 7.

17   *Walpole Journals*, II, 19.

18   *Walpole Journals*, I, 554–8; *Walpole Journals*, II, 86; GIV/P, 8.

19   *Papendiek Journals*, I, 132.

20   Ibid., 91-2; *Devonshire Correspondence*, 291; Wraxall, V, 383.

21   Leslie, *George the Fourth*, 19.

22   P/Corr., I, 4; *Hamilton Letters*, 71–7.

23   *Devonshire Correspondence*, 290.

24   GIV/P, 16.

25   *Hamilton Letters*, 88–90, 193.

26   P/Corr., I, 34, 35–6.

27   Levy, *The Mistresses of King George IV*, 27–8; *Devonshire Correspondence*, 290–91.

28   Levy, *The Mistresses of King George IV*, 28; GIV/P, 18–19.

29   Ibid., 29.

30   P/Corr., I, 36–8.

31   Ibid., 41, 43.

32   Ibid., 79.

33   Ibid., 44–5.

34   Ibid., 61n.

35   *Devonshire Correspondence*, 292; P/Corr., I, 55.

36   *Minto Letters*, III, 361.

37   P/Corr., I, 65–8, 72–3; *Fulke Greville Diaries*, 27.

2 – Into Opposition

1   P/Corr., I, 73, 75.

2   *Walpole Journals*, I, xix.

3   'George III "had secret son and heir"', *Sunday Times*, 29 June 1997.

4   *Walpole Journals*, I, xx–xxi.

5   *Walpole Journals*, II, 384.

6   Ibid., 404–5.

7   P/Corr., I, 86.

8   Clarke, *George III*, 103.

9   Ayling, *Fox*, 95.

10   Clarke, *George III*, 104.

11   Walpole, *Fox*, 6.

12   Clarke, *George III*, 106.

13   Ayling, *Fox*, 97.

14   Ibid., 103–4.

15   P/Corr., I, 95.

16   Ibid., 103.

17   *Walpole Journals*, II, 496–7.

18   Ayling, *Fox*, 111.

19   P/Corr., I, 104.

20   *Walpole Journals*, II, 497.

21   Ayling, *Fox*, 110–11.

22   *Walpole Journals*, II, 509; Ayling, *Fox*, 111.

23   *Walpole Journals*, II, 510.

24   P/Corr., I, 99, 113, 116–17

25   *Walpole Journals*, II, 525.

26   P/Corr., I, 125–6.

27   Ibid., 113, 99.

28   *Walpole Correspondence*, XXXIII, 499; Gronow, II, 255.

29   GIV/P, 35.

30   Cobbett, XXIII, 1123–5.

31   *Morning Chronicle*, 12 November 1783.

32   Ayling, *Fox*, 118–23.

33   Wraxall, III, 151.

34   *Devonshire Correspondence*, 70.

35   *Hamilton Letters*, 170–71.

36   Ayling, *Fox*, 131.

37   *Papendiek Journals*, I, 209–11.

38   Ayling, *Fox*, 134–8.

39   Walpole, *Fox*, 91.

3 – Mrs Fitzherbert

1   *Devonshire Correspondence*, 76.

2   Leslie, *Mrs Fitzherbert*, 21.

3   GIV/P, 47.

4   Leslie, *Mrs Fitzherbert*, 22.

5   GIV/P, 48.

6 *Devonshire Correspondence*, 86–7; GIV/P, 48–9; Leslie, *Mrs Fitzherbert*, 35–6.
7 *Fitzherbert Letters*, 24.
8 *Holland Memoirs*, II, 126.
9 *Devonshire Correspondence*, 87–8.
10 P/Corr., I, 153.
11 Ibid., 155–8, 160–61.
12 Ibid., 162, 164–7.
13 *Malmesbury Diaries*, II, 123, 125, 127–30.
14 GIV/P, 51.
15 P/Corr., I, 189–201.
16 GIV/P, 51.
17 *Fox Correspondence*, II, 278–85.
18 P/Corr., I, 174; P/Corr., II, 144, 213.
19 P/Corr., I, 216.
20 DENBIGH, CR 2017/C244, 340–44, WRO.
21 GIV/P, I, 56.
22 P/Corr., I, 228–9, 231, 232, 233–4.
23 *D'Arblay Diary*, III, 46.
24 Macalpine, 310–12.
25 Leslie, *Mrs Fitzherbert*, 59, 62.
26 *Fitzherbert Letters*, 68, 74.
27 *Memoranda concerning James Ord*, Georgetown University Library, 8–22, CAMPBELL.
28 Cadet Papers (1803), 129, WHEELER; *Indian Army List: 1760–1834*, WHEELER.
29 P/Corr., VIII, 483.
30 Copy of Lady Anne Barnard's will, dated 17 May 1823, and subsequent codicils, 22 December 1824, 23 April 1825, WHEELER.
31 Charles Hervey to Albert Hervey, undated, ibid.; Gerald Hervey to Albert Hervey, 24 June 1845, ibid.
32 GIV/P, 256; Levy, *The Mistresses of King George IV*, 102.
33 Cobbett, XXVI, 1009–56
34 GIV/P, 66–7.
35 Cobbett, XXVI, 1064–74.
36 Leslie, *Mrs Fitzherbert*, 72.
37 *Croker Papers*, I, 214; GIV/P, 68.
38 *Fox Correspondence*, 288–9.
39 Ibid., 288.

40 Wraxall, IV, 463.
41 Cobbett, XXVI, 1075
42 Ibid., 1074–80.
43 Leslie, *Mrs Fitzherbert*, 74.
44 P/Corr., I, 287, 289.
45 Cobbett, XXVI, 207–10.
46 P/Corr., I, 313.
47 Macalpine, 231.
48 Wraxall, V, 362.
49 *D'Arblay Diary*, III, 417.
50 *Cornwallis Correspondence*, I, 360.
51 Tomalin, *Mrs Jordan's Profession*, 104.
52 *Cornwallis Correspondence*, I, 374–5.
53 P/Corr., I, 321.

4 – *The Mad King*

 1 Leslie, *Mrs Fitzherbert*, 80.
 2 Macalpine, 3–4.
 3 Wraxall, III, 133.
 4 Macalpine, 4–5, 11.
 5 GIII/Corr., I, 384.
 6 Macalpine, 16.
 7 P/Corr., I, 358.
 8 *D'Arblay Diary*, IV, 273–4; Macalpine, 19.
 9 P/Corr., I, 360.
10 Macalpine, 20.
11 *D'Arblay Diary*, IV, 278.
12 Macalpine, 23.
13 *D'Arblay Diary*, IV, 284.
14 Macalpine, 25.
15 *D'Arblay Diary*, IV, 299–300.
16 Macalpine, 34–5; *Papendiek Journals*, II, 12.
17 *Harcourt Papers,* IV, 25–8.
18 Ibid., 28.
19 Buckingham, *Memoirs,* I, 436.
20 P/Corr. I, 366–7.
21 Macalpine, 172–5, 180–81, 229.
22 *D'Arblay Diary*, IV, 304.

23 Macalpine, 31.
24 Buckingham, *Memoirs*, I, 445.
25 *D'Arblay Diary*, IV, 316; Buckingham, *Memoirs*, II, 21.
26 Macalpine, 44.
27 Ibid., 47–8.
28 *D'Arblay Diary*, IV, 346; Macalpine, 50–51.
29 Macalpine, 51–2.
30 *Fulke Greville Diaries*, 119–23.
31 Macalpine, 54, 79.
32 Wraxall, V, 203.
33 P/Corr., I, 383–4.
34 GIV/P, 93–4
35 Macalpine, 54–5.
36 Cobbett, XXVII, 692–704; Macalpine, 55–7.
37 Cobbett, XXVII, 705–16.
38 *Fox Correspondence*, II, 263.
39 Ayling, *Fox*, 163; Cobbett, XXVII, 717–28.
40 Ayling, *Fox*, 163–4.
41 P/Corr., I, 421, 423.
42 *Devonshire Correspondence*, 140.
43 Aspinall, *Politics and the Press*, 6–7, 66–75, 274–5.
44 Macalpine, 60, 78–81.
45 *Minto Letters*, I, 271.
46 Buckingham, *Memoirs*, 106–7.
47 Ayling, *Fox*, 164; P/Corr., I, 490.
48 Macalpine, 82.
49 Cobbett, XXVII, 1294.
50 P/Corr., I, 491–2; *The Times*, 21 February 1789.
51 *Minto Letters*, I, 274–5.
52 Macalpine, 85–6.

5 – Rakes and Revolutionaries

1 Macalpine, 90–91; Wraxall, III, 369–70.
2 *Minto Letters*, I, 325.
3 Macalpine, 92.
4 P/Corr., II, 6–10.
5 *Fox Correspondence*, 307, GIV/P, 99.
6 Somerset, *William IV*, 53.

7   Macalpine, 96.

8   P/Corr., II, 15n; GIV/P, 100n.

9   P/Corr., II, 14n.

10   Ibid., 15.

11   *The History of the Times*, I, 54–60; Aspinall, *Politics and the Press*, 74–5.

12   *The Times*, 26 July 1790.

13   P/Corr., II, 68.

14   Ayling, *Fox*, 167.

15   *Devonshire Correspondence*, 163.

16   P/Corr., II, 3–4.

17   Leslie, *Mrs Fitzherbert*, 127–8; P/Corr., I, 357.

18   P/Corr., I, 146; Wraxall, V, 311; *Raikes Journal*, III, 200.

19   Pasquin, *Earl Barrymore*, 7–10, 23, 27, 40–41, 89–90, 105, 112–14; Leslie, *Mrs Fitzherbert*, 84.

20   P/Corr., II, 285–7.

21   Ibid., 59, 95–7.

22   Ibid., 128.

23   *The Times*, 13 August 1791.

24   P/Corr., II, 215n; GIV/P, 110.

25   Ayling, *Fox*, 170–75.

26   Cobbett, XXIX, 1516–17.

27   P/Corr., II, 285.

28   Ibid., 334–6.

29   Cole, *Beau Brummell*, 38.

30   Ehrman, *The Younger Pitt*, II, 254.

31   P/Corr., II, 339; GIV/P, 120.

32   P/Corr., II, 348.

33   Ibid., 327, 363–4.

34   *The Times*, 5 August 1793.

35   P/Corr., II, 394.

6 – Caroline of Brunswick

1   Wilkins, *Mrs Fitzherbert*, I, 274.

2   Wraxall, V, 357–8.

3   GIV/P, 130–31.

4   Wraxall, V, 36; Huish, *Memoirs of George IV*, I, 263.

5   P/Corr., II, 443n.

6   Ibid.

7   DENBIGH, CR 2017/C244, 448, WRO.
8   *Gower Correspondence*, I, 93.
9   *Fitzherbert Letters*, 120; Leslie, *Mrs Fitzherbert*, 95.
10 *The Times*, 7 August 1794; P/Corr., III, 139.
11 Oman, *Gascoyne Heiress*, 207.
12 P/Corr., II, 407.
13 Leslie, *Mrs Fitzherbert*, 95.
14 P/Corr., II, 453.
15 P/Corr., III, 9.
16 P/Corr., II, 454, 492.
17 *Malmesbury Diaries*, III, 153.
18 *Bury Diary*, I, 4.
19 MALMES, *Extracts from Diary*, 22 November 1794, 9M73/252, HRO.
20 P/Corr., II, 511.
21 Ibid., 508n, 511.
22 MALMES, Malmesbury Diary, 5, 9, 16 and 20 December 1794, 9M73/G2008, HRO.
23 MALMES, *Extracts from Diary*, 9M73/252, HRO.
24 MALMES, Letter from anonymous 'Englishman' to Duchess of Brunswick, 12 December 1794, 9M73/G1800/18, HRO.
25 MALMES, Malmesbury Diary, 28 December 1794, 9M73/G2008, HRO.
26 *Malmesbury Diaries*, III, 195–7.
27 Ibid., 203.
28 MALMES, Malmesbury Diary, 18 February and 6 March 1795, 9M73/G2008, HRO.
29 MALMES, *Extracts from Diary*, 28, 29 March and 2 April 1795, 9M73/252, HRO.
30 MALMES, Malmesbury Diary, 5 April 1795, 9M73/G2008, HRO.
31 MALMES, *Extracts from Diary*, 5 April 1795, 9M73/252, HRO.
32 *Bury Diary*, I, 13–14.
33 P/Corr., III, 38–9, 45.
34 GIII/Corr., II, 328.
35 *Devonshire Correspondence*, 209; GIV/P, 146.
36 Ibid., 147.
37 P/Corr., III, 3.
38 Ibid.
39 *Bury Diary*, I, 21.
40 P/Corr., III, 122–3.

41 Cole, *Brummell*, 40.
42 MALMES, *Detailed Account,* op. cit., 9M73/G2031, HRO.
43 MALMES, *Extracts from Diary*, 9M73/252, HRO.
44 MALMES, *Detailed Account,* op. cit., 9M73/G2031, HRO.
45 Cobbett, XXXI, 1464.
46 P/Corr., III, 4–5.
47 Ibid., 5, 71.
48 Ibid., 69.
49 Fraser, 70.
50 *Colchester Diary*, I, 2–3.

7 – *A Royal Separation*

1 P/Corr., III, 126–7.
2 Ibid., 132–8.
3 *Colchester Diary*, I, 37.
4 MALMES, *Detailed Account*, op. cit., 9M73/G2031, HRO.
5 P/Corr., III, 159.
6 *Colchester Diary*, I, 52.
7 P/Corr., III, 168.
8 Ibid., 168–71.
9 Ibid., 179.
10 Ibid., 181–3.
11 Fraser, 84–5.
12 P/Corr., III, 185–6
13 *The Times*, 24 May and 1 June; *Leeds Memoranda*, 221.
14 *Colchester Diary, I,* 59.
15 P/Corr., III, 190–93.
16 Ibid., 195–8.
17 Ibid., 194, 202–3.
18 *True Briton*, 2 June 1796.
19 Fraser, 90.
20 *Gower Correspondence*, I, 122–3.
21 P/Corr., III, 246, *The Times*, 25 July 1796.
22 P/Corr., III, 276.
23 *Glenbervie Diaries*, I, 71
24 P/Corr., III, 313–16.
25 Watson, *The Reign of George III*, 397.
26 Ayling, *Fox*, 197–8.

27   *Glenbervie Diaries*, I, 134.
28   Ehrman, *The Younger Pitt*, III, 44.
29   Ibid., 43–5.
30   P/Corr., III, 345.
31   Ibid., 379.
32   Fraser, 112–13; GIII/Corr., III, 6.
33   Wraxall, V, 353–61; *Farington Diary*, IV, 98.
34   Cole, *Beau Brummell*, 35.
35   Ibid., 47.
36   Ibid., 40, 42, 44.
37   *Farington Diary*, I, 156.
38   Cole, *Beau Brummell*, 44–5.
39   *Raikes Journal*, III, 55.
40   P/Corr., III, 451–3.
41   Ibid., 501.
42   *Greville Memoirs*, I, 270–71.
43   *Glenbervie Diaries*, II, 98.
44   *Minto Letters*, III, 36.
45   P/Corr., IV, 91.
46   Ibid., IV, 13, 16.
47   Ibid., 48; *Glenbervie Diaries*, II, 13–14.
48   P/Corr., IV, 57; GIV/P, 172–3.
49   *Leslie, Mrs Fitzherbert*, 115.
50   P/Corr., IV, 3; *Glenbervie Diaries*, II, 121.
51   Leslie, *Mrs Fitzherbert*, 116.
52   *Holland Journal*, II, 83.
53   Leslie, *Mrs Fitzherbert*, 117.

8 – The Reversionary Interest

1   Ehrman, *The Younger Pitt*, III, 496–509.
2   GIV/P, 185.
3   O'Toole, *A Traitor's Kiss*, 359.
4   GIII/Corr., III, 525.
5   Macalpine, 111–12, GIII/Corr., III, 496.
6   *Rose Diaries*, I, 315–17.
7   P/Corr., IV, 183–5.
8   Ibid., 184.
9   Ibid., 183; Macalpine, 117–19.

10 GIV/P, 187–8; *Colchester Diary*, I, 256; P/Corr., IV, 185.
11 *Glenbervie Diaries*, I, 170–71.
12 Watson, *The Reign of George III*, 411.
13 P/Corr., IV, 248.
14 Ibid., 249.
15 Ibid., 346; Cobbett, XXXVI, 1197–1209.
16 Ibid., 36, 1209–1229; P/Corr., IV, 134.
17 *Rose Diaries*, II, 14–15.
18 Cobbett, XXXVI, 1230.
19 HASTINGS, Add. MS 29179.f.146, BL.
20 P/Corr., IV, 396.
21 Ibid., 425.
22 Ibid., 427.
23 Ibid., 428–34.
24 *Rose Diaries,* II, 58–9.
25 P/Corr., IV, 351.
26 Ibid.
27 Ibid., 481–2.
28 *Glenbervie Diaries*, I, 369; Hylton, *The Paget Brothers*, 17.
29 *Colchester Diary*, I, 479–80; Macalpine, 131–2.
30 *Colchester Diary*, I, 481–2, 494.
31 *Malmesbury Diaries*, IV, 494.
32 *Colchester Diary*, I, 502–3.
33 Ibid., 506–7.
34 *Rose Diaries,* II, 124.
35 Ehrman, *The Younger Pitt,* III, 654.
36 Twiss, *Eldon*, I, 449.
37 *Rose Diaries,* II, 128.
38 Aspinall, *English Historical Documents*, 190.
39 Ehrman, *The Younger Pitt*, III, 656.
40 MISC, Add. MSS. 40102.ff.135–7, BL.
41 P/Corr., V, 10.
42 Ibid.
43 Ibid., 11.
44 Ibid., 167; *Colchester Diary*, I, 558.
45 Ibid., 557–8.
46 P/Corr., V, 165.
47 Watson, *The Reign of George III*, 428–30.
48 *Colchester Diary*, II, 226.

49 Hibbert, *Nelson*, 375–7.
50 P/Corr., V, 272.
51 *Creevey Papers*, I, 173; Hibbert, *Nelson*, 228.
52 P/Corr., V, 283.
53 Ibid., 281–2.
54 Hibbert, *Nelson*, 391.
55 P/Corr., V, 276.
56 *Colchester Diary*, II, 28.
57 Ibid., 32.
58 P/Corr., V, 299.

9 – *The Delicate Investigation*

1 Hinde, *Canning*, 117.
2 *Gower Correspondence*, I, 251, 255, *Lieven Letters*, 98.
3 Hinde, *Canning*, 88; Fraser, 124.
4 Fraser, 136.
5 *Delicate Investigation*, 213, 220–21.
6 GIV/P, I, 211.
7 *Glenbervie Diaries*, II, 107.
8 *Stanhope Memoirs*, I, 308.
9 *Dillon Memoirs*, II, 18–20.
10 *Glenbervie Diaries*, II, 133–4.
11 K/Corr., I, 523.
12 *Colchester Diary*, I, 529; Cockayne, *The Complete Peerage*, I, 460.
13 *Delicate Investigation*, 282–3.
14 Ibid., 284.
15 Fraser, 150.
16 P/Corr., V, 169, 202.
17 Ibid., 182; C/Corr., IX.
18 Ibid., IX–X.
19 Twiss, *Eldon*, I, 481.
20 *Minto Letters*, III, 371.
21 *Gower Correspondence*, II, 203.
22 Ibid., 203–4; New, *Brougham*, 81.
23 *Gower Correspondence*, II, 204.
24 Ibid., 187.
25 Ibid., 204; *Delicate Investigation*, 144, 150.
26 *Gower Correspondence*, II, 204.

27 *Delicate Investigation*, 2.
28 Ibid., 199, 203, 253–5, 265, 268–9.
29 Ibid., 205–6.
30 Ibid., 208.
31 Ibid., 209–10.
32 Ibid., 220–21.
33 Ibid., 204, 223.
34 Ibid., 211, 224–9, 240.
35 P/Corr., V, 396.
36 *Delicate Investigation,* 4–5.
37 K/Corr., II, 282, 359.
38 GIV/P, 217; Fraser, 169.
39 *Delicate Investigation,* 295; RA Geo. IV, Box 8 (Cole's evidence about Roberts); GIV/P, 219.
40 *Croker Papers,* II, 89; P/Corr, V, 407.
41 Ibid., 408.
42 *Delicate Investigation,* 6–7.
43 P/Corr., V. 425.
44 *Holland Journal,* II, 174, 179.
45 P/Corr., V, 427–8; *Holland Journal,* II, 180–81.
46 P/Corr., V, 428.
47 Ibid., 459.
48 *Holland Journal,* II, 186–7.
49 P/Corr., V, 459n.
50 *Delicate Investigation,* 16–141.
51 P/Corr., VI, 39.
52 Ibid., 41–2.
53 Ibid., 104–5, 110.
54 Ibid., 125–7.
55 Fraser, 187; *Glenbervie Diaries,* II, 83.
56 Fraser, 187; P/Corr., VI, 137n.
57 Ibid.
58 *Delicate Investigation,* 162–78.
59 RA Geo. IV, Box 8/20, 7 March 1807; Ibid., Box 12/39. Evidence in support of the charge of recrimination [1820]; Fraser, 189.
60 P/Corr., VI, 156–7.
61 Ibid., 162–3; RA Geo. IV, Box 8/3, 21 April 1807; Fraser, 190.
62 P/Corr., VI, 181.
63 RA Geo. IV, Box 8/3, 18 May 1807; Fraser, 192.

10 – Minney and Prinny

1 SEYMOUR, Lord Hugh to Lady Horatia Seymour, 23 July 1801, CR 114A/366, WRO.
2 Ibid., 15 August 1801.
3 Ibid., CR 114A/536/1.
4 Ibid., CR 114A/536/2.
5 Ibid., CR 114A/281A, CR 713/7, CR 114A/284.
6 Ibid., CR 114A/536/2.
7 Rutherford, *The Royal Pavilion*, 2.
8 *Glenbervie Diaries*, I, 250, 330–31.
9 Calvert, *An Irish Beauty of the Regency*, 162.
10 *Gower Correspondence*, II, 120.
11 Wilkins, *Mrs Fitzherbert and George IV*, II, 74, 69–70.
12 Albemarle, *Fifty Years*, I, 239–40.
13 Romilly, *Memoirs*, II, 146.
14 Swynnerton Papers, quoted in Leslie, *Mrs Fitzherbert*, 165.
15 *Fitzherbert Papers*, 178, 207.
16 Wraxall, IV, 137–8.
17 *Holland Memoirs*, II, 72.
18 Levy, *The Mistresses of King George IV*, 130.
19 K/Corr., VI, 95.
20 *Gower Correspondence*, II, 232.
21 Ibid, 297–8.
22 *Glenbervie Diaries*, II, 5.
23 *Gower Correspondence*, II, 349–50.
24 *Fitzherbert Letters*, 129–31.
25 Ibid., 133–4.
26 Ibid., 135.
27 Cole, *Brummell*, 80.
28 Ibid.; Sales, *Jane Austen*, 77.
29 Ibid., 74.
30 Raikes, *Journal*, II, 206.
31 *Wilson Memoirs*, 32, 64–5.
32 K/Corr., III, 368.
33 Fraser, *Black Ajax*, 178.
34 Ford, *Prizefighting*, 72.
35 Low, *Thieves' Kitchen*, 137.
36 Cole, *Brummell*, 56–7.

37   Southey, *Letters from England*, I, 122.
38   Low, *Thieves' Kitchen*, 25–6.
39   Ibid., 53.
40   Southey, *Letters from England*, I, 66–7, 74–5, 77.
41   *Greville Memoirs*, I, 60.
42   Low, *Thieves' Kitchen*, 163; Hansard, 1st series, XII, 583.
43   Low, *Thieves' Kitchen*, 166; Hansard, 1st series, XII, 179–87.
44   P/Corr., IV, 348.
45   Low, *Thieves' Kitchen*, 166–8; Hansard, 1st series, XII, 477, 583.
46   P/Corr., VI, 349.
47   Ibid.
48   Hansard, 1st series, XII, 663–708.

11 – *The Restricted Regency*

1   *Croker Papers,* I, 20.
2   Khan, *A Persian at the Court of King George,* 112–13, 131, 103, 137–8, 151, 154–5, 245, 289, 249.
3   P/Corr., VII, 378–405.
4   Ibid., 373–7.
5   Austen, *Mansfield Park* (1814), 91.
6   *Farington Diaries*, VI, 70.
7   Knight, *Autobiography*, I, 174–5.
8   *Glenbervie Diaries*, II, 94.
9   Macalpine, 144–6.
10   *Holland Journal*, II, 266; P/Corr., VII, 61.
11   *Rose Diaries*, II, 458–9.
12   *Glenbervie Diaries*, II, 106.
13   P/Corr., VII, 110–11.
14   Ibid., 62, 114.
15   Ibid., 124–5.
16   Ibid., 158–9.
17   Ibid., 128.
18   Ibid., 135–6, 190–91.
19   *Holland Journal*, II, 289–90.
20   P/Corr., VII, 137, 191, 200–201.
21   *Farington Diary*, VII, 19.
22   *Colchester Diary*, II, 336–7.
23   *Moore Letters*, I, 152–3.

24 *Gentleman's Magazine*, LXXXI, 587.

25 *Shelley Letters*, 99–100, Romilly, *Memoirs*, II, 409.

26 *Farington Diary*, VII, 22.

27 Buckingham, *Memoirs*, I, 145–61, 178–9.

28 Ibid., IV, 458.

29 P/Corr, VIII, 11–12.

30 Ibid., 370–71.

31 Buckingham, *Memoirs*, I, 224–5, 228, 231–4.

32 P/Corr., VIII, 307.

33 GIV/K, 18.

34 Buckingham, *Memoirs*, I, 239, 250–51.

35 Albemarle, *Fifty Years*, I, 329.

36 'Lines to a Lady Weeping', March 1812, *Byron Works*, 65.

37 Hansard, 1st Series, XXII, 85.

38 Byron to Walter Scott, 6 July 1812, *Byron Letters*, 123–4.

39 Raphael, *Byron*, 63.

40 *Byron Letters*, 177, 179.

12 – The Two Princesses

1 K/Corr., I, 74.

2 Watson, *George III*, 499.

3 *Moore Letters*, 196, 217.

4 K/Corr., I, 202, 203.

5 Ibid., 517.

6 C/Corr., XIII.

7 K/Corr., I, 518.

8 *Berry Correspondence*, II, 499.

9 *Bury Diary*, I, 36.

10 Ibid., 101.

11 Knight, *Autobiography*, I, 184.

12 Ibid., 200, 202, 219.

13 *Austen Letters*, 504.

14 *Colchester Diary*, II, 421.

15 *Annual Register*, 1813, 344–7.

16 Aspinall, *Politics and the Press*, 90–91.

17 *Berry Correspondence*, II, 532–4; *Colchester Diary*, II, 435.

18 Longford, *Wellington*, I, 323–4.

19 Gronow, I, 41–2.

20 *Greville Memoirs*, II, 341, 378.

21 C/Corr., 55, 711 89, 94.

22 *Farington Diary*, VII, 244; Fraser, 238–9.

23 Nicolson, *The Congress of Vienna*, 110–11.

24 *Berry Correspondence*, III, 26–7; *Moore Letters*, 319–20.

25 *Bury Diary*, I, 180–81.

26 Ibid., 173–4.

27 *Creevey Papers*, I, 198.

28 *Brougham Memoirs*, II, 208–9.

29 C/Corr., 117–19.

30 Fraser, 250.

31 C/Corr., 137–8.

32 *Bury Diary*, II, 158.

33 Gronow, I, 31–2.

34 Fraser, *Black Ajax*, 61.

35 Gronow, I, 32.

36 Ibid, 267–8.

37 K/Corr., I, 516–20.

38 *Greville Memoirs*, I, 29, 30–34.

39 *Croker Papers*, I, 59–60.

40 GIV/K, 80.

41 Anglesey, *One–Leg*, 149, 151–2.

42 K/Corr., II, 141.

43 C/Corr., 225.

44 *Bury Diary*, II, 104.

45 *The Prince and his Pleasures*, 79.

13 – The Milan Commission

1 *Edgeworth Letters*, I, 287.

2 *Lieven Letters*, 277.

3 *Croker Papers*, I, 125.

4 GIV/K, 84.

5 *Wheatley, London Past and Present*, III, 177; *Farington Diary*, VI, 264.

6 Sales, *Jane Austen*, 70–72

7 *Papendiek Journals*, II, 134–5, 139.

8 Fryer, *Staying Power*, 428–30.

9 Gronow, II, 126.

10 K/Corr., II, 43–4.

11 *Colchester Diary*, II, 600.

12 Gronow, I, 308–9.

13 K/Corr., II, 185.

14 *Harcourt Papers*, X, 82.

15 K/Corr., II, 203–5.

16 Macalpine, 241.

17 K/Corr., II, 210.

18 Ibid., 211.

19 *Farington Diary*, VIII, 152.

20 *The Times*, 20 November 1817.

21 *Croker Papers*, I, 105.

22 Ibid., 104; *Fraser*, 298.

23 *Croker Papers*, I, 105–6.

24 K/Corr., II, 212–13.

25 Macalpine, 242–3, *Farington Diary*, VIII, 152.

26 Macalpine, 243.

27 K/Corr., I, 497; C/Corr., 160.

28 Macalpine, 244.

29 *Croker Papers*, I, 108.

30 Ibid., 110.

31 *Creevey Papers*, 277.

32 Woodham-Smith, *Queen Victoria,* 51; Stockmar, *Memoirs*, I, 78.

33 Cleric, *A Queen of Indiscretions*, 41.

34 RA Geo. Box 8/6, 25 October 1814.

35 Ibid., 2 March 1815.

36 New, *Brougham*, 117.

37 RA Add. 21/102/10, 28 November 1815.

38 *Brougham Memoirs*, II, 298.

39 K/Corr., II, 252

40 Ibid.

41 Ibid., 280–81.

42 LIVERPL, Add. MSS. 38565, ff. 20–21, BL.

43 Add. MSS. 38190, f.31, 16 June 1819; RA Geo. Box 8/8, 17 and 22 June 1819.

44 New, *Brougham*, 230.

45 RA Geo., Box 9/1, 13 July 1819.

46 *Queen's Trial*, I, 25–96, 305–421, 450–59.

47 *Croker Papers*, I, 120, 123, 127.

48 Gronow, II, 256.

49 *Bury Diary*, II, 197–8; Levy, *The Mistresses of King George IV,* 153.

50 New, *Brougham*, 193.
51 *Brougham Memoirs*, II, 342–3.

14 – The Queen's Trial

1   *Croker Papers*, I, 155; *Lieven Letters*, 8.
2   *Croker Papers*, I, 156–7; *Lieven Letters*, 11.
3   *Greville Memoirs*, I, 87; *Lieven Letters*, 11; *Croker Papers*, I, 158–60.
4   Ibid., 160; RA Geo. IV, Box 8/10, 10 February 1820.
5   *Croker Papers*, I, 160.
6   *Greville Memoirs*, I, 88; RA Geo. IV, Box 8/10, 14 February 1820.
7   New, *Brougham*, 232.
8   Add. MSS. 38565, ff.93–4.
9   *Greville Memoirs*, I, 94.
10 Ibid., 95; Hansard, 2nd Series, I, 87.
11 *Lieven Letters*, 38; *Greville Memoirs*, I, 95.
12 *Hobhouse Diary*, 26; *Greville Memoirs*, I, 100.
13 Arnould, *Denman*, I, 154.
14 Hansard, 2nd Series, II, 167–8
15 Ibid., 212–13.
16 *Greville Memoirs*, I, 100; *Berry Correspondence*, III, 245.
17 Albemarle, *Fifty Years*, II, 117.
18 Fraser, 418; *Creevey Papers*, I, 307–8; Albemarle, *Fifty Years*, II, 121–2.
19 Hansard, 2nd Series, II, 644–5.
20 New, *Brougham*, 248.
21 Hansard, 2nd Series, II, 742–83.
22 *Lieven Letters*, 65.
23 Albemarle, *Fifty Years*, II, 122–3.
24 *Granville Letters*, 138.
25 *Berry Correspondence*, III, 253–4.
26 Hansard, 2nd Series, II, 801–25.
27 *Greville Memoirs*, I, 105.
28 *Granville Letters*, 138, Arnould, *Denman*, I, 165.
29 Hansard, 2nd Series, II, 841–73.
30 *Lieven Letters*, 66.
31 Hansard, 2nd Series, II, 895–1213, 1274–5.
32 *Arbuthnot Journal*, 36; *Lieven Letters*, 71–2; *Granville Letters*, 142–3.
33 K/Corr., II, 361–3, 366.

34   GIV/K, 172–3.
35   Hansard, 2nd Series, II, 112–210.
36   Arnould, *Denman*, I, 169; *Berry Correspondence*, III, 255; *Greville Memoirs*, I, 105; GIV/K, 173.
37   Hansard, 2nd Series, III, 303–26.
38   K/Corr., II, 371.
39   Hansard, 2nd Series, III, 436–523.
40   K/Corr., II, 371; *Greville Memoirs*, I, 106–7.
41   Hansard, 2nd Series, III, 641–2; New, *Brougham*, 258.
42   Hansard, 2nd Series, III, 1184.
43   *Arbuthnot Correspondence*, 20.
44   *Lieven Letters*, 91.
45   New, *Brougham*, 259; GIV/K, 184–5.
46   *Bury Diary*, II, 234–5.
47   *Lieven Letters*, 94.
48   *Colchester Diary*, III, 164.
49   *Hobhouse Diary*, 40; *Arbuthnot Correspondence*, 21.
50   RA Geo. IV Box 8/16, Denham Report, 16 November 1820; Fraser, 446.

15 – *Blackguard or Gentleman?*

1   *Bury Diary*, II, 265.
2   K/Corr., II, 406.
3   *Lyttelton Correspondence*, 235; Buckingham, *Memoirs*, II, 183.
4   *Colchester Diary*, III, 233.
5   *Arbuthnot Journal*, 108–9.
6   Albemarle, *Fifty Years*, I, 327; *Lyttelton Correspondence*, 237–8.
7   GIV/K, 204; *Arbuthnot Correspondence*, 25; *Croker Papers*, I, 200–201.
8   *Raikes Journal*, III, 57.
9   Gronow, II, 311–12.
10   *Raikes Journal*, III, 58.
11   GIV/K, 335.
12   *The Times*, 30 June 1830.
13   Ibid., 16 July 1830.
14   Albemarle, *Fifty Years*, II, 304–5.
15   *The Times*, 16 July 1830.
16   Ibid., 28 June 1830.

17   Ibid.
18   Byron to Walter Scott, 6 July 1812, *Byron Letters*, 123–4.
19   Leslie, *George the Fourth*, 19; *Raikes Journal*, I, 92.
20   *D'Arblay Diary*, VI, 333–4.

Bibliography

Airlie, Mabell, Countess of, *In Whig Society* (1921).

Albermarle, George Keppel, Earl of, *Fifty Years of My Life* (2 vols, 1876).

Anglesey, 7th Marquess of, *One-Leg: The Life and Letters of Henry William Paget, First Marquess of Anglesey 1768–1854* (Jonathan Cape, 1961).

Arbuthnot Correspondence: Aspinall, A. (ed.), *The Correspondence of Charles Arbuthnot* (Royal Historical Society, 1941).

Arbuthnot Journal: Bamford, Francis, and Wellington, Duke of, (eds), *The Journal of Mrs Arbuthnot, 1820–1832* (2 vols, 1950).

Arnould, Sir Joseph, *Memoir of Thomas First Lord Denman* (2 vols, 1873).

Aspinall, A., *The Correspondence of George, Prince of Wales 1770–1812* (8 vols, Cassell, 1963–71).

———, *The Later Correspondence of George III* (5 vols, C.U.P., 1962–70).

———, *Letters of the Princess Charlotte 1811–1817* (Home & Van Thal, 1949).

———, *The Letters of King George IV, 1812–1830* (3 vols, C.U.P., 1938).

———, *Politics and the Press: 1780–1850* (Home & Van Thal, 1949).

Aspinall, A., and Smith, E. (eds.), *English Historical Documents, 1783–1832* (Eyre & Spottiswoode, 1959).

Austen, Jane, *Mansfield Park* (Penguin, 1994).

———, *Emma* (Penguin, 1995).

Austen Letters: Chapman, R.W. (ed.), *Jane Austen's Letters to her Sister Cassandra and others* (1952).

Austen-Leigh, J.E., *A Memoir of Jane Austen* (1970).

Ayling, Stanley, *Fox: The life of Charles James Fox* (John Murray, 1991).

Barnard Letters: Powell, Anthony (ed.), *Barnard Letters 1778–1824* (Duckworth, 1928).

Berry Correspondence: Lewis, Lady Theresa (ed.), *Extracts of the Journals and Correspondence of Miss Berry from the year 1783 to 1852* (3 vols, Longman, 1865).

Brady, Frank, *James Boswell: The Later Years 1769–1795* (Heinemann, 1984).

Brougham Memoirs: Brougham, Henry, *The Life and Times of Henry Lord Brougham written by himself,* (3 vols, 1871).

Bruce, John, *The History of Brighton* (1831).

Bryant, Arthur, *The Age of Elegance* (1950).

Buckingham and Chandos, Duke of, *Memoirs of the Courts and Cabinets of George III* (4 vols, 1853–5).

Bury Diary: Bury, Lady Charlotte, *The Court of England under George IV – Founded on a Diary* (2 vols, John Macqueen, 1896).

Byron Letters: Moore, Thomas (ed.), *Letters and Journals of Lord Byron* (Galignani, 1831).

Byron Works: Byron, Lord, *The Works of Lord Byron* (Wordsworth, 1994).

Calvert, Hon. Frances, *An Irish Beauty of the Regency* (1911).

Campbell, Cynthia, *The Most Polished Gentleman: George IV and the Women in his Life* (Kudos, 1995).

Campbell, Lord, *Lives of the Lord Chancellors* (10 vols, John Murray, 1857).

Cannon, Richard, *The Historical Records of the 10th (Prince of Wales's Own) Royal Hussars* (1837).

Clarke, John, *The Life and Times of George III* (Weidenfeld & Nicolson, 1972).

Clarke, Mary Anne, *The Rival Princes* (2 vols, 1810).

Cleric, Graziani, *A Queen of Indiscretions: The Tragedy of Caroline of Brunswick,* trans. by Frederic Chapman (John Lane, 1907).

Cobbett's Parliamentary History (36 vols, 1066–1803).

Cockayne, G.E., *The Complete Peerage* (6 vols, 1987).

Colchester Diary: Colchester, Lord, *The Diary and Correspondence of Charles Abbot, Lord Colchester* (3 vols, 1861).

Cole, Hubert, *Beau Brummell* (Granada, 1977).

Cook, Chris, and Stevenson, John, *British Historical Facts 1760–1830* (Macmillan, 1980).

Cornwallis Correspondence: Ross, Charles (ed.), *Correspondence of Charles, First Marquess Cornwallis* (3 vols, 1859).

Craven, Lady, *The Beautiful Lady Craven,* Broadley, A.M., and Melville, Lewis (eds.), (1913).

Croker Papers: Jennings, Louis J. (ed.), *The Correspondence and Diaries of the Late Right Honourable John Wilson Croker* (3 vols, 1884).

Dale, Antony, *Fashionable Brighton 1820–1860* (Country Life, 1947).

D'Arblay Diary: ed. by her Niece, *Diary and Letters of Madame D'Arblay (Fanny Burney)* (7 vols, 1842).

de Bellaigue, Sir Geoffrey, *Carlton House: The Past Glories of George IV's Palace* (1991).

Delicate Investigation: Perceval, Hon. Spencer, *The Genuine Book – An Inquiry, or Delicate Investigation into the Conduct of Her Royal Highness the Princess of Wales* (1813).

Devonshire Correspondence: Bessborough, Earl of (ed.), *Georgiana: Extracts from the Correspondence of Georgiana, Duchess of Devonshire* (1955).

Dillon Memoirs: Lewis, Michael (ed.), *Memoirs of William Henry Dillon, 1780–1839* (1953).

Edgeworth Letters: Hare, Augustus (ed.), *The Life and Letters of Maria Edgeworth* (1894).

Ehrman, John, *The Younger Pitt* (3 vols, Constable, 1969, 1983 and 1996).

Farington Diary: Greig, James (ed.), *The Farington Diary* (8 vols, Hutchinson, 1922–8).

Fitzherbert Letters: Leslie, Shane (ed.), *The Letters of Mrs Fitzherbert and Connected Papers* (1940).

Foord-Kelcey, Jim and Philippa, *Mrs Fitzherbert and Sons* (Book Guild, 1991).

Ford, John, *Prizefighting: The Age of Regency Boximania* (David & Charles, 1971).

Fox Correspondence: Russell, Lord John (ed.), *Memorials and Correspondence of Charles James Fox* (2 vols, 1853).

Fraser, Flora, *The Unruly Queen: The Life of Queen Caroline* (Macmillan, 1996).

Fraser, George MacDonald, *Black Ajax* (HarperCollins, 1997).

Fryer, Peter, *Staying Power: The History of the Black People in Britain* (Pluto, 1984).

Fulke Greville Diaries: Bladon, F. McKno (ed.), *The Diaries of Colonel the Hon. Robert Fulke Greville* (Bodley Head, 1930).

George, M. Dorothy, *English Political Caricature to 1792* (Clarendon Press, 1959).

———, *English Political Caricature 1793–1832* (Clarendon Press, 1959).

Glenbervie Diaries: Bickley, Francis (ed.), *The Diaries of Sylvester Douglas, Lord Glenbervie* (2 vols, Constable, 1928).

Gower Correspondence: Granville, Castalia, Countess (ed.), *Lord Granville Leveson-Gower (First Earl Granville): Private Correspondence, 1781–1821* (2 vols, John Murray, 1916).

Granville Letters: Surtees, Virginia (ed.), *A Second Self: The Letters of Harriet Granville 1810–1845* (Michael Russell, 1990).

Gray, Robert, *The King's Wife: Five Queen Consorts* (Secker & Warburg, 1990).

Greville Memoirs: Strachey, Lytton and Fulford, Roger (eds.), *The Greville Memoirs 1814–1860* (3 vols, Macmillan, 1938).

Gronow, Rees Howell, *The Reminiscences and Recollections of Captain Gronow 1810–60* (2 vols, 1892).

Hamilton, Lady Anne, *Secret History of the Court of England, from the accession of George III to the death of George IV* (2 vols, 1832).

Hamilton Letters: Anson, Elizabeth and Florence (eds.), *Mary Hamilton: At Court and at Home from Letters and Diaries 1756 to 1816* (1925).

Hansard's Parliamentary Debates, 1st Series (41 vols, 1803–20), 2nd Series (1820–30).

Harcourt Papers: Harcourt, Edward William (ed.), *The Harcourt Papers* (14 vols, 1880–1905).

Hibbert, Christopher, *George IV: Prince of Wales 1762–1811* (Longmans, 1972).

———, *George IV: Regent and King 1811–1830* (Allen Lane, 1973).

———, *Nelson: A Personal History* (Penguin, 1995).

———, *Wellington: A Personal History* (HarperCollins, 1997).

Hinde, Wendy, *George Canning* (Blackwell, 1973).

History of the Times, The: Vol. 1 'The Thunderer in the Making' 1785–1841 (London, 1935).

Hobhouse Diary: Aspinall, A. (ed.), *The Diary of Henry Hobhouse: 1820–1827* (1947).

Holland, Sir Henry, *Recollections of Past Life* (1872).

Holland Memoirs: Holland, Henry Edward, Lord (ed.), *Henry Richard, Lord Holland: Memoirs of the Whig Party during my time (2* vols, 1852–4).

Holland Journal: Ilchester, Earl of (ed.), *The Journal of Elizabeth Lady Holland (1791-1811)* (2 vols, 1908).

Holmes, Geoffrey, and Szechi, Daniel, *The Age of Oligarchy: Pre-industrial Britain 1722–1783* (Longman, 1993).

Hone, J. Ann, *For the Cause of Truth: Radicalism in London, 1796–1821* (Oxford, 1982).

Huish, Robert, *Memoirs of George IV* (2 vols, 1831).

Hylton, Lord (ed.), *The Paget Brothers, 1790–1840* (1918).

Jerningham Letters: Castle, Egerton (ed.), *The Jerningham Letters, 1780–1843, Being excerpts from the correspondence and diaries of . . . Lady Jerningham and her daughter Lady Bedingfield* (2 vols, 1896).

Jesse, Captain, *The Life of Beau Brummell* (1854).

Jockey Club, The, or a Sketch of the Manners of the Age (1792).

Khan, Mirza Abul Hassan, *A Persian at the Court of King George 1809–10* (Barrie & Jenkins, 1988).

Knight, Cornelia, *Autobiography of Miss Cornelia Knight: With extracts from her Journals and Anecdote Books* (2 vols, 1861).

Leeds Memoranda: Browning, Oscar (ed.), *The Political Memoranda of Francis Fifth Duke of Leeds* (1884).

Leslie, Anita, *Mrs Fitzherbert* (Hutchinson, 1960).

Leslie, Shane, *George the Fourth* (Ernest Benn, 1926).

Levy, Peter, *The Mistresses of King George IV* (Peter Owen, 1994).

Lieven Letters: Quennell, Peter (ed.), *The Private Letters of Princess Lieven to Prince Metternich 1820–26* (1948).

Lindstrum, Derek, *Sir Jeffrey Wyatville: Architect to the King* (1973).

Londonderry, Charles, 3rd Marquess of, *Memoirs and Correspondence of Viscount Castlereagh, 2nd Marquess of Londonderry* (12 vols, 1853).

Longford, Elizabeth, *Wellington: Vol. 1 – Years of the Sword* (1970).

———, *Wellington: Vol 2 – Pillar of State* (Weidenfeld, 1972).

Low, Donald, *Thieves' Kitchen* (1993).

Lyttelton Correspondence: Wyndham, Hon. Mrs Hugh (ed.), *Correspondence of Sarah Spencer Lady Lyttelton, 1787–1870* (1912).

Macalpine, Ida, and Hunter, Richard, *George III and the Mad-Business* (Pimlico, 1991).

Malmesbury Diaries: Malmesbury, 3rd Earl of (ed.), *The Diaries and Correspondence of James Harris, First Earl of Malmesbury* (4 vols, 1844).

Marchand, Leslie (ed.), *Byron's Letters and Journals* (12 vols, 1873–82).

Marples, Morris, *Six Royal Sisters: Daughters of George III* (1969).

Marshall, Dorothy, *Eighteenth Century England* (Longman, 1968).

Melville, Lewis, *Beau Brummel, His Life and Letters* (1924).

———, *The Berry Papers: being the correspondence, hitherto unpublished, of May and Agnes Berry, 1763–1852* (1912).

Memes, J.S., *Memoirs of Antonio Canova* (1825).

Minto Letters: Minto, Countess of (ed.), *Life and Letters of Sir Gilbert Elliot, 1st Earl of Minto* (3 vols, 1874).

Mitchell, Austin, *The Whigs in Opposition, 1815–1830* (O.U.P., 1967).

Mitchell, L.B.J., *Charles James Fox and the Disintegration of the Whig Party, 1782–1794* (1970).

Moore, Thomas, *Letters and Journals of Lord Byron* (Galignani, 1831).

Moore Letters: Dowden, Wilfrid S. (ed.), *The Letters of Thomas Moore* (2 vols, O.U.P., 1964).

Moore Memoirs: Russell, Lord John (ed.), *Memoirs, Journal and Correspondence of Thomas Moore* (8 vols, 1853–6).

Murray, Hon. Amelia, *Recollections of the Early Years of the Present Century* (1868).

New, Chester W., *The Life of Henry Brougham to 1830* (O.U.P., 1961).

Nicolson, Sir Harold, *The Congress of Vienna* (1940).

Nightingale, J., *Memoir of the Public and Private Life of . . . Caroline, Queen of Great Britain* (1820).

Northumberland Diaries: Greig, James (ed.), *The Diaries of a Duchess: Extracts from the Diaries of the First Duchess of Northumberland, 1716–1776*.

Oman, Carola, *The Gascoyne Heiress: The Life and Diaries of Frances Mary Gascoyne-Cecil, 1802–39* (Hodder & Stoughton, 1968).

O'Toole, Fintan, *A Traitor's Kiss: The Life of Richard Brinsley Sheridan* (Granta, 1997).

Paget Papers: Paget, Sir Augustus B. (ed.), *The Paget Papers: Diplomatic and other Correspondence of the Rt. Hon. Sir Arthur Paget* (2 vols, 1896).

Palmer, Alan, *The Life and Times of George IV* (Weidenfeld & Nicolson, 1972).

Papendiek Journals: Delves Broughton, Mrs Vernon (ed.), *Court and Private Life in the Time of Queen Charlotte: Being the Journals of Mrs Papendie* (2 vols, 1887).

Pasquin, Anthony, *The Life of the Late Earl of Barrymore* (1793).

Peel Memoirs: Stanhope, Earl, and Cardwell, E. (eds.), *The Memoirs of Sir Robert Peel* (2 vols, 1857).

Pellew, George, *The Life and Correspondence of the Rt. Hon. Henry Addington, First Viscount Sidmouth* (3 vols, 1847).

Plowden, Alison, *Caroline and Charlotte* (Sidgwick & Jackson, 1989).

Plumb, J.H., *The First Four Georges* (1956).

Prince and his Pleasures, The: Satirical Images of George IV and his Circle (1997).

Pyne, W.H., *The History of the Royal Residences* (1819).

Queen's Trial: Report of the Proceedings before the House of Lords on a Bill of Pains and Penalties, ed. by J. Nightingale (3 vols, 1821).

Raikes Journal: Raikes, Thomas, *A Portion of the Journal kept by Thomas Raikes Esq: 1831–1847* (4 vols, Longman, 1856–7).

Raphael, Frederic, *Byron* (Cardinal, 1988).

Romilly, Sir Samuel, *Memoirs of the Life of Sir Samuel Romilly* (3 vols, 1840).

Rose Diaries: Harcourt, Rev. Levenson (ed.), *The Diaries and Correspondence of the Rt. Hon. George Rose* (2 vols, 1860).

Rudé, George, *Hanoverian London 1714–1808* (Secker & Warburg 1971).

Russell, Lord John, *Memorials and Correspondence of Charles James Fox* (2 vols, 1853).

Rutherford, Jessica, *The Royal Pavilion* (1997).

Sales, Roger, *Jane Austen and Representations of Regency England* (Routledge, 1994).

Shelley Diary: Edgcumbe, Richard (ed.), *The Diary of Frances, Lady Shelley* (2 vols, 1912–13).

Shelley Letters: Ingpen, R. (ed.), *The Letters of Percy Bysshe Shelley* (1912).

Sheridan Letters: Price, Cecil (ed.), *The Letters of Richard Brinsley Sheridan* (1960).

Smith, E.A., *A Queen on Trial: The Affair of Queen Caroline* (Alan Sutton, 1993).

Southey, Robert, *Letters from England* (2 vols, 1807).

Somerset, Anne, *The Life and Times of William IV* (Weidenfeld & Nicholson, 1980).

Stanhope Memoirs: Memoirs of the Lady Nester Stanhope as related by herself in conversation with her physician (3 vols, 1845).

Stockmar, E. von (ed.), *Memoirs of Baron Stockmar* (2 vols, 1872–3).

Stuart Letters: Johnson, B.B.(ed.), *The Letters of Lady Louisa Stuart* (1926).

Tomalin, Claire, *Mrs Jordan's Profession* (Viking, 1994).

Twiss, Horace, *The Public and Private Life of Lord Chancellor Eldon* (3 vols, 1844).

Walpole, B.C., *Recollections of The Life of Charles James Fox* (1806).

Walpole Correspondence: Lewis, W.S. (ed.), *The Yale Edition of Horace Walpole's Correspondence* (34 vols, O.U.P., 1937–65).

Walpole Journals: Steuart, A. Francis (ed.), *The Last Journals of Horace Walpole During the Reign of George III* (2 vols, 1910).

Watson, J. Steven, *The Reign of George III 1760–1815* (O.U.P, 1960).

Wellington Letters: Wellington, 7th Duke of (ed.), *Wellington and His Friends: Letters of the First Duke of Wellington* (Macmillan, 1965).

Wheatley, Henry B., *London Past and Present* (3 vols, John Murray, 1891).

Wilkins, W.H., *Mrs Fitzherbert and George IV* (2 vols, 1905).

Williams, E.N., *Life in Georgian England* (Batsford, 1962).

Wilson Memoirs: Blanch, Lesley (ed.), *The Game of Hearts: Harriette Wilson and her Memoirs* (Gryphon, 1957).

Windham, Rt. Hon. William, *The Windham Papers* (2 vols, 1913).

Woodham-Smith, Cecil, *Queen Victoria: Her Life and Times 1819–1861* (Penguin, 1994).

Wraxall, Nathaniel, *Memoirs of Sir Nathaniel William Wraxall: 1772–1784,* Wheatley, Henry (ed.), (5 vols, 1884)

Index